# SUSTAINABILITY: DYNAMICS AND UNCERTAINTY

FONDAZIONE ENI ENRICO MATTEI (FEEM) SERIES ON ECONOMICS, ENERGY AND ENVIRONMENT

This series serves as an outlet for the main results of FEEM's research programmes in the areas of economics, energy and environment.

The Scientific Advisory Board of the series is composed as follows:

Kenneth J. Arrow
Department of Economics,
Stanford University, Stanford, California, USA

William J. Baumol
C.V. Starr Center for Applied Economics,
New York University, New York City, USA

Partha Dasgupta
Cambridge University, Cambridge, United Kingdom

Siro Lombardini
University of Turin, Turin, Italy

Karl-Göran Mäler
The Beijer Institute, Stockholm, Sweden

Ignazio Musu
University of Venice, Venice, Italy

James M. Poterba
Department of Economics,
Massachusetts Institute of Technology, Cambridge, Massachusetts, USA

Domenico Siniscalco (Series Editor)
Director, Fondazione Eni Enrico Mattei, Milan, Italy
and
University of Turin, Turin, Italy

Giorgio Barba Navaretti (Series Associate Editor)
Fondazione Eni Enrico Mattei
and
University of Milan, Milan, Italy

*The titles published in this series are listed at the end of this volume.*

# Sustainability: Dynamics and Uncertainty

*edited by*

GRACIELA CHICHILNISKY

GEOFFREY HEAL

and

ALESSANDRO VERCELLI

KLUWER ACADEMIC PUBLISHERS
DORDRECHT / BOSTON / LONDON

Library of Congress Cataloging-in-Publication Data

```
Sustainability : dynamics and uncertainty / edited by Graciela
  Chichilnisky, Geoffrey Heal, and Alessandro Vercelli.
       p.    cm. -- (Economics, energy and environment ; 9)
  Includes index.
  ISBN 0-7923-4698-X
  1. Sustainable development. 2. Environmental policy. 3. Economic
development--Environmental aspects.   I. Chichilnisky, Graciela.
II. Heal, G. M.  III. Vercelli, Alessandro.  IV. Series.
HC79.E5S8664  1997
338.9--dc21                                                97-23951
```
ISBN 0-7923-4698-X

---

Published by Kluwer Academic Publishers,
P.O. Box 17, 3300 AA Dordrecht, The Netherlands

Sold and distributed in the U.S.A. and Canada
by Kluwer Academic Publishers,
101 Philip Drive, Norwell, MA 02061, U.S.A.

In all other countries, sold and distributed
by Kluwer Academic Publishers,
P.O. Box 322, 3300 AH Dordrecht, The Netherlands

*Printed on acid-free paper*

All rights reserved
©1998 Kluwer Academic Publishers
No part of the material protected by this copyright notice may be reproduced or
utilized in any form or by any means, electronic or mechanical,
including photocopying, recording or by any information storage and retrieval system,
without written permission from the copyright owner.

Printed in the Netherlands

# Table of Contents

Editors' Introduction — vii

List of Contributors — xv

SECTION 1: OVERVIEW — 1

1.1. Interpreting Sustainability, G. M. Heal — 3

1.2. Global Environmental Risks, G. Chichilnisky and G. M. Heal — 23

SECTION 2: DYNAMICS — 47

2.1. Sustainable Use of Renewable Resources, A. Beltratti, G. Chichilnisky and G. M. Heal — 49

2.2. North South Trade and the Dynamics of the Environment, R. Abraham, G. Chichilnisky and R. Record — 77

2.3. Trade, Migration, and Environment: A General Equilibrium Analysis, G. Chichilnisky and M. Di Matteo — 109

2.4. A Simple Model of Optimal Sustainable Growth, G. Cazzavillan and I. Musu — 129

2.5. Environmental Externalities, Disconnected Generations and Policy, G. Marini and P. Scaramozzino — 139

2.6. Stochastic Sustainability, M. P. Tucci — 151

2.7. Sustainable Development and the Freedom of Future Generations, A. Vercelli — 171

SECTION 3: UNCERTAINTY                                              189

3.1. Hard Uncertainty and Environmental Policy, A. Vercelli         191

3.2. Environmental Option Values, Uncertainty Aversion and
     Learning, M. Basili and A. Vercelli                            223

3.3. Environmental Bonds: A Critical Assessment,
     L. Torsello and A. Vercelli                                    243

3.4. Uncertain Future Preferences and Conservation,
     A. Beltratti, G. Chichilnisky and G. M. Heal                   257

3.5. Financial Markets for Unknown Risks, G. Chichilnisky
     and G. M. Heal                                                 277

3.6. Stochastic Sustainability in the Presence of
     Unknown Parameters, M. P. Tucci                                295

3.7. Climate Change and Emission Permits, A. Beltratti              319

GRACIELA CHICHILNISKY, GEOFFREY HEAL AND
ALLESSANDRO VERCELLI

# Introduction

What is sustainable development? A fashionable phrase, certainly: but are there substantive issues behind it? There are, in fact, several. This volume is organized about two of them, one relating to long-run dynamics, and the other to uncertainty.

The adjective "sustainable" derives from the following concern: Can our current patterns of economic activity be continued over long periods without disastrous consequences for the environment, or for us? Do existing institutions and decision criteria lead us to select patterns of activity which we can safely continue over very long periods of time, or are they somehow too "myopic" to detect and avoid harmful long-run consequences? Most of the non-economic discussions of sustainability are concerned about this dimension: they address the issue of discriminating against the future, of depriving future generations of certain environmentally-based benefits which we enjoy today, or of destruction by the present generation of the environmental and ecological infrastructures which support important aspects of human activity. In a much-quoted phrase the Brundtland Report (1987) refers to sustainable development as "development that meets the needs of the present without compromising the ability of future generations to meet their own needs." Sustainability is anchored in the concept of basic needs, introduced in Chichilnisky (1977). Current threats to the ecological infrastructures of human activities are reviewed by McMichael (1993) and Daily (1997).

Underlying such concerns is the issue of modelling and evaluating alternative long-term dynamic paths open to an economy which in an essential way is dependent on environmental inputs. How to model and evaluate alternative development paths of an economic-environmental system, especially with reference to their long-run properties, is the theme of the papers in Section 2 of this volume.

Evidently, a concern about the long-run, and especially about environment in the long-term, must acknowledge uncertainty about many of the underlying processes and relationships. What is the nature of this uncertainty? How do we model it? What does it mean to enquire whether patterns of economic activity will lead to disastrous environmental consequences when we are uncertain of some of the underlying relationships? How should such a question be posed? This is the subject matter of the papers in Section 3.

Both of these topics – sustainability and long-run dynamics, and sustainability and uncertainty – are hard to model and analyze. There is a paucity of analytical work on sustainability, particularly relative to the volume of applied and policy-oriented discussion. So in some respects the collection here aims to break new ground by addressing the issue of sustainability within mainstream analytical economic models, using tools from welfare economics, a broad range of resource allocation theory and decision theory. The paper by Heal in Section 1 reviews some strands of the earlier literature on dynamics and sustainability: however, mention should also be made here of the important earlier contributions by Asheim (1994), Barbier and Markandya (1994), Hartwick (1977), Pearce et al. (1990) and Pezzey (1989), who are amongst the first to have worked to bring some formal precision to the concept of sustainable development.

Section 1 contains two papers – "Interpreting Sustainability" and "Global Environmental Risks" – which provide non-technical overviews of some of the key questions in each of the areas of dynamics and uncertainty, respectively. Rather than repeat that material here, the reader is referred to those papers for general introductions to the two fields.

What conclusions emerge from this collection of studies? A thorough analysis of sustainability requires that we understand better how economic and environmental (i.e., ecological or biological) systems interact over the long run. The paper by Abraham, Chichilnisky and Record shows that, even for the very simplest ecological and economic systems, these interactions can be so complex as to span the entire range of known dynamic behaviors, including phenomena not previously noted in economics, such as fractal attractor basins. They show that the nature of the interactions between the economic and ecological systems depends on the system of property rights in effect. Ill defined property rights induce chaotic dynamics. Confronted with such a range of outcomes, we clearly need to know more precisely what kinds of systems and what ranges of parameter values are reasonable. Only then can we have an idea of the types of dynamic behavior which we need to study in evaluating the long-run responses of linked economic and ecological systems to alternative policies.

The Abraham–Chichilnisky–Record paper is purely descriptive: it does not seek to define an "optimal" or "sustainable" path. But what it describes, namely the set of possible dynamics for interacting economic and ecological systems, provides the choice set from which a best path must be chosen. Formally, and very simplistically, we have a set of economic variables $e$ whose values at time $t$ are represented by the vector $e_t$ and similarly a vector of ecological (also biological) variables $b_t$ which interact in their dynamic evolution:

$$\frac{de_t}{dt} = f(e_t, b_t), \quad \frac{db_t}{dt} = g(e_t, b_t).$$

Among the solution paths to this interaction between economic and ecological variables, we look for those which are sustainable. Sustainable paths are typically those along which the values of certain key stocks are always positive, these key stocks being important environmental resources. The types of paths on which certain variables can be positive forever include stationary solutions with appropriate positivity conditions, or limit cycles or chaotic attractors satisfying the same positivity conditions. These paths, and the paths which approach them, constitute the set of sustainable paths. From amongst these we have to choose one or more which are in some sense the best. Note that rather than imposing positivity of certain stocks in the long run as a condition for sustainability, we would prefer to derive this as a characteristic of optimal solutions from more fundamental judgements about the valuation of stocks and flows: this is the route pursued by the papers in this volume.

The introductory paper by Heal in Section 1 reviews these matters in general terms, not going into technical details: it discusses the precedents for a concept of sustainability in welfare economics, and reviews alternative optimality concepts and their connection to sustainability. The paper by Beltratti, Chichilnisky and Heal in Section 2 then focuses in detail on the problem of characterizing optimal paths which are in some sense sustainable when a renewable resource interacts with a standard neoclassical one sector model of economic growth, a model simpler than the two sector economic growth model in the paper by Abraham, Chichilnisky and Record (which is drawn from Chichilnisky, 1981). Beltratti, Chichilnisky and Heal reach the interesting conclusion that for such a model to yield a well-defined sustainable optimal path in the sense of Chichilnisky (1996a), it is necessary that the rate at which future benefits are discounted relative to the present should fall asymptotically to zero. This is a conclusion surprisingly consonant, as Heal points out, with a growing body of empirical evidence on individual attitudes towards the future. This body of evidence (see, for example, Lowenstein and Thaler, 1989, or Cropper et al., 1994) suggests that individuals do not discount the future at a constant rate: rather, they practice what has come to be called "hyperbolic discounting" (Henderson and Bateman, 1995) or "slow discounting" (Harvey, 1994). The discount rate which they apply falls with the length of the period to which they apply it.

As the papers by Heal and Beltratti, Chichilnisky and Heal note, recognizing the contributions made by biological resource stocks to human welfare, and so the need to preserve positive quantities of these stocks, is also a key move in analyzing options for sustainable development. These two papers, and that of Cazzavillan and Musu, pursue this matter. They address the implications of recognizing that the stock of a resource, which may be renewable or exhaustible, can itself be a source of value to society, in addition to the flow of goods and services derived by consuming it. The Beltratti–Chichilnisky–Heal paper on uncertain preferences also addresses the importance of environmental stocks as a source of social value, in this case in the context of uncertainty and option values. The paper by Cazzavillan and Musu is also of interest in that it explores the issue of sustainability in the context of an endogenous growth model, a category of model which has recently been fashionable but within which little attention has been paid to environmental matters.

The chapter by Tucci on stochastic sustainability works out a simple dynamic model which combines an economic system with a climate system incorporating stochastic elements. Contrary to much of the literature in this area, which is interested in the optimal sustainable development over an infinite horizon, the goal here is to find a stochastically sustainable development period by period. Therefore, no maximization is needed and no assumptions about the existence of an intergenerational social welfare function are required.

The paper by Marini and Scaramozzino broadens further the types of dynamic model considered, pursuing the issue of sustainability in the context of an overlapping generations model. It raises important dynamic issues which relate more directly to public finance and taxation policy. And that of Chichilnisky and di Matteo places on the economic agenda a new and powerful issue, one already concerning political scientists: the link between environmental abuse and international migration, a link which leads directly to discussions of environmental conflicts and international security. As they note in their introduction, migration induced by environmental pressures is today a very real phenomenon in may of the poorer parts of the world, and is an increasing source of global political stress. The paper by Vercelli on sustainability suggests a new formalization of sustainability: development is considered sustainable when it does not reduce the range of options open to future generations.

In the area of uncertainty and sustainability, the contributors also raise complex and important questions, several of which connect with issues raised by the discussion of dynamics and sustainability. The papers by Vercelli, Basili and Vercelli, and Torsello and Vercelli explore the impact that different hypotheses about uncertainty may have on the themes discussed in this book. The authors of these chapters stress the crucial importance of the distinction between two basic kinds of uncertainty faced by the decision-maker when she looks for the solution to environmental problems. Uncertainty is here considered to be "soft" when it is possible to represent the beliefs of the decision-maker in terms of a unique additive, fully reliable, probability distribution, and "hard" when it is possible to represent the beliefs of the decision-maker only in terms of a non-additive probability distribution, or of a plurality of priors none of which can be considered as fully reliable. Particular emphasis is put by the authors of the these chapters on the case of hard uncertainty because it is their conviction that environmental problems involve this sort of uncertainty. Problems of this type are completely neglected by the standard approach of environmental economics since it is based on the traditional decision theory which routinely assumes soft uncertainty.

The first paper of the third section of the book ("Hard Uncertainty and Environmental Policy") surveys recent contributions to decision theory which explore the foundations of decision theory under hard uncertainty. These theories have implications for environmental policy which are briefly outlined by the author. A first example is the paper by Vercelli mentioned above ("Sustainable Development and the Freedom of Future Generations") where some implications of hard uncertainty for the definition of sustainable development are briefly indicated; in particular the author maintains that hard uncertainty about the preferences of future generations suggests a definition of long-run sustainability based upon the conservation of the freedom of future generations. In the paper by Basili and Vercelli ("Environmental Option Values, Irreversibility and Learning") it is shown that the distinction between soft and hard uncertainty also affects the valuation of environmental goods. In particular the authors argue that the presence of hard uncertainty adds to the option value two further components based upon the aversion towards hard uncertainty and upon potential structural learning under irreversibility. The paper by Torsello and Vercelli is a case study of one interesting instrument of environmental policy recently advocated by Perrings and Costanza for countering environmental risks. Also in this case the distinction between soft and hard uncertainty proves to be crucial. While Perrings and Costanza believe that environmental bonds are designed exactly to cope with situations characterized by hard uncertainty, the debate about the limits of the applicability of e-bonds has often assumed the more traditional case of soft uncertainty. A clear distinction between the above types of uncertainty may help to clarify the issues raised in the debate.

Chichilnisky and Heal, in "Global Environmental Risks" in Section 1, also make an argument for the distinctiveness of environmental uncertainty, in this case in terms of the novelty and indeed uniqueness of some of the risks involved. In their subsequent paper "Financial Markets for Unknown Risks" in Section 3, they suggest how conventional risk-management institutions must be altered in order to provide economic mechanisms for insurance in the face of such risks. In simple terms, they recommend a securitization of the insurance function in the face of catastrophic environmental risks, something which is right now being actively considered by the insurance and investment banking industries (see Chichilnisky, 1996b).

A second main theme of the papers on uncertainty, is the importance of "option values", a classic concept introduced into the environmental conservation literature by Arrow and Fisher (1974) and Henry (1974a, b). The essence of this concept is, of course, well known. The basic point is that if we are uncertain about the value of an asset, and may learn more about that value with the passage of time, then there is value in holding on to it until we have learned as much as we can. This point was originally developed in a series of relatively simple, two-period models: the papers by Beltratti, Chichilnisky and Heal, and Basili and Vercelli in Section 3 investigate the robustness of this conclusion and survey the literature on this matter. The contributions of Tucci address a very fundamental matter: how can we define sustainability in the presence of substantial uncertainty about the underlying economic and ecological relationships? He shows that an ingenious application of statistical concepts can give some rather powerful insights into this matter. In particular he presents a simulation based on Nordhaus (1994).

The papers in this volume cover many aspects of the dynamics and uncertainty associated with sustainability. What else would be needed to offer complete coverage of the analytical dimension of sustainability? Two topics come to mind. One is the management of the "global commons", by which we refer to the assignment of property rights in and management of the use of global public goods such as the atmosphere, the oceans and reserves of biodiversity. There are many complex and interesting economic issues which arise when one considers how best to manage these. They are, of course, public goods, so that we have to be concerned about the possibility of "free riding": they are in fact a very particular type of public goods, namely privately produced public goods. They are privately produced in that the amounts of carbon dioxide or of chlorofluorocarbons in the atmosphere are the results of large numbers of decisions made by individuals and firms about life-styles, technologies, etc. This introduces an element into the attainment of efficient allocations which is absent from conventional public goods such as defence or law and order, and has interesting implications for the use of tradeable permits, a method of establishing property rights and harnessing market forces in the service of the environment which is rapidly gaining attention. In particular, it implies that the initial distribution of property rights amongst participants in the permit market determines whether or not the equilibrium attained by the market after trading will be Pareto efficient. (There is an echo here of the significance of property rights in the Abraham–Chichilnisky–Record paper.) These issues are studied in detail in Chichilnisky and Heal (1994) and Chichilnisky et al. (1993). In this volume, only Beltratti's paper in Section 2 addresses the behavior of permit markets. In keeping with the theme of the volume, it focuses on the behavior of these markets in the long run, and under conditions of uncertainty, aspects which had hitherto been completely neglected in the literature.

A second set of issues which are integral to any complete understanding of sustainability, and which we do not study in detail in this volume, are those relating to national income accounting and to project evaluation. There is a general recognition that the way we measure national income does not properly account for interactions between economy and environment: an influential early study of this was that by Nordhaus and Tobin in 1972, and subsequently there has been a growing literature addressing the need to reform national accounting systems to reflect the consumption of non-market environmental assets. Contributions here include those by Dasgupta and Heal (1979), Repetto (1987), Pearce (1990) and others. The intellectual basis for reform of national income accounting lies in an analysis of the shadow prices associated with environmental resources, and these shadow prices arise from models such as those of Beltratti, Chichilnisky and Heal, Cazzavillan and Musu, and Marini and Scarramozzini. So the type of models studied here can provide an important input to the design of conventions for measuring national income properly. This issue is discussed at length by Heal (1996). The same is true of cost-benefit analysis: again, the intellectual basis lies in the study of optimal development models and the shadow prices associated with their solutions, so that the models studied in Section 2 can contribute to the development of a new environmentally conscious foundation of cost-benefit analysis, even though they do not themselves discuss the methods of cost-benefit analysis. Again, these issues are developed at length in Heal (1996).

This volume has evolved over five years as the outcome of a series of research projects and workshops sponsored by the Fondazione ENI Enrico Mattei, begun initially in 1991, with workshops in Milan in 1992 and 1994. The enthusiasm and support of the staff and research associates of the Fondazione, and especially the intellectual and organizational input of Andrea Beltratti, have been invaluable.

## References

1. Arrow, K. J. and A. C. Fisher (1974). "Environmental Preservation, Uncertainty and Irreversibility", *Quarterly Journal of Economics* 88, 312–319.
2. Asheim, G. B. (1994). "Net National Product as an Indicator of Sustainability", *Scandinavian Journal of Economics* 1994, 96.
3. Barbier, E. and A. Markandya (1990). "The Conditions for Achieving Environmentally Sustainable Development", *European Economic Review* 34(2–3), 659–669.
4. Chichilnisky, G. (1977). "Economic Development and Efficiency Criteria in the Satisfaction of Basic Needs", *Applied Mathematical Modelling* 1, 290–297.
5. Chichilnisky, G. (1981). "Terms of Trade and Domestic Distribution: Export-Lead Growth with Abundant Labor", *Journal of Development Economics* 8, 163–192.
6. Chichilnisky, G. (1996a). "Sustainable Development: An Axiomatic Approach", *Social Choice and Welfare* 13(2), 231–257.
7. Chichilnisky, G. (1996b). "Catastrophe Bundles Hedge Unknown Risks", *Best's Review*, February, 44–48.
8. Chichilnisky, G. and G. M. Heal (1994). "Who Should Abate Carbon Emissions? An International Viewpoint", *Economics Letters* 44, 443–449.
9. Chichilnisky, G., G. M. Heal and D. Starrett (1993). "International Emission Permits: Equity and Efficiency", Working Paper, Stanford Institute for Theoretical Economics. Forthcoming in *Environmental Markets*, G. Chilchilnisky and G. M. Heal (eds.).

10. Cropper, M. L., S. K. Aydede and P. R. Portney (1994). "Preferences for Life-Saving Programs: How the Public Discounts Time and Age", *Journal of Risk and Uncertainty* 8, 243–265.
11. Daily, G. (1997). *Nature's Services: Societal Dependence on Natural Ecosystems*, Island Press, Washington DC.
12. Dasgupta, Partha S. and Geoffrey Heal (1979). *Economic Theory and Exhaustible Resources*, Cambridge University Press.
13. Hartwick, J. M. (1977). "Intergenerational Equity and Investing the Rents from Exhaustible Resources", *American Economic Review* 66, 972–974.
14. Harvey, C. (1994). "The Reasonableness of Non-Constant Discount Rates", *Journal of Public Economics* 53, 31–51.
15. Heal, G. M. (1995). *Valuing the Future: Economic Theory and Sustainability*, Lief Johansen Lectures, University of Oslo. Circulated as a working paper of the Department of Economics, University of Oslo, Columbia University Press, forthcoming.
16. Henderson, N. and I. Bateman (1995). "Empirical and Public Choice Evidence for Hyperbolic Social Discount Rates and the Implications for Intergenerational Discounting", *Environmental and Resource Economics* 5, 413–423.
17. Henry, C. (1974a). "Option Values in the Economics of Irreplaceable Assets", *Review of Economic Studies, Symposium on the Economics of Exhaustible Resources*, 89–104.
18. Henry, C. (1974b). "Investment Decisions under Uncertainty: The Irreversibility Effect", *American Economic Review* 64, 1005–1012.
19. Lowenstein, G. and R. Thaler (1989). "Intertemporal Choice", *Journal of Economic Perspectives* 3, 181–193.
20. McMichael, A. J. (1993). *Planetary Overload*, Cambridge University Press.
21. Nordhaus, W. D. (1994). *Managing the Global Commons: The Economics of the Greenhouse Effect*, Cambridge, MA, MIT Press.
22. Nordhaus, W. D. and J. Tobin (1972). "Is Economic Growth Obsolete?" in *Economic Growth*, 5th Anniversary Colloquium, National Bureau of Economic Research.
23. Repetto, R., M. Wells, C. Beer and F. Rossini (1987). *Natural Resource Accounting for Indonesia*, Washington, DC, World Resource Institute.
24. Pearce, D. W., A. Markandya and E. Barbier (1990). *Sustainable Development: Economy and Environment in the Third World*, London, Earthscan Publications.
25. Pezzey, J. (1989). *Economic Analysis of Sustainable Growth and Sustainable Development*, Washington, DC, The World Bank. Now reprinted as Pezzey, J. (1992). *Sustainable Development Concepts: An Economic Analysis*, World Bank Environment Paper No. 2.
26. Solow, R. M. (1992). "An Almost Practical Step Towards Sustainability", Invited Lecture on the Occasion of the Fortieth Anniversary of Resources for the Future, Resources and Conservation Center, Washington, DC.
27. Thaler, R. (1981). "Some Empirical Evidence on Dynamic Inconsistency", *Economics Letters* 8, 201–207.
28. World Commission on Environment and Development (1987). *Our Common Future* (The Brundtland Report), Oxford, Oxford University Press.

# List of Contributors

R. H. Abraham, Visual Math Institute, Mathematics Department, 303 Potrero Street 63, Santa Cruz, CA 96060, U.S.A.

M. Basili, Dipartimento Economia Politica, Università di Siena, Piazza S. Francesco 7, 53100 Siena, Italy

A. Beltratti, Istituto di Economia Politica, Facolta di Economia e Commercio, Università di Torino, Corso Unione Sovietica 218 Bis, 10134 Torino (TO), Italy

G. Cazzavillan, Dipartimento Scienze Economiche, Università Ca' Foscari, Fondmento S. Giobbe, Canneregio 873, 30121 Venezia, Italy

G. Chichilnisky, Program on Information and Resources, Columbia University, 405 Low Library, New York, NY 10027, U.S.A.

M. Di Matteo, Dipartimento Economia Politica, Università di Siena, Piazza S. Francesco 7, 53100 Siena, Italy

G. M. Heal, Graduate School of Business, Columbia University, 405 Low Memorial Library, New York, NY 10027, U.S.A.

G. Marini, Dipartimento Economia E Istit., Università degli Studi di Roma "Tor Vergata", Via di Tor Vergata, 00133 Roma, Italy

I. Musu, Dipartimento di Economia, Università di Venezia, Cà Fosari, Dorsoduro 3246, I-30123 Venezia, Italy

R. Record, The Santa Cruz Operation Inc., Santa Cruz, California, U.S.A.

P. Scaramozzino, Department of Economics, University College London, Gower Street, London WC1E 6BT, U.K.

L. Torsello, Dipartimento di Economia Politica, Istituto di Economia, Università degli Studi di Siena, Piazza S. Francesco 7, 53100 Siena, Italy

M. P. Tucci, Facolta di Scienze Economiche e Sociali, Università di Siena, Piazza S. Francesco 7, 53100 Siena, Italy

A. Vercelli, Dipartimento Economia Politica, Università di Siena, Piazza S. Francesco 7, 53100 Siena, Italy

# SECTION 1. OVERVIEW

GEOFFREY HEAL*

## 1.1. Interpreting Sustainability

### 1. Interpretations of Sustainability

"Sustainability" had become quite an influential and widely-used word. At the Earth Summit in Rio considerable attention was devoted to sustainability, and the concept is embodied in the resulting UN Framework Convention on Sustainable Development. In addition, the OECD, the UNCTAD, and the U.S. Presidential Council on Sustainable Development, and many other domestic and international policy-oriented institutions, are devoting time and energy to the analysis of sustainable policies. An economic theorist or a public policy economist could easily find this very worrying, for sustainability is not part of our lexicon, as Solow has lucidly noted [41]: it has as yet no established meaning. There is a literature on sustainable development, which I shall review later, but this is recent and partial at best, and one could certainly not say that it represents an economic consensus on how to formalize the ideas associated with sustainability. However, it seems important to try to find a formalization with which both economists and biological and geological scientists are comfortable, as the ideas and intuitions linked to sustainability represent a very real set of concerns which need to be addressed.

My aim in this paper is to review the conceptual literature on sustainability, and in particular to summarize current research by Chichilnisky [9], Beltratti et al. [5, 6] and Heal [24]. I hope to use this to suggest that we can give a clear conceptual content to the idea of sustainability, and can build on this conceptual content to establish a framework for project evaluation, shadow pricing and environmental accounting all of which are consistent with the

---

* This research was supported by grant number 93-09610 from the NSF, and by a grant from the Fondazione Eni Enrico Mattei. I am grateful to Graciela Chichilnisky for valuable comments on this paper, and to Andrea Beltratti and Bob Solow for insightful discussions of the issue of sustainability. This is a development of a plenary talk given at the 1994 Annual Meetings of Social Science Federation of Canada in Ottawa, and subsequently presented at the Stanford Environment Forum. I have benefitted from the comments of participants at both meetings, especially Paul Ehrlich, Bill Reilly and Jonathan Roughgarden.

underlying theoretical framework, in just the way that current approaches to project evaluation and national income accounting are consistent with and draw their intellectual justification from the discounted utilitarian approach to optimal growth theory. In the next section, I review the existing literature on sustainability, and certain existing concepts which, although not explicitly linked to sustainability, can nevertheless contribute to the formalization of this concept. In Section 3 I then give a preliminary definition of sustainability, which is formalized in Section 4. Section 5 contains applications of this framework to several different growth models, and Section 6 considers its implications for accounting, project evaluation and shadow prices.

## 2. History of Sustainability

The concepts and observations which underlie sustainability are not new. Certainly, they go back at least to the 1970s: the Bariloche model (Chichilnisky [8], Herrera et al. [26], emphasized relevant issues in 1972:

... underdeveloped countries cannot advance by retracing the steps of ... the developed countries ... it would imply repeating those errors that have lead to ... deterioration of the environment ... The solution ... must be based on the creation of a society intrinsically compatible with its environment.

In this same model Chichilnisky [8] introduced the concept of "Basic Needs" as a way of formalizing the minimum requirements needed for successful participation in society, and linked the satisfaction of these basic needs with "the creation of a society intrinsically compatible with its environment."

More recently, the Brundtland report [42] produced the following widely-quoted remark:

Sustainable development is development that meets the needs of the present without compromising the ability of future generations to meet their own needs.

The ease with which this rolls off one's tongue has much to do with the attention given to the concept in recent years. This ease is, however, a little misleading. Certainly, there is no corresponding ease of intellectual assimilation: this is Solow's point [41].

If one were to summarize the key concerns expressed by Chichilnisky and Brundtland, they would seem to be twofold:
- recognition of the long-run impact of resource and environmental constraints on patterns of development and consumption.
- concern for the well-being of future generations, particularly in so far as this is affected by their access to natural resources and to environmental goods.

The framework which I will develop in Sections 3 and 4 below will meet both of these concerns, which seem well founded.

## 2.1. Possible Formalizations

Back at the dawn of modern microeconomics, Hicks [27] defined income as "the maximum amount that could be spent without reducing real consumption in the future." Clearly, there is a concept of sustainability here, one which has points of contact with the Brundtland report's concern for "meet(ing) the needs of the present without compromising the ability of future generations to meet their own needs." In Hicksian terms, Brundtland may be saying no more than that we, the present, should consume within our income. However, for this to be true, the concept of income involved would have to be a sophisticated one indeed, encompassing income of all types, psychic as well as monetary, from environmental assets, and adjusting monetary income to allow for the depletion of environmental assets. This observation raises naturally the issue of "green accounting", i.e., national income accounting conventions which reflect adequately the services provided by environmental assets and the depletion of natural resources. Developing a satisfactory set of conventions in this area is intimately linked to provision of a satisfactory definition of sustainability: in fact, the former is the mathematical dual of the latter.[1] A review of the work to date in this field is given by Dasgupta et al. [16].[2]

Hicks' definition of income is often paraphrased as "the maximum consumption that maintains capital intact". In the context of this paraphrase of Hicks, it is natural to mention recent work by Daley [15] and Pearce et al. [36], in which they have argued for constancy of *natural* capital stocks as a condition for sustainability. Sustainable paths for them are paths which maintain intact, in some sense, our stock of environmental assets.

Solow and Hartwick [20, 41] have generalized this in the direction of Hicks' concept of income and argued that sustainability is captured by a Rawlsian definition of intertemporal welfare: from a Rawlsian perspective, welfare is maximized by maximizing the welfare of the least-well-off generation. One can write this formally and succinctly as

$$\left\{ \max_{\text{feasible paths}} \left\{ \min_{\text{generations } t} \{\text{Welfare}_t\} \right\} \right\}, \quad (1)$$

where $\text{Welfare}_t$ is the welfare level of generation $t$, so that we are required by (1): (i) for any feasible path to find the welfare level of the least-well-off generation on that path, and then (ii) to seek the feasible path which gives the greatest value of this minimal level.

An interesting result due Hartwick and extended by Dixit et al. [18] and Solow shows, under fairly strong assumptions, that if a country invests an amount equal in value to the market value of its use of exhaustible resources, then it solves the Rawlsian problem (1) and achieves the highest possible level of utility for the least-well-off generation. Remarkably, it also achieves the highest constant level of utility over time that is feasible given the economy's initial stocks of capital and resources. Now, investing an amount equal in value to the market value of the use of exhaustible resources is of course maintaining the value of all capital stocks, including natural capital stocks, intact. It is, in other words, living within our Hicksian income, and a generalization of the Daley–Pearce concept, allowing for the substitution of natural by produced capital of equal market value. As my colleague Graciela Chichilnisky has observed,[3] while this result is fascinating and surprising, it is also slightly suspect from an environmental perspective: imagine all trees replaced by buildings of equivalent value. It is not clear that this is what we mean by sustainable development! Perhaps supply and demand would take care of this problem: as we approach such a situation, the price of trees might rise, and that of dwellings fall, to a point where it is impossible to replace trees by dwellings of equal market value.

In the 1960s, Meade [33], Phelps [37] and Robinson [39] introduced the concept of the "Golden Rule of Economic Growth", which was defined as the configuration of the economy giving "the highest indefinitely maintainable level of consumption per capita". In the standard one-sector neoclassical growth model – the "Solow model" – this configuration is characterized by equality of the rate of rate of return on capital to the rate of population growth:

$$\text{rate of return} = \text{pop'n growth rate}.$$

The definition of the "golden rule" as giving "the highest indefinitely maintainable level of consumption per capita" is clearly a statement about sustainability, but made in a framework devoid of any environmental and resource constraints. It is natural to extend this concept to dynamic economic models incorporating these constraints: I review recent work on such an extension, the "green golden rule", later in this paper (see also [5]).

Note that finding the configuration of the economy which gives the highest indefinitely maintainable level of consumption per capita is *not* the same as achieving the highest constant level of utility over time that is feasible given the economy's initial stocks of capital and resources. This latter is, according to Hartwick, Dixit et al., and Solow, the outcome of investing in produced capital so as to maintain intact the total value of natural and produced capital. It is maximization subject to specific initial conditions: the former – the golden rule – is the selection of the configuration which maximizes over all maintainable configurations, independently of initial conditions.

It emerges from this review that there are elements of formal frameworks which seem to capture aspects of what we mean by sustainability, with Hicks' definition of income and the golden rule foremost among them. But none of them seem to address fully the concerns articulated in the quotes above from the Bariloche model or the Brundtland report.

## 2.2. Limitations of Earlier Approaches

Consider each of the approaches just listed. They all have limitations. The Rawlsian approach ties us to the historical accident of initial conditions (see [40] or [17]): if, as is typically the case in developing countries, the present generation is also the poorest, then this approach does not legitimize saving now for the future. Such saving involves a transfer from the poor present to the presumably richer future, which cannot be sanctioned by a Rawlsian view of justice.

As we shall see in detail below, the golden rule does just the opposite of Rawls: it disregards the present totally provided we get the long-run right. It could justify a very Stalinist approach to economic development. I shall suggest its use in combination with other elements, in an approach proposed by Chichilnisky [9].

Stationarity of natural capital as a criterion, as suggested by Daley and Pearce, seems arbitrary, although it does avoid scenarios under which all natural capital is replaced by produced capital of equal value. But given ecological thinking about resilience, and spontaneous change in natural systems (see, for example, [28]), stationarity seems inappropriate to characterize sustainability. It appears that in the biological world, stillness describes death not life!

## 2.3. Discounted Utilitarianism

The default approach to the evaluation of development paths is the discounted utilitarian framework: the best path is that which provides the greatest present discounted value of benefits. Many authors have expressed reservations about the balance this strikes between present and future. Cline [13] and Broome [7] have argued for the use of a zero discount rate in the context of global warming, and Ramsey and Harrod were scathing about the ethical dimensions of discounting in a more general context, commenting respectively that discounting "is ethically indefensible and arises merely from the weakness of the imagination" and that it is a "polite expression for rapacity and the conquest of reason by passion" (see [19, 38, 22][4]). It may be fair to say that discounted utilitarianism dominates our approach more for lack of convincing alternatives than because of the conviction that it inspires. It has proven particularly controversial with non-economists concerned with environmental valuations.

A positive discount rate forces a fundamental asymmetry between present and future generations, particularly those very far into the future. This asymmetry is troubling when dealing with environmental matters such as climate change, species extinction and disposal of nuclear waste, as many of the consequence of these may be felt only in the very long run indeed, a hundred or more years into the future. At any positive discount rate these consequences will clearly not loom large (or even at all) in project evaluations. If one discounts present world GNP over two hundred years at 5% per annum, it is worth only a few hundred thousand dollars, the price of a good apartment. Discounted at 10%, it is equivalent to a used car. On the basis of such valuations, it is irrational to be concerned about global warming, nuclear waste, species extinction, and other long-run phenomena. Yet societies are worried about these issues, and are actively considering devoting very substantial resources to them. So part of our concern about the future is not captured by discounted utilitarianism. It is this that is driving an interest in formalizing the concept of sustainability.

## 3. Sustainability: A Preliminary Definition

We have now reviewed earlier approaches to sustainability and the intuition behind this concept. The time has come to build on this. I suggest that the essence of sustainability lies in two axioms:
- a symmetric treatment of the present and of the long-term future, which places a positive value on the very long run, together with
- explicit recognition of the intrinsic value of environmental assets.

The first of these points is captured in a definition of sustainability proposed by Chichilnisky [9], and we will build on this. The second point relates to the way in which we value environmental assets: in their own right, rather than instrumentally, for their capacity to provide services to humanity. I will formalize this approach, and develop its implications in what I shall call "resource constrained" economies: resource-constrained means what physicists know as "dissipative" systems.

### 3.1. Valuing Environmental Assets

There are (at least) four ways in which environmental assets are sources of value.
1. They may be valuable as sources of knowledge: this is a source of value in biodiversity, the source which is tapped in biological prospecting and in the famous Merck-InBio deal.[5]
2. Environmental assets may have value as life-support systems: green plants produce oxygen, bacteria clean water and fertilize soil, insects pollinate plants. All of these activities are crucial in the maintenance of human life.
3. Environmental assets, such as animals, plants, and even landscapes, may have an intrinsic value, a value in and of themselves independently of their anthropocentric value, and similarly they may have a right to exist independently of their value to humanity.[6]
4. There may be a cultural value to environmental assets. Animals, plants or even ecosystems are often important in societies' self-images – as with the American eagle, the Russian bear, Hinduism and the elephant, or heather moors and Scotland. Each of these societies would in some measure fell diminished by the loss of its emblematic flora or fauna.

Items 1 and 2 are instrumental values – they may vanish if we find synthetic substitutes for natural resources in these roles. They value the environment as a means rather than as an end. Explicit recognition of the intrinsic value seems to me an essential element of the concept of sustainability. Formally, this means that utility is derived not just from a flow of consumption that can be produced from the environment, used either as a consumption good or as an input to production, but also from the existence of a stock, so that instantaneous utility at each point in time can be expressed as a function $u(c_t, s_t)$ where $c_t$ is a flow of consumption at time $t$ and $s_t$ an environmental stock at that date, as, for example, in [5, 31].

My sense is that if we value the long-run adequately, and recognize the intrinsic value of environmental assets, then everything else that is associated with sustainability in the areas of climate change, biodiversity, nuclear waste disposal, etc., is logically implied. Valuing the long-run, and valuing the environment as more than an input to human activity, will lead to the selection of what one thinks of intuitively as "sustainable" policy options when considering policies towards global warming, species preservation and the management of nuclear waste. There is no need for a formal definition of sustainability: it is a derived concept, and the best strategy is to "go behind" it and understand and model the concerns underlying it. These appear to be quite amenable to economic analysis.

The point is that valuing the long-run implies concern for social costs that will occur one hundred years or more ahead, and hence a concern about the long-run consequences of climate change, of nuclear waste disposal, and of loss of biodiversity. Such concerns are only rational if we place more weight on the very long run than is consistent with discounted utilitarianism. So although valuing the long-run and valuing environmental assets do not themselves describe precise sustainable policies on issues such as climate change, biodiversity, they are necessary conditions for the systematic and consistent selection of such policies as "optimal".

This framework is consistent with the attitudes of Bariloche, Brundtland, Solow and the other authors mentioned earlier, namely that sustainability is about intergenerational equity, about resource constraints and about concern for the impact of human activity on the environment.

## 4. Sustainability

Chichilnisky [9] suggests a set of principles or axioms for ranking alternative development paths which imply that we place positive weight on the very long run properties of a path. Technically, her axioms lead to a way of ranking paths which places positive weight on the limiting properties of a path: it also places positive weight on its properties in the near term. This formulation is in tune with the concerns being voiced by those who write about sustainability in the context of our responsibilities to future generations.

Chichilnisky views the problem of choosing amongst alternative paths as a social choice problem: each generation has in principle different preferences

over alternative developments of the economy, and the social choice problem is to combine in these in a way which respects certain basic ethical principles, as formalized by Arrow [1]. Chichilnisky uses two main axioms, which rule out "dictatorial" solutions. Recall that a dictatorial solution is one in which the will of one individual always prevails. Chichilnisky loosens this concept somewhat, requiring that the wills of certain groups, rather than individuals, should not always prevail. In particular, she distinguishes between "the present" and "the future". "The present" she defines as any finite set of periods: the future is what remains after the present. Given this terminology, two axioms underlie her approach:
- no dictatorship of the present (no finite set of generations should be dictatorial), and
- no dictatorship of the future ("the very long run" should not be dictatorial).

Somewhat surprisingly, these two axioms, plus several more technical axioms relating to continuity and linearity, suffice to characterize the valuation of alternative developments of the economy uniquely as the sum of two terms, one that is a *discounted integral of utilities* ($\int_0^\infty u(c_t, s_t) \delta(t) dt$, where $\delta(t)$ is a discount factor) and *one that depends on the long-run properties of the stream* (for example, $\lim_{t \to \infty} u(c_t, s_t)$).[7] Formally, Chichilnisky's criterion is to rank alternative paths of the economy according to the value of the number given by[8]

$$\left\{ \theta \int_0^\infty u(c_t, s_t) \delta(t) dt + (1-\theta) \lim_{t \to \infty} u(c_t, s_t) \right\}. \tag{2}$$

In the formulation I am giving here, the instantaneous valuation of the economy's state at date $t$ depends, as discussed above, on both the flow of consumption $c_t$ and on the stock $s_t$ of environmental assets. Nothing in the Chichilnisky axioms requires that we value the stock in this way: the presence of the term $s_t$ in the valuation function is dictated by the need to recognize the intrinsic value of environmental assets.

Although the derivation of this ranking requires technical arguments, there is in fact an intuitive explanation. Note first that the first element in this expression is just a discounted sum of utilities: this is precisely the standard approach beloved of economists and questioned by environmentalists. However, the criterion as a whole is a generalization of this by the addition of a term which values the very long run (or limiting) behavior of the economy. Of course, if only short periods of time are at stake, this will make no difference. Similarly, if the economy's limiting behavior is totally determined by technological and resource constraints, the presence of the additional term will have no impact. It counts only if the time horizon is unlimited and there are several alternative behavior patterns available over that period.

Another way of understanding this approach is to note that we would probably like to weight consumption in all periods – present and future – equally. However, this is not possible: one cannot weight all elements of an arbitrarily long stream equally and positively, for if one did, the weights would sum to infinity. A natural response is, therefore, to concentrate some weight on "the present" ($\int_0^\infty u(c_t, s_t) \delta(t) dt$) and some on "the future" ($\lim_{t \to \infty} u(c_t, s_t)$). This is precisely what the expression (2) does.

## 5. Sustainable Development

The use of the Chichilnisky criterion (2) in models of optimal economic development is investigated by Beltratti et al. [5, 6] and Heal [24]. It leads to problems which are technically more challenging than the dynamic optimization problems usual in economics. There are two general observations which we can make about solutions.

One is that any solution must satisfy the "usual" Ramsey–Hotelling first order or local optimality conditions, reviewed at length in, for example, [17, 21]. These conditions are the mathematical expression of the observation that on any path which maximizes the criterion (2) it cannot be possible to shift consumption between two finite proximate dates and thereby increase the discounted integral of utilities, for if this were possible one could increase the first term in the maximand. The local behavior of a solution over finite periods of time will therefore be quite familiar to economists from the earlier literature on optimal resource management.

A second observation is that the influence of the extra term $\lim_{t \to \infty} u(c_t, s_t)$ is felt in the choice of a right hand end point for the differential equations which embody the first order or local optimality conditions necessary for the maximization of (2). The right hand end point for these equations is now influenced by what Beltratti et al. term the "green golden rule", referred to above. This is the configuration of the economy which gives the highest indefinitely maintainable level of the function $u(c_t, s_t)$. It is a generalization of the earlier golden rule of economic growth, due to Meade, Phelps and Robinson, to reflect the valuation of environmental assets and the role played by environmental resources in maintaining the viability of the economy.

A final general observation: any path which maximizes the criterion (2) for some model of the economy has associated with it so-called shadow prices or adjoint variables which play the role of prices: they value the various components of the economy in a way which reflects fully their contributions to the maximand. These adjoint variables are therefore precisely the prices which we want for sustainable accounting: they reflect the values of various goods and services from the perspective of sustainable development. Interestingly, it may not be the case that an optimal development schedule will maximize the present value of profits at these prices: I shall return to this later.

## 5.1. Sustainability and Exhaustibility

The next step is to set out in more detail the implications of our formalization of sustainability in the context of some specific models of economic dynamics. First I shall look at the simplest possible model, a model of the optimal depletion of a finite stock of a non-renewable resource. This is an extension of the so-called cake-eating problem first posed and solved by Hotelling [29]. An economy is given a fixed, known initial stock $s_0$ of a non-renewable resource, which provides its only source of consumption. The question posed is: how fast should it use this up? What principles should determine the balance struck between present and future consumption, given that each is at the expense of the other? Hotelling, in a prescient paper that went unrecognized for many years, analyzed this issue when the instantaneous utility of the economy depends only on current consumption and the objective is to maximize the discounted sum of utilities:

$$\max \int_0^\infty u(c_t) e^{-\delta t} dt \text{ subject to } \int_0^\infty c_t dt \leq s_0. \tag{3}$$

We are in fact interested in a more complex problem, in which optimality is defined by the more complex criterion (2):

$$\max \left\{ \theta \int_0^\infty u(c_t, s_t) e^{-\delta t} dt + (1-\theta) \lim_{t \to \infty} (c_t, s_t) \right\},$$

$$0 \leq \theta \leq 1, \text{ s.t. } \int_0^\infty c_t dt \leq s_0. \tag{4}$$

In going from the more complex criterion in (4) to the simpler one in (3), one deletes two elements of problem (4): the presence of the stock of the resource as an argument of the utility function, and the presence of the term $\lim u(c_t, s_t)$ which places value on the limiting behavior of the economy. I shall introduce the solution to the general problem (4) by considering the solutions of several simpler problems, of which (3) is one.

The solution of (3) is well known (see [17]): it involves a price $p_t$ for the resource which rises over time at the discount rate (the "Hotelling Rule")

$$\frac{1}{p_t} \frac{dp_t}{dt} = \delta \tag{5}$$

and a consumption level for the resource which falls over time to zero according to

$$\frac{1}{c_t} \frac{dc_t}{dt} = \eta \delta, \tag{6}$$

where

$$\eta = c_t \frac{d^2 u / dc_t^2}{du / dc_t} < 0$$

which is known to economists as the elasticity of the marginal utility of consumption or the degree of risk aversion and to mathematicians as the Gaussian curvature of the function $u(c)$. This number is a constant for a number of widely-used functional forms: I shall assume it to be constant for the rest of this paper. This solution involves the depletion of the entire stock of the resource, with its price rising over time exponentially.

Consider next a variant of this problem due to Krautkraemer:

$$\max \int_0^\infty u(c_t, s_t) e^{-\delta t} dt \text{ subject to } \int_0^\infty c_t dt \leq s_0 \text{ or } \frac{ds}{dt} = -c_t \quad (7)$$

which differs only in the inclusion of the stock of the resource as an argument of the valuation function. Consider for simplicity the special case in which $u(c_t, s_t) = u(c_t) + v(s_t)$. This case is solved by Heal [24]: the solution is characterized by a stock $s^*$ satisfying

$$\frac{dv(s^*)/ds}{du(0)/dc} = \delta.$$

The optimal path is then to have consumption fall to zero, reaching zero when the remaining stock is $s^*$. At this stock, which is then maintained intact for ever, the marginal rate of substitution between the stock, which is $s^*$, and the flow,[9] which is 0, is equal to the rate of discount $\delta$. So explicit recognition of the value of the stock may lead to permanent conservation of the stock.[10] This is a move in the direction of sustainable solutions. The determination of the stock $s^*$ which is maintained for ever is illustrated in Figure 1: it is clear from this that this stock is larger, the lower is the discount rate.

The simple model embodied in (7) can be used to illustrate the "green golden rule" concept mentioned several times above. This is the configuration of the economy which gives the greatest indefinitely maintainable level of utility. Make the very reasonable assumption that $u(c, s)$ is increasing in $s$ for any $c$. Utility levels which can be maintained for ever are those corresponding to zero consumption levels: $u(0, s)$. Amongst these, the greatest is $u(0, s_0)$. The green golden rule is therefore a development path on which consumption is zero for ever and the entire initial stock is maintained completely intact for ever. This is certainly an environmentally-friendly solution, possibly overly so! With different and more sophisticated models, the green golden rule is less extreme: details are given in [24, 6].

Finally, I review the implications of the approach to sustainability developed in the last section and based on the Chichilnisky criterion. For this we seek a solution of (4), without any of the foregoing simplifications. As we are already familiar with solutions to various simplifications of (4), it is not difficult to appreciate the structure of a solution to the full problem. It is in fact a cross between a solution to (7) and the green golden rule: it involves maintaining intact for ever a stock of the resource larger than would be prescribed by the solution to (7), but nevertheless smaller than the entire initial stock. This is in fact a very general property of solutions to optimal development programs

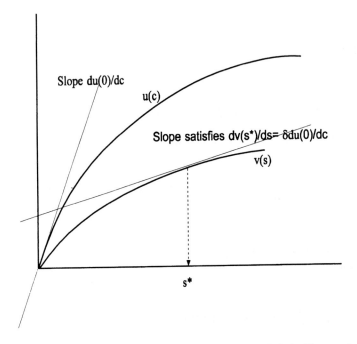

*Figure 1.* The determination of the stock which is preserved indefinitely. The marginal utility of the stock equals the discount rate times that of the flow at zero.

with the Chichilnisky criterion: for problems which are resource-constrained or "dissipative" in physicists' terminology, they are typically between the solution to the utilitarian problem when the stock of the resource is valued in the utility function, and the green golden rule. They satisfy the same differential equations as the utilitarian solution, but have a different right hand end point and are more "future oriented", as one would expect. We will see below an example of a problem which is not resource-constrained in the same sense, and for which the solution with the Chichilnisky criterion does not lie between the green golden rule and the utilitarian solution.

The solutions of the different problems and the relationships between them are illustrated in Figure 2: in all of them, consumption falls to zero, as it has to because of the finite initial stock. Differences arise with respect to how much of that stock is held intact.

### 5.2. Sustainability with Renewable Resources

A more complex version of the problem just analyzed arises if the resource is renewable, with its own dynamics, rather than exhaustible. Examples are natural populations of fish or animals, or of trees. Several inanimate resources also have the capacity to renew themselves: soil fertility is renewed by micro-

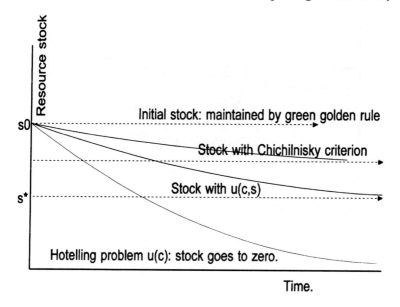

*Figure 2.* The time-paths of the environmental asset under alternative definitions of optimality.

bial action if the soil is not used, and the air and bodies of water have the capacity to cleanse themselves as long as pollution is below a threshold level. In all of these cases the rate of change of the stock of the resource contains a positive term reflecting the capacity of the resource to renew itself. In these cases the equivalent to problem (4) is now

$$\max \left\{ \theta \int_0^\infty u(c_t, s_t) e^{-\delta t} dt + (1-\theta) \lim_{t \to \infty} (c_t, s_t) \right\},$$

$$0 \leq \theta \leq 1 \text{ s.t } \frac{ds}{dt} = f(s) - c, \tag{8}$$

where $f(s)$ is the rate of renewal of the resource, which is a function of the existing stock of the resource. In biological terms, it is a population growth function. Population growth for this resource is reduced by the rate at which it is consumed: hence the subtraction of the term $c$ in the population growth equation.

The problem (8) is studied at length by Beltratti et al. [6]. The green golden rule for this model is illustrated in Figure 3: it is the tangency $T^*$ of a contour of $u(c_t, s_t)$ with the curve $f(s)$, which is often taken to be quadratic[11] and is drawn quadratic in Figure 3. This point of tangency gives the highest maintainable utility level. Beltratti Chichilnisky and Heal show that any path which is a solution to the utilitarian problem

$$\max \left\{ \int_0^\infty u(c_t, s_t) e^{-\delta t} dt \right\} \text{ subject to } \frac{ds}{dt} = f(s) - c \tag{9}$$

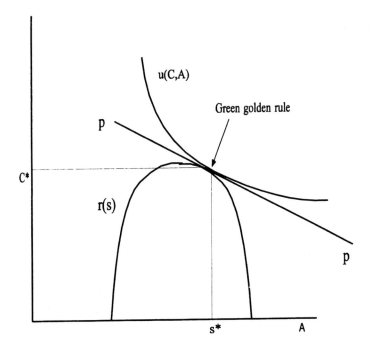

*Figure 3.* The green golden rule or highest sustainable utility level is characterized by a tangency between an indifference curve and the set of stationary points.

will asymptote to a point on the locus $c = f(s)$ which is to the left of the green golden rule, unless $\delta = 0$: in this case the purely utilitarian solutions have the green golden rule as their right hand end point. We show in [6] that in general there is no solution to the problem (8): there is, however, a solution if the discount rate is not constant but is a function of time and goes asymptotically to zero. In this case the overall objective function is

$$\left\{ \theta \int_0^\infty u(c_t, s_t) \gamma(t) \, dt + (1 - \theta) \lim_{t \to \infty} (c_t, s_t) \right\}, \tag{10}$$

where $\gamma(t)$ is the discount factor at time $t$ which satisfies

$$\lim_{t \to \infty} \frac{1}{\gamma(t)} \frac{d\gamma(t)}{dt} = 0. \tag{11}$$

A particular case of this is the usual exponential discount factor with the discount rate declining to zero:

$$\exp -\delta(t) t, \quad \text{with} \quad \lim_{t \to \infty} \delta(t) = 0.$$

In fact, Heal [25] shows that having the maximand of the form given in (10) with the discount factor satisfying (11) is necessary and sufficient for the existence of a solution to the Chichilnisky optimization problem (8) with a renewable rather than an exhaustible resource. This indicates that there is a major qualitative difference between the behavior of exhaustible and renewable systems with respect to this definition of sustainability.

It is rather interesting that there is now considerable experimental evidence that individuals considering intertemporal decisions do in fact display a discount rate which declines with the futurity of the event concerned [14, 32]. This evidence suggests behavior with respect to the future of precisely the type needed to ensure that Chichilnisky's axioms can define optimal paths, which asymptote to the green golden rule. The behavior observed by [32] and [14] is actually consistent with a more general body of observations on human behavior – the well-known Weber–Fechner law of physics. This can be summarized as follows: consider a stimulus $s$ to which a human has a response $r$: then the change in the response resulting from a change in the stimulus is inversely proportional to the pre-existing stimulus. Formally,

$$\frac{dr}{ds} = \frac{K}{s},$$

where $K$ is a constant of proportionality. This is just the pattern observed in the studies mentioned above, and indeed extensively confirmed in the psychology literature. In the present context it says that the effect of postponing an event by one year is less, the further that event is in the future. In the notation of (10) above,

$$\frac{d\gamma}{dt} = \frac{K}{t} \quad \text{or} \quad \gamma(t) = K \ln t.$$

This means that in measuring futurity, people respond to the logarithm of time and not to time itself – just as in acoustics, the original domain of the Weber–Fechner law, they respond to the log of sound intensity.[12]

## 6. Sustainable Accounting

A solution to any of the problems in the last section will have associated with it a set of adjoint variables or shadow prices with the property that if agents choose their actions so as to maximize value at these prices, then they will select the actions which implement the solution. In other words, these prices can decentralize the solution, the optimal sustainable development path. They fully reflect the contributions of various inputs and outputs to the optimal sustainable development of the economy, and so are adequate guides for individual decisions and form a basis for sustainable accounting and valuation.

In decentralizing dynamic problems, economists are used to thinking of the maximization of the present discounted value of actions. In the case of decentralizing optima according to the Chichilnisky criterion, there is an important difference: agents' optimal actions may not maximize the present value of actions at the associated prices. In fact, these prices may not define present values. In this context, it is necessary to distinguish between maximization of the present value of profits, and maximization of intertemporal profits. Maximization of intertemporal profits means that during each period, profits are maximized. A fundamental result in intertemporal welfare economics (due to Chichilnisky and Kalman [12]) states that maximization of present value profits and of intertemporal profits are the same at a given set of prices if and only if at those prices present values are well defined. But prices may not define a present value: in this case intertemporal profit maximization is well defined even though present value maximization is not.

The prices associated with sustainable optima will frequently not define present values. In these cases, optimal actions may maximize intertemporal profits at the associated prices without there being a single number representing total profit in present value terms which is maximized. The simplest illustration of this is probably provided by the green golden rule solution of the renewable resource problem (8) considered above and illustrated in Figure 3. Consider the line $pp$ in this figure: recognizing that the set of points on or below the curve $c = f(s)$ is the set of points which are indefinitely feasible, i.e., are sustainable, we note that the line $pp$ behaves like a set of prices, separating the feasible set on or below the locus $f(s)$ from the set of points preferred to the tangency point $T^*$ which is the green golden rule. An economy choosing between different points on the $c = f(s)$ at relative prices for $c$ and $s$ given by the slope of $pp$ will choose the point $T^*$: these prices therefore guide the trade-off between consumption $c$ and conservation $s$ correctly. However, they do not define a present value: on the green golden rule prices are constant over time as is the point $T^*$ chosen, so that if $(c^*, s^*)$ are the coordinates of $T^*$ and $(p_c, p_s)$ the prices given by the line $pp$, then the "present value" $\int_0^\infty \{c^* p_c + s^* p_s\}$ is clearly infinite. In such cases one may need to replace the goal of maximizing the present discounted value of profits by the maximization of sustainable profits: this is an area for further research.

## 7. Final Remarks

I have argued, following some convincing precedents, that the key aspects of sustainability are a concern for the future – putting the welfare of the future on a more or less symmetric basis with our own – and a recognition of the intrinsic value of environmental assets. It emerges that these two principles, simple and obvious though they seem, imply substantial changes in our existing way of analyzing economic development and of accounting for value.

There are, of course, aspects of the problem which have been omitted. One is uncertainty. Uncertainty is a key feature of most major environmental problems, reviewed in detail in [11]. Uncertainty is also an inevitable aspect of long-run decisions, which are particularly at issue in discussing sustainability.

So it must feature in a comprehensive review of sustainability. There are, presumably, two main categories of uncertainty.

One is uncertainty about the preferences of future generations: they may value environmental goods more highly than we do, they may live more at harmony with the natural environment. There again, they may not. In either case, it may be wrong to assume, as we do in formulae such as (4), that the valuation of consumption streams and stocks is unchanged over time. If we believe that the environment is likely to matter more to them than to us, this is presumably an additional reason for being conservative in its use. Issues if this type are studied in Chapter 3.4 of this volume: there Beltratti, Chichilnisky and Heal study problem (3), depletion of an exhaustible resource with utility derived only from the flow of consumption, when future preferences are unknown, and in particular inquire whether this provides a motive for conservation of the resource. They also extend the analysis to problem (7), in which the stock is an argument of the utility function.

A second category of uncertainty is uncertainty about future resources, technologies and in general future constraints on economic activity. Both resources and technologies may be discovered, changing radically the constraints under which we operate. This has been the driving force behind economic development for many centuries, although it may be changing. A loosening of these constraints will make it easier to meet the needs of future generations: the competition between their needs and ours is reduced in intensity.

Considerations of this type do not change the basic principles of sustainability, but they will affect their implementation. They will for example affect the computation of shadow prices: preliminary steps in this direction are taken by Beltratti Chichilnisky and Heal for a simple model in [4].

## Notes

1. Duality here is used in the sense of functional analysis: the dual of a space is the set of all real-valued continuous linear functions defined on it.
2. See also Asheim [2].
3. Private communication.
4. Heal [22] has argued that a zero consumption discount rate can be consistent with a positive utility discount rate in the context of environmental projects.
5. For details of this and similar deals, see [10].
6. A discussion of some of these philosophical issues can be found in [30]. A fascinating recent paper by Ng is also recommended [34].
7. This term does not have to be the limit of the sequence of utilities: it can be any purely finitely additive measure defined on the sequence of utilities. Another example, widely used in the theory of repeated games, is the longrun average utility value.
8. In the text I use as the second term the expression $\lim_{t \to \infty} u(c_t, s_t)$. In fact the limit of a sequence is not always well defined. Technically the second term, which values the long run aspects of an economy's performance, is a purely finitely additive measure, a measure which places all its weight on the terms at infinity. The limit of a sequence is

such a measure: we could use the limit when it is defined, which is on a closed subspace, and then extend it to the whole space by the Hahn–Banach theorem.
9. For non-economists, this marginal rate of substitution between stock and flow is just the slope of a contour of $u(c_t, s_t) = u(c_t) + v(s_t)$ in the $c - s$ plane.
10. $s^*$ is not always strictly positive: for details, see [24, 31].
11. A quadratic growth function gives rise to a logistic curve for total population.
12. This, of course, is why sound intensity is usually measured on a log scale, as with decibels.

## References

1. Arrow, Kenneth J. *Social Choice and Individual Values*, Cowles Foundation Monograph, John Wiley and Sons, 1953.
2. Asheim, Geir B. "Net National Product as an Indicator of Sustainability", *Scandinavian Journal of Economics* 96, 1994, 257–265.
3. Beltratti, Andrea and Geoffrey Heal. "Depletion and Uncertain Preferences", Working Paper, Columbia Business School, 1994.
4. Beltratti, Andrea, Graciela Chichilnisky and Geoffrey Heal. "Uncertain Future Preferences and Conservation", Working Paper, Columbia Business School, 1992: Chapter 3.4 of this volume.
5. Beltratti, Andrea, Graciela Chichilnisky and Geoffrey Heal. "The Green Golden Rule", Working Paper, Columbia Business School, 1994.
6. Beltratti, Andrea, Graciela Chichilnisky and Geoffrey Heal. "The Green Golden Rule and Sustainable Growth", in *Approaches to Sustainable Development*, Ian Goldin and Alan Winters (eds.), Paris, OECD, 1994, pp. 147–166.
7. Broome, John. *Counting the Cost of Global Warming*, London, White Horse Press, 1992.
8. Chichilnisky, Graciela. "Economic Development and Efficiency Criteria in the Satisfaction of Basic Needs", *Applied Mathematical Modeling* 1, 1977, 290–297.
9. Chichilnisky, Graciela. "What Is Sustainable Development?", Paper presented at the 1993 Workshop of the Stanford Institute for Theoretical Economics, 1993. Published as "An Axiomatic Approach to Sustainable Development", *Social Choice and Welfare* 13(2), 1996, 231–257.
10. Chichilnisky, Graciela. "Property Rights and the Pharmaceutical Industry: A Case Study of Merck and InBio", Case Study, Columbia Business School, 1993.
11. Chichilnisky, Graciela and Geoffrey Heal. "Global Environmental Risks", *Journal of Economic Perspectives* 7(4), 1993, 65–86.
12. Chichilnisky, Graciela and Peter Kalman. "Application of Functional Analysis to Models of Efficient Allocation of Economic Resources", *Journal of Optimization Theory and Applications* 30(1), 1980, 19–32.
13. Cline, William R. *The Economics of Global Warming*, Washington DC, Institute for International Economics, 1992.
14. Cropper, Maureen L., Sema K. Aydede and Paul R. Portney. "Preferences for Life-Saving Programs: How the Public Discounts Time and Age", *Journal of Risk and Uncertainty* 8, 1994, 243–265.
15. Daley, Herman E. *Steady State Economics: Second Edition with New Essays*, Washington DC, Island Press, 1991.
16. Dasgupta, Partha S., Bengt Kriström and Karl-Göran Mäler. "Current Issues in Resource Accounting", in *Current Issues in Environmental Economics*, P.-O. Johansson, B. Kriström, and K.-G. Mäler (eds.) (forthcoming).
17. Dasgupta, Partha S. and Geoffrey M. Heal. *Economic Theory and Exhaustible Resources*, London, Cambridge University Press, 1979.

18. Dixit, Avinash K., Peter Hammond and Michael Hoel. "On Hartwick's Rule for Regular Maximin Paths of Capital Accumulation and Resource Depletion", *Review of Economic Studies* XLVII(3) No. 148, 1980, 551–556.
19. Harrod, Roy. *Towards a Dynamic Economy*, London, Macmillan Press, 1948.
20. Hartwick, John M. "Intergenerational Equity and Investing the Rents from Exhaustible Resources", *American Economic Review* 66, 1977, 972–974.
21. Heal, Geoffrey M. *The Theory of Economic Planning*, Amsterdam, North-Holland, 1973.
22. Heal, Geoffrey M. "The Optimal Use of Exhaustible Resources", Chapter 18 in *Handbook of Natural Resource and Energy Economics*, Vol. III, A. Kneese and J. Sweeney (eds.), Amsterdam, New York and Oxford, North-Holland, 1993, pp. 855–880.
23. Heal, Geoffrey M. *The Economics of Exhaustible Resources*, International Library of Critical Writings in Economics, Edward Elgar, 1993.
24. Heal, Geoffrey M. "Valuing the Very Long Run", Working Paper, Columbia Business School, 1993.
25. Heal, Geoffrey M. "Lectures on Sustainability", the text of the Lief Johansen Memorial Lectures, given in Oslo in March 1995 and distributed as a Working Paper of the Department of Economics, University of Oslo, 1995.
26. Herrera, Amilcar O., Hugo D. Scolnik, Graciela Chichilnisky. *Catastrophe or New Society*, Ottawa, Canada, International Development Research Centre, 1976.
27. Hicks, John R. *Value and Capital*, Oxford University Press, 1939.
28. Hollings, C.S. "Resilience and Stability of Ecological Systems", *Annual Review of Ecological Systems* 4, 1973, 1–24.
29. Hotelling, Harold. "The Economics of Exhaustible Resources", *Journal of Political Economy* 39, 1931, 137–175.
30. Kneese, Alan V. and William D. Schultze. "Ethics and Environmental Economics", in *Handbook of Natural Resource and Energy Economics*, Chapter 5, Vol. I, Alan Kneese and James Sweeney (eds.), Amsterdam, New York and Oxford, North Holland, 1985, pp. 191–220.
31. Krautkraemer Jeffrey A. "Optimal Growth, Resource Amenities and the Preservation of Natural Environments." *Review of Economic Studies* LII, 1985, 153–170.
32. Lowenstein, George and Richard Thaler, "Intertemporal Choice", *Journal of Economic Perspectives* 3, 1989, 181–193.
33. Meade, James E. "The Effect of Savings on Consumption in a State of Steady Growth", *Review of Economic Studies* 29, 1962, 227–234.
34. Ng, Yew-Kwang. "Towards Welfare Biology: Evolutionary Economics of Animal Consciousness and Suffering", Working Paper, Monash University, Australia 3168, forthcoming in *Biology and Philosophy*.
35. Nordhaus, William D. "Is Growth Sustainable? Reflections on the Concept of Sustainable Economic Growth", Paper presented to the International Economic Association Conference, Varenna, Italy, 1992.
36. Pearce, David W., Anil Markandya and Edward Barbier. *Sustainable Development: Economy and Environment in the Third World*, London, Earthscan Publications, 1990.
37. Phelps, Edmund S. "The Golden Rule of Accumulation: a Fable for Growthmen." *American Economic Review* 51(4), 1961, 638–643.
38. Ramsey, Frank. "A Mathematical Theory of Saving", *Economic Journal* 38, 1928, 543–559.
39. Robinson, Joan. "A Neoclassical Theorem", *Review of Economic Studies* 29(80), 1962, 219–226.
40. Solow Robert M. "Intergenerational Equity and Exhaustible Resources", *Review of Economic Studies* (Symposium on the Economics of Exhaustible Resources), 1974, 29–45.

41. Solow Robert M. "An Almost Practical Step Towards Sustainability", Invited Lecture on the Occasion of the Fortieth Anniversary of Resources for the Future, Washington DC, Resources and Conservation Center, 1992.
42. World Commission on Environment and Development, *Our Common Future* (The Brundtland Report), Oxford University Press, 1987.

GRACIELA CHICHILNISKY AND GEOFFREY HEAL

## 1.2. Global Environmental Risks

### 1. Introduction

The need to manage climate risks is not a new: it has shaped social institutions for many centuries. In medieval England, a peasant farmer's land was broken into many widely-dispersed parcels. Economic historians interpret this as a way of hedging climate risk (see references in Bromley [9]). Land in different locations would be affected differently by droughts, floods and frosts. By spreading land holdings over different locations, as well as by organizing agricultural cooperatives and buying insurance, farmers have managed climate risk for many centuries.

Today's concerns about global climate change break new ground in two ways. One is the worldwide scope of the potential changes considered. The second is that these changes appear to be driven by human activity, which has now reached levels at which it can affect the earth's climate. Climate has always been unpredictable, but the inclusion of these two new elements has extended this uncertainty both qualitatively and quantitatively. Classical formulations of uncertainty in economics no longer provide an adequate basis for analysis.

The uncertainty about climate has several sources. There is uncertainty about basic scientific relationships, such as the link between gaseous emissions and global mean temperature. There is also uncertainty about the connection between global mean temperature and climate. Clearly it is climate, a variable encompassing wind patterns, humidity and rain patterns, and not just temperature, that matters from a socio-economic perspective. The floods of 1997 in the U.S. and Central Europe have reminded us of the profound vulnerability of human settlement to climate. Climatologists link these to El Nino, the ocean current off the coast of Chile, confirming the global linkages within the earth's climate system.

Future emissions of greenhouse gases and future climate are also highly uncertain. In addition, these can be driven by economic activity and by policy measures: hence the risks faced are endogenous.

There are two standard ways in which societies can respond to the risks associated with such uncertainty. One way is *mitigation*. The other is *insurance*. We can think of them as broadly equivalent to prevention and cure respectively in the medical field.

Mitigation means taking measures to reduce the possible damage. One way of doing this is to take steps that minimize the damage if the harmful event occurs. Building levees, canals and flood drainage systems to reduce the impact of flood waters is an example. An alternative approach to mitigation is to reduce the incidence of harmful events. Of course, if steps are taken to reduce the risk of climate change, then the risks become endogenous, determined by our policy measures. This contrasts with most models of resource-allocation under uncertainty, in which probabilities are about acts of nature and are therefore exogenous.[1] In an Arrow–Debreu framework, there is no scope for mitigation in the second sense of improving odds. The probabilities of states in an Arrow–Debreu framework may be subjective and an agent's subjective probabilities may be altered by learning. However, the frequency of incidence of harmful events cannot be altered by agents in the Arrow–Debreu model. The same is true in the classical models of insurance, where the incidence of harmful events is again taken to be exogenous. Mitigation acquires a new meaning when risks are endogenous.

Insurance in contrast to mitigation does nothing to reduce the chances of damage due to climate change. It only arranges for those who are adversely affected to receive compensation after the event, as in the case of federal disaster relief for flood victims in the U.S. Insurance is a major economic activity, involving both the insurance industry and large parts of the securities industry. Can the existing and very extensive private sector organizations provide those at risk from climate change with adequate insurance cover? If not, why not? What changes in market institutions might be appropriate in this case?

This paper is about these and related questions. In attempting to answer them, we deal with many different aspects of the theory of risk-bearing. There are four key issues which recur in our analysis.

The first issue concerns the difficulty in assessing risks. Most climate-related risks are difficult to quantify. Indeed, in a classical statistical sense the probabilities describing them are unknowable. We may never be able to observe experiments to approximate the probability of global climate change in the relative frequency sense: such events are inherently unique. It is possible to evaluate the frequency of occurrence of a health risk from morbidity or mortality data, as the outcomes of repeated experiments are available. However, we cannot evaluate the risks from $CO_2$ emissions in this way.[2]

The second issue is endogeneity of risks. The risks that we face are affected by our actions.[3]

The third issue is correlation of risks. Climate changes will affect large numbers of people in the same way. A rise in sea level, for example, will affect low-level coastal communities in most countries. Insurance in the traditional sense of risk-pooling works best for large numbers of small statistically independent risks. We thus have to ask what types of markets work best with collective risks.

Irreversibility is the final issue. In this area, many major economic decisions and their consequences are likely to be irreversible. Climate changes, the melting of ice caps, desertification, species extinction, are all processes not reversible, or at least not on relevant time scales.

In summary, we are dealing with risks that are *poorly understood, endogenous, collective and irreversible*. In policy terms, the nature and extent of uncertainty about global climate change implies that society's position will be dominated by two questions:
- What cost is it worth incurring to reduce the poorly-understood risk of climate change, or to improve our understanding of that risk?; and
- How may existing social institutions, such as insurance contracts and securities markets, be used to provide the most efficient allocation of the risks associated with global climate change?

## 2. Risk-Allocation in a General Equilibrium Framework

Economists have two standard models of risk-allocation in a market economy. The more general is that of Arrow and Debreu, in which agents trade "contingent commodities". The alternative is the model of insurance via risk-pooling in large populations. Neither case addresses the issue of mitigation via a reduction in the incidence of harmful events.

In the Arrow–Debreu framework there is a set of exogenous "states of nature" whose values are random and represent the sources of uncertainty. Classically, one thinks of events such as earthquakes and meteor strikes. Agents in the economy are allowed to trade commodities contingent on the values of these exogenous variables. These are called "state-contingent commodities". With a complete set of markets for state-contingent commodities, the first theorem of welfare economics holds for economies under uncertainty: an *ex-ante* Pareto efficient allocation of resources can be attained by a competitive economy with uncertainty about exogenous variables.

Arrow [1] showed that efficiency can, in fact, be attained by using a mixture of securities markets and markets for non-contingent commodities, so that a complete set of contingent commodity markets is not required. This observation provides a natural and important role for securities markets in the allocation of risk-bearing. The securities used are contracts that pay one unit if and only if a particular state occurs. While the contingent contract approach is in principle all-inclusive and covers most conceivable cases of uncertainty, in practical terms there are cases where it can be impossible to implement. It can be very demanding in terms of the number of markets required. For example, if agents face individual risks (i.e., risks whose probabilities vary from individual to individual), then in a population of 100 similar agents each of whom faces two possible states, the number of markets required would be $2^{100}$ (see the subsequent paper by Chichilnisky and Heal [17] in this volume). The number of markets required is so large as to make the contingent contract approach unrealistic.

The use of insurance markets for pooling risks is a less general but more practical alternative. This requires that populations be large and that the risks be small, similar and statistically independent. The law of large numbers then operates and the frequency of occurrence of an insured event in a large sample of agents approximates its frequency in the population as a whole. There is thus a role for insurance companies to act as intermediaries and pool large numbers of similar but statistically independent risks. In so doing, they are able via aggregation and the use of the law of large numbers to neutralize the risks faced by many similar agents. The main references on this are [3, 36, 37].

The insurance approach is at a disadvantage when risks are correlated. When large numbers are likely to be affected at once, risk-pooling will not work. However, it does have the advantage relative to the contingent market approach of economizing dramatically on the number of markets needed. In the above example, only two mutual insurance contracts and 2809 securities would be needed instead of $2^{100}$ contingent contracts [12, 17].

When risks are allocated by trading state-contingent commodities securities, or by risk-pooling and insurance, *it is very important that agents know, or believe that they know, the relative frequencies of the states of nature, at least approximately.* This is obvious when trading insurance contracts. The actuarial calculations needed to set insurance premia can only be performed if the parties believe that the relative frequencies of the insured events are approximately known.

In the Arrow–Debreu approach, it suffices to think of agents maximizing expected utility to appreciate the need for them to know, or at least behave as if they know, the relative frequencies of exogenous states. These frequencies are the weights placed on their utilities from state-dependent consumption. The point is simple: if agents can not assign relative frequencies then their preferences are not well defined and they cannot act to maximize expected utility.

In the context of climate change this may be too demanding. Agents do not know the frequencies of different states, and recognize that they do not know them. They recognize that there are several different opinions about what these are, but feel unable to choose definitively between these alternatives. If they were expected utility maximizers, they would be uncertain about their own preferences. In such a case, it is natural to think of the frequency distribution over climate changes as a state of the world, a risk, in the Savage sense: we do not know what value it will assume, and whatever value this is, it affects economic activity. As shown below, ignorance then assumes the role of a collective risk, and can be treated by the use of state-contingent markets. One sometimes thinks of uncertainty about probabilities being resolved by learning. This is an avenue which is not open when scientific knowledge is incomplete and experiments are not possible. In this case an alternative approach is the opening of new markets (see [17], and Sections 3.1 and 3.2 below).

In sum: the Arrow–Debreu approach to risk allocation via state-contingent markets is in principle universally applicable. However, it is cumbersome and perhaps unrealistic in the case of risks with individual components. Insurance markets are more manageable, but leave uncovered collective risks such as the risk induced by ignorance of the true frequency distribution of harmful events. So it would be natural to allow agents to trade securities contingent on such collective risks, and cover the individual components of risks by mutual insurance contracts. This is precisely the approach that we develop below. Although new to the economics literature, it is by no means new in practice: we argue below that some of the oldest risk-bearing institutions recorded, agricultural cooperatives, have exactly this structure.

## 3. Ignorance as Collective Risk

Consider an economy in which agents face risks whose relative frequencies they know that they cannot evaluate. Such risks could derive from the impact of global climate change on income levels via floods, storms or droughts, or from the effects on health of ozone depletion, acid rain, or air pollution. What market structure would suffice to assure efficient allocations in this situation? There are widely differing opinions about these impacts, on which there is inadequate information.

Chichilnisky and Heal [17] formalize this type of situation in a simple general equilibrium model. Each agent faces the risk of being in one of several states (e.g. healthy or sick, productive or unproductive). No-one knows what will be the true frequency distribution of affected agents. A probability is assigned to each possible frequency. A typical probability distribution of this type might state for example that there is a 10% chance that 90% of the population will be harmed by global warming, a 25% chance that 50% of the population will be harmed, etc. The probability distribution over alternative frequency distributions may be different from individual to individual.

In this framework, we have two levels of uncertainty:

The first level of uncertainty is collective: what is the distribution of agents who are harmed in the economy? Will 90% be harmed, or only 30%? This is a question about the aggregate incidence of the phenomenon over the population as a whole.

The second level of uncertainty is individual: it is uncertainty about whether a given agent is harmed or not by climate change. It devolves about questions such as: given that 90% of the population will be harmed, will a particular agent be harmed or not?

In our example of the impact of the depletion of the ozone layer on cancer or the impact of climate change on agricultural productivity the two levels of uncertainty are: firstly, uncertainty about the true relationship between ozone depletion and the incidence of individual disease in the population as a whole, or about the true relationship between climate change and agricultural productivity; and secondly, uncertainty about whether any given person or community will be affected.

Our ignorance of scientific processes (e.g., the relation between ozone depletion and skin cancer or between $CO_2$ emission and climate change) causes the collective risk, by which we mean the uncertainty about the relative frequency of harmed agents in the population. Uncertainty about this frequency is central to the problem. When this is resolved we will still not know who is damaged and who is not, but we will at least know the frequency describing this. Once frequencies are known, actuarial calculations can be conducted and the problem is insurable.

We propose an institutional structure which uses two types of financial instruments which are tailored to these two aspects of the problem. These can lead to efficient allocation in the face of such risks. We follow a framework established by Cass et al. [12] and Chichilnisky and Heal [17].

One instrument is a *mutual insurance contract* to deal with the risks faced by agents or communities contingent on each possible distribution of harmful effects worldwide. A mutual insurance contract is an agreement between parties subject to similar risks that those who are harmed will be compensated by the others. Examples are agricultural cooperatives of the type recorded in Europe at least since the fifteenth century, and the nineteenth century U.K. workers' associations and friendly societies. These involved agreements between a group of workers that if one were sick and unable to work, he or she would be compensated by the others. In the present context, one could think of groups of communities subject to the possible impact of climate change, with those unharmed compensating the others. Making the terms of such a mutual insurance contract contingent on the distribution of harmful effects worldwide means that there is a different compensation agreement between the parties for each possible aggregate distribution of harmful effects. To know what compensation is due in any particular case, the parties have first to assess the distribution of harmful effects globally, and on the basis of this decide which mutual insurance contract to apply.

Having dealt with individual risks by mutual insurance, we still face collective risks. We need *statistical securities* to deal with these collective risk induced by uncertainty about the overall distribution of adverse effects. Arrow securities are defined as securities that pay one dollar if and only if a particular state of the world occurs. Statistical securities pay one dollar if and only if there is a particular frequency of affected parties in the population. As already

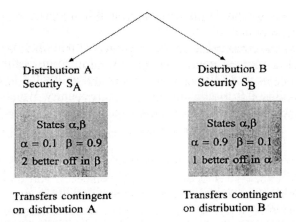

*Figure 1.* Statistical securities pay dependent on the distribution of states. Insurance contracts make transfers given a distribution of states.

noted, the incidence of impacts on the population as a whole is being treated as a "state of the world" in the Arrow–Debreu sense. We treat each possible distribution of adverse affects as a distinct collective state (called a statistical state), and use securities markets to enable parties to transfer wealth between these states. One Arrow security is needed for each possible distribution of adverse effects worldwide, because to attain Pareto efficiency each separate state must be covered by a security.

The following example will help to make this framework concrete. It is illustrated in Figure 1. Consider a world of two countries 1 and 2, in which the climate may be in one of two states $\alpha$ or $\beta$. There are two possible probability distributions over these two climate states. These distributions are called $A$ and $B$, with distribution $A$ giving a probability of 0.1 to climate state $\alpha$ and a probability of 0.9 to climate state $\beta$. Distribution $B$ gives the reverse probabilities, i.e., it gives probability 0.9 to climate state $\alpha$ and probability 0.1 to climate state $\beta$. The endowments of the two countries depend on the climate state, and are as follows: $\omega_1(\alpha)$ is country 1's endowment vector if the climate is in state $\alpha$, and $\omega_2(\alpha)$ is the corresponding endowment for country 2. Similarly, endowments in climate state $\beta$ are given by $\omega_1(\beta)$ and $\omega_2(\beta)$ respectively. Endowments satisfy $\omega_1(\alpha) > \omega_2(\alpha)$ and $\omega_1(\beta) < \omega_2(\beta)$, so that country 1 is relatively better off in state $\alpha$ and country 2 in state $\beta$.

To reach an efficient allocation of risks we need two Arrow securities. One, $S_A$, pays \$1 if and only if the probability distribution over states of the climate is $A$. The other, $S_B$, pays \$1 if and only if the probability distribution over states of the climate is $B$. In practice of course probability distributions are not observable, and we cannot condition contracts on unobservable events. So conditioning on probability distributions means conditioning on frequency distributions consistent with that probability distribution in a sampling sense.

Countries can spread the risk arising from not knowing which is the true distribution over states of the climate by trading these two securities. In addition they make mutual insurance contracts conditional on states of the climate. Such a contract could take the following form. If the distribution over climate states is $A$ (distribution $A$ gives probability 0.1 to climate state $\alpha$ and probability 0.9 to climate state $\beta$) then country 1 makes a transfer $\Delta^{\alpha}_{1,2}$ to country 2 if the state of the climate is $\alpha$, and country 2 makes a transfer $\Delta^{\beta}_{2,1}$ to country 1 if the climate state is $\beta$. These transfers satisfy $0.1\Delta^{\alpha}_{1,2} + 0.9\Delta^{\beta}_{2,1} = 0$ so that the expected transfer is zero and the mutual insurance contract is actuarially fair. There would be a similar contract to cover the case when the distribution over climate states is $\dot{B}$.

To summarize the argument:

*Our ignorance of the frequency of the impacts of climate change constitutes a collective risk. This collective risk can be allocated through markets for statistical securities, which pay off contingent on that frequency. For the individual risks that remain, it is more practical to use mutual insurance contracts: this is done by having a different individual insurance contract for each possible frequency of impacts.*

There are two features of the results which are of general interest. One is the development of a framework for achieving efficient allocations in the face of uncertain individual risks. Given rapid changes in technology with potentially far-reaching environmental impacts and health effects, the problem of providing insurance against such risks is particularly important. It is a matter of very active concern in the insurance industry. The second interesting feature is the way a combination of securities markets and insurance markets can be used to provide a relatively simple institutional structure for dealing with unknowable risks. Current trends in the securitization of certain risks are consistent with this analysis.

### 3.1. *An Institutional Framework*

Our analysis suggests that although the risks associated with global climate change are very difficult to evaluate, there is, nevertheless, a market framework within which insurance can be provided. It involves, firstly, identifying the set of possible descriptions of the collective risks. Natural descriptions of risk are frequencies of occurrence of climate-related events such as floods, tropical storms or certain temperature patterns.

Secondly, this framework involves introducing statistical securities whose payoffs depend on which description of the risk is correct. This amounts to allowing agents to bet on which model of the risk is correct. Betting on which of several alternative descriptions of the way the world works is correct, is in effect what one does when choosing one research strategy over another. Corporations, individuals and governments all do this regularly.

For example, a market for the securities of high-technology firms pursuing different research strategies towards the same goal is a financial market in which these bets are made.

Finally, our approach involves establishing compensation agreements between harmed and unharmed regions that depend on which description of the risk turns out to be correct. Mutual insurance contracts or mutual compensation agreements are already part of our institutional framework. In fact, they date back to the nineteenth century and beyond, and were the foundations of many current insurance companies and trade unions. Consider, for example, agricultural cooperatives, probably the oldest risk-allocation institutions in the world. In fact, one of the largest banks in Italy, the Monte dei Paschi di Siena, was founded to play this role in 1473. They have insured against weather risks since then,[4] and have provided mutual insurance contracts for their members, in that they have arranged transfers from the less to the more fortunate in any given season, the size of the transfer depending on the overall level of prosperity. They have also provided an elementary form of insurance against the overall frequency of poor crop yields in their community by building up reserves to carry over from good to bad years. So they have actually fulfilled both of the insurance functions outlined above – making transfers between agents contingent on the overall incidence of negative events, and allowing a mechanism for transferring wealth between states in the sense of high or low overall incidences of negative events in the population.

## 3.2. Trading Risks

An interesting aspect of the markets just described is that they can provide a natural mechanism for reconciling differences in assessments of the likelihood of important climate changes between countries, and for testing the conviction behind publicly-stated positions.

Suppose, for example, the U.S.A. believes it most likely that there will be little climate change, and the European Community believes otherwise. Then through the market for securities whose payoffs depend on which description of climate change is correct, the U.S.A. will naturally sell insurance to the E.C. The U.S.A. would wish to be a seller of securities which pay if climate change is serious, because of its belief that this event will not occur, and a buyer of securities that pay if it is not, because of its belief that this will be the outcome. The E.C. would be on the opposite sides of these markets.

International markets for the risks of climate change would also provide an objective test of the seriousness with which countries adhere to their publicly-professed positions on the risk of climate change. It is possible that a country might publicly profess to a lack of concern about the risks of climate change, in spite of actually being concerned about these risks, in order to free ride on $CO_2$ abatement policies introduced by others. These issues are discussed in detail in [27] and the references cited there. The existence of markets for the risks of climate change would place such a country in a dilemma. The country's true beliefs would incline it to sell securities paying off in the event of climate change not being serious, and buy those paying off if it is serious. Consistency with its public positions would require that it be on exactly the opposite sides of these markets. There would, therefore, be a cash cost to convincing and consistent misrepresentation of true beliefs. These cash costs could offset some of the incentive to free ride on other countries' efforts to reduce greenhouse emissions.

Note that trading risks is different from the trading of emission permits. The recognition of uncertainty suggests the need to consider state-contingent emission permits, where the state is defined in terms of the frequency of climate-change related events. Such contingent emission permits could play the role of securities whose payoffs depend on the collective risk.

In the context of emission permits, it is worth noting the public good nature of the climate. Climate is a public good. However, it does not fit fully the conventional paradigm because emission abatement, which is the production of the public good "unchanged climate", is conducted independently in the various countries of the world. It is not produced in a central production facility, as assumed in the usual treatments of public goods. A consequence is that economic efficiency will only imply equalization of the marginal costs of emission abatement across countries if lump-sum transfers between countries are made to equalize the marginal utility of income in all countries. Equalization of the marginal costs of emission abatement across countries is often taken as justification of the superiority of tradeable permits as a method for controlling emissions. This point is developed in [14, 18]. More generally, a key issue is that an efficient allocation of a public good such as unchanged climate must be supported by a Lindahl equilibrium and not a competitive equilibrium. In general competitive markets for tradeable emission permits may not decentralize Pareto efficient allocations of abatement.

## 4. Optimal Allocation with Endogenous Risks

What is it worth spending to reduce the probability of harmful climate change? Only if we can answer this question can we judge properly proposals for carbon taxes, alternative energy strategies, and $CO_2$-reduction protocols. Careful judgment is crucial, as all of these involve very considerable costs, as indicated by Cline [20] and others. Here we shall summarize one approach to this problem, based on Heal [25, 26]. This is a model that examines the extent to which the consumption of fossil fuels should be curtailed because it increases the probability of a change in climate. The model in [25] is based on three assumptions. Firstly, the atmosphere may be in one of two states, one favorable to economic activity and one unfavorable (there is a possibility of a future climate catastrophe). The favorable and unfavorable states are denoted $A_f$ and $A_u$, respectively. Secondly, the atmosphere transits stochastically from the favorable state to the unfavorable, and once there remains there for ever, so that atmospheric change is irreversible: $A_u$ is an absorbing state. The probability of transiting to the unfavorable state is endogenous and increases with the level of cumulative emissions from the use of fossil fuels.

Fossil fuels (use rate $R_t$), capital equipment (stock $K_t$) and the atmosphere ($A = A_f$ or $A_u$) are used to produce output $Q_t$, which may be consumed $C_t$ or reinvested $\dot{K}_t$ to augment the capital stock. Production generates emissions, which affect the probability of a change in the state of the atmosphere. The atmosphere is a resource that enters into the economy's production function, which may be in a favorable or an unfavorable state. Initially, the atmosphere is in the favorable state but may change stochastically to the unfavorable state, and once in this state will remain there forever. The source of emissions which affect the probability of climate change is the use of an exhaustible resource in production. The remaining input to production is the capital stock. An obvious example of this structure is the emission of $CO_2$ by the use of fossil fuels.

$$\left. \begin{array}{c} Q_t = Q\left(K_t, R_t, A\right) = C_t + \dot{K}_t \\ A = A_f \text{ or } A_u \\ Q\left(K_t, R_t, A_f\right) > Q\left(K_t, R_t, A_u\right) \text{ for all } K_t, R_t. \end{array} \right\}.$$

The probability of a change of atmospheric state depends on cumulative emissions, and emissions are assumed proportional to current use of the fossil fuel. For simplicity we therefore identify emissions and fossil fuel consumption $R_t$. Let

$$Z_t = \int_0^t R_\tau d\tau, \quad \frac{dZ_t}{dt} = R_t.$$

The evolution of the climate is as follows. There is a date $T > 0$ such that $A = A_f$, $t \leq T$, and $A = A_u$, $t > T$. Here $T$ is a random variable whose marginal density function $f$ has as its argument cumulative emissions $Z_t$, $f = f(Z_t)$ The probability that the climate changes, i.e., the date $T$ occurs, in an interval $(t_1, t_2)$, is

$$\Pr T \in (t_1, t_2) = \int_{Z_{t1}}^{Z_{t2}} f(Z_t) dt.$$

It follows that if $Z_{t1} = Z_{t2}$, so that there is no depletion or emission in the interval $(t_1, t_2)$, then the probability of climate change in that interval is zero. When there is emission in an interval $(t_1, t_2)$, the chance of climate change depends on emissions in that interval and also on cumulative emissions up to that interval. All of this makes good sense.

Output may be consumed or invested. Consumption yields utility and the objective is to maximize the expected present discounted utility of consumption. There is a constraint on the total amount of the resource that can be used, as this is exhaustible. The overall problem solved involves maximizing expected utility subject to the resource and national income constraints, where the expectation is over the process governing climate change. Formally:

$$\left. \begin{array}{l} \max E \int_0^\infty U\left(C_t\right) e^{-\delta t} dt \\ \text{s.t. } \int_0^\infty R_t dt \leq S_0 \\ \dot{K}_t = Q\left(K_t, R_t, A\right) - C_t \end{array} \right\}.$$

The expectation here is over the distribution of the date of change of the climate, $T$.

Heal [25] characterizes optimal paths of consumption, capital accumulation and use of fossil fuel for this problem. He compares these with those that are optimal in the absence of an atmospheric impact, and also studies the impact of changes in parameters such as the discount rate and degree of risk aversion and uses this to isolate the key parameters in determining the optimal rate of use of fossil fuels. The introduction of atmospheric impact makes a fundamental difference.

The time profile of resource use which emerges is flatter than that which emerges from an optimal depletion problem with no atmospheric impact. Initial levels of resource use are lower, and they fall more slowly, than in the no-atmospheric-impact case. The difference depends on the degree of risk aversion and on the parameters of the probability distribution relating cumulative emission to climate change.

The behavior of the shadow price of the resource is also of interest. In the pure depletion case this price rises at the rate of discount: in [25] it may fall and even become negative. We can interpret the difference between the shadow price of the resource in the no-atmospheric-impact case and the current case as an optimal carbon tax. This tax depends on the country's degree of risk aversion and on the parameters of the probability distribution describing the risk of climate change as a function of carbon emissions, as well as on the damage resulting from climate change. The model thus leads to a distinctive approach to characterizing an optimal carbon tax and its evolution over time. Because it is an intertemporal model, it provides this characterization in terms of the internalization of probabilistic intergenerational externalities. Hartwick [24] gives an analysis of carbon taxes using this framework.

The likelihood of climate change as a function of economic activity is a key relationship in evaluating the choices posed in this model. This is a functional relationship rather than a parameter. Global change R&D leads us to a better understanding of this relationship. It is worth stressing that proper economic analysis requires not just the likelihood of climate change as a result of one particular emission scenario, which is what most scientific analyses are providing, but rather *a systematic evaluation of how the nature and likelihood of climate change varies with the pattern of economic activity*. The study and characterization of this likelihood function is an important topic for interdisciplinary research.

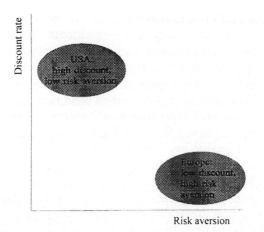

*Figure 2.* Possible systematic differences in parameters determining attitudes towards the risk of climate change.

It is not surprising that what it is worth paying to reduce the risk of climate change depends inter alia on a society's degree of risk aversion and discount rate. However, this has an interesting and important implication. Even if there were complete agreement about all of the scientific aspects of the global change problem, there could still be disagreement about policy responses. Because of the international externalities associated with climate, so that all countries "consume" the same climate, $CO_2$ abatement policies only make sense if coordinated internationally ( [4, 10, 29].

The fact that different countries need not agree on policy choices even if they agree on the scientific evaluation of the problem could clearly make such agreement difficult to obtain. Different countries' positions with respect to measures to restrict greenhouse gas emissions depend on their discount rates and degrees of risk aversion. The U.S., for example, has been against global abatement agreements, while Germany has been in favor. This fits with the conventional wisdom that the financial and industrial community in the U.S. has both a higher discount rate and a lower degree of risk aversion (greater willingness to take risks) than that in Germany. The differences in policy positions could then be attributed to differences in preferences rather than, or in addition to, different interpretations of the current scientific evidence. Figure 2 portrays such an interpretation of differences in the attitudes underlying policy choices toward global warming.

Different perceptions of the risk involved do not, however, preclude efficient solutions. Economics is about differences in preferences leading to trade. In this case differences in attitudes towards risk could be grounds for the introduction of markets in which different risk positions are traded, with efficiency gains. This was discussed in Section 3.2.

## 5. Option Values and Irreversibility

In valuing environmental resources such as current climate conditions, biodiversity, or complex ecological systems, the irreversibility of decisions and events can be central. A key aspect of these resources is that once altered they cannot easily be restored to their current conditions, at least on a relevant timescale. The decision not to preserve a rich reservoir of biodiversity such as the 60 million year old Korup forest in Nigeria is irreversible. The alteration or destruction of a unique asset of this type has an awesome finality, and analysts have sought to capture this in a framework for cost-benefit analysis. This has led to the concept of "option value": preserving a unique asset in its present state allows us the possibility of changing our minds later. Altering it irreversibly does not. Preserving it has thus to be credited with an "option value" because it keeps open to us the option of reconsidering our decision. Altering it leaves us no such option in the future.

A concept related to option value is that of non-use value or existence value. We may value environmental goods for which we have no immediate economic use. The existence of certain species is in this category: the Californian condor, the spotted owl, and various snails and fish come to mind. There is no sense in which we can currently use these species: possibly one could argue that the condor and the owl have consumption value for those willing to make the effort needed to see them, but few people come into this category. One doubts that this is a significant issue with the snail.

The two concepts, option value and non-use value, seem to overlap. Many goods which exemplify one also exemplify the other. At the same time, there are no doubt differences. Non-use values stem in some degree from ethical considerations, from a recognition that a species has a right to exist even if humanity places no direct value on it. But one suspects that behind many non-use valuations there lurks an option value: many non-use valuations stem from an unstated belief that a use value may emerge.

In this section we review two distinct formulations of this issue, one in which the returns to a preservation project are uncertain at present but will be revealed in the future, and one in which the preferences of future generations for environmental facilities are uncertain. The first framework is the one in which the issue of option values has traditionally been studied. We provide an outline of the argument in this case and illustrate the fact that one needs three conditions for an option value to exist. These are irreversibility, the acquisition of information with the passage of time, and an asymmetry of the underlying probability distribution. Similar results apply to the case of uncertainty about the preferences of future generations.

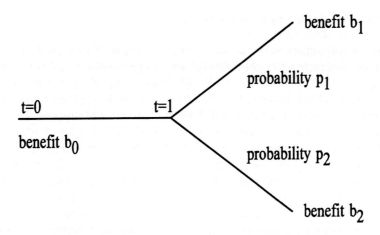

*Figure 3.* The benefits from conservation in different states.

## 5.1. *Waiting for Information*

The option value of preserving an environmental or ecological asset has been explored in the context of uncertainty about the future benefits associated with its existence. A review of the literature can be found in [23].[5] The central issue is that there are benefits that will accrue in the future from the preservation of a resource, but these are currently unknown. If the resource is preserved into the future, then in the future the decision about whether to preserve it can be reconsidered in the light of better information then available about the benefits from its existence. If it is not preserved, then there is no chance of reconsideration when we have better information. In this case conventional decision rules will underestimate the value of preserving the asset. The following example (from [21]) illustrates the key point in a simple framework. It is illustrated in Figure 3.

We shall show that with irreversible decisions there is an option value to conservation in the initial period if and only if there is a positive expected payoff from conservation in that period given that we follow an optimal policy. We contrast this with the reversible case, in which we never conserve in the first period and there is no option value.

Consider two dates, $t = 0$ and $t = 1$. We have one unit of an environmental asset. The benefit from preserving this at time $t = 0$ is $b_0$. At time $t = 1$ there are two possible states of nature $s_1$ and $s_2$. The state of nature is revealed at time $t = 1$. If the state is $s_1$, the benefit of preserving the asset is $b_1$: if $s_2$ is the state, the benefit is $b_2$. The probabilities of $s_1$ and $s_2$ are $p$ and $(1-p)$, respectively. Decisions about preservation are made at times $t = 0$ and $t = 1$. At $t = 0$ a decision is made on how much of the asset to preserve until $t = 1$ : at that date we may either conserve everything conserved at $t = 0$, or conserve less. Given that destruction is irreversible, we cannot at $t = 1$ conserve more than was conserved at $t = 0$. Our options at $t = 1$ are, therefore, constrained by the decision made at $t = 0$. This data is summarized in Figure 3.

We shall compare the case already described where the decision made at time $t = 0$ is irreversible with an alternative case in which this decision can in fact be reversed. In this case the decision made at time $t = 0$ no longer constrains the options available at time $t = 1$. We look at this alternative case first, as it is simpler and provides a benchmark. Let $c_0$ be the amount of the resource conserved at time $t = 0$, and $c_1$ and $c_2$ be the amounts conserved at time $t = 1$ in states 1 and 2 respectively. The expected benefit from development (assuming a zero discount rate) is

$$b_0 c_0 + p b_1 c_1 + (1-p) b_2 c_2. \tag{1}$$

We have to choose consumption levels $c_0$, $c_1$ and $c_2$ to maximize (1). We assume that there is currently no benefit to preservation,[6] $b_0 < 0$, nor is there any benefit in state 1 in the future, $b_1 < 0$. However, there is the possibility of state 2 in which there are positive benefits from preservation, i.e., $b_2 > 0$. If decisions are reversible, we preserve nothing at time $t = 0$, i.e., we set $c_0 = 0$. Then at time $t = 1$, we conserve nothing in state 1 and everything in state 2, i.e., we set $c_1 = 0$ and $c_2 = 1$. In the reversible case we *can* set $c_2 = 1$ because by assumption decisions made at $t = 0$ *are* reversible.

Now consider the real case in which the decision at time $t = 0$ cannot be reversed later. In this case the choice made at $t = 0$ does constrain the choices open at $t = 1$. We have to satisfy the constraint that what is conserved at time $t = 1$ cannot exceed that which was conserved initially, i.e., $0 \leq c_1$, $c_2 \leq c_0 \leq 1$. In particular, if everything is destroyed in the first period, then we have no options in the second. What policies now maximize (1)? Is there a value to carrying the option to conserve into the second period? Clearly, if in the second period the state of the world is one in which there are positive benefits to conservation, then we will conserve everything left to us by our earlier decisions, that is we will always set $c_2 = c_0$. If, however, the state is unfavorable to conservation, then we will conserve nothing and set $c_1 = 0$. Hence the maximand (1) reduces to

$$\{b_0 + (1-b_2)p)\}c_0 + p b_1 c_1 = \{b_0 + (1-p)b_2\}c_0$$

and the initial conservation level is positive if and only if

$$\{b_0 + (1-p)b_2\} > 0. \tag{2}$$

The inequality (2) has a simple interpretation: the left hand side is the expected payoff from conservation in the first period. It is the certain payoff in the first period plus the expected payoff from conservation in the second, given that if the state unfavorable to conservation occurs there will be no conservation in the second period. It is the expected payoff to conservation in period one given that an optimal policy is followed subsequently.

It is optimal to conserve in the first period if and only if there is a positive expected payoff from conservation given that we follow an optimal policy. Contrast this with the decision in the reversible case, in which we never conserve and always chose $c_0 = 0$. These two decisions are different if the expected payoff to conservation in the first period is positive.[7] In this case there is an option value to conservation as a means of carrying the resource into the second period and taking advantage of future information.

## 5.2. Option Values

Note that the existence of an "option value"[8] does not depend on risk aversion, as we assumed throughout the previous subsection that the maximand is the expected value of benefits. The key issues here are: firstly, the irreversibility of the decision; secondly, the fact that delaying a decision can let one take advantage of better information, and thirdly, the asymmetry represented by (2). This latter condition implies that on average there will be benefits from conservation in the first period, provided that we choose optimally later.

There are important practical implications of the analysis that we have just completed. Climate change is likely to be irreversible if it occurs. So in a cost-benefit analysis of preventing climate change (i.e., preserving the atmospheric environment), it may be appropriate to credit preservation (preventing climate change) with an option value. This will be the case if the passage of time is likely to bring significant new information about the likelihood of climate change or about its consequences and the expected payoffs satisfy (2) above.

The most thorough study of the costs and benefits of reducing climate change is [20]. It seems worth noting that although this study refers many times to the scientific uncertainties associated with predicting climate change, it at no point attributes an option value to preservation, i.e., to preventing climate change. This means that it may systematically underestimate the benefit-cost ratio of preservation of the atmosphere in its status quo. There is also an analysis in [38] of the value of waiting for scientific information about the greenhouse effect. They consider two possibilities: acting strongly now to reduce the emission of greenhouse gases, or taking very limited action now and waiting until there is further scientific evidence. Taking major steps towards emission abatement now amounts to conserving the atmospheric environment in its present state, and should again be credited with an option value. Manne and Richels fail to do this, and so again underestimate the value of buying insurance against the greenhouse effect by acting strongly now. As the value of an option generally increases with increasing uncertainty about the future, and as uncertainty looms large in any projections regarding global warming, the extent of the underestimate could be important.

### 5.3. Uncertainty about Future Generations

There are several ways of generalizing or refining the concept of option value. A key consideration seems to be the possibility that future generations will value environmental resources more than we do. If this is simply a statement that these resources will be scarcer, and so more valuable on the margin, then this effect is captured in the usual approach to cost-benefit analysis [28].

It may, however, be a statement that future generations could have different preferences from us, and might value environmental assets differently. Because they might value them more, we should, it is argued, attribute a value to leaving them the option of high consumption levels. Solow [41] argues that an important element in the definition of sustainability is recognizing the possibility that the preferences of future generations about environmental assets may be very different from ours. This seems close to the concept of option value set out above, and indeed it is, though there are some differences that are revealing. We next study this problem, drawing heavily on results in [6], and using a highly simplified version of that model.[9]

We shall illustrate the conclusion that uncertainty about future preferences alone is not sufficient to produce an "option value" case for increasing the resource left to the next generation. In addition to pure uncertainty, there must be asymmetry in the distribution of possible changes in preferences. Neutral uncertainty with increases and decreases in intensity of preferences equally likely does not generate a case for leaving more to the future in case their preferences for the resource are more intense than ours. Uncertainty makes a case for conservation only when the expected return to postponement of consumption is positive.

Consider a two period world where there is a fixed total stock of a natural resource to be consumed in the two periods. The initial stock is known to be $s_0$. The amounts consumed in the first and second periods are $c_1$ and $c_2$, respectively: these must obviously satisfy $c_1 + c_2 = s_0$. As the stock is irreplaceable, anything that is consumed in the first period is not available in the second, so that consumption here is an irreversible depletion of the stock. The utility from period one consumption is $u(c_1)$, which is an increasing strictly concave function. The utility from second period consumption is unknown: it may be either $(1 + \alpha)u(c_2)$ with probability $p$ or $(1 - \beta)u(c_2)$ with probability $(1 - p)$. Here $0 < \alpha, \beta < 1$. So there is a probability $p$ that the utility derived from future consumption will be "scaled up" by a factor $\alpha$, and a probability $(1 - p)$ that it will be "scaled down" by a factor $\beta$.

Consider first as a benchmark the case in which there will be no change in preferences, so that we just have to pick $c_1$ and $c_2$ to maximize $u(c_1) + u(c_2)$. Figure 4 shows this situation: the length of the horizontal axis is $s_0$, the initial stock of the resource. Consumption in the first period $c_1$ is measured to the right from the left hand origin and consumption in the second period to the left from the right hand origin. Marginal utility in each period is plotted, and

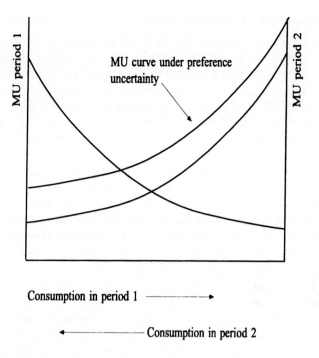

*Figure 4.* A possible increase in the marginal utility of consumption leads to a more conservative depletion policy.

the optimal levels of $c_1$ and $c_2$ are those at which the marginal utility curves cross. In the absence of discounting, and with utility functions the same in each period, these curves will of course be equal, as shown in Figure 4.

Now suppose that there is uncertainty about preferences in the second period – think of this as uncertainty about the preferences of a future generation. Also simplify matters by assuming that $\beta = 0$, so that the only possible change in preferences is a "scaling up" of the utility of consumption. This corresponds to the case that we mentioned at the start of this section, namely the possibility of an increase in the appreciation that people have for the resource. Now we have to choose $c_1$ and $c_2$ to maximize the expectation of utility, which is $u(c_1) + p(1 + \alpha)u(c_2) + (1 - p)u(c_2)$. The solution to this requires that the marginal utility of consumption in the first period equals the expected marginal utility in the second, i.e.,

$$\frac{\partial u}{\partial c_1} = \{p\alpha + 1\}\frac{\partial u}{\partial c_2}. \tag{3}$$

Clearly, $\{p\alpha + 1\} > 1$, so that the expected marginal utility curve for second period consumption is now above the certain second period marginal utility curve, as shown in Figure 4.

The optimal first period consumption level is now lower than before, as a result of the possibility of a shift in future preferences towards the natural resource. Generally one can show that the amount of this reduction depends on the probability distribution governing the change in preferences, the discount rate and the degree of risk aversion. Does this reduction in period one consumption reflect an "option value" in the sense of the previous section?

To understand this, we have to consider the more general case that we posed initially. In this case, $\beta$ is no longer zero, and equalization of expected marginal utilities in the two periods requires that

$$\frac{\partial u}{\partial c_1} = \{p(1+\alpha) + (1-p)(1-\beta)\}\frac{\partial u}{\partial c_2}.$$

Now the period two expected utility curve may lie above or below the first period curve: it will be exactly the same as the first period curve, i.e., the curve in the absence of uncertainty, if and only if

$$\{p(1+\alpha) + (1-p)(1-\beta)\} = 1. \tag{4}$$

This condition means that the expected shift in period two utility is zero. The period two expected utility curve will lie above (below) the certain curve if the left hand side of (4) is greater than (less than) unity. So if there is uncertainty about future preferences but on average we expect no net change, i.e., if an increase in preference for the resource is as likely as a decrease in the sense that (4) holds, then first and second period consumption levels will be exactly as in the certain case. Uncertainty about future preferences will not lead to a reduction in present consumption. Indeed it will lead to no changes in any consumption levels, even if agents are strictly risk averse in the sense that their utility functions are strictly concave.[10]

If on the other hand there is an expectation of an increase in the utility of consumption in the second period, so that the left hand side of (4) exceeds one, then the period two expected utility curve will lie above that under certainty and consequently the optimal period one consumption level will be lower than under certainty. Conversely, if there is an expectation of a decrease in the utility of consumption in the second period, i.e., the left hand side of (4) is less than one, then there will be a decrease in the period one consumption relative to its level under certainty.

In conclusion, uncertainty about future preferences alone is not sufficient to produce an "option value" case for increasing the resource left to the next generation. In addition to pure uncertainty, there must be asymmetry in the distribution of possible changes in preferences. Neutral uncertainty with increases and decreases equally likely, in the sense of (4), does not generate a case for leaving more to the future in case their preferences for the resource are more intense than ours. Uncertainty makes a case for conservation only when the expected return to postponement of consumption is positive (in the sense of the left hand side of (4) being positive).[11]

The Beltratti–Chichilnisky–Heal results on option values summarized here apply to the case in which utility is derived only from the flow of consumption of the environmental resource. In practice the stock may also enter as an argument of the utility function. For example, we value the current climate as an asset: we value the current stock of species or of rainforests. In this case, which is studied in Chapter 3.4, there are likely to be two qualitatively different types of optimal consumption path, depending on the size of the initial stock of the resource. If this is large, the optimal path will involve the maintenance of positive stocks of the resource indefinitely: if it is small, then the entire stock will eventually be consumed. The size of the critical initial stock at which this qualitative change in solution occurs, will depend on preferences. In this case, it is possible that a change in uncertainty about future preferences will tip the economy from one optimal consumption regime to another. Such a phenomenon would make a dramatic difference to the computation of the option value. These issues are investigated in Chapter 3.4 of this volume.

## 6. Conclusions and Open Questions

While some of the foundations are in place for an understanding of the economics of global environmental risks, there are certain aspects that require more attention. From a policy perspective, the endogeneity of the risk faced is important. The purpose of many recommended policies is precisely to change the risks that we face. An example is the global carbon tax investigated by the OECD and reviewed in [14]. Only recently has there been systematic study of the welfare economics of markets with endogenous risks, and many questions remain open.

The policy implications of many of the issues that we have reviewed need further attention. How important, for example, are the option values associated with global changes? It would be interesting to see some of the large models reviewed in [43] used to address this question. We need to study further the institutional implications of trading environmental risks on financial markets such as contingent claims markets and mutual insurance markets. The public good aspect of the global climate has not been analyzed adequately. The structure of emissions permit markets needed for efficiency is still not understood. Our analyses of option values are still based on very limited assumptions, in spite of a long and distinguished literature in this area. Finally, economists clearly need more exchange of information with physical scientists: it is fair to say that the two areas fail to make any significant contact in a field that needs the skills of both.

The prospect of climate change induced by human activity faces societies with demanding issues in risk management and risk assessment: at the same time, it faces economics with challenges and opportunities. The challenge is to develop intellectual tools, communicate them to society at large and prove that they can add value to the analysis of a complex and possibly fundamental problem.

## 7. Acknowledgments

Both Chichilnisky and Heal acknowledge financial support from the NSF (grants 92-16028 and 91-0460, respectively), the Fondazione Mattei and the Monte dei Paschi di Siena. Both authors appreciate valuable comments from Ken Arrow, Andrea Beltratti, Mordecai Kurz and Bob Solow. A shorter version of this paper was published as symposium in *Journal of Economic Perspectives*, Fall, 1993.

## Notes

1. Kurz [33] set out a framework for endogenous uncertainty: recently, this has been an active field, e.g., [13, 15, 16, 34, 35].
2. In this respect, there may be a difference between the various aspects of climate risk. There is historical data on the relation between atmospheric $CO_2$ and climate from tree ring and ice core studies. With ozone depletion the phenomenon is so new that such data is not available.
3. Endogeneity of risks leads to moral hazard when risks to agents depend on their actions, which cannnot be observed by the insurers and will be influenced by the insurance offered. This leads to arguments for coinsurance. In the present context such problems are not central to the analysis: asymmetric information is not a characteristic of climate risks. Endogenous uncertainty is more general than moral hazard.
4. They also supported part of this research.
5. Amongst the studies of this issue are Weisbrod [42], Krutilla [32], Cichetti and Freeman [19], Schmalensee [40], Arrow and Fisher [2], Henry [30, 31] and Bohm [8].
6. If $b_0 > 0$, there are benefits to conservation in the first period, so that $c_0 = 1$, i.e., we conserve in the first period. We concentrate on the interesting case of $b_0 < 0$, when the only incentive to conserve in period 1 is the possibility of a positive return in period 2.
7. An important simplifying assumption in this example is the linearity of payoffs in the level of preservation. Fisher and Krutilla [23] discuss the role of linearity.
8. Pindyck [39] considers a similar example in the case of irreversible investment decisions, and shows that the option value of delaying an investment decision to take advantage of information that will become available in the future, can be computed using the formula used in finance for valuing an option to buy a stock. See also [22].
9. The full model is radically different from most other models in which option values have been studied. It is an infinite-horizon stochastic dynamic optimization model in which the maximand is the expected present value of utility and future preferences evolve stochastically.
10. Technically, this is because uncertainty here is about the utility functions, and the maximand is linear in these. Society is not risk-averse about utility levels, even though it is about consumption levels.
11. The same was true in the analysis of option values in the previous subsection, where the assumption of asymmetry in the returns to postponement was embodied in the inequality (2).

# References

1. Arrow, Kenneth J. "The role of securities in an optimal allocation of risk-bearing", in *Econometrie, Proceedings of the Colloque sur les Fondements et Applications de la Theorie du Risque en Econometrie*, Centre National de la Recherche Scientifique, Paris, 1953. English translation in *Review of Economic Studies* 31, 1964, 91–96.
2. Arrow, Kenneth J. and Anthony C. Fisher. "Environmental Preservation, Uncertainty and Irreversibility", *Quarterly Journal of Economics* 88, 1974, 312–319.
3. Arrow, Kenneth J. and Robert C. Lind. "Uncertainty and the Evaluation of Public Investments", *American Economic Review* 60(3), 1970, 364–378.
4. Barrett, Scott. Paris, Environment Directorate, OECD, 1990.
5. Barrett, Scott. "The Paradox of International Environmental Agreements", Paris, Environment Directorate, OECD, 1990.
6. Beltratti, Andrea, Graciela Chichilnisky and Geoffrey M. Heal. "Uncertain Future Preferences and Conservation", Stanford Institute for Theoretical Economics, Technical Report No. 53, 1992. Chapter 3.4 of this volume.
7. Beltratti, Andrea, Graciela Chichilnisky and Geoffrey M. Heal. "Sustainable Growth and the Green Golden Rule", Working Paper, Columbia Business School, 1993. Presented at the OECD conference on "Sustainable Economic Development: Domestic and International Policy", Paris, May 1993.
8. Bohm, Peter. "Option Demand and Consumer's Surplus: Comment", *American Economic Review* 65, 1975, 733–736.
9. Bromley, Daniel W. *Making the Commons Work*, San Francisco, CA, ICS Press, 1992.
10. Carraro, Carlo and Domenico Siniscalco. "Strategies for International Protection of the Environment", Working Paper, Fondazione Eni Enrico Mattei, Milano, 1991.
11. Chichilnisky, Graciela and Ho-Mou Wu. "Financial Innovation and Default in Incomplete Markets", Working Paper, Columbia University, Department of Economics.
12. Cass, David, Graciela Chichilnisky and Ho-Mou Wu. "Individual Risks and Mutual Insurance", CARESS Working Paper #91-27, Department of Economics, University of Pennsylvania, 1991. Also appeared in *Econometrica* 64(2), 1996, 333–341.
13. Chichilnisky, Graciela. "Existence and Optimality of Equilibrium with Endogenous Uncertainty", Working Paper, Columbia University, Department of Economics, 1992. Chapter 3.5 of this volume.
14. Chichilnisky, Graciela. "The Abatement of Carbon Emissions in Industrial and Developing Countries", Paper presented at the International Conference on the Economics of Climate Change, OECD/IEA, Paris, June 1993.
15. Chichilnisky, Graciela, Jayasri Dutta and Geoffrey M. Heal. "Price Uncertainty and Derivative Securities in a General Equilibrium Model", First Boston Working Paper, Columbia Business School, 1992.
16. Chichilnisky, Graciela, Frank H. Hahn and Geoffrey M. Heal. "Price Uncertainty and Incomplete Markets", First Boston Working Paper, Columbia Business School, 1992.
17. Chichilnisky, Graciela and Geoffrey M. Heal. "Financial Markets for Unknown Risks", First Boston Working Paper Series, Columbia Business School, 1992.
18. Chichilnisky, Graciela and Geoffrey M. Heal. "Who Should Abate Carbon Emissions? An International Viewpoint", First Boston Working Paper, Columbia Business School, 1993.
19. Cichetti, Charles J. and A. Myric Freeman III. "Option Demand and Consumer Surplus: Further Comment", *Quarterly Journal of Economics* 85, 1971, 528–539.
20. Cline, William R. *The Economics of Global Warming*, Washington, DC, Institute for International Economics, 1992.
21. Dasgupta, Partha S. and Geoffrey M. Heal. *Economic Theory and Exhaustible Resources*. Cambridge, Cambridge University Press, 1979.

22. Dixit, Avinash K. "Investment and Hysteresis", *Journal of Economic Perspectives* 6(1), 1992, 107–132.
23. Fisher, Anthony C. and John V. Krutilla. "Economics of Nature Preservation", in *Handbook of Natural Resource and Energy Economics*, Vol. I, Alan. V. Kneese and James L. Sweeney (eds.), Amsterdam, North-Holland, 1985, pp. 165–188.
24. Hartwick, John M. "Decline Biodiversity and Risk-Adjusted NNP", Working Paper, Queens University, Department of Economics, 1992.
25. Heal, Geoffrey M. "Interaction between Economy and Climate: A Framework for Policy Design under Uncertainty", in *Advances in Applied Microeconomics*, Vol. 2, V. Kerrry Smith and Ann Dryden White (eds.), J.A.I. Press, 1984, pp. 119–147.
26. Heal, Geoffrey M. "Economy and Climate: A Preliminary Framework for Microeconomic Analysis", in *Commodity and Resource Policies in Agricultural Systems*, Richard E. Just and Nancy Bockstael (eds.), Berlin, Springer-Verlag, 1991, pp. 196–212.
27. Heal, Geoffrey M. "Risk Management and Global Change", Presented at *First Nordic Conference on the Greenhouse Effect*, 1991.
28. Heal, Geoffrey M. "Optimal Resource Use", in *Handbook of Natural Resource and Energy Economics*, Alan V. Kneese and James L. Sweeney (eds.), Amsterdam, North-Holland, 1992, pp. 855–880.
29. Heal, Geoffrey M. "International Negotiations on Emission Control", *Economic Development and Structural Change* 1(1), 1993, 1–19.
30. Henry, Claude. "Option Values in the Economics of Irreplaceable Assets", *Review of Economic Studies*, Special issue on *Symposium on the Economics of Exhaustible Resources*, 1974, 89–104.
31. Henry, Claude. "Investment Decisions under Uncertainty: The Irreversibility Effect", *American Economic Review* 64, 1974, 1005–1012.
32. Krutilla, John V. "Conservation Reconsidered", *American Economic Review* 57, 1967, 777–786.
33. Kurz, Mordecai. "The Kesten–Stigum Model and the Treatment of Uncertainty in Equilibrium Theory", in *Essays on Economic Behavior Under Uncertainty*, M. S. Balch, D. L. McFadden and S. Y. Wu (eds.), Amsterdam: North-Holland, 1974, pp. 389–399.
34. Kurz, Mordecai. "On the Structure and Diversity of Rational Beliefs", Technical Report No. 39, Stanford Institute for Theoretical Economics, 1990.
35. Kurz, Mordecai. "General Equilibrium with Endogenous Uncertainty", in *The Formulation of Economic Theory: Essays in Honor of Kenneth Arrow*, Graciela Chichilnisky (ed.), Cambridge, Cambridge University Press (forthcoming).
36. Malinvaud, Edmond. "The Allocation of Individual Risk in Large Markets", *Journal of Economic Theory* 4, 1972, 312–328.
37. Malinvaud, Edmond. "Markets for an Exchange Economy with Individual Risk", *Econometrica* 3, 1973, 383–412.
38. Manne, Alan S. and Richard G. Richels. *Buying Greenhouse Insurance*, Cambridge, MA, MIT Press, 1992.
39. Pindyck, Robert S. "Irreversibility, Uncertainty and Investment", *Journal of Economic Literature* XXIX(3), 1991, 1110–1148.
40. Schmalensee, Richard. "Option Demand and Consumers' Surplus: Valuing Price Changes under Uncertainty", *American Economic Review* 62, 1972, 813–824.
41. Solow, Robert M. *Sustainability: An Economist's Perspective*, The Eighteenth J. Seward Johnson Lecture, Woods Hole Oceanographic Institution, Woods Hole, MA, 1992.
42. Weisbrod, Burton A. "Collective Consumption Services of Individual Consumption Goods", *Quarterly Journal of Economics* 77, 1964, 71–77.
43. Weyant, John P. "Costs of Reducing Global Carbon Emissions", *Journal of Economic Perspectives* 7(4), 1993, 27–46.

# SECTION 2. DYNAMICS

ANDREA BELTRATTI, GRACIELA CHICHILNISKY AND GEOFFREY HEAL

# 2.1. Sustainable Use of Renewable Resources*

## 1. Introduction

We consider here optimal use patterns for renewable resources. Many important resources are in this category: obvious ones are fisheries and forests. Soils, clean water, landscapes, and the capacities of ecosystems to assimilate and degrade wastes are other less obvious examples.[1] All of these have the capacity to renew themselves, but in addition all can be overused to the point where they are irreversibly damaged. Picking a time-path for the use of such resources is clearly important: indeed, it seems to lie at the heart of any concept of sustainable economic management.

We address the problem of optimal use of renewable resources under a variety of assumptions both about the nature of the economy in which these resources are embedded and about the objective of that economy. In this second respect, we are particularly interested in investigating the consequences of a definition of sustainability as a form of intertemporal optimality recently introduced by Chichilnisky [7], and comparing these consequences with those arising from earlier definitions of intertemporal optimality. In terms of the structure of the economy considered, we review the problem initially in the context of a model where a renewable resource is the only good in the economy, and then subsequently we extend the analysis to include the accumulation of capital and the existence of a productive sector to which the resource is an input.

Although we focus here on the technical economic issues of defining and characterizing paths which are optimal, in various senses, in the presence of renewable resources, one should not loose sight of the very real motivation underlying these exercises: many of the earth's most important biological and ecological resources are renewable, so that in their management we confront

---

* This paper draws heavily on earlier research by one or more of the three authors, namely Beltratti, Chichilnisky and Heal [1–3], Chichilnisky [7, 8], and in particular many of the results here were presented in Heal [18].

the fundamental choice which underlies this paper, namely their extinction, or their preservation as viable species. In this context the recent discussion of sustainability or sustainable management of the earth's resources is closely related to the issues of concern to us. (For a more comprehensive discussion of issues relating to sustainability and its interpretation in economic terms, see [18]. For a review of the basic theory of optimal intertemporal use of resources, see [10, 11, 15].)

We assume, as in [19] and in earlier work by some or all of us [1–3] that the renewable resource is valued not only as a source of consumption but also as a source of utility in its own right: this means that the existing stock of the resource is an argument of the utility function. The instantaneous utility function is therefore $u(c, s)$, where $c$ is consumption and $s$ the remaining stock of the resource. This is clearly the case for forests, which can be used to generate a flow of consumption via timber, and whose stock is a source of pleasure. Similarly, it is true for fisheries, for landscapes, and probably for many more resources. Indeed, in so far as we are dealing with a living entity, there is a moral argument, which we will not evaluate here, that we should value the stock to attribute importance to its existence in its own right and not just instrumentally as a source of consumption.

## 2. The Utilitarian Case without Production

We begin by considering the simplest case, that of a conventional utilitarian objective with no production: the resource is the only good in the economy. For this framework we characterize the utilitarian optimum, and then extend these results to other frameworks. The maximand is the discounted integral of utilities from consumption and from the existence of a stock, $\int_0^\infty u(c, s) e^{-\delta t} dt$, where $\delta > 0$ is a discount rate. As the resource is renewable, its dynamics are described by

$$\dot{s}_t = r(s_t) - c_t.$$

Here $r$ is the growth rate of the resource, assumed to depend only on its current stock. More complex models are of course possible, in which several such systems interact: a well-known example is the predator-prey system. In general, $r$ is a concave function which attains a maximum at a finite value of $s$, and declines thereafter. This formulation has a long and classical history, which is reviewed in [11]. In the field of population biology, $r(s_t)$ is often taken to be quadratic, in which case an unexploited population (i.e., $c_t = 0 \ \forall t$) grows logistically. Here we assume that $r(0) = 0$, that there exists a positive stock level $\bar{s}$ at which $r(\bar{s}) = 0 \ \forall s \geq \bar{s}$, and that $r(s)$ is strictly concave and twice continuously differentiable for $s \in (0, \bar{s})$. The overall problem can now be specified as

$$\max \int_0^\infty u(c, s) e^{-\delta t} dt \text{ s.t. } \dot{s}_t = r(s_t) - c_t, s_0 \text{ given.} \qquad (1)$$

The Hamiltonian in this case is

$$H = u(c_t, s_t) e^{-\delta t} + \lambda_t e^{-\delta t} [r(s_t) - c_t].$$

Maximization with respect to consumption gives as usual the equality of the marginal utility of consumption to the shadow price for positive consumption levels:

$$u_c(c_t, s_t) = \lambda_t$$

and the rate of change of the shadow price is determined by

$$\frac{d}{dt}\left(\lambda_t e^{-\delta t}\right) = -\left[u_s(c_t, s_t) e^{-\delta t} + \lambda_t e^{-\delta t} r'(s_t)\right].$$

To simplify matters we shall take the utility function to be separable in $c$ and $s$: $u(c, s) = u_1(c) + u_2(s)$, each taken to be strictly concave and twice differentiable. In this case a solution to the problem (1) is characterized by

$$\left.\begin{array}{l} u_1'(c_t) = \lambda_t \\ \dot{s}_t = r(s_t) - c_t \\ \dot{\lambda}_t - \delta \lambda_t = -u_2'(s_t) - \lambda_t r'(s_t) \end{array}\right\}. \tag{2}$$

In studying these equations, we first analyze their stationary solution, and then examine the dynamics of this system away from the stationary solution.

### 2.1. Stationary Solutions

At a stationary solution, by definition $s$ is constant so that $r(s_t) = c_t$: in addition, the shadow price is constant so that

$$\delta u_1'(c_t) = u_2'(s_t) + u_1'(c_t) r'(s_t).$$

Hence:

PROPOSITION 1. *A stationary solution to the utilitarian optimal use pattern (2) satisfies*

$$\left.\begin{array}{l} r(s_t) = c_t \\ \frac{u_2'(s_t)}{u_1'(c_t)} = \delta - r'(s_t) \end{array}\right\}. \tag{3}$$

The first equation in (3) just tells us that a stationary solution must lie on the curve on which consumption of the resource equals its renewal rate: this is obviously a prerequisite for a stationary stock. The second gives us a relationship between the slope of an indifference curve in the $c$–$s$ plane and the slope of the renewal function at a stationary solution: the indifference curve cuts the renewal function from above. Such a configuration is shown in Figure 1. This is just the result that the slope of an indifference curve should equal the discount rate if $r'(s) = 0 \; \forall s$, i.e., if the resource is non-renewable [17, 18].

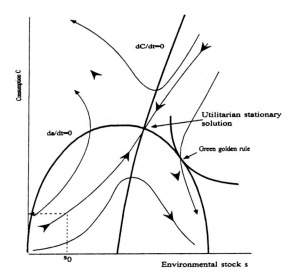

*Figure 1.* Dynamics of the utilitarian solution.

There is a straightforward intuitive interpretation to the second equation in (3). Consider reducing consumption by an amount $\Delta c$ and increasing the stock by the same amount. The welfare loss is $\Delta c u_1'$: there is a gain from increasing the stock of $\Delta c u_2'$, which continues for ever, so that we have to compute its present value. But we also have to recognize that the increment to the stock will grow at the rate $r'$: hence the gain from the increase in stock is the present value of an increment which compounds at rate $r'$. Hence the total gain is

$$\Delta c \int_0^\infty u_2' e^{r't} e^{-\delta t} dt = u_2' \Delta c / (r' - \delta).$$

When gains and losses just balance out, we have

$$u_1' + u_2'/(r' - \delta) = 0$$

which is just the second equation of (3). So (3) is a very natural and intuitive characterization of optimality.

### 2.2. Dynamic Behavior

What are the dynamics of this system outside of a stationary solution? These are also shown in Figure 1. They are derived by noting the following facts:
1. beneath the curve $r(s) = c$, $s$ is rising as consumption is less than the growth of the resource.
2. above the curve $r(s) = c$, $s$ is falling as consumption is greater than the growth of the resource.

3. on the curve $r(s) = c$, $s$ is constant.
4. from (2), the rate of change of $c$ is given by

$$u_1''(c)\dot{c} = u_1'(c)[\delta - r'(s)] - u_2'(s).$$

The first term here is negative for small $s$ and vice versa: the second is negative and large for small $s$ and negative and small for large $s$. Hence $c$ is rising for small $s$ and vice versa: its rate of change is zero precisely when the rate of change of the shadow price is zero, which is on a line of positive slope containing the stationary solution.

5. by linearizing the system

$$\left. \begin{array}{l} u_1''(c)\dot{c} = u_1'(c)[\delta - r'(s)] - u_2'(s) \\ \dot{s}_t = r(s_t) - c_t \end{array} \right\}$$

around the stationary solution, one can show that this solution is a saddle point. The determinant of the matrix of the linearized system is

$$r'(s)\{\delta - r'(s)\} - \frac{1}{u_1''}\{u_1'r'' + u_2''\}$$

which is negative for any stationary stock in excess of the maximum sustainable yield.

Hence the dynamics of paths satisfying the necessary conditions for optimality are as shown in figure 1, and we can establish the following result:

PROPOSITION 2.[2] *For small values of the discount rate $\delta$ or large values of the derivatives $r'$, $r''$ or $u_1'$, all optimal paths for the utilitarian problem (1) tend to the stationary solution (3). They do so along a path satisfying the first order conditions (2), and follow one of the two branches of the stable path in Figure 1 leading to the stationary solution. Given any initial value of the stock $s_0$, there is a corresponding value of $c_0$ which will place the system on one of the stable branches leading to the stationary solution. The position of the stationary solution depends on the discount rate, and moves to higher values of the stationary stock as this decreases. As $\delta \to 0$, the stationary solution tends to a point satisfying $u_2'/u_1' = r'$, which means in geometric terms that an indifference curve of $u(c,s)$ is tangent to the curve $c = r(s)$ given by the graph of the renewal function.*

This result characterizes optimal paths for the problem (1). It does not prove the existence of such paths. The Appendix gives an argument which establishes that an optimal path exists for all of the problems whose solutions are characterized in this paper.

Note that if the initial resource stock is low, *the optimal policy requires that consumption, stock and utility all rise monotonically over time.* The point is that because the resource is renewable, both stocks and flows can be built up over time provided that consumption is less than the rate of regeneration, i.e., the system is inside the curve given by the graph of the renewal function $r(s)$. In practice, unfortunately, many renewable resources are being consumed at a rate greatly in excess of their rates of regeneration: in terms of Figure 1, the current consumption rate $c_t$ is much greater than $r(s_t)$. So taking advantage of the regeneration possibilities of these resources would in many cases require sharp limitation of current consumption. Fisheries are a widely-publicized example: another is tropical hardwoods and tropical forests in general. Soil is a more subtle example: there are processes which renew soil, so that even if it suffers a certain amount of erosion or of depletion of its valuable components, it can be replaced. But typically human use of soils is depleting them at rates far in excess of their replenishment rates.

Proposition 2 gives conditions necessary for a path to be optimal from problem (1). Given the concavity of $u(c, s)$ and of $r(s)$, one can invoke standard arguments to show that these conditions are also sufficient (see, for example, [22]).

## 3. Renewable Resources and the Green Golden Rule

We can use the renewable framework to ask the question: what configuration of the economy gives the maximum sustainable utility level?[3] There is a simple answer.

First, note that a sustainable utility level must be associated with a sustainable configuration of the economy, i.e., with sustainable values of consumption and of the stock. But these are precisely the values that satisfy the equation

$$c_t = r(s_t)$$

for these are the values which are feasible and at which the stock and the consumption levels are constant. Hence in Figure 1, we are looking for values which lie on the curve $c_t = r(s_t)$. Of these values, we need the one which lies on the highest indifference curve of the utility function $u(c, s)$: this point of tangency is shown in the figure. At this point, the slope of an indifference curve equals that of the renewal function, so that the marginal rate of substitution between stock and flow equals the marginal rate of transformation along the curve $r(s)$. Hence:

PROPOSITION 3.[4] *The maximum sustainable utility level (the green golden rule) satisfies*

$$\frac{u_2'(s_t)}{u_1'(c_t)} = -r'(s_t).$$

Recall from (3) that as the discount rate goes to zero, the stationary solution to the utilitarian case tends to such a point. Note also that any path which approaches the tangency of an indifference curve with the reproduction function, is optimal according to the criterion of maximizing sustainable or long-run utility. In other words, this criterion of optimality only determines the limiting behavior of the economy: it does not determine how the limit is approached. This clearly is a weakness: of the many paths which approach the green golden rule, some will accumulate far more utility than others. One would like to know which of these is the best, or indeed whether there is such a best. It transpires that in general there is not. We return to this later.

## 3.1. Ecological Stability

An interesting fact is that the green golden rule, and also for low enough discount rates the utilitarian solution, require stocks of the resource which are in excess of that giving the maximum sustainable yield, which is of course the stock at which the maximum of $r(s)$ occurs. This is important because only resource stocks in excess of that giving the maximum sustainable yield are stable under the natural population dynamics of the resource [21]: they are ecologically stable. To see this, consider a fixed depletion rate $d$, so that the resource dynamics is just

$$\dot{s} = r(s) - d.$$

For $d < \max_s r(s)$, there are two values of $s$ which give stationary solutions to this equation, as shown in Figure 2. Call the smaller $s_1$ and the larger $s_2$. Clearly for $s > s_2$, $\dot{s} < 0$, for $s_1 < s < s_2$, $\dot{s} > 0$, and for $s < s_1$, $\dot{s} < 0$, as shown in Figure 2. Only the stock to the right of the maximum sustainable yield is stable under the natural population adjustment process: high discount rates, and utilitarian optimal policies when the stock of the resource is not an argument of the utility function, will give stationary stocks below the maximum sustainable yield.

## 4. The Rawlsian Solution

Consider the initial stock level $s_1$ in Figure 1: the utilitarian optimum from this is to follow the path that leads to the saddle point. In this case, as noted, consumption, stock and utility are all increasing. So the generation which is least well off, is the first generation. What is the Rawlsian solution in the present model, with initial stock $s_1$? It is easy to verify that this involves setting $c = r(s_1)$ for ever: this gives a constant utility level, and gives the highest utility level for the first generation compatible with subsequent levels being no lower. This remains true for any initial stock no greater than that associated with the green golden rule: for larger initial stocks, the green golden rule is a Rawlsian optimum. Formally,

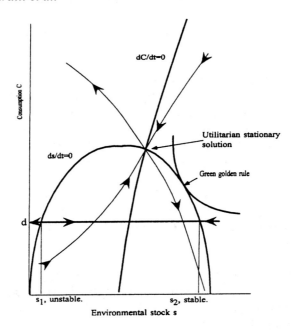

*Figure 2.* The dynamics of the renewable resource under a constant depletion rate.

PROPOSITION 4. *For an initial resource stock $s_1$ less than or equal to that associated with the green golden rule, the Rawlsian optimum involves setting $c = r(s_1)$ for ever. For $s_1$ greater than the green golden rule stock, the green golden rule is a Rawlsian optimum.*

## 5. Chichilnisky's Criterion

Next, we ask how the Chichilnisky criterion [7, 8] alters matters when applied to an analysis of the optimal management of renewable resources. Recall that Chichilnisky's criterion ranks paths according to the sum of two terms, one an integral of utilities against a finite countably additive measure and one a purely finitely additive measure defined on the utility stream of the path. The former is just a generalization of the discounted integral of utilities (generalized in the sense that the finite countably additive measure need not be an exponential discount factor). The latter term can be interpreted as a *sustainable utility level*: Chichilnisky shows that any ranking of intertemporal paths which satisfies certain basic axioms must be representable in this way. The problem now is to pick paths of consumption and resource accumulation over time to:

$$\max \alpha \int_0^\infty u(c_t, s_t) f(t)\, dt + (1-\alpha) \lim_{t\to\infty} u(c_t, s_t) \bigg\}, \quad (4)$$
$$\text{s.t. } \dot{s}_t = r(s_t) - c_t, s_0 \text{ given.}$$

where $f(t)$ is a finite countably additive measure.

The change in optimal policy resulting from the change in the criterion of optimality is quite dramatic. With the Chichilnisky criterion and the measure $f(t)$ given by an exponential discount factor, i.e., $f(t) = e^{-\delta t}$, *there is no solution to the overall optimization problem.*[5] There is a solution only if $f(t)$ takes a different, non-exponential form, implying a non-constant discount rate which tends asymptotically to zero. Chichilnisky's criterion thus links in an unexpected way with recent discussions of individual attitudes towards the future: there is empirical evidence that individuals making intertemporal choices act as if they have non-constant discount rates which decline over time. Formally:

PROPOSITION 5.[6] *The problem (4) has no solution, i.e., there is no optimal pattern of use of a renewable resource using the Chichilnisky criterion with a constant discount rate.*

*Proof.* Consider first the problem

$$\max \int_0^\infty u(c_t, s_t) e^{-\delta t} dt \text{ s.t. } \dot{s}_t = r(s_t) - c_t, s_0 \text{ given.}$$

The dynamics of the solution is shown in Figure 1, reproduced here as Figure 3.

It differs from the problem under consideration by the lack of the term in limiting utility in the maximand. Suppose that the initial stock is $s_0$ in Figure 3. Pick an initial value of $c$, say $c_0$, below the path leading to the saddle-point, and follow the path from $c_0$ satisfying the utilitarian necessary conditions given above:

$$u_1''(c)\dot{c} = u_1'(c)[\delta - r'(s)] - u_2'(s),$$
$$\dot{s}_t = r(s_t) - c_t.$$

Denote by $v_0$ the 2-vector of initial conditions: $v_0 = (c_0, s_0)$. Call this path $\{\bar{c}_t, \bar{s}_t\}(v_0)$. Follow this path until it leads to the resource stock corresponding the green golden rule, i.e., until the $t'$ such that on the path $\{\bar{c}_t, \bar{s}_t\}(v_0)$, $\bar{s}_{t'} = s^*$, and then at $t = t'$ increase consumption to the level corresponding to the green golden rule, i.e., set $c_t = r(s^*)$ for all $t \geq t'$. This is feasible because $c_t < r(s_t)$ along such a path. Such a path is shown in Figure 3. Formally, this path is $(c_t, s_t) = \{\bar{c}_t, \bar{s}_t\}(v_0) \ \forall t \leq t'$ where $t'$ is defined by $\bar{s}_{t'} = s^*$, and $c_t = r(s^*), s_t = s^* \ \forall t > t'$.

Any such path will satisfy the necessary conditions for utilitarian optimality up to time $t'$ and will lead to the green golden rule in finite time. It will therefore attain a maximum of the term $\lim_{t\to\infty} u(c_t, s_t)$ over feasible paths. However, the utility integral which constitutes the first part of the maximand

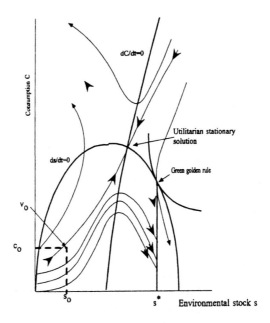

*Figure 3.* A sequence of consumption paths with initial stock $s_0$ and initial consumption level below that leading to the utilitarian stationary solution and converging to it. Once the stock reaches $s^*$ consumption is set equal to $r(s^*)$. The limit is a path which approaches the utilitarian stationary solution and not the green golden rule.

can be improved by picking a slightly higher initial value $c_0$ for consumption, again following the first order conditions for optimality and reaching the green golden rule slightly later than $t'$. This does not detract from the second term in the maximand. By this process it will be possible to increase the integral term in the maximand without reducing the limiting term and thus to approximate the independent maximization of both terms in the maximand: the discounted utilitarian term, by staying long enough close to the stable manifold leading to the utilitarian stationary solution, and the limit (purely finitely additive) term by moving to the green golden rule very far into the future.

Although it is possible to *approximate* the maximization of both terms in the maximand independently by postponing further and further the jump to the green golden rule, there is no feasible path that actually *achieves* this maximum. The supremum of the values of the maximand over feasible paths is approximated arbitrarily closely by paths which reach the green golden rule at later and later dates, but the limit of these paths never reaches the green golden rule and so does not achieve the supremum. More formally, consider the limit of paths $(c_t, s_t) = \{\bar{c}_t, \bar{s}_t\}(v_0) \ \forall t \leq t'$ where $t'$ is defined by $\bar{s}_{t'} = s^*$, and $c_t = r(s^*), s_t = s^* \ \forall t > t'$ as $c_0$ approaches the stable manifold of the utilitarian optimal solution. On this limiting path $s_t < s^* \ \forall t$.

Hence there is no solution to (4). □

Intuitively, the non-existence problem arises here because it is always possible to postpone further into the future moving to the green golden rule, with no cost in terms of limiting utility values but with a gain in terms of the integral of utilities. This is possible because of the renewability of the resource. There is no equivalent phenomenon for an exhaustible resource [18].

### 5.1. Declining Discount Rates

With the Chichilnisky criterion formulated as

$$\alpha \int_0^\infty u(c_t, s_t) e^{-\delta t} dt + (1-\alpha) \lim_{t \to \infty} u(c_t, s_t),$$

there is no solution to the problem of optimal management of a renewable resource. In fact as noted the discount factor does not have to be an exponential function of time. The criterion can be stated slightly differently, in a way which is still consistent with Chichilnisky's axioms and which is also consistent with solving the renewable resource problem. This reformulation builds on a point that we have noted before, namely that for the discounted utilitarian case, as the discount rate goes to zero, the stationary solution goes to the green golden rule. We shall, therefore, consider a modified objective function

$$\alpha \int_0^\infty u(c_t, s_t) \Delta(t) dt + (1-\alpha) \lim_{t \to \infty} u(c_t, s_t),$$

where $\Delta(t)$ is the discount factor at time $t$, $\int_0^\infty \Delta(t) dt$ is finite, the discount rate $q(t)$ at time $t$ is the proportional rate of change of the discount factor:

$$q(t) = -\frac{\dot{\Delta}(t)}{\Delta(t)}$$

and we assume that the discount rate goes to zero with $t$ in the limit:

$$\lim_{t \to \infty} q(t) = 0. \tag{5}$$

So the overall problem is now

$$\max \alpha \int_0^\infty u(c_t, s_t) \Delta(t) dt + (1-\alpha) \lim_{t \to \infty} u(c_t, s_t)$$
$$\text{s.t. } \dot{s}_t = r(s_t) - c_t, \ s_0 \text{ given,}$$

where the discount factor $\Delta(t)$ satisfies the condition (5) that the discount rate goes to zero in the limit. We will show that for this problem, there is a solution:[7] in fact, it is the solution to the utilitarian problem of maximizing just the first term in the above maximand, $\int_0^\infty u(c_t, s_t) \Delta(t) dt$. As before we take the utility function to be separable in its arguments: $u(c, s) = u_1(c) + u_2(s)$. Formally,

PROPOSITION 6.[8] *Consider the problem*

$$\max \alpha \int_0^\infty \{u_1(c) + u_2(s)\} \Delta(t)\, dt + (1-\alpha) \lim_{t\to\infty} \{u_1(c) + u_2(s)\},$$
$$0 < \alpha < 1, \text{ s.t. } \dot{s}_t = r(s_t) - c_t, s_0 \text{ given},$$

*where* $q(t) = -(\dot{\Delta}(t)/\Delta(t))$ *and* $\lim_{t\to\infty} q(t) = 0$. *A solution to this problem is identical to the solution of "*$\max \int_0^\infty \{u_1(c) + u_2(s)\} \Delta(t)\, dt$ *subject to the same constraint". In words, the conditions characterizing a solution to the utilitarian problem with the variable discount rate which goes to zero also characterize a solution to the overall problem.*

*Proof.* Consider first the problem $\max \alpha \int_0^\infty \{u_1(c) + u_2(s)\} \Delta(t)\, dt$ s.t. $\dot{s}_t = r(s_t) - c_t$, $s_0$ given. We shall show that any solution to this problem approaches and attains the green golden rule asymptotically, which is the configuration of the economy which gives the maximum of the term $(1-\alpha) \lim_{t\to\infty} u(c_t, s_t)$. Hence this solution solves the overall problem. The Hamiltonian for the integral problem is now

$$H = \{u_1(c) + u_2(s)\} \Delta(t) + \lambda_t \Delta(t) [r(s_t) - c_t]$$

and maximization with respect to consumption gives as before

$$u_1'(c_t) = \lambda_t.$$

The rate of change of the shadow price $\lambda_t$ is determined by

$$\frac{d}{dt}(\lambda_t \Delta(t)) = -[u_2'(s_t) \Delta(t) + \lambda_t \Delta(t) r'(s_t)].$$

The rate of change of the shadow price is, therefore,

$$\dot{\lambda}_t \Delta(t) + \lambda_t \dot{\Delta}(t) = -u_2'(s_t) \Delta(t) - \lambda_t \Delta(t) r'(s_t). \tag{6}$$

As $\dot{\Delta}(t)$ depends on time, this equation is not autonomous, i.e., time appears explicitly as a variable. For such an equation, we cannot use the phase portraits and associated linearization techniques used before, because the rates of change of $c$ and $s$ depend not only on the point in the $c$–$s$ plane but also on the date. Rearranging and noting that $\dot{\Delta}(t)/\Delta(t) = q(t)$, we have

$$\dot{\lambda}_t + \lambda_t q(t) = -u_2'(s_t) - u_1'(c_t) r'(s_t).$$

But in the limit $q = 0$, so in the limit this equation is autonomous: this equation and the stock growth equation form what has recently been called in dynamical systems theory an asymptotically autonomous system [4]. According to proposition 1.2 of [4], the asymptotic phase portrait of this non-autonomous system

$$\left. \begin{array}{l} \dot{\lambda}_t + \lambda_t q(t) = -u_2'(s_t) - u_1'(c_t) r'(s_t) \\ \dot{s}_t = r(s_t) - c_t \end{array} \right\} \tag{7}$$

is the same as that of the autonomous system

$$\left.\begin{array}{l}\dot{\lambda}_t = -u_2'(s_t) - u_1'(c_t)r'(s_t) \\ \dot{s}_t = r(s_t) - c_t\end{array}\right\} \qquad (8)$$

which differs only in that the non-autonomous term $q(t)$ has been set equal to zero.[9] The pair of Equations (8) is an autonomous system and the asymptotic stability properties of original system (7) will be the same as those of the associated limiting autonomous system (8). This latter system can be analyzed by the standard techniques used before. At a stationary solution of (8), $\dot{\lambda}_t = 0$ and $c_t = r(s_t)$, so that

$$\frac{u_2'}{u_1'} = -r' \quad \text{and} \quad c_t = r(s_t)$$

which is just the definition of the green golden rule. Furthermore, by the arguments used above we can establish that the green golden rule is a saddlepoint of the system (8), as shown in Figure 3. So the optimal path for the problem

"maximize $\int_0^\infty \{u_1(c) + u_2(s)\}\Delta(t)\,dt$

subject to $\dot{s}_t = r(s_t) - c_t$, $s_0$ given"

is for any given initial stock $s_0$ to select an initial consumption level $c_0$ such that $(c_0, s_0)$ is on the stable path of the saddle point configuration which approaches the Green Golden Rule asymptotically. But this path also leads to the maximum possible value of the term $\lim_{t\to\infty}\{u_1(c) + u_2(s)\}$, and therefore leads to a solution to the overall maximization problem. □

Figure 4 shows the behavior of an optimal path in this case. Intuitively, one can see what drives this result. The non-existence of an optimal path with a constant discount rate arose from a conflict between the long-run behavior of the path that maximizes the integral of discounted utilities, and that of the path that maximizes the long-run utility level. When the discount rate goes to zero in the limit, that conflict is resolved. In fact, one can show that it is resolved only in this case, as stated by the following proposition.

PROPOSITION 7.[10] *Consider the problem*

$$\max \alpha \int_0^\infty \{u_1(c) + u_2(s)\}\Delta(t)\,dt + (1-\alpha)\lim_{t\to\infty}\{u_1(c) + u_2(s)\},$$
$$0 < \alpha < 1, \text{ s.t. } \dot{s}_t = r(s_t) - c_t, s_0 \text{ given,}$$

*where $q(t) = -(\dot{\Delta}(t)/\Delta(t))$. This problem has a solution only if $\lim_{t\to\infty} q(t) = 0$. In this case, the solution is characterized by the conditions which characterize the solution to "$\max \int_0^\infty \{u_1(c) + u_2(s)\}\Delta(t)\,dt$ subject to the same constraint".*

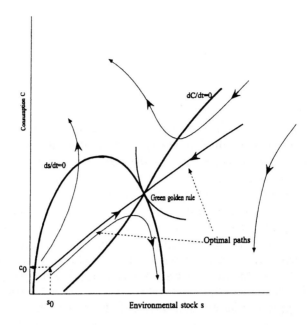

*Figure 4.* Asymptotic dynamics of the utilitarian solution for the case in which the discount rate falls to zero.

*Proof.* The "if" part of this was proven in the previous proposition, Proposition 6. The "only if" part can be proven by an extension of the arguments in Proposition 5, which established the non-existence of solutions in the case of a constant discount rate. To apply the arguments there, assume contrary to the proposition that $\liminf_{t\to\infty} q(t) = \bar{q} > 0$, and then apply the arguments of Proposition 5. □

Existence of a solution to this problem is established in the Appendix.

### 5.2. Examples

To complete this discussion, we review some examples of discount factors which satisfy the condition that the limiting discount rate goes to zero. The most obvious is

$$\Delta(t) = e^{-\delta(t)t}, \quad \text{with} \quad \lim_{t\to\infty} \delta(t) = 0.$$

Another example[11] is

$$\Delta(t) = t^{-\alpha}, \quad \alpha > 1.$$

Taking the starting date to be $t = 1$,[12] we have

$$\int_1^\infty t^{-\alpha} dt = \frac{1}{\alpha - 1}$$

and

$$\frac{\dot{\Delta}}{\Delta} = \frac{-\alpha}{t} \to 0 \quad \text{as} \quad t \to \infty.$$

## 5.3. Empirical Evidence on Declining Discount Rates

Proposition 7 has substantial implications. It says that when we seek optimality with a criterion sensitive to the present and the long-run future, then with non-renewable resources existence of a solution is tied to the limiting behavior of the discount rate: in the limit, we have to treat present and future utilities symmetrically in the evaluation of the integral of utilities. In a certain sense, the treatment of present and future in the integral has to be made consistent with the presence of the term $\lim_{t \to \infty} \{u_1(c) + u_2(s)\}$ which places positive weight on the very long run.

There is a growing body of empirical evidence that people actually behave like this in evaluating the future (see, for example, [20]; see also [18] for a more comprehensive discussion). The evidence suggests that the discount rate which people apply to future projects depends upon, and declines with, the futurity of the project. Over relatively short periods up to perhaps five years, they use discount rates which are higher even than commercial rates – in the region of 15% or more. For projects extending about ten years, the implied discount rates are closer to standard rates – perhaps 10%. As the horizon extends the implied discount rates drops, to in the region of 5% for 30 to 50 years and down to of the order of 2% for 100 years. It is of great interest that a framework for intertemporal optimization that is sensitive to both present and future generates an implication for discounting that may rationalize a form of personal behavior that hitherto has been found irrational.

This empirically-identified behavior is consistent with results from natural sciences which find that human responses to a change in a stimulus are non-linear, and are inversely proportional to the existing level of the stimulus. This is an example of the Weber–Fechner law, which is formalized in the statement that human response to a change in a stimulus is inversely proportional to the pre-existing stimulus. In symbols,

$$\frac{dr}{ds} = \frac{K}{s} \quad \text{or} \quad r = K \log s,$$

where $r$ is a response, $s$ a stimulus and $K$ a constant. This has been found to apply to human responses to the intensity of both light and sound signals. We noted that the empirical results on discounting cited above suggest that something similar is happening in human responses to changes in the futurity of an event: a given change in futurity (e.g., postponement by one year) leads to a smaller response in terms of the decrease in weighting, the further the event already is in the future. In this case, the Weber–Fechner law can be applied to responses to distance in time, as well as to sound and light intensity, with the result that the discount rate is inversely proportional to distance into the future. Recalling that the discount factor is $\Delta(t)$ and the discount rate $q(t) = -\dot{\Delta}(t)/\Delta(t)$, we can formalize this as

$$q(t) = \frac{1}{\Delta}\frac{d\Delta}{dt} = \frac{K}{t} \quad \text{or} \quad \Delta(t) = e^{K\log t} = t^K$$

for $K$ a positive constant. Such a discount factor can meet all of the conditions we required above: the discount rate $q$ goes to zero in the limit, the discount factor $\Delta(t)$ goes to zero and the integral $\int_1^\infty \Delta(t)\,dt = \int_1^\infty e^{K\log t}\,dt = \int_1^\infty t^K\,dt$ converges for $K$ positive, as it always is. In fact, this interpretation gives rise to the second example of a non-constant discount rate considered in the previous section. A discount factor $\Delta(t) = e^{K\log t}$ has an interesting interpretation: the replacement of $t$ by $\log t$ implies that we are measuring time differently, i.e. by equal proportional increments rather than by equal absolute increments.

### 5.4. Time Consistency

An issue which is raised by the previous propositions is that of *time consistency*. Consider a solution to an intertemporal optimization problem which is computed today and is to be carried out over some future period of time starting today. Suppose that the agent formulating it – an individual or a society – may at a future date recompute an optimal plan, using the same objective and the same constraints as initially but with initial conditions and starting date corresponding to those obtaining when the recomputation is done. Then we say that the initial solution is *time consistent* if this leads the agent to continue with the implementation of the initial solution. Another way of saying this is that a plan is time consistent if the passage of time alone gives no reason to change it. The important point is that the solution to the problem of optimal management of the renewable resource with a time-varying discount rate, stated in Proposition 7, is not time-consistent. A formal definition of time consistency is:[13]

DEFINITION 8. Let $(c_t^*, s_t^*)_{t=0,\infty}$ be the solution to the problem

$$\max \alpha \int_0^\infty \{u_1(c) + u_2(s)\}\Delta(t)\,dt + (1-\alpha)\lim_{t\to\infty}\{u_1(c) + u_2(s)\},$$
$$0 < \alpha < 1, \text{ s.t. } \dot{s}_t = r(s_t) - c_t, s_0 \text{ given.}$$

Let $(\hat{c}_t, \hat{s}_t)_{t=T,\infty}$ be the solution to the problem of optimizing from $T$ on, given that the path $(c_t^*, s_t^*)_{t=0,\infty}$ has been followed up to date $T$., i.e., $(\hat{c}_t, \hat{s}_t)_{t=T,\infty}$ solves

$$\max \alpha \int_T^\infty \{u_1(c) + u_2(s)\}\Delta(t-T)\,dt + (1-\alpha)\lim_{t\to\infty}\{u_1(c) + u_2(s)\},$$
$$0 < \alpha < 1, \text{s.t. } \dot{s}_t = r(s_t) - c_t, s_T^* \text{ given.}$$

Then the original problem solved at $t = 0$ is time consistent if and only if $(\hat{c}_t, \hat{s}_t)_{t=T,\infty} = (c_t^*, s_t^*)_{t=T,\infty}$, i.e., if the original solution restricted to the period $[T, \infty]$ is also a solution to the problem with initial time $T$ and initial stock $s_T^*$, for any $T$.

It is shown in [14] that the solutions to dynamic optimization problems are in general time consistent only if the discount factor is exponential. The following result is an illustration of this fact.

PROPOSITION 9.[14] *The solution to the problem of optimal management of a renewable resource with a discount rate falling asymptotically to zero is not time consistent, i.e., the solution to*

$$\max \alpha \int_0^\infty \{u_1(c) + u_2(s)\} \Delta(t)\, dt + (1-\alpha) \lim_{t\to\infty} \{u_1(c) + u_2(s)\},$$

$0 < \alpha < 1$, s.t. $\dot{s}_t = r(s_t) - c_t$, $s_0$ given, $q(t) = -\frac{\dot{\Delta}(t)}{\Delta(t)}$, $\lim_{t\to\infty} q(t) = 0$.
*is not time consistent.*

*Proof.* Consider the first order condition for a solution to this problem, which are given in (7) and repeated here with the substitution $\lambda = u_1'$:

$$\left. \begin{array}{c} u_1''(c_t)\dot{c}_t + u_1'(c_t)q(t) = -u_2'(s_t) - u_1'(c_t)r'(s_t) \\ \dot{s}_t = r(s_t) - c_t \end{array} \right\}. \quad (9)$$

Let $(\tilde{c}_t, \tilde{s}_t)_{t=0,\infty}$ be a solution computed at date $t = 0$. The rate of change of consumption on this at a date $T > 0$ will be given by (9). Now let $(\bar{c}_t, \bar{s}_t)_{t=\Upsilon,\infty}$ be a solution to the problem with starting date $\Upsilon$, $0 < \Upsilon < T$, and initial conditions at $\Upsilon$ given by $(\tilde{c}_\Upsilon, \tilde{s}_\Upsilon)$. When the problem is solved again with starting date $\Upsilon$, the value of $\Delta(t)$ at calendar time $\Upsilon$ is $\Delta(0)$, the initial value of the discount factor. Hence on this path the value of $\Delta(t)$ at date $T$ is $\Delta(T - \Upsilon)$, while it is $\Delta(T)$ on the initial path. Hence $q(T)$ will differ, and the two paths will have different rates of change of consumption for all dates in excess of $\Upsilon$. This establishes that if the optimum is recomputed at any date $T > 0$, then the initial plan will no longer be followed. □

These are interesting and surprising results: to ensure the existence of an optimal path which balances present and future "correctly" according to Chichilnisky's axioms, we have to accept paths which are not time consistent. Of course, the empirical evidence cited above implies that individual behavior must also be inconsistent, so society in this case is only replicating what individuals apparently do. Traditionally, welfare economists have always regarded time consistency as a very desirable property of intertemporal choice. More recently, this presumption has been questioned: philosophers and psychologists have noted that the same person at different stages of her or his life can reasonably be thought of as different people with different perspectives on life and different experiences.[15] The implications of working with inconsistent choices clearly need further research.

## 6. Capital and Renewable Resources

Now we consider the most challenging, and perhaps most realistic and rewarding, of all cases: an economy in which a resource which is renewable and so has its own dynamics can be used together with produced capital goods as an input to the production of an output. The output in turn can as usual in growth models be reinvested in capital formation or consumed. The stock of the resource is also a source of utility to the population. So capital accumulation occurs according to

$$\dot{k} = F(k, \sigma) - c$$

and the resource stock evolves according to

$$\dot{s} = r(s) - \sigma,$$

where $k$ is the current capital stock, $\sigma$ the rate of use of the resource in production, and $F(k, \sigma)$ the production function. As before $r(s)$ is a growth function for the renewable resource, indicating the rate of growth of this when the stock is $s$.

As before, we shall consider the optimum according to the utilitarian criterion, then characterize the green golden rule, and finally draw on the results of these two cases to characterize optimality according to Chichilnisky's criterion.

## 7. The Utilitarian Optimum

The utilitarian optimum in this framework is the solution to

$$\left. \begin{array}{l} \max \int_0^\infty u(c_t, s_t) e^{-\delta t} dt \text{ subject to} \\ \dot{k} = F(k, \sigma) - c \text{ and } \dot{s} = r(s) - \sigma \end{array} \right\}. \tag{10}$$

We proceed in the by-now standard manner, constructing the Hamiltonian

$$H = u(c, s) e^{-\delta t} + \lambda e^{-\delta t} \{F(k, \sigma) - c\} + \mu e^{-\delta t} \{r(s) - \sigma\}$$

and deriving the following conditions which are necessary for a solution to (10):

$$u_c = \lambda, \tag{11}$$

$$\lambda F_\sigma = \mu, \tag{12}$$

$$\dot{\lambda} - \delta\lambda = -\lambda F_k, \tag{13}$$

$$\dot{\mu} - \delta\mu = -u_s - \mu r_s, \tag{14}$$

where $r_s$ is the derivative of $r$ with respect to the stock $s$.

## 7.1. Stationary Solutions

A little algebra shows that the system (11) to (14), together with the two underlying differential equations in (10), admits the following stationary solution:

$$\delta = F_k(k, \sigma), \tag{15}$$

$$\sigma = r(s), \tag{16}$$

$$c = F(k, \sigma), \tag{17}$$

$$\frac{u_s(c, s)}{u_c(c, s)} = F_\sigma(k, \sigma)(\delta - r_s). \tag{18}$$

This system of four equations suffices to determine the stationary values of the variables $k$, $s$, $\sigma$ and $c$.

It is important to understand fully the structure of stationary states in this model, and in particular the trade-off between consumption $c$ and the resource stock $s$ across alternative stationary states.

First, consider this relationship across stationary states for a given value of the capital stock $k$: in this case we can write

$$c = F(k, \sigma(s)),$$

and so we have

$$\left.\frac{\partial c}{\partial s}\right|_{k \text{ fixed}} = F_\sigma r_s. \tag{19}$$

As $F_\sigma$ is always positive, this has the sign of $r_s$, which is initially positive and then switches to negative: hence we have a single-peaked relationship between $c$ and $s$ for fixed $k$ across stationary states. The $c$–$s$ relationship across stationary states for a fixed value of $k$ replicates the shape of the growth function $r(s)$ and so has a maximum for the same value of $s$.

In general, however, $k$ is not fixed across stationary states, but depends on $\sigma$ via Equation (15). Taking account of this dependence and treating (15) as an implicit function, we obtain the total derivative of $c$ with respect to $s$ across stationary states:

$$\frac{dc}{ds} = r_s \left( -\delta \frac{F_{k\sigma}}{F_{kk}} + F_\sigma \right), \tag{20}$$

which, maintaining the assumption that $F_{k\sigma} \geq 0$, also has the sign of $r_s$ and again inherits the shape of $r(s)$. Note that for a given value of $s$: $|(dc/ds)| \geq |(\partial c/\partial s)_k \text{ fixed}|$ and that the two are equal only if the cross derivative $F_{k\sigma}$ is zero. The various curves relating $c$ and $s$ across stationary solutions are shown in Figure 5: for $F_{k\sigma} > 0$ the curve corresponding to $k$ fully adjusted to $s$ both rises and falls more sharply than the others, and crosses each of these twice, from below while increasing and from above while decreasing, as shown. A stationary solution with a capital stock $\hat{k}$ must lie on the intersection of the

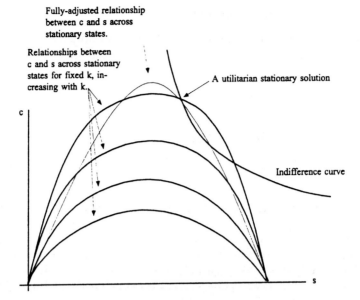

*Figure 5.* A utilitarian stationary solution occurs where the fully-adjusted $c$–$s$ relationship crosses the same relationship for the fixed value of $k$ corresponding to the stationary solution.

curve corresponding to a capital stock fixed at $\hat{k}$ with the curve representing the fully-adjusted relationship. At this point, $c$, $s$ and $k$ are all fully adjusted to each other. (In the case of $F_{k\sigma} = 0$ the curves relating $c$ and $s$ for $k$ fixed and fully adjusted are identical, so that in the case of a separable production function the dynamics are simpler, although qualitatively similar.)

The stationary first order condition (18) relates most closely to the curve connecting $c$ and $s$ for a fixed value of $k$ (the only relevant curve for $F_{k\sigma} = 0$), and would indicate a tangency between this curve and an indifference curve if the discount rate $\delta$ were equal to zero. For positive $\delta$, the case we are considering now, the stationary solution lies at the point where the $c$–$s$ curve for the fixed value of $k$ associated with the stationary solution crosses the $c$–$s$ curve along which $k$ varies with $s$. At this point, an indifference curve crosses the fixed-$k$ $c$–$s$ curve from above: this is shown in Figure 5. Note that as we vary the discount rate $\delta$, the capital stock associated with a stationary solution will alter via Equation (15), so that in particular lowering the discount rate will lead to a stationary solution on a fixed-$k$ $c$–$s$ curve corresponding to a larger value of $k$ and therefore outside the curve corresponding to the initial lower discount rate.

## 7.2. Dynamics of the Utilitarian Solution

The four differential equations governing a utilitarian solution are

$$\left.\begin{array}{l} \dot{k} = F(k,\sigma) - c(s_t, \lambda_t) \\ \dot{s} = r(s) - \sigma(\mu_t, \lambda_t, k_t) \\ \dot{\lambda} - \delta\lambda = -\lambda F_k \\ \dot{\mu} - \delta\mu = -u_s - \mu r_s \end{array}\right\}.$$

The matrix of the linearized system is

$$\begin{bmatrix} \delta - F_\sigma \lambda \frac{F_{\sigma k}}{F_{\sigma\sigma}} & \frac{u_{cs}}{u_{cc}} & -\frac{F_\sigma F_\sigma}{\lambda F_{\sigma\sigma}} - \frac{1}{u_{cc}} & \frac{F_\sigma}{\lambda F_{\sigma\sigma}} \\ \frac{F_{\sigma k}}{F_{\sigma\sigma}} & r_s & \frac{F_\sigma}{\lambda F_{\sigma\sigma}} & -\frac{1}{\lambda F_{\sigma\sigma}} \\ -\lambda F_{kk} + F_{k\sigma}\lambda \frac{F_{\sigma k}}{F_{\sigma\sigma}} & 0 & \delta + \frac{F_{k\sigma} F_\sigma}{F_{\sigma\sigma}} & -\frac{F_{k\sigma}}{F_{\sigma\sigma}} \\ 0 & \frac{u_{sc}u_{cs}}{u_{cc}} - u_{ss} - \mu r_s & -\frac{u_{sc}}{u_{cc}} & \delta - r_s \end{bmatrix}.$$

To establish clear general results on the signs of the eigenvalues of this matrix, we have to make simplifying assumptions. If $F_{\sigma\sigma}$ is large, so that the marginal productivity of the resource drops rapidly as more of it is employed, then the eigenvalues of the above matrix are: $r_s$, $\delta - r_s$, $1/(2u_{cc})(2u_{cc}\delta \pm \sqrt{u_{cc}^2\delta^2 + 4u_{cc}\lambda F_{kk}}$. There are two negative roots in this case, as $r_s < 0$ at a stationary solution. In this case the utilitarian stationary solution is locally a saddle point.

PROPOSITION 10.[16] *A sufficient condition for the utilitarian stationary solution to be locally a saddle point is that $F_{\sigma\sigma}$ is large, so that the marginal productivity of the resource diminishes rapidly in production.*

There are other cases in which the stationary solution is locally a saddle point, involving additive separability of the utility function.[17] Existence of a solution to the utilitarian problem is established in the Appendix.

## 8. The Green Golden Rule with Production and Renewable Resources

Across stationary states, the relationship between consumption and the resource stock satisfies the equation

$$c = F(k, r(s)),$$

so that at the green golden rule we seek to maximize the sustainable utility level with respect to the inputs of capital $k$ and the resource stock $s$:

$$\max_{s,k} u(F(k, r(s)), s).$$

Maximization with respect to the resource stock gives

$$\frac{u_s}{u_c} = -F_\sigma r_s, \qquad (21)$$

which is precisely the condition (18) characterizing the stationary solution to the utilitarian conditions for the case in which the discount rate $\delta$ is equal to zero. So, as before, the utilitarian solution with a zero discount rate meets the first order conditions for maximization of sustainable utility with respect to the resource stock. Of course, in general the utilitarian problem may have no solution when the discount rate is zero. Note that the condition (21) is quite intuitive and in keeping with earlier results. It requires that an indifference curve be tangent to the curve relating $c$ to $s$ across stationary states for $k$ fixed at the level $\overline{k}$ defined below: in other words, it again requires equality of marginal rates of transformation and substitution between stocks and flows.

The capital stock $k$ in the maximand here is independent of $s$. How is the capital stock chosen? In a utilitarian solution the discount rate plays a role in this through the equality of the marginal product of capital with the discount rate (15): at the green golden rule there is no equivalent relationship.

We close the system in the present case by supposing that the production technology ultimately displays satiation with respect to the capital input alone: for each level of the resource input $\sigma$ there is a level of capital stock at which the marginal product of capital is zero. Precisely,

$$\overline{k}(\sigma) = \min k : \frac{\partial F}{\partial k}(k, \sigma) = 0. \tag{22}$$

We assume that $\overline{k}(\sigma)$ exists for all $\sigma \geq 0$, is finite, continuous and non-decreasing in $\sigma$. Essentially assumption (22) says that there is a limit to the extent to which capital can be substituted for resources: as we apply more and more capital to a fixed input of resources output reaches a maximum above which it cannot be increased for that level of resource input. In the case in which the resource is an energy source, this assumption was shown by Berry et al. [5] to be implied by the second law of thermodynamics: this issue is also discussed by Dasgupta and Heal [11]. In general, this seems a very mild and reasonable assumption. Given this assumption, the maximization of stationary utility with respect to the capital stock at a given resource input,

$$\max_{k} u\left(F\left(k, r(s)\right), s\right)$$

requires that we pick the capital stock at which satiation occurs at this resource input, i.e., $k = \overline{k}(r(s))$. Note that

$$\frac{\partial \overline{k}(r(s))}{\partial s} = \frac{\partial \overline{k}(\sigma)}{\partial \sigma} r_s;$$

so that $\overline{k}$ is increasing and then decreasing in $s$ across stationary states: the derivative has the sign of $r_s$. In this case, the green golden rule is the solution to the following problem:

$$\max_{s} u\left(F\left(\overline{k}(r(s)), r(s)\right), s\right),$$

where at each value of the resource stock $s$ the input and the resource and the capital stock are adjusted so that the resource stock is stationary and the capital stock maximizes output for that stationary resource input. The relationship between consumption and the resource stock across stationary states when at each resource stock the capital stock is adjusted to the level $\overline{k}(r(s))$ has the following slope:

$$\frac{dc}{ds} = F_k \frac{\partial \overline{k}}{\partial \sigma} r_s + F_\sigma r_s$$

and by the definition of $\overline{k}$ the first term on the right is zero, so that the slope of the curve relating $c$ and $s$ when the capital stock is given by $\overline{k}$ is the same as the slope when the capital stock is fixed. This curve is thus the outer envelope of the curves for fixed values of the capital stock.

The total derivative of the utility level with respect to the stock of the resource is now

$$\frac{du}{ds} = u_c F_k \frac{\partial \overline{k}}{\partial \sigma} r_s + u_c F_\sigma r_s + u_s.$$

By assumption (22) and the definition of $\overline{k}$, $F_k = 0$ here: hence equating this to zero for a maximum sustainable utility level gives the earlier expression (21). The green golden rule is characterized by a tangency between an indifference curve and the outer envelope of all curves relating $c$ to $s$ across stationary states for fixed capital stocks.

PROPOSITION 11.[18] *In an economy with capital accumulation and renewable resources, under the assumption (22) of satiation of the production function with respect to capital, the green golden rule satisfies the first order condition $u_s/u_c = -F_\sigma r_s$ which defines a tangency between an indifference curve and the outer envelope of c–s curves for fixed values of k. It has a capital stock of $\overline{k}(\sigma(s^*))$, where $s^*$ is the green golden rule value of the resource stock and $\overline{k}$ denotes the capital stock at which the marginal product of capital first becomes zero for a resource input of $\sigma(s^*)$.*

What if production does not display satiation with respect to the capital stock? In this case there is no maximum to the output which can be obtained from a given resource flow and so from a given resource stock. Unless we assume satiation of preferences with respect to consumption, the green golden rule is not well defined.[19]

## 9. Optimality for the Chichilnisky Criterion

Now we seek to solve the problem

$$\left. \max \alpha \int_0^\infty u(c_t, s_t) e^{-\delta t} dt + (1-\alpha) \lim_{t\to\infty} u(c_t, s_t) \right\} . \quad (23)$$
$$\text{s.t. } \dot{k} = F(k_t, \sigma_t) - c_t \ \& \ \dot{s}_t = r(s) - \sigma_t, s_t \geq 0 \quad \forall t.$$

In the case of satiation of the production process with respect to capital, as captured by assumption (22), the situation resembles that with the Chichilnisky criterion with renewable resources above: there is no solution unless the discount rate declines to zero. Formally:

PROPOSITION 12.[20] *Assume that condition (22) is satisfied. Then problem (23) has no solution.*

*Proof.* The structure of the proof is the same as that used above. The integral term is maximized by the utilitarian solution, which requires an asymptotic approach to the utilitarian stationary state. The limit term is maximized on any path which asymptotes to the green golden rule. Given any fraction $\beta \in [0, 1]$ we can find a path which attains the fraction $\beta$ of the payoff to the utilitarian optimum and then approaches the green golden rule. This is true for any value of $\beta < 1$, but not true for $\beta = 1$. Hence any path can be dominated by another corresponding to a higher value of $\beta$. □

We now consider instead optimization with respect to Chichilnisky's criterion with a discount rate which declines to zero over time:

PROPOSITION 13.[21] *Consider the problem*

$$\max \alpha \int_0^\infty u_1(c,s) \Delta(t) \, dt + (1-\alpha) \lim_{t \to \infty} u_1(c,s), \, 0 < \alpha < 1,$$

$$\text{s.t. } \dot{k} = F(k_t, \sigma_t) - c_t \, \& \, \dot{s}_t = r(s_t) - c_t, \, s_0 \text{ given.}$$

*where $q(t) = -(\dot{\Delta}(t)/\Delta(t))$ and $\lim_{t \to \infty} q(t) = 0$. Any solution to this problem is also a solution to the problem of maximizing $\int_0^\infty u_1(c,s) \Delta(t) \, dt$ subject to the same constraint. In words, solving the utilitarian problem with the variable discount rate which goes to zero solves the overall problem.*

*Proof.* The proof is a straightforward adaptation of the proof of Proposition 6, and is omitted. □

As before, the existence of a solution is established in the Appendix.

What does the Chichilnisky-optimal path look like in this case? It is similar in general terms to the set of paths shown in Figure 4, except that the graph of the growth function $r(s)$ is replaced by the outer envelope of the curves relating $c$ and $s$ for fixed values of $k$. The optimal path moves towards the green golden rule, which is a point of tangency between an indifference curve and the outer envelope of the curves relating $c$ and $s$ for fixed values of $k$. This point is the limit of utilitarian stationary solutions as the associated discount rate goes to zero.

## 10. Conclusions

A review of optimal patterns of use of renewable resources has suggested interesting conclusions. The green golden rule is an attractive configuration: it gives the highest sustainable utility level. Utilitarian solutions with a positive discount rate will accumulate a smaller stock of the resource than that associated with the green golden rule, although the difference goes to zero as the discount rate used in the utilitarian formulation gets smaller. Of course, for a zero discount rate, there is typically no utilitarian optimum. Investigation of Chichilnisky's criterion in some measure bridges the gap between these two concepts of optimality: a solution exists if and only if the discount rate in the integral term of Chichilnisky's maximand declines asymptotically to zero, in which case maximization of the integral term alone – the sum of discounted utilities – leads one to the green golden rule. This result remains true even with the inclusion of production: matters are more complex in that case, but not qualitatively different. Interestingly, there is empirical evidence that people display declining discount rates in their behavior towards the future. Such behavior is quite consistent with behavior patterns found in other aspects of human choice and summarized as the Weber–Fechner law.

## 11. Appendix

In this appendix we establish conditions sufficient for the existence of solutions to the various intertemporal optimization problems considered in Propositions 2, 6, 7, 10 and 13 of the text. We use an approach and a set of results developed initially by Chichilnisky [6] and applied by Chichilnisky and Gruenwald [9]. This is a very direct and intuitive approach: we show that the set of feasible solutions to the constraints is a compact set, and that the objective function is a continuous function, and invoke the standard result that a continuous function on a compact set attains a maximum. The delicate step here is to find a topology in which we have compactness and continuity under reasonable assumptions about the problem: for this we use weighted $L_p$ spaces, as introduced in Chichilnisky [6].

We consider the utilitarian optimality problem analyzed in Section 7, as this is the most complex of the problem in the paper. Earlier problems in the paper are special cases of this, so that the existence of a solution to this implies the existence of solutions to the earlier problems. The optimization problem is:

$$\left. \begin{array}{l} \max \int_0^\infty u\left(c_t, s_t\right) e^{-\delta t} dt \text{ subject to} \\ \dot{k} = F\left(k, \sigma\right) - c \text{ and } \dot{s} = r\left(s\right) - \sigma \end{array} \right\}. \qquad (24)$$

We make the following *assumptions*:

1. $u(c,s)$ is concave, increasing and differentiable. It satisfies the Caratheodory condition, namely it is continuous with respect to $c$ and $s$ for almost all $t$ and measurable with respect to $t$ for all values of $c$ and $s$.
2. $r(0) = 0$, $\exists \bar{s} > 0$ s.t. $r(s) = 0 \,\forall s \geq \bar{s}$, $\max_s r(s) \leq b_1 < \infty$, and $r(s)$ is concave for $s \in [0, \bar{s}]$.
3. For any $\sigma \exists b_2(\sigma) < \infty$ s.t. $F(k, \sigma) \leq b_2(\sigma)$.
4. $\exists b_3 < \infty$ s.t. $|\dot{s}| \leq b_3$.
5. $\exists b_4 < \infty$ s.t. $|\dot{k}| \leq b_4$.

The first two conditions are conventional. The third implies that bounded resource availability implies bounded output: it is a form of the assumption made by Dasgupta and Heal [10] that the resource is essential to production. It is a restatement of assumption (22) in the text. The final two assumptions imply that it is not possible for either the resource stock or the capital stock to change infinitely rapidly. These seem to be very reasonable assumptions. However, we shall in the end not require them: we shall prove the existence of an optimal path under these assumptions, and then note that a path which is optimal without these assumptions is still feasible and optimal with them.

PROPOSITION 14. *Under assumptions (1) to (5) above, the utilitarian optimization problem (24) has a solution.*

*Proof.* Under the above assumptions, the set of feasible time paths of the resource stock $s$ and consumption $c$ are uniformly bounded above. (Note that $s$ is bounded by (2), and $c$ by (3) and (5).) They are non-negative and so bounded below. Hence the paths of $s$ and $c$ are integrable against some finite measure and so are elements of a weighted $L_1$ space. Denote by $P$ the set of feasible paths $s_t$ and $c_t$, $0 \leq t \leq \infty$: as a subset of $L_1$, $P$ is closed and norm bounded, so that by the Banach–Aloaglu theorem it is weak-* compact. By Lebesgue's bounded convergence theorem, it is also compact in the norm of $L_1$.

The objective $U = \int_0^\infty u(c_t, s_t) e^{-\delta t} dt$ maps $P$ to the real line $\Re$. To complete the proof we need to show that $U$ is continuous in the norm of $L_1$. This follows immediately from the characterization of $L_p$ continuity given in [6]:

LEMMA 15 (Chichilnisky). *Let $W = \int_\Re u(c_t, t) d\nu(t)$ for a finite measure $\nu(t)$, with $u(c_t, t)$ satisfying the Caratheodory condition. Then $W$ defines a norm-continuous function from $L_p$ to $\Re$ for some coordinate system of $L_p$ if and only if $|u(c_t, t)| \leq a(t) + b|c_t|^p$, where $a(t) \geq 0$, $\int_\Re a(t) d\nu(t) < \infty$ and $b > 0$.*

In the case of our objective the role of $u(c_t, t)$ is played by $u(c_t, s_t) e^{-\delta t}$. An extension of Chichilnisky's lemma to functions $u$ defined on $\Re^2$ is straightforward. As $u$ is defined only on $\Re_+^2$, concavity implies that Chichilnisky's inequality is satisfied for $p = 1$. This completes the proof of existence of an optimum. □

We have now proven the existence of an optimal path for the most complex of the optimization problems discussed in the paper: existence of an optimum for the simpler problems can be deduced from this. Our proof used assumptions (4) and (5) above, which bound respectively $\dot{s}$ and $\dot{k}$, the rates of change of the resource and capital stocks. These assumptions were not made in the body of the paper. However, note from the characterization results in the paper that solutions to the problems without bounds on the rates of change of stocks do in fact have bounded rates of change of the stocks of the resource and of capital. Hence for sufficiently large bounds, the imposition of bounds on the rates of change of stocks cannot change the solutions to the optimization problems. It follows that we have also established the existence of solutions for the unbounded optimization problems.

## Notes

1. See [12] for a detailed listing of many more examples.
2. This proposition, which was first proved in [18], is a strengthening of results in [3].
3. Elsewhere we have called this the green golden rule [3].
4. This result, and the associated concept of the green golden rule, were introduced in [1] and [3].
5. We are grateful to Kenn Judd for this observation.
6. This result was introduced in [18].
7. We are grateful to Harl Ryder for suggesting this result and outlining the intuition behind it.
8. This result was first proven in [18].
9. This equality is not always true: it requires locally uniform convergence of the non-autonomous system to the autonomous system. For details, see [4].
10. This result was first proven in [18].
11. Due to Harl Ryder.
12. This discount factor is infinite when $t = 0$: hence the need to start from $t = 1$.
13. Further discussions of time consistency can be found in [14].
14. This result was first proven in [18].
15. For a further discussion, see [13] and references therein.
16. This result was first proven in [18].
17. See [18] for details.
18. This result was first proven in [18].
19. See [18] for details.
20. This result was first proven in [18].
21. This result was first proven in [18].

## References

1. Beltratti, A., G. Chichilnisky and G. M. Heal. "Sustainable growth and the green golden rule", in *Approaches to Sustainable Economic Development*, Ian Goldin and Alan Winters (eds.), Paris, Cambridge University Press for the OECD, 1993, pp. 147–172.
2. Beltratti, A., G. Chichilnisky and G. M. Heal. "The Environment and the Long Run: A Comparison of Different Criteria", *Ricerche Economiche* 48, 1994, 319–340.
3. Beltratti, A., G. Chichilnisky and G. M. Heal. "The Green Golden Rule", *Economics Letters* 49, 1995, 175–179.
4. Benaïm, M. and M. W. Hirsch. "Asymptotic Pseudotrajectories, Chain Recurrent Flows and Stochastic Approximations", Working Paper, Department of Mathematics, University of California at Berkeley, 1994.
5. Berry, S., G. M. Heal and P. Salomon. "On the Relation between Economic and Thermodynamic Concepts of Efficiency in Resource Use", *Resources and Energy* 1, 1978, 125–137. (also reprinted in [16]).
6. Chichilnisky, G. "Nonlinear Functional Analysis and Optimal Economic Growth", *Journal of Optimization Theory and Applications* 61(2), 1977, 504–520.
7. Chichilnisky, G. "What Is Sustainable Development?", Working Paper, Stanford Institute for Theoretical Economics, 1993.
8. Chichilnisky, G. "Sustainable Development: An Axiomatic Approach", *Social Choice and Welfare* 13(2), 1996, 219–248.
9. Chichilnisky, G. and P. F. Gruenwald. "Existence of an Optimal Growth Path with Endogenous Technical Change", *Economics Letters* 48, 1995, 433–439.
10. Dasgupta, P. S. and G. M. Heal. "The Optimal Depletion of Exhaustible Resources", *Review of Economic Studies*, Special Issue on Exhaustible Resources, 1974, 3–28.
11. Dasgupta, P. S. and G. M. Heal. *Economic Theory and Exhaustible Resources*, Cambridge University Press, 1979.
12. Daily, G. *Nature's Services, Societal Dependence on Natural Ecosystems*, Island Press, Washington DC, 1997.
13. Harvey, C. "The Reasonableness of Non-Constant Discounting", *Journal of Public Economics* 53, 1994, 31–51.
14. Heal, G. M. *The Theory of Economic Planning*, Advanced Texts in Economics, Amsterdam, North-Holland, 1973.
15. Heal, G. M. "The Optimal Use of Exhaustible Resources" *Handbook of Natural Resource and Energy Economics*, Vol. III, Alan Kneese and James Sweeney (eds.), Amsterdam, New York and Oxford, North-Holland, 1993, pp. 855–880.
16. Heal, G. M. *The Economics of Exhaustible Resources*, International Library of Critical Writings in Economics, Edward Elgar, 1993.
17. Heal, G. M. "Interpreting Sustainability", in *Social Sciences and the Environment*, L. Quesnel (ed.), University of Ottawa Press, 1995, pp. 119–143.
18. Heal, G. M. *Lectures on Sustainability*, Lief Johansen Lectures, University of Oslo, 1995. Circulated as a working paper of the Department of Economics, University of Oslo, and forthcoming as *Valuing the Future: Economic Theory and Sustainability*, Columbia University Press.
19. Krautkramer, J. A. "Optimal Growth, Resource Amenities and the Preservation of Natural Environments", *Review of Economic Studies* 52, 1985, 153–170 (also reprinted in [16]).
20. Lowenstein, G. and R. Thaler. "Intertemporal Choice", *Journal of Economic Perspectives* 3, 1989, 181–193.
21. Roughgarden, J. and F. Smith. "Why Fisheries Collapse and What to Do about It", in *Proceedings of the National Academy of Sciences*, forthcoming.
22. Seierstad, A. and K. Sydsæter. *Optimal Control Theory with Economic Applications*, Advanced Texts in Economics, Amsterdam, North-Holland, 1987.

RALPH ABRAHAM, GRACIELA CHICHILNISKY AND RON RECORD

## 2.2. North-South Trade and the Dynamics of the Environment

### 1. Introduction

This paper develops a dynamic model of North-South trade in which the environment plays an important role. Our model is based on Chichilnisky's North-South model for the macroeconomic interaction between two regions of the world economy. The latter was introduced in a static context in [1]. We introduce dynamics in the original North-South model by allowing the endogenous accumulation of capital. As a second extension of [1], we introduce here a variable which represents the system of property rights on an environmental asset which is used as an input to production.[1] This variable could represent, for example, the property rights on forests from which wood is extracted to be used as an input to the production of traded goods, or the property rights on water which is similarly used, perhaps for agricultural goods for export.

The paper explains mathematically and through simulations the dynamics of a two-region world. There are two produced goods and two inputs to production. Capital is one input: it accumulates in the two regions through time as a function of profits. We show that as we vary the property rights on the environment the dynamics of the system changes. The less well defined are the property rights, the more chaotic are the model's dynamics.

The models which result bear some similarity to one created by John von Neumann in 1932 and extended by Richard Goodwin in 1990 [12, chapter 3]. We establish, in a sequence of steps, that these models are variants of the coupled logistic maps studied in several recent papers, for example, [11]. The idea is to alter [1] to allow capital accumulation through time, assuming that the approach to equilibrium follows rapidly. New equations are introduced in our model, which are not found in [1] or [3]. These equations describe the evolution of capital stock through time by accumulation and depreciation.[2]

The outline of the paper[3] and the main results are as follows. In Section 2 we introduce some useful notation, and in Section 3 the static North-South model [1] is recalled. Following that, we develop in Section 4 a rather simple one-dimensional model which is pedagogically useful because it anticipates the mathematical structure of our main model. We analyze its dynamical behavior in a sequence of propositions, and confirm this behavior through simulation. This dynamical behavior is essentially equivalent to the logistic map, and is similar to that which will be found later in our main model. In Section 5.2 we introduce our main (two-dimensional) model, and establish its dynamic behavior through simulation. We find a very rich dynamic behavior, with an extensive web of bifurcations controlled by the environmental property rights parameters. We find chaotic attractors, and chaotic separatrices. That is, the basins of attraction form a fractal structure. In Section 6, the conclusions, we interpret our results in the broader context of North-South trade and the environment.

### 1.1. *The Dynamic North-South Model*

Our dynamic model is based on [1], but with a major extension. Two fundamental equations are added to those of [1], which endogenize the changes in capital stock in the two regions through time. We first explain intuitively how the dynamical model is defined, and following this we provide the mathematical definitions.

The dynamical model is constructed iteratively as follows. Start from given values of the exogenous parameters of the North-South model[4] of [1]. The vector of initial levels of capital stocks in the two regions is a two-dimensional parameter, which will be the initial value (for $t = 1$) of our dynamical system in the plane. Now solve the static North-South model analytically.[5] The solution gives us, *inter alia*, the equilibrium value of *GNP* in each region.[6] So far the model is static, and identical to that in [1]. How does our dynamical system move in the plane from period $t = 1$ to period $t = 2$? To define the dynamics we will introduce two new equations, one in each region, both depending on the corresponding equilibrium level of *GDP* in the region in period $t = 1$. These equations explain how capital accumulates: a proportion of *GDP* in $t = 1$ is saved and increases previous period capital stock, while some of the old capital depreciates. From these equations one updates capital stocks and obtains a new set of exogenous parameters for the (static) North-South model for $t = 2$. These differ from the previous set (for $t = 1$) only with respect to the initial capital stocks, which have now varied according to our two new equations. The new capital stocks for the North and the South define a two-dimensional vector describing the period $t = 2$ value of our dynamical system. Now solve the (static) North-South model for this new set of exogenous parameters, and obtain *GDP* for period $t = 2$. Iterating this procedure defines the dynamical system in the plane for every period $t \geq 1$.

The following is the mathematical formulation of the procedure explained above.

Our first goal is to define the two new capital accumulation equations which add to the equations of the (static) North-South model and obtain, from these two new equations, a two-dimensional discrete dynamical system, generated by an endomorphism of the plane, $T : \Re^2 \mapsto \Re^2$. The two new equations are:

$$K_N(t+1)^+ = s_N(GNP_N) + (1 - \delta_N)K_N(t), \qquad (1.1.1)$$

$$K_S(t+1)^+ = s_S(GNP_S) + (1 - \delta_S)K_S(t). \qquad (1.1.2)$$

Equation (1.1.1) describes capital accumulation through time in the North, and (1.1.2) in the South. These equations are standard, and are interpreted as follows. Equation (1.1.1) explains *capital stock* at time $t+1$ in the North (N) as the sum of capital stock in the previous period in the North, $K_N(t)$, minus the part of this which is depreciated ($\delta_N$ is the depreciation factor in the North) plus *savings*, which is the savings rate in the North, $s_N$, times the *gross national product* in the North, $GNP_N$.

In order to determine our two-dimensional discrete dynamic system we need to define from these equations an endomorphism of the plane, $T : \Re^2 \mapsto \Re^2$. The depreciation and savings rate are exogenously given parameters. But how do we determine *GNP* in the two regions for any given values of the capital stocks in each, considering that they trade with each other through the international market?

The solution to this problem is one of the main contributions of our paper: the specifications of the *GNP* variables as the solutions of two simultaneous market equilibrium problems. Here is where we use [1]. The combination of Equations (1.1.1) and (1.1.2) with the North-South trade model is done here for the first time, and we call this the *dynamic North-South model*.

How do we obtain an endomorphism of the plane from the two equations for capital accumulation? We start with initial values of the two capital stocks, one for each region, $K_N$ and $K_S$. The *static* North-South model solves the world economy equations from the following initial parameters: *capital* and *labor supply, technologies* and *demand* in each region. Here, for the dynamic North-South model, we assume instead that *capital* and *labor supply* and *technologies* are initially given in each region.

In each region, at time $t$, we solve fully the static North-South model at time $t$ and obtain *GNP* at time $t$. From this, in turn, we compute the capital stocks, at time $t+1$, using our new dynamic equations for capital accumulation, (1.1.1) and (1.1.2).

The procedure can be summarized as follows. The static North-South model determines endogenously five price variables and sixteen quantity variables. It has two goods traded internationally (basic goods, $B$, and industrial goods, $I$) and two factor of production (capital, $K$, and labor, $L$). The price variables are the *international terms of trade* for the two traded goods $B$ and $I$, denoted by $p_B$ and $p_I$, (these are reduced to one by the normalizing assumption $p_I = 1$, and henceforth $p = p_B$), and the *prices of labor* and *rental of capital* in each region, denoted $w$ and $r$. Technologies are different in the two regions so that the rewards to labor and to capital are also different. The sixteen quantities which are endogenously determined are: *supply* and *demand* for the basic and industrial goods, *employment of factors* in the two sectors, imports and exports of both goods, all in each of the two regions. From these endogenous variables we obtain an expression for the desired *GNP* in each region. By definition, *GNP* is the value of the gross national product, that is, the value of all outputs minus all inputs (of $B$ and $I$) computed at the equilibrium market prices, $p$. These are the prices at which all markets clear. Recall that part of the production of each country is consumed in the other country, and that relative prices $p$ have adjusted to permit this trade and to clear markets, so that imports equal exports in each of the two traded goods. The result is an equilibrium level of *GNP* in each region,

$$GNP_N = pB_N^S + I_N^S, \qquad (1.1.3)$$

$$GNP_S = pB_S^S + I_S^S. \qquad (1.1.4)$$

Here $p$, $B^S$, and $I^S$ are determined as the solution of a system of 22 simultaneous equations in 22 variables, as in the *static* North-South model, This is explained in Section 5.2 below. *Therefore, for each value of capital stock we have assumed an instantaneous adjustment to an equilibrium in the static North-South model.*

From all this we obtain the *GNP* in each region at time $t$. The two dynamic equations (1.1.1) and (1.1.2) then provide capital stocks in the two regions at the next period, $t + 1$. Our plane endomorphism, $T$, is now well defined.

The equations describing *GNP* in each region are nonlinear. Therefore, the endomorphism $T$ is nonlinear as well. In the following we shall study its qualitative properties and experiment with simulations depicted graphically. But before analyzing the model, it will be useful to explain the connections with the environment.

### 1.2. North-South Trade and the Environment

The environment appears in this model as one of the inputs, or *factors* of production. While in the original North-South model the two factor of production are *labor* and *capital*, recently [4] the model has been extended to three factors of production, one of which is a *natural resource*, such as water from an aquifer, or fish from a common body of water, or wood from a common forest. In the original North-South model the behavior of a certain parameter $\alpha$ – representing the supply response of a factor to its price – is shown to be crucial in explaining the patterns of trade between the two regions, including the terms of trade and the gains from trade. Furthermore, in [4], the absolute value of this parameter in the South, $\alpha_S$, is proven to vary with the *property rights regime* for the resource (such as land). This resource is used as an input for the production of the traded goods (such as cash crops: coffee, cotton palm oil). It is, therefore, of interest to simulate the behavior of the North-South model with *different property rights* for this environmental resource, that is, different values of $\alpha_N$ and $\alpha_S$. These parameters contain crucial information about property rights. It was shown in [4–6] that $\alpha_S$ is smaller when the property rights are well defined, and is larger when they are ill-defined. As an example, [4] predicts that a regime of property rights which gives better rights to the locals of the rainforest (for example, in Guatemala and Ecuador) could improve the terms of trade on cash crops and control the overexploitation of its rainforest.

We now apply our model to explain the fundamental connection between the environment and trade. We will look at the environment as a common property resource which is used as an input to production in both regions. Examples are: rainforests, bodies of water, or fisheries. These are inputs to the production of environmentally intensive goods which are internationally traded, such as: wood products, industrial output, cash crops (cotton, coffee, soya beans, palm oil). In our model, we shall now reinterpret $L$ as an *environmental input* used, together with the other input, $K$, to produce basic and industrial goods, $B$ and $I$. Thus, we rename $L$ as $E$ for the remainder of this section.

As already mentioned, a crucial parameter in the North-South model is $\alpha$, the response of the supply of $E$ to it relative price, $w/p$. In [1] and [3], this parameter was shown to determine the properties of the solutions (equilibria). Here, $\alpha$ will play a similar role: it represents the *property rights* on the environmental resource, $E$: $\alpha$ is smaller when the property rights are well defined, and larger when they are ill-defined. For example: if the local population has well-defined property rights on the biodiversity of a rainforest, which is an input to the production of pharmaceuticals, then the wood input $E$ will be harvested more carefully. Obtaining a larger supply of $E$ requires a larger increase of the price of $E$, $p_E$. Thus, $\alpha$ is smaller when the property rights on the rainforest are well defined. The theory and the analytics proving this fact appear in [5] as lemma 1. When property rights on the rainforest are ill-defined, $\alpha$ is large: this means that a lot more wood will be harvested, and the forest may be destroyed, for smaller increases in prices. The *price* represents the value of the input.

It has been shown in [4, 6] that well-defined property rights lead to better valuation of scarce resources. Good examples are provided by Merck Pharmaceuticals, Inc. and Shaman Pharmaceuticals, Inc. These companies have entered into agreements to advance cash and to share the profits from prospecting biodiversity samples in Costa Rica and in South American countries. The biodiversity samples are an input to the production of valuable pharmaceuticals (examples: *curare* and the more recently discovered *periwinkle* which treats Hodgkins disease and leukemia in children) sharing the profits with the locals. This amounts to improving the property rights of the local population on the common property resource: the rainforest's biodiversity. This scheme is not too different from the venture capital agreements which advance working capital to use intellectual property (software ideas) and share the rights subsequently with the entrepreneurs. By increasing the realized value of the common property input, these agreements increase the interest in conservation by those who would otherwise overuse or overexploit the resource beyond its biological steady-state extraction rate.

All of these considerations may be represented in the North-South model by varying the parameter $\alpha_S$ in the South. This variation simulates the input of property right agreements in developing countries for their valuable common property resources. For the theories explaining the general impact of varying in the static North-South model in [3], see [5]. In this paper we address the *dynamic* North-South model, and ask the same questions. The problem is more complex since our model is dynamic, and we rely on simulation to provide our answers.

### 1.3. *Organization of the Paper*

We begin by recalling the static North-South model. Then we will develop the equations for the general form of the dynamic North-South model in the sequence of steps. To reveal the mathematical structure of the problem, we will present, in the first of these steps, a very simplified one-dimensional dynamic version of our two-dimensional dynamic system. This is only a mathematical artifice, as the economics are embodied only in the full two-dimensional version, our main model, of Section 5.2. We then explain some properties of the dynamical model and present simulations which confirm our results and suggest possible extensions. We end with a proposal for a dynamical system linking our dynamic North-South model with the atmospheric chemistry of the carbon cycle.

## 2. Notational Conventions

We will write $K_N$ in place of $K(N)$ used in [3]. We are going to encounter symbolic expressions in the variables:

$$K_N, K_S, s_N, s_S, \ldots,$$

and so on. We will refer to $K$ for example as a *root symbol*, and only when accompanied by a subscript $N$ or $S$ will the symbol denote a variable. Thus, we may write expressions or equations in these root variables, but they are symbolic only. When the appropriate subscripts are adjoined, they become expressions or equations of variables defined in our models. Let $A$ be an expression of root symbols. Then $A_N$ will denote the same expression in the corresponding variables of the North system, and likewise for $A_S$ for the South, while $A_T$ will be defined to mean $A_N + A_S$.

Note: Equation (GC2.21b) denotes equation 2.21b in [3].

## 3. Recalling the North-South Model

We begin with the parameters, variables, and notations of the static North-South model as defined in [3]. The root symbols of the eight parameters in each region are: $a_1, a_2, c_1, c_2, \alpha, \beta, \bar{K}$ and $\bar{L}$. Thus, we will encounter $a_1 = a_{1N}, a_{1S}$, etc. The crucial variables which determine the model are five price variables and sixteen quantity variables. The price variables are:

1. $p = p_B$ denotes the *price of basic goods*, $B$. Since the *price of industrial goods*, $I$, had been set to unity, $p_I = 1$, $p$ is the *relative price of basics with respect to industrial goods*. It is also called the *terms of trade* since $B$ and $I$ are the only two goods in the international market. In a market equilibrium, $p$ is the same in both regions, North and South, but all other price variables may differ in the two regions.
2. $w$ denotes *wages*.
3. $r$ denotes the *capital rental price*.

    Since labor and capital are *not* traded internationally (that is, between the two regions), their values are determined by $p$ according to local conditions (Equations GC2.21b, GC2.4a) which are unequal in the two regions (because two regions have different production technologies). The five price variables, or *prices*, are $p, r_N, r_S, w_N, w_S$.

    The *quantity variables* are the following.

4. $K$ denotes *capital stock*. This is determined by $r$, see (GC2.4) and Figure 1. This relationship is for the static model only. This $K$ will be determined, in the dynamic models of this paper, by a discrete dynamical system modeling the annual variation of capital stock in each region.
5. $L$ denotes *labor*. This is determined by $w$ and $p$, see (GC2.3).
6. $B^S$ and $B^D$ denote quantities of *basic goods supplies* and *basic goods demanded*.
7. $I^S$ and $I^D$ denote quantities of industrial goods supplied and demanded.
8. $X_B^S = B^S - B^D$ and $X_I^S = I^S - I^D$ denote exports of goods, the excess of what is supplied over what is consumed in each region.

The sixteen quantity variables are: $L, K, B^S, B^S, I^S, I^D, X_B^S, X_I^S$, in each region. The diagram of Figure 1 shows how $p$ (and the parameters in each region) determine all of these other variables. Labor, $L$, and capital, $K$, are the inputs to production. Using labor can capital the two economies produce the two goods, or commodities, $B^S$ and $I^S$. In each region, $B^S$ is produced using labor and capital according to

$$B^S = \min(L/a_1, K/c_1). \tag{3.1}$$

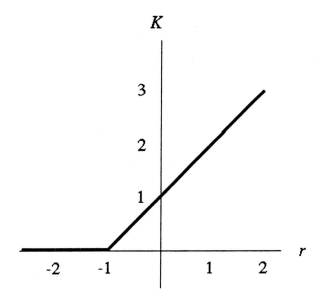

Figure 1. Grahp of $K(r)$. The y-intercept is at $\bar{K}$, and the slope is $\beta$.

Therefore, efficient use of $L$ and $K$ requires that

$$B^S = L/a_1 = K/c_1,$$

that is, labor and capital are used in fixed proportions for each level of output of $B^S$, or

$$L/K = a_1/c_1,$$

where $a_1$ is called the *labor-output ratio* (since $B^S = L/a_1$) and $c_1$ is called the *capital output ratio* (since $B^S = K/c_1$). Equation (3.1) is the *production technology* which determines how much $B$ can be produced with the available $K$ and $L$. Similarly, each region has a production technology for $I$,

$$I^S = \min(L/a_2, K/c_2) \tag{3.2}$$

with the same interpretation for the parameters $a_2$ and $c_2$. Equations (3.1) and (3.2) give rise to (GC2.20). (GC2.20 indicates equation number 20 from section 2 of [3].)

Now $\alpha$ and $\beta$ represent the responses of labor and capital supplies to changes in their prices: $w$ and $r$. We postulate:

$$L = \alpha w/p_B + \bar{L} \tag{GC2.3}$$

with $\bar{L} < 0$, and

$$r = (K - \bar{K})/\beta \tag{GC2.4}$$

with $\bar{K} > 0$. Equation (GC2.3) means that as the real wage $w/p_B$ increases, so does the supply of labor. And Equation (GC2.4) means the same for capital. The negative value of $\bar{L}$ indicates the minimum wage needed for survival before people supply positive labor.

Note: these relationships are particular to the static model. Later in this paper, while retaining the static relationship (GC2.3), we shall replace (GC2.4) with a dynamic rule of capital accumulation.

Some further relationships are the following, all from [3]:

$$p_B = (a_1 - rD)/a_2, \tag{GC2.21}$$

$$B^S = (c_2 L - a_2 K)/D \tag{GC2.20}$$

$$I^S = (a_1 K - c_1 L)/D \tag{GC2.20}$$

$$w = (p_B c_2 - c_1)/D, \tag{GC2.21}$$

all of which are non-negative, and

$$D = a_1 c_2 - a_2 c_1.$$

All remaining symbols denote constants defined in [3]. Note that the superscript $S$ in $B^S$ and $I^S$ and denotes Supply (vs Demand), not South (vs North). Also the subscript $B$ in $p_B$ indicates Basic (vs the subscript $I$ for Industrial). Henceforth, we will omit these subscripts when no confusion results (esp. in Section 4). Hence: $L$ for $L^S$ (we will not use $L^D$), $p$ for $p_B$ (we will not use $p_I$), $B$ for $B^S$ (we will not use $B^D$), and $I$ for $I^S$ (we will write $I^D$ when we mean demand for industrial goods). Thus the equations above become:

$$p = (a_1 - rD)/a_2 \tag{GC2.21a}$$

$$B = (c_2 L - a_2 K)/D \tag{GC2.20a}$$

$$I = (a_1 K - c_1 L)/D \tag{GC2.20b}$$

$$L = \alpha w/p + \bar{L} \tag{GC2.3a}$$

$$w = (pc_2 - c_1)/D \tag{GC2.21b}$$

$$r = (K - \bar{K})/\beta \tag{GC2.4a}$$

all non-negative, and

$$D = a_1 c_2 - a_2 c_1.$$

To close the static model in [3], two more variables were fixed:

$$I = \bar{I}^D$$

exogenously in each region.

This "closure" corresponds to the demand specification derived from assuming a simple preference form, which was defined and illustrated in

[3]. One can consider several other demand specifications without changing the structure of the model or its behavior, as shown in [1, 3]. Indeed, in the specification of our dynamical North-South model, the two-dimensional endomorphism is defined using a demand specification (5.3.1) which amounts to requiring that the demand for industrial goods $I^D$ is a proportion $1 - \gamma$ of *GNP*. This last specification is useful in a North-South world, because typically industrial countries consume a higher proportion of their *GNP* in the form of industrial goods, while developing countries consume proportionately more basic goods. With our specification (5.2.6) it is also possible to simulate an economy where the proportion $\gamma$ depends on the *GNP* level, with $\gamma$ decreasing as a function of *GNP*. We now begin a step-by-step development of our two-dimensional dynamical system. The first step will be a simple one-dimensional model.

## 4. One-Dimensional Models

In preparation for our main model, the two-dimensional map defined in Section 5.2, we now study a preliminary, one-dimensional model. This simple model is less realistic in economic terms than our main model of Section 5.2. Our purpose in introducing a simple model first is pedagogic: this serves to anticipate and explain the mathematical behavior of the larger model in a transparent fashion. It is important to note that the results of this paper do not depend on this simple model but rather on the main model, which is introduced and developed in Section 5.2.

We now introduce dynamics for the macroeconomic variables of the North region. The variables of the South will then be obtained as functions of those of the North, as follows.

PROPOSITION 1. *In the North-South model, the South capital is obtained from the North by the affine isomorphism,*
$$K_S = H_0 + H_1 K_N,$$
where
$$H_1 = \frac{\beta_S a_{2S} D_N}{\beta_N a_{2N} D_S}$$
and
$$H_0 = \frac{\beta_S}{D_S} \left[ -\frac{a_{1N}}{a_{2N}} a_{2S} + a_{1S} \right] - H_1 \bar{K}_N + \bar{K}_S.$$

*Proof.* From (GC2.4) we have
$$K_N = \beta_N r_N + \bar{K}_N \tag{4.0.1}$$
and
$$K_S = \beta_S r_S + \bar{K}_S. \tag{4.0.2}$$

As we assume the terms of trade $p = p_B$ are the same in each region, $p_S = p_N$, or from (GC2.21a),

$$p = (a_{1S} - r_S D_S)/a_{2S} = (a_{1N} - r_N D_N)/a_{2N}, \quad (4.0.3)$$

or, solving for $r_S$,

$$r_S = \frac{1}{D_S}\left\{(r_N D_N - a_{1N})\frac{a_{2S}}{a_{2N}} + a_{1S}\right\}, \quad (4.0.4)$$

we now substitute (4.0.1) into (4.0.2) and obtain

$$K_S = \beta_S r_S + \bar{K}_S = \frac{\beta_S}{D_S}\left\{(r_N D_N - a_{1N})\frac{a_{2S}}{a_{2N}} + a_{1S}\right\} + \bar{K}_S.$$

Using (GC2.4a) to replace $r_N$ we have

$$K_S = \frac{\beta_S}{D_S}\left\{\frac{a_{2S}D_N}{a_{2N}}\left[\frac{K_N - \bar{K}}{\beta_N}\right] - \frac{a_{1N}}{a_{2N}} + a_{1S}\right\} + \bar{K}_S$$

and simplifying, we get the proposition. □

Henceforth in Section 4, we will write $K$ in place of $K_N$, and so forth.

### 4.1. The Dynamics of the One-Dimensional Model

We envision a dynamic in which changes in the capital stock in the North result, after a rapid transit to new static equilibrium, in new equilibrium values of the variables. We use discrete dynamics to model the annual reports of these variables. And now, Equation (4.0.1) is understood as a demand equation, so that $\beta < 0$. *This differs from* [3]. The annual increments of $K$ will be defined by a function, $f : \mathbf{R}\setminus\{\bar{x}\} \to \mathbf{R}$ (we will identify the excluded point $\bar{x}$ subsequently), so that for year $n+1$, we have $K(n+1) = f(K(n))$. Also, we write $K^+$ for $f(K)$. This function is assumed to be defined by

$$f(K) = (1 - \delta)K + s(GNP), \quad 0 < \delta, \quad s < 1, \quad (4.1.1)$$

where the depreciation rate, $\delta$, and the rate of savings, $s$, are constants with small, positive values, and

$$GNP = pB + I. \quad (4.1.2)$$

As usual, GNP is the inner product of goods and prices, and again, $p_I = 1$ (GC2.16).

After substitution of the expressions in the preceding section, the endomophism $f$ may be written in the following form.

PROPOSITION 2. *The function defined in (4.1.1) may be expressed as*

$$f(K) = A_0 + A_1 K + A_2 K^2 + A_*/(K - K_0), \quad (4.1.3)$$

where the coefficients are given by
$$A_0 = (s/a)[1 + c_2\bar{K}/\beta](\bar{L} + \alpha c_2/D) - sa_2^2 c_1,$$
$$A_1 = (1 - \delta) + (s/\beta)\{-\bar{K} - (c_2/a_2)(\bar{L} + \alpha c_2/D)\},$$
$$A_2 = s/\beta,$$
$$A_* = -s(c_1^2 a_2 \beta/D),$$
and the singular point ($\bar{x}$ above) is
$$K_0 = \bar{K} + a_1\beta/D.$$

## 4.2. Proof of Proposition 2

We will demonstrate the dynamical rule given above in six steps.

**Step 1.** First we observe:
$$p = u_1(K - K_0),$$
where $u_1 = -D/a_2\beta$, and $K_0 = \bar{K} + a_1\beta/D$.
*Proof.* From (GC2.21a) of Section 2 we have
$$p = (a_1 - rD)/a_2$$
and substituting for $r$ from (GC2.4a) above,
$$p = \frac{a_1}{a_2} - \frac{(K - \bar{K})D}{a_2\beta},$$
from which we obtain
$$p = u_0 + u_1 K,$$
where $u_1$ is defined above, and
$$u_0 = \frac{a_1\beta + D\bar{K}}{a_2\beta}.$$
Then Step 1 follows, with
$$K_0 = -u_0/u_1 = \frac{a_1\beta + D\bar{K}}{a_2\beta} + \frac{a_2\beta}{D} = \frac{a_1\beta}{D} + \bar{K}.$$

**Step 2.** Continuing, we find:
$$pL = -\frac{\alpha c_2 + \bar{L}D}{a_1\beta}K + \frac{\alpha c_2 + \bar{L}D}{a_1\beta}\bar{K} + \bar{L} + \frac{\alpha}{D}(c_2 - c_1).$$

Note: Combining Steps 1 and 2, we have expressed $L$ as a function of $K$. Combining with Proposition 1, we see that the evolution of all four of the primary variables, $K_N, L_N, K_S$ and $L_S$, are determined from our one-dimensional model.

*Proof.* From (GC2.3a) of Section 2 we have

$$pL = p\left(\alpha\frac{w}{p} + \bar{L}\right) = \alpha w + p\bar{L}$$

and substituting for $W$ from (GC2.21b),

$$pL = \alpha\frac{pc_2 - c_1}{D} + p\bar{L} = \left(\frac{\alpha c_2}{D} + \bar{L}\right)p - \frac{\alpha c_1}{D}.$$

Using Step 1,

$$pL = \left(\frac{\alpha c_2}{D} + \bar{L}\right)p_1(K - K_0) - \frac{\alpha c_1}{D}$$

$$= -\left(\frac{\alpha c_2}{D} + \bar{L}\right)\frac{D}{a_1\beta}K + \left(\frac{\alpha c_2}{D} + \bar{L}\right)\frac{D}{a_1\beta}K_0 - \frac{\alpha c_1}{D}$$

$$= -\frac{\alpha c_2 + \bar{L}D}{\beta a_1}K + \frac{\alpha c_2 + \bar{L}D}{\beta a_1}\left(\bar{K} + \frac{a_1\beta}{D}\right) - \frac{\alpha c_1}{D}$$

$$= -\frac{\alpha c_2 + \bar{L}D}{\beta a_1}K + \frac{\alpha c_2 + \bar{L}D}{\beta a_1}\bar{K} + \frac{\alpha c_2}{D} + \bar{L} - \frac{\alpha c_1}{D}$$

$$= -\frac{\alpha c_2 + \bar{L}D}{\beta a_1}K + \frac{\alpha c_2 + \bar{L}D}{\beta a_1}\bar{K} + \bar{L} + \frac{\alpha}{D}(c_2 - c_1),$$

completing the derivation.

**Step 3.** Next, see that:

$$pK = -\frac{D}{a_2\beta}K^2 + \left[\frac{D}{a_2\beta}\bar{K} + \frac{a_1}{a_2}\right]K.$$

*Proof.* From Step 1 we have

$$pK = p_1(K - K_0)K$$

$$= p_1K^2 - p_1K_0K$$

$$= -\frac{D}{a_2\beta}K^2 + \frac{D}{a_2\beta}\left[\bar{K} + \frac{a_1\beta}{D}\right]K$$

$$= -\frac{D}{a_2\beta}K^2 + \left[\frac{D}{a_2\beta}\bar{K} + \frac{a_1}{a_2}\right]K.$$

**Step 4.** Putting these together, we have

$$pB = C_0 + C_1 K + C_2 K^2,$$

where

$$C_0 = \frac{\alpha c_2 + \bar{L}D}{a_1 \beta} \bar{K} + \bar{L} + \frac{\alpha}{D}(c_2 - c_1),$$

$$C_1 = -\frac{\alpha c_2^2}{a_1 \beta D} - \frac{c_2 \bar{L}}{a_1 \beta} - \frac{\bar{K}}{\beta} - \frac{a_1}{D},$$

$$C_2 = 1/\beta.$$

*Proof.* From Section 2 (GC2.20a) we have

$$pB = p \frac{c_2 L - a_2 K}{D}$$

$$= \frac{c_2}{D} pL - \frac{a_2}{D} pK,$$

in which we may replace $pL$ with Step 2, and $pK$ by Step 3, obtaining

$$pB = \frac{c_2}{D} \left\{ -\frac{\alpha c_2 + \bar{L}D}{a_1 \beta} K + \frac{\alpha c_2 + \bar{L}D}{a_1 \beta} \bar{K} + \bar{L} + \frac{\alpha}{D}(c_2 - c_1) \right\}$$

$$- \frac{a_2}{D} \left\{ -\frac{D}{a_2 \beta} K^2 + \left[ \frac{D}{a_2 \beta} \bar{K} + \frac{a_1}{a_2} \right] K \right\}$$

$$= \frac{1}{\beta} K^2 - \left\{ \frac{\alpha c_2^2}{a_1 \beta D} + \frac{c_2 \bar{L}}{a_1 \beta} + \frac{\bar{K}}{\beta} + \frac{a_1}{D} \right\} K$$

$$+ \left\{ \frac{\alpha c_2 + \bar{L}D}{a_1 \beta} \bar{K} + \bar{L} + \frac{\alpha}{D}(c_2 - c_1) \right\},$$

which is Step 4.

**Step 5.** Similarly, see that:

$$I = I_0 + I_1 K + I_*/(K - K_0),$$

where

$$I_0 = -\left[ \frac{c_1 \bar{L}}{D} + \frac{\alpha c_1 c_2}{D^2} \right],$$

$$I_1 = \frac{a_1}{D},$$

$$I_* = -\frac{\alpha \beta a_2 c_1^2}{D^3}.$$

*Proof.* From Section 2 (GC2.20b) we have

$$I = \frac{a_1 K - c_1 L}{D}$$

$$= \frac{a_1}{D} K - \frac{c_1}{D}[\frac{\alpha w}{p} + \bar{L}]$$

$$= \frac{a_1 K - c_1 \bar{L}}{D} - \frac{\alpha c_1}{D} \frac{w}{p}$$

$$= \frac{a_1 K - c_1 \bar{L}}{D} - \frac{\alpha c_1}{D^2}\left[c_2 - \frac{c_1}{p}\right]$$

$$= \frac{a_1 K - c_1 \bar{L}}{D} - \frac{\alpha c_1 c_2}{D^2} + \frac{\alpha c_1^2}{D^2} \frac{1}{p}$$

$$= \frac{a_1}{D} K - \left[\frac{c_1 \bar{L}}{D} + \frac{\alpha c_1 c_2}{D^2}\right] + \frac{\alpha c_1^2}{D^2} \frac{1}{p_1(K - K_0)},$$

which is Step 5

$$GNP = G_0 + G_1 K + G_2 K^2 + G_*/(K - K_0),$$

where

$$G_0 = C_0 + I_0 = \frac{\alpha c_2 + \bar{L}D}{a_1 \beta} \bar{K} + (1 - \frac{c_1}{D})\bar{L} + \frac{\alpha}{D}(c_2 - c_1) - \frac{\alpha c_1 c_2}{D^2}$$

$$G_1 = C_1 + I_1 = -\left[\frac{\alpha c_2^2}{a_1 \beta D} + \frac{c_2 \bar{L}}{a_1 \beta} + \frac{\bar{K}}{\beta}\right]$$

$$G_2 = C_2 = 1/\beta,$$

$$G_* = I_* = -\alpha \beta a_2 c_1^2 / D^3.$$

*Proof.* From Section 4 (4.1.2) we have

$$GNP = pB + I,$$

in which we may replace $pB$ by Step 4, and $I$ by Step 5, obtaining

$$GNP = C_2 K^2 + (C_1 + I_1) K + (C_0 + I_0) + I_* \frac{1}{K - K_0}.$$

which completes our derivation. □

## 4.3. Preliminaries on Quadratic Maps

In the preceding sections we have obtained an endomorphism of real numbers, generating a semi-cascade (discrete dynamical system), for the dynamics of the North-South model. This one-dimensional model will be useful to us, as we will see later in the study of our main (two-dimensional) model. This is because dynamics in one dimension has been extensively studies, whereas dynamics in two dimension is a current frontier. To relate this one-dimensional model to the well known logistic map, we will make use of the following.

PROPOSITION 3. *A quadratic function, $f : \Re \to \Re$, defined by*
$$f(x) = A_0 + A_1 x + A_2 x^2$$
*with $A_2 \neq 0$, and the discriminant $\Delta = (A_1 - 1)^2 - 4 A_0 A_2 > 0$, has a repelling fixed point at*
$$B_0 = -\frac{(A_1 - 1)}{2 A_2} + \frac{\Delta}{2 A_2}$$
*with its distinct preimage at $B_0 + B_1$, where*
$$B_1 = -A_1/A_2 - 2 B_0.$$
*The affine function*
$$x : \Re \to \Re; \ y \mapsto x(y) = B_0 + B_1 y$$
*is an affine isomorphism, and conjugates $f$ into the canonical form for the quadratic family*
$$g(y) = x^{-1}(f(x(y))) = \mu y(1 - y),$$
*with*
$$\mu = 1 + \Delta.$$
*Furthermore, the usual domain of this logistic function, $y \in J = [0, 1]$, is mapped to an interval $x \in I = [B_0, B_0 + B_1]$, in the orientation preserving case $B_0 > 0$, else $x \in I = [B_0 + B_1, B_0]$, by this affine isomorphism.*

*Proof.* To compute the next value of $y$ under the conjugate map, we apply the inverse map to $y^+$,
$$y^+ = -\frac{B_0}{B_1} + \frac{1}{B_1} x^+$$
$$= -\frac{B_0}{B_1} + \frac{1}{B_1} f(x)$$
$$= -\frac{B_0}{B_1} + \frac{1}{B_1}[A_0 + A_1 x + A_2 x^2],$$
and then with $x \mapsto y$,
$$y^+ = -\frac{B_0}{B_1} + \frac{A_0}{B_1} + \frac{A_1}{B_1}(B_0 + B_1 y) + \frac{A_2}{B_1}(B_0 + B_1 y)^2$$
$$= \left[ -\frac{B_0}{B_1} + \frac{A_0}{B_1} + \frac{A_1}{B_1} B_0 + \frac{A_2}{B_1} B_0^2 \right]$$
$$+ [A_1 + 2 A_2 B_0] y + (A_2 B_1) y^2.$$

Now we equate this with the desired canonical form,
$$y^+ = g(y) = \mu y(1-y) = 0 + \mu y + (-\mu)y^2$$
term by term.

For degree zero,
$$-\frac{B_0}{B_1} + \frac{A_0}{B_1} + \frac{A_1}{B_1}B_0 + \frac{A_2}{B_1}B_0^2 = 0,$$
and as $A_2 \neq 0$ and $B_1 \neq 0$
$$A_2 B_0^2 + (A_1 - 1)B_0 + A_0 = 0$$
from which, by the binomial formula,
$$B_0 = -\frac{(A_1 - 1 \pm \Delta)}{2A_2}.$$

Note: The quadratic equation for $B_0$ here is the condition for a fixed point of the map $f$, so the $\pm$ yields the two fixed points. As the slope of $f$ at these two possible values for $B_0$ is
$$f'(B_0) = A_1 + 2A_2 B_0 = 1 \pm \Delta$$
we choose the positive sign for the repelling fixed point. If $B_0^-$ denotes the other root, with the minus sign, then this is the paired fixed point, created by a fold bifurcation, and initially attractive, for $\Delta$ small and positive. Then its distinct preimage is $B_0^- + B_1^-$, where $B_1^- = -A_1/A_2 - 2B_0^-$. Also, note that the critical point is $x_e = -A_1/2A_2$.

For degree one,
$$\mu = A_1 + 2A_2 B_0$$
and for degree two,
$$\mu = -A_2 B_1.$$

Subtracting these two expressions and solving for $B_1$,
$$B_1 = -\frac{A_1}{A_2} - 2B_0$$
completing the specification of the affine isomorphism. From the first expression for $\mu$ above we obtain its form in the proposition. □

COROLLARY 4. *Given the function* $f : \Re\setminus\{\bar{x}\} \to \Re$, *defined by*
$$f(x) = A_0 + A_1 x + A_2 x^2 + A_*/(x - \bar{x})$$
*with* $A_2 \neq 0$, *and* $(A_1 - 1)^2 > 4A_0 A_2$, *then* $y \mapsto x = B_0 + B_1 y$ *with*
$$B_0 = -\frac{A_1 - 1 + \Delta}{2A_2}$$

and

$$B_1 = -A_1/A_2 - 2B_0$$

is an affine isomorphism, and conjugates $f$ to the canonical form $g : \Re\backslash\{\bar{y}\} \to \Re$, with

$$g(y) = x^{-1}(f(x(y))) = \mu y(1-y) + \nu/(y-\bar{y})$$

with $\nu = A_*/B_1^2$, $\bar{y} = \bar{x}/B_1 - B_0/B_1 = x^{-1}(\bar{x})$, and $\mu + \Delta$ as above. And as above, the usual domain of the logistic function, $y \in J = [0, 1]$, assuming $\bar{y} \notin J$, is again mapped to the interval, $x \in I = [B_0, B_0 + B_1]$, by the affine isomorphism.

*Proof.* The quadratic terms are conjugated as shown, according to Proposition 3 above. For the last term, see that

$$(1/B_1)\frac{A_*}{x-\bar{x}} = \frac{\nu}{y-\bar{y}}$$

with which, the formula for $g$ is obtained. □

*Remark.* If the singular point lies outside the interval $J$, then this interval as approximately the invariant interval defined by the initially repelling fixed point and its distinct preimage. In case the point $\bar{y}$ lies to the right of the interval $J$, the domain of $g$ should be reduced to the subinterval $J^*$ defined by the expanding fixed point and its nearby preimage. In case $\bar{y}$ lies to the left of $J$, then the interval may be increased to $J^*$. The case with $\bar{y}$ in the interval shown in Figure 2.

The invariant interval of $g$, $J^*$, is not identical to the reference interval, $J = [0, 1]$ unless $\nu = 0$. Likewise, we have an interval for $f$, $I^*$, not identical to the corresponding reference interval, $I = [B_0, B_0 + B_1]$.

In summary, we see that in the case in which the singular point is outside the interval of interest, our one-dimensional model must behave exactly like the well-known logistic (or quadratic) map, with a convergent sequences of period-doubling bifurcations, and chaotic attractors. In the other case (which occurs with reasonable values of our numerous parameters) the behavior should be similar. This is difficult (but possible) to establish analytically, but we will use simulation instead.

### 4.4. Simulations

We now establish that, indeed, the behavior of our one-dimensional model is that of the familiar logistic function, even though the singularity falls in the domain of the map. We begin by fixing values for the many parameters appearing in this dynamical system. First, let $\delta = 0.1$ and $s = 0.08$. For the

North-South Trade and the Dynamics of the Environment    95

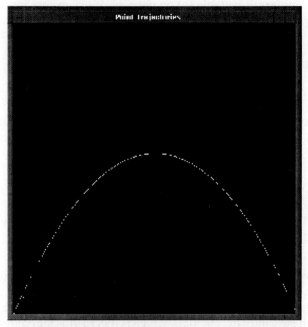

*Figure 2a.* Graph of the one-dimensional model with $0 < x < 163$. Note the gap in the graph at the left. This is the singularity, shown enlarged in Figure 3.

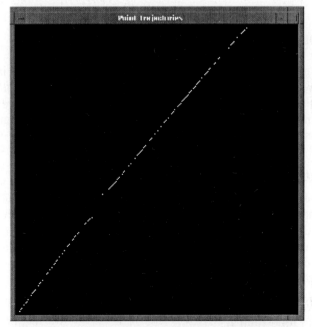

*Figure 2b.* Graph of the one-dimensional model with $0 < x < 20$, illustrating the singularity in the map.

others, our guide will be table (c) on page 44 of [3], except for the sign of $\beta$ which we reverse. Thus, in the North,

$$a_1 = 2, \quad \bar{K} = 12,$$
$$a_2 = 0.15, \quad \bar{L} = 0.5,$$
$$c_1 = 1.8, \quad \alpha = 6,$$
$$c_2 = 1.7, \quad \beta = -9.7.$$

These are chosen so that $p, r, w, L, K, B, I > 0$ in each region. Note that the control parameter $\mu$ in the transformed dynamical system depends upon all of these values. The derived constants are then approximately:

$$D = 3.13$$
$$A_0 = -0.058524, \quad B_0 = 0.167727,$$
$$A_1 = 1.350306, \quad B_0^- = 42.306847,$$
$$A_2 = -0.008247, \quad B_1^- = 79.110881,$$
$$A_* = 0.1201, \quad B_1 = 163.389119,$$

with the singularity at $\bar{x} = 5.801917$ and the attracting fixed point at 42.316339, see Figures 2a and 2b.

The response diagram for function $f$ of (4.1.1) – with all the parameters fixed with these values except for $\alpha$, which is regarded as the control parameter in the simulation – is the familiar orbit diagram for the quadratic family, as shown in Figure 3.

## 5. Two-Dimensional Models

In the first dynamical system studied above, we had an evolution in the North variables, while the South variables were to be determined from their Northern siblings by an algebraic relation. We now want to consider a more symmetric dynamic, in which the corresponding variables in both regions are in mutual coevolution.

### 5.1. *A Preliminary Model*

Here we rewrite the one-dimensional model as a two-dimensional model without changing the dynamics for $K_N$. That is, instead of obtaining $K_S$ from $K_N$ after each timestep by conjugation with the affine isomorphism of Proposition 1, which assumed a rapid settling to static equilibrium, we will derive a semi-cascade for $K_S$ parallel to that of $K_N$.

From Proposition 1 we have

$$K_S = H_0 + H_1 K_N, \tag{5.1}$$

while from Proposition 2,

$$K_N(n+1) = f(K_N(n)),$$

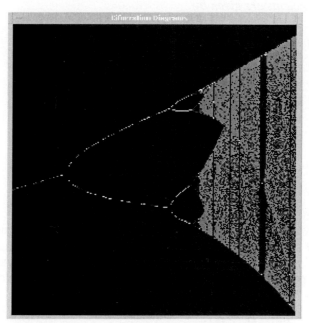

*Figure 3.* Response diagram for the one-dimensional model with $6 < \alpha < 8$. This is the familiar figure for the quadratic family. The vertical axis is the domain of the one-dimensional dynamical system. Each value of the control parameter $\alpha$ determines a vertical interval, and a particular map generating the dynamic. The white point (or set of points) is the unique attractor of the dynamical system for the given value of the control parameter: a point attractor (as in equilibrium theory), periodic attractor (as in business cycles), or a chaotic attractor (as in economic data).

or writing $f_N$ in place of $f$,
$$K_N^+ = f_N(K_N). \tag{5.2}$$
Note that the inverse of Proposition 1 is
$$K_N = \frac{K_S - H_0}{H_1}. \tag{5.3}$$
We now apply the map of (5.1) to the left-hand side of (5.2), and its inverse (5.3) to the rights-hand side, as in the proof of Proposition 3, with the following result.

PROPOSITION 5. *The dynamic (5.2) for $K_N$ implies a conjugate dynamic for $K_S$, which may be expressed,*
$$K_S(n+1) = f_S(K_S(n)) \quad \text{or} \quad K_S^+ = f_S(K_S),$$
*where the generating endomorphism is*
$$f_S(y) = A_{0S} + A_{1S}y + A_{2S}y^2 + A_{*S}\frac{1}{y - \bar{y}}$$

and the coefficients are given by

$$A_{0S} = H_0 + H_1 A_0 - A_1 H_0 + A_2 \frac{H_0^2}{H_1},$$

$$A_{1S} = A_1 - 2A_2 \frac{H_0}{H_1},$$

$$A_{2S} = \frac{A_2}{H_1},$$

$$A_{*S} = H_1^2 A_*,$$

$$\bar{y} = H_0 + K_N^0 H_1.$$

Note: Given $K_S$ and all the parameters, we obtain all the variables. But, we will use different values for the parameters in the South: again, as in Section 4.4, we let $\delta = 0.1$ and $s = 0.08$. For the others, we again refer to table (c) on page 44 of [3], except for the sign of $\beta$ which we reverse. Thus, in the South,

$$a_1 = 4.5, \quad \bar{K} = 2.7,$$
$$a_2 = 0.02, \quad \bar{L} = -2,$$
$$c_1 = 0.01, \quad \alpha = 75,$$
$$c_2 = 3, \quad \beta = -0.025.$$

These are chosen so that $p, r, w, L, K, B, I > 0$ in each region. Note that the control parameter $\mu$ in the transformed dynamical system depends upon all of these values. The derived constants are then approximately:

$$D = 13.5$$
$$A_0 = -750.642844, \quad B_0 = 2.691218,$$
$$A_1 = 558.498719, \quad B_0^- = 2.694575,$$
$$A_2 = -103.512843, \quad B_1^- = 0.006303,$$
$$A_* = 0.0000000008, \quad B_1 = 0.013018,$$

with the singularity at $\bar{x} = 2.691667$ and the attracting fixed point at $2.694576$.

*Proof.* From Proposition 1 we have

$$K_S = H_0 + H_1 K_N$$

with inverse

$$K_N = \frac{K_S - H_0}{H_1},$$

while from Proposition 2,

$$K_N(n+1) = f_N(K_N(n)).$$

As in the proof of Proposition 3, we now apply the affine isomorphism and its inverse to this equation, getting

$$K_S^+ = H_0 + H_1 K_N^+$$
$$= H_0 + H_1 f(K_N)$$
$$= H_0 + H_1 f\left(\frac{K_S - H_0}{H_1}\right)$$
$$= H_0 + H_1 A_0 + H_1 A_1 \frac{K_S - H_0}{H_1} + H_1 A_2 \left[\frac{K_S - H_0}{H_1}\right]^2$$
$$+ H_1 A_* \frac{1}{(K_S - H_0)/H_1 - K_0}$$
$$= H_0 + H_1 A_0 + A_1(K_S - H_0) + \frac{A_2}{H_1}(K_S^2 - 2H_0 K_S + H_0^2)$$
$$+ H_1^2 A_* \frac{1}{K_S - H_0 - K_0 H_1}$$

from which the proposition follows. □

We may apply the Corollary of Proposition 3 independently to each of the dynamical systems (4.2) and (5.1), obtaining the (uncoupled) two-dimensional logistic endomorphism,

$$k_N^* = \mu_N k_N (1 - k_N) + \nu_N/(k_N - k_{N0}),$$
$$k_S^* = \mu_S k_S (1 - k_S) + \nu_S/(k_S - k_{S0}),$$

both on the unit interval, with

$$\mu_N = 1 + \sqrt{(A_{1N} - 1)^2 - 4 A_{0N} A_{2N}} = 1 + \Delta_N,$$
$$\mu_S = 1 + \sqrt{(A_{1S} - 1)^2 - 4 A_{0S} A_{2S}} = 1 + \Delta_S,$$
$$\nu_N = A_{*N}/B_{1N}^2,$$
$$\nu_S = A_{*S}/B_{1S}^2.$$

That is, we have in this model a minor modification of two (uncoupled) logistic maps, each of the form

$$f(K) = (1 - \delta)K + s(GNP),$$

or equivalently,

$$f(K) = (1 - \delta)K + s(pB + I).$$

We now seek to couple them through $p$.

## 5.2. The Main Model

We will work with an endomorphism of the plane

$$T : \mathbf{R}^2 \to \mathbf{R}^2; (K_N, K_S) \mapsto (K_N^+, K_S^+)$$

defined as in the one-dimensional model by

$$K_N^+ = s_N(pB_N + I_N) + (1 - \delta_N)K_N, \quad (5.2.1)$$

$$K_S^+ = s_S(pB_S + I_S) + (1 - \delta_S)K_S, \quad (5.2.2)$$

where the terms of trade, $p$, are the same in both regions, because markets are competitive. These equations predict growth of capital stock in one fiscal period. As before, $pB + I$ is the *GNP* (gross national product), $s$ is the savings rate, and $\delta$ is depreciation. In our simulations, we will use $s \approx 12/100$, and $\delta \approx 10/100$, and for both regions.

The time evolution of all of the variables in each system is to be found by the iteration of the mapping $T$, beginning with any initial state, $(K_N^0, K_S^0)$. To complete the definition of the endomorphism $T$ and thus the dynamics of the model, we explain the determination of the intermediate variables, $p, B, I$, in each region. These are determined by equation (GC2.22) of [3] modified as follows:

$$\beta_N = 0, \quad \bar{K}_N = K_N; \quad \beta_S = 0, \quad \bar{K}_S = K_S.$$

We recall, from [3], the equation

$$A_T p^2 + (C_T + I_T^D)p - V_T = 0, \quad \text{(GC2.22)}$$

where here $A = \beta a_1 a_2/D^2$, and $C$ and $V$ are defined below. Equation (GC2.22) then becomes, with $\beta = 0$ in each region,

$$(C_T + I_T^D)p - V_T = 0, \quad (5.2.3)$$

using the convention of Section 2. Here, the symbolic expressions $C$, $V$ and $I^D$, are defined by

$$C = (1/D)[c_1 \bar{L} - a_1 K + \alpha c_1 c_2/D], \quad (5.2.4)$$

$$V = \alpha c_1^2 / D^2, \quad (5.2.5)$$

$$I^D = GNP(1 - \gamma), \quad (5.2.6)$$

where $\gamma \in (0, 1)$. In fact, we will choose $\gamma \approx 60/100$. In any case, we would like $s + (1 - \gamma) \ll 1$. Note that $C$ is a function of $K$ in each region, $V$ is a constant, and *GNP* in the expression for $I^D$ is to be determined from the formula $GNP = pB + I$. Equation (5.2.6) is the assumption that demand for industrial goods is proportional to *GNP*, as described above, in each region. This treats the two goods, $B$ and $I$, symmetrically. Note that the values of $B$ and $I$ are directly computed as function of $K$ (in each region) by

Equations (3.1) and (3.2), but the value of $p$ in this expression is not directly available. We obtain this value, assuming the rapid approach to equilibrium in the static model as described in Section 1, as described below.

Once $p$ is determined, we obtain the *GNP*, which is given by Equation (4.1.2), and equations (GC2.20a,b), (GC2.21a), and (GC2.3) from [3], as:

$$GNP = p(c_2 L - a_2 K)/D + (a_1 K - c_1 L)/D$$
$$= p(\alpha c_2^2/D^2 + c_2 \bar{L}/D - a_2 K/D]$$
$$+ [-2\alpha c_1 c_2/D^2 + a_1 K/D - c_1 \bar{L}/D] + \alpha c_1^2/D^2 p \quad (5.2.7)$$

for each region. Note that Equation (5.2.3) determines $p$ if *GNP* is known, but our expression (5.2.7) above requires $p$. When this circularity is resolved, we obtain a quadratic equation for p with all coefficients known.

We begin by rewriting (5.2.3), using (5.2.6), in the form

$$p[C_T + (1-\gamma)GNP] - V_T = 0, \quad (5.2.8)$$

and using (5.2.7), this yields

$$E_T p^2 + (C_T + F_T)p + (G_T - V_T) = 0, \quad (5.2.9)$$

where

$$E = (1-\gamma)[\alpha c_2^2/D^2 - (a_2 K + c_2 \bar{L})/D],$$
$$F = (1-\gamma)[-2\alpha c_1 c_2/D^2 + a_1 K/D - c_1 \bar{L}/D],$$

and

$$G = (1-\gamma)\alpha c_1^2/D^2.$$

Thus, computing $L$ from $K$ in each region, all the coefficients of the quadratic equation (5.2.9) are known. We solve this equation, and in case of two real roots, we choose the larger one for the current value of $p$. Then from (5.2.7) we have *GNP* in each region, and the specification of the map $T$ is complete.

An interesting simplification to our main model results from substituting $rK$ for *GNP* in the dynamical rules for the 2D endomorphism, Equations (5.2.1) and (5.2.2). This third model has been studied by Di Matteo [10] and we may return to it in a future publication.

## 5.3. Simulation Results

For the first two-dimensional model, the response diagram is shown in Figure 4. Throughout this section, the values of all the constants are as given in Section 4.4 (for the North) and Section 5.1 (for the South) except as noted in the figure captions.

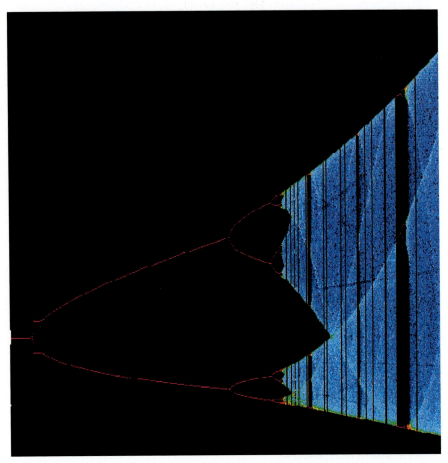

*Figure 4.* Response diagram for the first of the two-dimensional models. Here we vary $\alpha_N$ from 31 to 49 while holding $\alpha_S$ fixed at 20. The horizontal axis represents the control parameter, $\alpha_N$, while the vertical axis represents the North capital supply, $K_N$, after several iterations. The interpretation of this diagram is identical to that of Figure 3, except that here the vertical axis is the one-dimensional projection of a two-dimensional state space.

It is here that our experience with the one-dimensional model is pedagogically useful, as we see a strong similarity in the response diagrams. In this case, we have a two-dimensional state space, of the variables $K_N$ and $K_S$, and a one-dimensional control space, of the control parameter, $\alpha_N$. Thus, the response diagram is three-dimensional. But here we have reduced it to a two-dimensional graphic by projection. The vertical axis represents the two-dimensional state space (of the capital stocks in North only), and the horizontal axis is the control space of the environmental variable $\alpha_N$. As the two equations of the first two-dimensional model are uncoupled, this projection gives us exactly the response diagram of the one-dimensional model

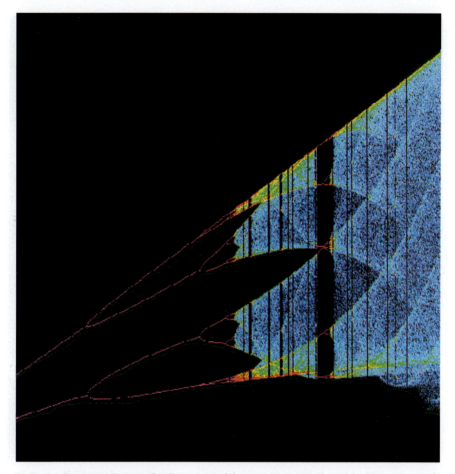

*Figure 5.* Response diagram for the second of the two-dimensional models. Here we vary the $\alpha_S$ from 40 to 90 while holding the $\alpha_N$ fixed at 6. The horizontal axis represents the control parameter, $\alpha_S$. Both North and South capitol stocks are plotted on the vertical axis. This view of the response diagram is constructed as follows. For each value of the control parameter (horizontal axis) there corresponds a dynamical system on the state space, a rectangle in the plane of the state variables $K_N$ and $K_S$. This discrete dynamical system has a single attractor, either a point (static attractor), a finite point set of $k > 1$ points (a $k$-periodic attractor), or an infinite set (chaotic attractor). In any case, we (step 1) project this attractor onto the $K_N$ axis, then (step 2) project this attractor onto the $K_S$ axis, and then (step 3) superimpose both projections onto the same interval of real numbers. Finally (step 4), this picture is inserted into the response diagram as a vertical line segment over the chosen value of the control parameter. Note that there are two figures, similar to Figure 4, which are superimposed here, one for each of the projections: $K_N$ and $K_S$.

studied above, that is, Figure 3. (Some of the parameters differ, however, between these two figures.) We see, at the left of the response diagram, a period doubling bifurcation, followed by the familiar convergent sequences

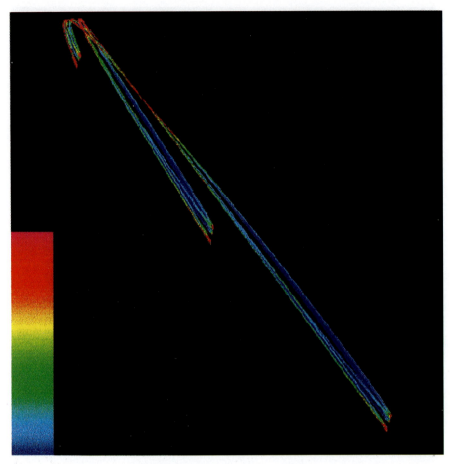

*Figure 6.* A histogram of the attractor in the two-dimensional state space of $K_N$ and $K_S$, for a particular value of the control parameter, $\alpha_S = 80$. The horizontal axis represents values of $K_N$, the vertical, $K_S$. The bar on the lower left shows the gray scale code, from black (no points of the trajectory in a unit area) to white (maximum number of trajectory points in a unit area).

of similar events. As we see this in projection, we may understand that there is a periodic attractor in the two-dimensional state space of the variables $K_N$ and $K_S$, which progressively becomes more and more complex, and finally, fills a subset of the plane chaotically. Starting from any initial values of the two capital supplies, the time sequence of subsequent values approaches this attractor asymptotically.

But the second two-dimensional model is our main goal in this paper. And for this model, the bifurcation diagram is shown in Figure 5.

For some values of the various parameters, we find a single basin, with a chaotic attractor. The attractor portrait for one such case is shown in Figure 6.

*Figure 7.* The two basins of attraction using the second of the two-dimensional models with $\alpha_S$ set to 17.5 and $\alpha_N$ to 1.5. In addition, the South's $a_2$ and $c_1$ are set to 0.05 and 0.04 rather than 0.02 and 0.01 as in Figure 6. The darker bands belong to one basin. The wedges between them comprise the other basin, and are shaded according to how far each point is from the attractor, in terms of number of iterations.

Note that this attractor is closely approximated by a straight line segment, indicating that the one-dimensional model is surprisingly good, at least for these values of the parameters.

For other values of the parameters, we find multistability. That is, there are two or more basins. The basin portrait for one such case is shown in Figure 7. This portrait has two basins, each containing a point attractor. The two basins are separated by a fractal boundary. This portrait is radically nonlinear, and indicates a significant difference from the one-dimensional models, which are necessarily monostable (that is, they have a single attractor).

## 6. Conclusion

We introduced and developed a dynamic version of the North-South model and studied its global dynamics. Our methodology was to replace the static capital endowments in the North-South model by a process of capital accumulation and depretiation through time. After showing that this leads to a well-defined dynamical system on the plane, we studied the evolution of trade and the environment through the global dynamics of the system. We showed that there is a crucial parameter which explains global dynamics: this is the regime of property rights for environmental assets in developing countries, i.e. in the region we call the South. We showed that the less well-defined are these property rights, the more chaotic is the model. We studied the particular characteristics of this chaotic system.

In a future development we hope to explore the global climate in relation with international trade. In this context, the common property resource is the planet's atmosphere, which is used as an input to production, for example, in the combustion of fossil fuels (oil). A by-product of this combustion is $CO_2$. In this case we would study not one but *two* separate but closely interacting dynamical systems on the plane: international trade and the biosphere (atmospheric chemistry, solar radiation, biological gas exchange, ocean dynamics, water reservoirs, climate, etc.). Especially, we will explore the greenhouse gas exchange between (1) the atmosphere, (2) human populations (which inhale oxygen and exhale carbon dioxide, both by breathing and by industrial activities), and (3) biomass and bodies of water, which act as $CO_2$ reservoirs.

A simple biosphere model for beginning the study of this connection is the *daisy-world model* of Watson and Lovelock. This model achieves climate regulation with two cooperating species of "daisies": black daisies (preferring cool but making warmth) and white daisies (preferring warm but making cool). One can replace one species of daisies by human industry, and by doing so extend the analysis of this paper to consider two coupled dynamical systems: the dynamical North-South system and the modified daisy-world system just described. The dynamical North-South model will be extended to three dimensions: $K$, $L$ and $E$. See [2] for this extension in a static framework.

**Notes**

1. See also [6].
2. See Equation (4.1.1).
3. More details are given in Section 1.3 below.
4. These are standard exogenous parameters, common to all general equilibrium models: technologies, supplies of inputs, i.e. capital and environment, and the preferences in the two regions.
5. The North-South model can be solved analytically by a single "resolving" equation [1]. This means that, knowing the exogenous parameters we can compute explicitely the equilibrium values of the model.
6. GNP is the value of the outputs minus the value of the inputs. In other words: it is the inner product of the equilibrium prices with the difference between outputs and inputs at an equilibrium.

## References

1. Chichilnisky, G. "Terms of Trade and Domestic Distribution: Export-Led Growth with Abundant Labor Supply", *J. Development Economics* 8, 1981, 163–192.
2. Chichilnisky, G. "International Trade in Resources: A General Equilibrium Analysis", *Environmental and Natural Resource Mathematics, Short Course, Proc. Symp. Appl. Maths., Proc. Amer. Math. Soc.* 32, 1985, 75–125.
3. Chichilnisky, G. "A General Equilibrium Theory of North-South Trade", in *Essays in Honor of Kenneth Arrow, Vol. 2, Equilibrium Analysis*, W. Heller, R. Starr and D. Starrett (eds.), Cambridge, Cambridge University Press, 1986, pp. 3–56.
4. Chichilnisky, G. "North-South Trade and the Global Environment", Stanford Institute for Theoretical Economics, Technical Report No. 31, Stanford University, 1991. *American Economic Review* 84(4), 1994, 851–873.
5. Chichilnisky, G. "Global Environment and North-South Trade", Stanford Institute for Theoretical Economics, Working Paper No. 78, Stanford University, 1992.
6. Chichilnisky, G. "North-South Trade and the Dynamics of Renewable Resources", *Structural Change and Economic Dynamics* 4, 1993, 219–248.
7. Chichilnisky, G. and G. M. Heal *The Evolving International Economy*, Cambridge, Cambridge University Press, 1987.
8. Chichilnisky, G. and M. Di Matteo. "Migration of Labor and Capital in a General Equilibrium Model of North-South Trade", Working Paper, Columbia University, 1992.
9. Devaney, R. *An Introduction to Chaotic Dynamical Systems*, Second Edition, Reading, MA, Addison-Wesley, 1991.
10. Di Matteo, M. "Dynamical Properties of Chichilnisky's Model of North-South Trade", Working Paper, Università di Siena, 1992.
11. Gardini, L., R. Abraham, R. Record and D. Fournier-Prunaret. "A Double Logistic Map", *Int. J. Bifurcations and Chaos* 4, 1994, 145–176.
12. Goodwin, R. M. *Chaotic Economic Dynamics*, Oxford, Clarendon Press, Oxford University Press, 1990.

GRACIELA CHICHILNISKY AND MASSIMO DI MATTEO

## 2.3. Trade, Migration, and Environment: A General Equilibrium Analysis*

### 1. Introduction

Two major trends in the world economy are international migration and environmental degradation. The object of the paper is to analyze the connection between these two trends, which have generally been analyzed in isolation. Here we represent a world economy in which the exploitation of natural resources as well as the migration of labor have a global character. We discuss the welfare impact of migration and exploitation of natural resources and policies to address these issues.

Industrial development has reached a point where it adversely affects the natural environment. A large share of the world population could be harmed by the instability of the global climate caused by increased concentration of $CO_2$ in the atmosphere. The destruction of biodiversity on the planet has reached unprecedented proportions. Although these are world phenomena, Chichilnisky (1994) showed that environmental degradation can also be considered as a North-South issue. The international market is the vehicle through which the overproduction of natural resources by the South is reconciled with the overconsumption by the North. At the heart of this explanation there is the crucial role played by the different regimes of property rights prevailing in the resource extraction of the two regions.

Another world-wide phenomenon, the migration of labor, has recently intensified. Large migrant flows from Latin America to the USA and from North Africa and Middle East to Europe take place today. The collapse of the socialist economies in Eastern Europe has led to massive migration into the industrialized part of Europe.

Not surprisingly, governments and international organizations are concerned with these developments. Migrant labor has profound consequences

---

* We are indebted to the Fondazione Mattei for financial support and to R. Faini, G. Heal, M. Kurz, and A. Montesano for comments and suggestions.

not only on the host countries but also on the countries of origin. Besides social and political effects, the change in the availability of labor affects the employment structure and the distribution of income of the countries involved. Environmental damage can lead to disruptions of entire populations such as those caused by scarcity of water.

Migration is typically linked to wage and income differentials. Moreover, there is now evidence (e.g. Myers, 1993) that migration is particularly sensitive to the degradation of the environment and to the effects of climate change. Migrant flows are typically from the South to the North, since climate changes affect more the primary sector of the economy which is the basis of Southern economy. In addition developing countries have fewest (technical as well as economic) resources to confront the problem. It is also believed that environmental refugees, as they could aptly be called (Myers, 1993), are the result of tropical deforestation, soil erosion and desertification that occur in many areas of the South. Chichilnisky (1994) showed how all these phenomena are directly connected to trade and to the poor definition of property rights in the South.

Migration patterns reallocate production in the North and South economies, induce a change in trade patterns, and a modification of relative prices.

We develop a framework which follows Chichilnisky (1981, 1994), possessing the same logical structure as the Heckscher–Ohlin model that highlights the connection between labor migration and exploitation of natural resources. From our analysis we obtain answers to the following questions:

1. how does migration affect the exploitation of natural resources?
2. how do policies to check environmental degradation interact with migration flows?
3. how do trade policies affect migration flows and the exploitation of natural resources?

The main results of the paper are as follows. Migration is prompted by wage differentials as technology is different across countries. We show that migration from the South induces a decrease in the exploitation of the resource in the South. This increases the welfare of the South but can decrease that of the North. Migration can lead to higher prices of resources in the North and in the South, setting up a process of induced technical change in the North and better terms of trade for the South, altogether a positive outcome. As is intuitively obvious, migration reduces the wage differential between North and South in a model where, contrary to Heckscher–Ohlin assumptions, technologies differ between countries. Finally, we show that it is possible that a tax on the use of the resource in the South induces an increase in its extraction rather than a decrease. Trade policies could have a positive impact on resource extraction, could reduce the wage gap and therefore decrease the economic incentive to the mobility of labour.

The paper is organized as follows. Section 2 presents the basic model. Section 3 extends it to cover the case of migration and proves the main results on the effects of migration on the exploitation of the resource and the welfare of the South. Section 4 examines the tendency towards real wage equalization. Section 5 argues that tax policies on the use of the resource are unreliable in that they can have effects opposite from what is intended. Finally, we discuss how traditional trade policies could affect the degree of factor mobility and the exploitation of resources.

## 2. The Model

There are two regions, the industrialized countries (North) and the developing countries (South), two goods $A$ and $B$ and two factors. The formulation follows Chichilnisky (1981, 1994). The inputs are an environmental resource $E$ and labor $L$, that are used to produce the two goods. In both regions the $B$ good is more resource intensive than $A$. Constant returns to scale and fixed coefficients are assumed in the production of each good. Technology is different in the two countries:[1] there are four technical coefficients, $c_i(a_i)$, representing the quantity of labor (environmental resource) per unit of output of good $i$. Endowments of labor and environmental resource are not fixed but depend on relative rewards. Therefore, even if there are fixed coefficients in production, there is substitutability among factors in the economy as a whole as relative prices change.[2]

### 2.1. One Region Model

Consider first the economy of the South. Perfect competition in the goods market and constant returns to scale imply zero profits in equilibrium so that:

$$P_B = a_1 P_E + c_1 w, \qquad (1)$$

$$P_A = a_2 P_E + c_2 w, \qquad (2)$$

where $P_A$ (respectively $P_B$) is the price of good $A$ ($B$), $P_E(w)$ is the price of the environmental resource (labor), $a_i(c_i)$ ($i = 1, 2$) are the coefficients of the environmental resource (labor) respectively in industry 1 ($B$) and 2 ($A$).

The assumption that $B$ is more intensive in the use of the resource than $A$ translates into a positive value for $\mathsf{D} \equiv \mathsf{a_1 c_2 - a_2 c_1}$. For future reference we derive the relation between $P_B$ and the wage, $w$, and $P_B$ and $P_E$, the price of the resource.

From Equations (1) and (2) we obtain:

$$P_E = \frac{c_2 P_B - c_1}{D},$$

$$w = \frac{a_1 - a_2 P_B}{D},$$

and, therefore,

$$\frac{\partial(P_E/P_B)}{\partial P_B} = \frac{c_1 P_B^{-2}}{D},$$

$$\frac{\partial(w/P_B)}{\partial P_B} = \frac{-a_1 P_B^{-2}}{D}.$$

Labor and resource supplied are a function of their rewards. The labor supply depends positively on the real wage $w/P_B$ according to the following:

$$L^S = \beta w/P_B + L_0, \tag{3}$$

where $\beta$ and $L_0$ are positive.

For simplicity, we assume that the resource is extracted using labor as the only input and according to a strictly concave production function, $E = E(N)$. It was shown recently (Chichilnisky, 1994)[3] that under these circumstances the amount of resource supplied is an increasing function of the price of the resource and that the precise form of the supply curve depends on the prevailing structure of property rights. We will assume that the South has common property (in particular open access) regimes for the pools from which the resource is extracted.

To solve the model we need to know the relative price of the resource with respect to labor. However, there is no developed labor market in the extraction sector of the South that we label the subsistence sector of the economy: hence there is no market wage. We need to define the opportunity cost of labor. Let us denote this opportunity cost by $q$ and let us assume for the moment that it is a given quantity, equal for each worker. Later in the paper we will derive an expression for $q$ in a general equilibrium fashion.

How is the opportunity cost $q$ connected with the level of resource extraction? Following Chichilnisky (1994) a level of effort is chosen by the typical worker in such a way that $q$ equals the common property marginal product of labor times the market price of the resource. The common property marginal product (CMP) is the change in the average yield that a typical worker $i$ obtains as (s)he supplies one more unit of effort in a situation where the ownership of the pool is not restricted. We can express the relation that holds in the optimal situation as

$$P_E \cdot \text{CMP} = q,$$

As the price of the resource $P_E$ increases the optimal level of effort increases, given the assumption of strict concavity of the production function and the constancy of $q$. As a result the quantity supplied of the resource goes up as its price $P_E$ increases.

These considerations give rise to a supply curve of the natural resource in the South that depends positively on its price $P_E$, for any given $q$. Note how property rights matter. If there were well defined private property rights in the

South, then the supply curve would have been steeper, as in this case $q/P_E$ equals the private property marginal product which is lower than the CMP.[4]

This argument leads us to postulate a supply function of the resource (which is assumed to be linear for simplicity):

$$E^S = \alpha P_E/q + E_0, \tag{4}$$

where $E_0$ and $\alpha > 0$.

The parameter $\alpha$ is large when there is common property for the resource (as it is the case with the South) since it reflects the greater sensitivity of the supply of $E$ to its price in comparison to the case where property rights are well defined.[5] In the model a large value for $\alpha$ formalizes the so-called "tragedy of the commons" which is known to lead to an exploitation of the resource which is larger than the one occurring with a private property regime.

The situation is summarized in the following diagram, where $E_C^S$ is the common property supply curve and $E_P^S$ the private property supply curve:

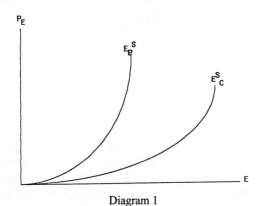

Diagram 1

The demand equations for the resources, $E^D$ and $L^D$, are:

$$E^D = a_1 B^S + a_2 A^S, \tag{5}$$

$$L^D = c_1 B^S + c_2 A^S, \tag{6}$$

where $B^S$ ($A^S$) is the supply of the $B$ ($A$) commodity respectively.

In equilibrium demand for resources equals supply so that:

$$L^D = L^S, \tag{7}$$

$$E^D = E^S. \tag{8}$$

The South exports the resource intensive good, $B$ and imports $A$. Indeed it has been shown (Chichilnisky, 1994) that when the two countries have identical technology and preferences, a sufficient reason for them to engage in trade is the difference in the property rights regime of the natural resource that is used as an input of production. In particular the South has an apparent comparative advantage in, and exports, the resource intensive good. The South exports good $B$, even if North and South share similar technology and preferences.

In the context of the present, more general model, where technologies and preferences may differ among countries, the assumed pattern of trade can always be sustained by a suitable choice of the value of the demand for the $A$ good in the two countries, as it is apparent from inspection of diagram 2 below.

Exports of the South equal the difference between domestic supply and demand, namely:

$$X_B^S = B^S - B^D, \tag{9}$$

whereas imports of commodity $A$ equal the difference between demand and domestic supply, namely:

$$X_A^D = A^D - A^S, \tag{10}$$

where $A^D$ ($B^D$) is the demand for the $A$ ($B$) good.

We assume that trade balances:

$$P_B X_B^S = P_A X_A^D. \tag{11}$$

### 2.2. Two Region Model

Equations for the North are similar except for different values of the parameters and of the exogenous variables, reflecting different technologies, preferences and property right regime. In the North it is possible that labor supply responds little to the real wage.[6] Property rights for the resources are well defined in the North so that the supply curve for the North is steeper reflecting the private property marginal product.

In Equation (4) we approximate $q$, the opportunity cost of labor, by $P_B$ for the South where subsistence labor is employed in the extraction sector.[7] For the North we approximate $q$ by $P_A$ as there is no subsistence sector in the North. Equation (4) now reads for the South:

$$E^s = \alpha P_E/P_B + E_0$$

and for the North:

$$E^s(N) = \alpha_N P_E/P_A + E_0(N).$$

The North imports the resource intensive good $B$ and exports the (skilled) labor intensive good $A$.

There are other self explanatory conditions to be fulfilled in an international equilibrium:

$$P_A(S) = P_A(N), \tag{12}$$

$$P_B(S) = P_B(N), \tag{13}$$

$$X_B^S(S) = X_B^D(N), \qquad (14)$$

$$X_A^D(S) = X_A^S(N). \qquad (15)$$

Finally, we choose the numeraire:

$$P_A = 1. \qquad (16)$$

To close the model we follow the original Chichilnisky's model (1981)[8] but we could equally consider other assumptions which would lead to similar results:[9]

$$A^D(S) = A_0^D(S), \qquad (17)$$

$$A^D(N) = A_0^D(N). \qquad (18)$$

The model is composed of 12 equations for the South ((1–11) and (17)) plus 12 analogous equations for the North (denoted (1'–11') and (18)) plus (12), (13), (15) and (16). Indeed, Equation (14) is always satisfied when trade is balanced and (12), (13), and (14) hold. There are 28 endogenous variables, 14 in each region: $P_B, P_A, w, P_E, L^S, L^D, E^S, E^D, B^S, B^D, A^S, A^D, X_B^S, X_A^D$.[10]

It turns out that the model can be solved analytically in a very simple way: it reduces to a quadratic equation in the Southern terms of trade, $P_B$. Starting from the equilibrium condition in the world market for the $A$ good

$$A_0^D(S) + A_0^D(N) = A^S(S) + A^S(N)$$

and using Equations (1–8) we obtain:

$$[A(N)] P_B^2 + \left[A_0^D(S) + A_0^D(N) + C(S) + C(N)\right] P_B$$
$$- [V(S) + V(N)] = 0, \qquad (19)$$

where

$$A(N) = \alpha_N (c_1 c_2)_N / D_N^2,$$
$$C(S) = (1/D)[c_1 E_0 - a_1 L_0 + (a_1 a_2 \beta + c_1 c_2 \alpha)/D],$$
$$C(N) = (1/D)_N [(c_1 E_0 - a_1 L_0)_N + (a_1 a_2 \beta - c_1^2 \alpha)_N / D_N],$$
$$V(S) = \beta a_1^2 / D^2 + \alpha c_1^2 / D^2,$$
$$V(N) = \beta_N (a_1^2)_N / D_N^2.$$

Equation (19) has one positive solution since the constant term is negative and the quadratic is positive.

Once the terms of trade are known all the other endogenous variables can be computed (Chichilnisky, 1981). The solution of the model is, therefore, complete.

116  G. Chichilnisky and M. Di Matteo

The market for the A good can be illustrated in the following diagram, where the continuous line indicates the equilibrium level of the terms of trade at which the Southern demand for exports equals the Northern supply of exports:

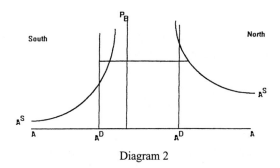

Diagram 2

## 2.3. The Opportunity Cost of Labor in the Subsistence Sector

Typically, the opportunity cost of labor, $q$ is equal to the wage but in the South there is no formal labor market in the subsistence sector. Therefore, in the following we will derive an endogenous value for $q$ in a general equilibrium fashion, following (Chichilnisky, 1994).

We assume that the typical worker maximizes a utility function $U = U(A, N_0 - N)$ depending on the consumption of good $A$ and on leisure, $N_0 - N$, subject to the following constraint: $P_A A = P_E E(N)$, where $E$ has already been defined in Section 2.1, and $N_0$ is the total available amount of time. In the preferred situation it is true for the typical worker that:

$$\frac{\partial U/\partial (N_0 - N)}{\partial U/\partial A} = \frac{P_E(\partial E/\partial N)}{P_A}.$$

Previously we have shown (in Section 2.1) that $q$ must be equal to the value of the common property marginal product; since in our North-South model $P_A = 1$, it follows that:

$$\frac{\partial U/\partial (N_0 - N)}{\partial U/\partial A} = q.$$

So $q$, which is a function of $P_E/P_A$, is the ratio of the marginal utilities of the typical worker. This fully defines an endogenous value for $q$, once $P_B$ is known. From the latter we can compute $P_E$ using Equations (1) and (2).

The next step is to show that as the price of the resource which the typical worker sells goes down, (s)he has to work more and not less to secure a minimum level of subsistence when the price of consumption goods has increased (in relative terms). Hence our next step is to ascertain what happens to the worker's choice of leisure and good $A$ when (s)he is confronted with a different price of the resource and we allow the opportunity cost $q$ to change.

For this purpose only, we assume that the utility function $U$ has an elasticity of substitution between leisure and $A$ less than one.[11] In this case an increase in the relative price of $A$ implies a reduction in the leisure consumed or, which is the same thing, an increase in the supply of effort. Hence we establish:

PROPOSITION 1. *If the elasticity of substitution between leisure and consumption is less than one, a worker in the subsistence sector who maximizes $U = U(A, N_0 - N)$ subject to $P_A A = P_E E(N)$, increases his (her) effort when the price of resource $E$ decreases vis-à-vis the price of good $A$.*

*Proof.* The supply curve $E^S$ we derived (Equation (4)) was parameterized by $q$. As $P_E/P_A$ decreases, the quantity of effort increases and with it the supply of the resource. By the strict concavity of the production function, also $(\partial E/\partial N)$ decreases so that $q$ has to decrease as well. In terms of our supply curve for the resource this means that such a curve shifts downwards signalling in equilibrium a higher supply of the resource as $P_E/P_A$ decreases, once changes in $q$ are taken into account. □

A geometrical explanation of the result is provided in the Appendix.

## 3. Why Does Labor Migrate?

Since technologies are different across countries factor prices are not equalized after trade, as the Heckscher–Ohlin theory (which is based on the assumption of equal technologies) asserts.[12] Indeed real wages are equal across countries only when the terms of trade take on a particular value, $P_B^M$, given by the following expression:

$$\frac{(a_1/D)_N - a_1/D}{(a_2/D)_N - a_2/D} \equiv P_B^M. \tag{20}$$

The value in this expression depends exclusively on technological parameters so that only by a coincidence does it equal the equilibrium terms of trade that reflects the solution of the general equilibrium model. In addition the value of the terms of trade given by (20) could be such as to entail a negative value for the equalized real wage.

A similar argument applies for the price of the resource, which in general is not equalized either. We can show that to have an equalized price for the resource $E$, the terms of trade should take on a value, $P_B^F$, given by the following expression:

$$\frac{(c_1/D)_N - c_1/D}{(c_2/D)_N - c_2/D} \equiv P_B^F. \tag{21}$$

While in equilibrium either (20) or (21) could occur by coincidence, both cannot occur at the same time, as it is clear by comparing them: hence simultaneous equalization of real wages and resource price across countries is ruled out.

If real wages are different across countries there is an incentive for workers to move from the low wage to the high wage region.[13] We can easily establish under which conditions labor moves to the North (South). As every endogenous variable can be computed when the terms of trade are determined, we know that $w/P_B < (>)(w/P_B)_N$ implies:

$$\left[\left(\frac{a_2}{D}\right)_N - \frac{a_2}{D}\right] P_B < (>) \left(\frac{a_1}{D}\right)_N - \frac{a_1}{D}.$$

Let us make the following by now standard[14]

ASSUMPTION 1. *In the South technologies are dual.*

By dual technologies in the South we mean that the B sector is much more resource intensive than in the North. This can be translated into the model by assuming a much larger value for $D$ with respect to $D_N$ (see the definition of $D$ in Section 2.1). If then $D \gg D_N$ then we can establish that labor leaves the South whenever

$$P_B < \frac{(a_1/D)_N - (a_1/D)}{(a_2/D)_N - (a_2/D)} \equiv P_B^M.$$

In a similar way we can establish (under the same conditions) that the price of the resource is lower in the South than in the North whenever

$$P_B > \frac{(c_1/D)_N - (c_1/D)}{(c_2/D)_N - (c_1/D)} \equiv P_B^F.$$

In addition to the real wage gap, other factors have recently been highlighted in the migration phenomenon. In particular there is evidence (Myers, 1993) that among the consequences of environmental damage is the fact that people move away from their homes. It is also believed that environmental refugees are due to tropical deforestation, soil erosion and desertification.

It is because migration is such a complex phenomenon that at first we do not intend to establish a strict, quantitative relation between the number of workers who migrate and the real wages gap in the two countries. Though we maintain that, among economic factors, real wages differential is a major force in shaping labor migration, at this stage our analysis can accommodate the case where (at least part of) migration occurs for environmental motivations.

In order to accommodate the analysis of migration in our framework we simply reinterpret the equilibrium described in the model of the previous section as an equilibrium occurring in an interval of time within which migration is not allowed.[15] At the end of each period workers check whether real wages are higher in the North than in the South and decide to move towards the higher wage country.

The number of workers who at the junction between one period and another leave any one country can be represented in the model as a change in $L_0$. If workers leave the South (North) it will be a fall (increase) in $L_0$ for the South and an increase (fall) of $L_0(N)$ in the North of exactly the same amount. Then a new equilibrium is reached within the second period at the end of which the story repeats itself.

## 4. The Effects of Migration on Wage Differential and Resource Extraction

Let us now suppose, quite reasonably, that real wages are lower in the South than in the North so that workers move from the South to the North. In our model this is captured by an increase in $L_0(N)$ and a fall in $L_0$ of exactly the same magnitude.

We can now establish the following

PROPOSITION 2. *If Assumption 1 holds, migration from the South to the North is associated with a higher level of the South's terms of trade.*

*Proof.* Using Equation (24) and the implicit function theorem we compute:

$$\frac{\partial P_B}{\partial L_0} = \frac{[a_1/D] P_B}{2P_B [A(N)] + [A_0^D(S) + A_0^D(N) + C(S) + C(N)]},$$

$$\frac{\partial P_B}{\partial L_0(N)} = \frac{[(a_1/D)_N] P_B}{2P_B [A(N)] + [A_0^D(S) + A_0^D(N) + C(S) + C(N)]}. \quad (22)$$

In the denominator when $\alpha$ is large in the South the sign of the term in $\alpha$ determines the sign of $C(S)$ and $C(N)$. Since the term in $\alpha$ in $C(S)$ is $c_1 c_2 \alpha$, a positive quantity, the denominator is positive in this case. If Assumption 1 holds, then the numerator of the second expression is larger in absolute value than the numerator of the first and the net effect will be dominated by the Northern component. As a consequence of the assumed changes in $L_0$, the change in the terms of trade will be positive. □

The intuitive economic explanation of the above result is as follows. An increase in $L_0(N)$ and a fall in $L_0(S)$ means that for any level of the terms of trade the supply of labor is larger in the North and smaller in the South. This triggers a shift in the production mix in each country, the North increasing the production of $A$ (at the expense of $B$), the South the production of the resource intensive good $B$ (at the expense of $A$). Take the market for the $A$ good: if the fall in production in the South is smaller than the increase in the North, then the terms of trade of the South increase. This happens precisely when, according to our terminology, technologies are dual in the South (using Equations (5–8)):

$$\frac{\partial A^S(S)}{\partial L^S(S)} = \frac{a_1}{D} < \left(\frac{a_1}{D}\right)_N = \frac{\partial A^S(N)}{\partial L^S(N)}.$$

The situation is illustrated in the diagram below where $P'_B$ is the new level of the terms of trade and $A'^S$ is the level of supply of $A$ after migration.

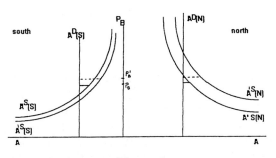

Diagram 3

To proceed with our analysis we need to determine whether the wage differential decreases after migration. When workers leave the South the terms of trade are lower than the level at which real wages are equalized. Since as a consequence of migration flows, the terms of trade increase, it is clear that the gap in the terms of trade will be lower:

PROPOSITION 3. *When Assumption 1 holds, migration will reduce the wage differential.*

*Proof.* When Assumption 1 holds, workers leave the South whenever $P_B < P_B^M$. As a consequence of migration from the South terms of trade increase. Ergo the gap in the terms of trade reduces. On the other hand, from the comparison of Equations (1) and (2) with the corresponding Northern equations, an increase in the terms of trade will induce a fall in the Southern real wage which is less than the fall in the Northern, if Assumption 1 holds. Therefore, there is a tendency towards wage rates equalization. A similar argument holds when real wages are higher in the South than in the North, namely when $P_B > P_B^M$. □

The situation[16] is illustrated in diagram 4 where the different slopes of the two curves depends on Assumption 1, namely on the large value of $D$ with respect to $D_N$:

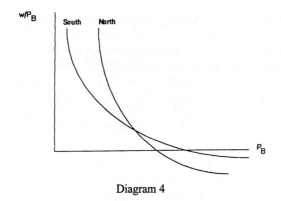

Diagram 4

The next point is to explore the impact of migration on the resources. We wish to determine whether differences in $P_E$ across countries *increase*.

The outcome depends on the sign of the differential gap before migration has taken place. We have established that after migration from the South, the terms of trade rise. This in turn will increase $P_E$ as is clear from Equations (1) and (2). In particular the price of the resource will increase more in the North than in the South, if Assumption 1 holds, thus increasing the difference in prices between the North and the South. Only if before migration the price of the resource were lower in the North than in the South, would migration result in reducing the differential in the resource price. In other words, if the equilibrium terms of trade are such that at the same time $P_B < P_B^M$ and $P_B < P_B^F$, then labor migration will induce a reduction in both the labor and the resource prices gaps.[17]

From the policy point of view the effects of a yawning gap between the price of the resource across regions could be to foster more direct investment from the North to exploit the lower level of the resource price in the South; secondly it could set up a process of induced technical progress in the North. These developments are not dealt with here and deserve further analysis.

The final point in this section is to examine the effects of migration on the exploitation of resources. What will be the general equilibrium effects of the migration pattern?

When migration takes place from South to North a new equilibrium is established with a higher level of the terms of trade. In turn this implies a new level for the price of the resource and a new value for the opportunity cost of labor employed in the subsistence sector to extract the resource. As a result the quantity supplied of the resource will change. In which direction it changes can be inferred by making use of a result already established (Proposition 1). It was shown there that as the price of the resource increases, the typical worker in the subsistence sector will supply less effort and therefore less of the resource will be extracted. Since after migration the terms of trade increase and, as is clear from Equations (1) and (2), the price of the resource increases as well, it follows:

PROPOSITION 4. *After migration from the South to the North, if Assumption 1 holds, the new equilibrium is characterized by a higher level of the resource price and a yawning gap in resources prices in the North and the South, potentially leading to induced technical change in the North. If the elasticity of substitution between leisure and the consumption good is less than one for the subsistence worker, this leads to a higher opportunity cost of subsistence labor in the South. At this new equilibrium the worker applies less effort and less resource is extracted in the South.*

*Proof.* This is a corollary of Propositions 1 and 2. From Proposition 2 migration from the South will increase the terms of trade. From Equations (1) and (2) the increase in the terms of trade will increase the price of the resource (relative to $P_A$). This, via Proposition 1, induces an increase in leisure and, therefore, a fall in effort of the typical worker and a decrease in the exploitation of the resource. □

## 5. The Effects of Migration on Welfare

We finally consider the effects on the welfare of the two countries. Since the quantity consumed of the $A$ good is given in each country, one has to look at the response of the demand for the $B$ good (when terms of trade change) to analyze welfare improvements. Indeed if, following migration, the demand for basic goods increases in the South, then South's welfare increases. To show this, first we recall that exports are the difference between domestic supply and demand. Secondly, we notice that the supply of $B$ depends positively on its price, $P_B$. If we can show that exports fall when the terms of trade increase, then it is clear that demand has to increase.

PROPOSITION 5. *Migration of labor from the South to the North increases the South's welfare, if Assumption 1 holds.*

*Proof.* From
$$X_B^S = B^S - B^D$$
using (5) and (6) and Walras' Law, we get
$$X_B^S = (c_2 E - a_2 L)/D - (P_E E + wL - A_0^D)/P_B.$$
This reduces to
$$X_B^S = \alpha c_1 c_2 / D^2 P_B - \alpha c_1^2 / D^2 P_B^2 + P_B^{-1}$$
$$\times [E_0 c_1/D - L_0 a_1/D + A_0^D - \beta a_1^2/D^2 P_B + \beta a_1 a_2/D^2].$$
If we differentiate with respect to $P_B$ we get
$$\partial X_B^S/\partial P_B = (\alpha/D^2 P_B^2)[-c_1 c_2 + 2c_1^2 P_B^{-1}] - P_B^{-2}$$
$$\times [A_0^D + E_0 c_1/D - L_0 a_1/D + \beta a_1 a_2/D^2 - \beta a_1^2/D^2 P_B].$$

The sign of the expression is dominated by the terms in $\alpha$ which is very large for the South. From Equations (1) and (2) it is immediate to see that the sign of the term in square brackets is negative if $c_2/D < 2P_E/P_B$. The latter is satisfied when Assumption 1 holds, namely $D$ is very large. On the other hand,

$$\partial B^S/\partial P_B = [\alpha c_1 c_2/D^2 + \beta a_1 a_2/D^2]P_B^{-2} > 0.$$

Therefore, when the terms of trade increase, supply of $B$ goods increases and exports decrease: hence demand for $B$, being the difference of the two, has to increase and the welfare of the South increases as well. □

Without more information it is impossible to determine the sign of the demand for basics in the North, as there $\alpha$ is not large. We conclude that as workers move from the South to the North, South's welfare increases and North's can either decrease or increase, if we measure welfare by the amount of consumption goods available in each economy.

To end this section we stress that dual technology in the South is a crucial assumption for some of our results. If the hypothesis were true for the North (an unlikely event, though) migration from the South would bring about a decrease in the terms of trade rather than an increase. Consequently, when labor leaves the South resource extraction would expand rather than contract. However, the conclusions about the tendency towards a reduction of the wage (and resource price) gap would be unaffected.

## 6. Effects of Tax and Trade Policies

In this section we examine the effects of a tax policy in the South aimed at reducing the exploitation of the resource and of a change in the property rights in the South. We will also consider the effects of trade policy in the South.

It is generally believed that taxes on the use of the resource will lead to a reduction in demand and therefore will help environmental preservation. However typically this kind of analysis assumes that all other prices remain constant. Here we would like to examine the effect of a tax on the use of the resource in the general equilibrium model we have just presented.

Let us assume that a unit tax $T$ on the use of the resource (paid by those who utilize it) is levied in the South. Assume also that the revenue from this tax is used to increase the domestic demand for the non-resource intensive good, $A$. In this case we establish:

PROPOSITION 6. *A unit tax $T$ on the use of the resource, whose proceeds are used to increase demand for the $A$ commodity, will reduce the terms of trade, the price of the resource, and increase the output of the resource in the South.*

*Proof.* Levying a unit tax on the use of the resource and allocating the revenue to the demand for good $A$ is tantamount to assuming a shift of demand in favor of good $A$. By using the implicit function theorem and (24), let us compute:

$$\frac{\partial P_B}{\partial A^D(S)} = \frac{-P_B}{2P_B\left[A(N)\right] + A_0^D(S) + A_0^D(N) + C(S) + C(N)}.$$

The above expression is negative since the denominator is positive as in (25). The decrease in the terms of trade induces a lower level of the resource price, via Equations (1) and (2), an increase in the output of the resource and a fall in the opportunity cost of subsistence labor via Proposition 1. □

We have shown that partial equilibrium result could be misleading since after the tax the price of the resource actually falls rather than increases and this leads to more extraction, not less. If the above policy were enacted when real wages were lower in the South, one further effect of this policy would be that of encouraging migration from the South as it widens the wage gap and induces more degradation.

Can one resort to some other policy to reduce the exploitation of the resource? An alternative policy in the South would be to define property rights in a better way so that the extraction of the resource is less sensitive to its price and the tendency to an overexploitation of the resource is kept in check (see Chichilnisky, 1994).

Finally, we discuss the effects of trade policy, in reference to results derived in a context of a similar model. Di Matteo (1993) proved that an export duty in the South increases its terms of trade.[18] Therefore, a move towards protectionism by increasing the terms of trade and the price of the resource will reduce the amount of resource produced and exported in the South.

In addition, Di Matteo (1993) proved that a tax on the production of the $B$ good in the South increases its terms of trade and therefore, as a result, exploitation of the resource falls.

As a result of these policy actions, the real wage differential is reduced and, other things equal, we also expect migration to reduce.

## 7. Conclusions

We have analyzed the relations between degradation of the environment and labor migration, two phenomena which are at the centre of today's economic debate. In the South, contrary to the North, property rights in the extraction sector are not well defined. The South exports the resource intensive good.

Migration occurs due to wage differentials. Under our conditions migration leads to better terms of trade for the South, the price of the resource goes up and less resource is extracted in the South: the welfare in the South increases.

Under our hypotheses migration from the South to the North helps reducing the extraction of the natural resources.

We also analyze the effect of a unit tax on the resource in the South with the revenue spent by the government in buying the less resource intensive good. This reduces the terms of trade and therefore increases the extraction of the resource. Our conclusion is that partial equilibrium analysis of taxes can be misleading in that the overall effects of the imposition of a tax are opposite from what is intended.

Finally, we notice that a less liberal trade policy has positive effects on the level of actual exploitation of the resource.

## 8. Appendix

To show that as the price of the resource falls relative to $P_A$ the typical worker will supply more effort as we claimed at the end of Section 2, we first examine the implication of such a change in the case of a utility function with a unitary elasticity of substitution. There are two goods, $A$ and leisure, $N_0 - N$. The definition of unitary elasticity of substitution is:

$$\frac{\partial(A/N_0 - N)}{\partial(P_A/q)} \frac{P_A/q}{A/(N_0 - N)} = 1.$$

In words the ratio between the proportionate rate of change of the demand ratio and the proportionate rate of change of the marginal rate of substitution (which in an ideal situation coincides with the price ratio) is equal to one.

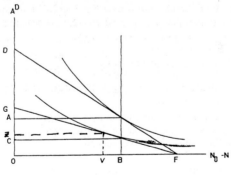

Diagram 5

In the diagram we postulate an increase in $P_A$, i.e. a move from $D$ to $G$: we know (using Thales's theorem) that in this case:

$$\frac{(OA - OC)/OB}{OA/OB} = \frac{(OD - OG)/OF}{OD/OF},$$

namely

$$1 - \frac{OC}{OA} = 1 - \frac{OG}{OD}.$$

However, the left-hand side of (28) is the proportionate rate of change of the demand ratio and the right-hand side is the proportionate rate of change of the price ratio, when the elasticity of substitution is equal to one. In this situation the worker will consume the same amount of leisure and a smaller amount of the $A$ good but in such a way that the proportion in value terms of the goods is unaltered after the increase in the price of $A$.

If, on the contrary, the elasticity is less than 1 then for the left-hand side to be less than the right-hand side, it is necessary that the amount of $A$ chosen, say $OZ$, is greater than the amount chosen in the case of unitary elasticity, i.e. $OC$. This means that at the new tangency point the amount of leisure will be to the left of $OB$, say $OV$: this entails a higher level of $A$ consumed and a smaller level of leisure than in the case of unitary elasticity. Therefore, more resources are extraced.

## Notes

1. Here we deal with the interdependence between migration and environmental degradation, whereas in (Chichilnisky, 1994) the focus was on how differences solely in the property rights regime in the extraction of the resource could lead to an overexploitation of the resource in the South.
2. Capital is not explicitly included among the factors of producton. However, one can consider that labour is skilled and embodies a certain degree of training and use of capital. Such training could have been acquired by working with machines.
3. The reader is referred to (Chichilnisky, 1994, appendix A) for a detailed proof.
4. The latter equals the average product when the number of workers is very large, as it is sensible to assume in the South. In this case it is immediate to notice that for a strictly concave production fuction the average product is greater than the marginal. For a more general argument, see (Chichilnisky, 1994, appendix A).
5. See (Chichilnisky, 1994, section 3).
6. A very low value for $\beta$ does not affect results.
7. Following (Chichilnisky, 1994, appendix B).
8. They imply a given structure of the indifference curves as shown in (Chichilnisky, 1986, appendix f).
9. The assumption about demand is not in contrast with the hypothesis (as expressed at the end of this section) about the behaviour of the subsistence workers in the South, as the latter are not part of the rest of the market economy.
10. The last two for the North are $X_B^D$ and $X_A^S$.
11. In the case of a developing country the assumption can be justified on the following grounds. Suppose on the contrary, and take an extreme case, that the good $A$ and leisure were perfect substitutes. The worker would be indifferent between consuming no $A$ and enjoying leisure only: in a situation where the typical worker has only labour to sell this implication is totally unrealistic. On the other hand, to suppose that $A$ and leisure were perfect complements would go too far, as it implies that, no matter what prices are, the typical worker will consume a given proportion between $A$ and leisure (in physical terms). The case we are considering takes into account the fact that as the price of the resource the typical worker sells go down, (s)he has to work more and not less to secure a minimum level of subsistence whose price has gone up (in relative terms).
12. We have analyzed the effects of labour and capital migration and its relation with H–O model in (Chichilnisky and Di Matteo, 1992).

13. Probably migration flows respond to differences in real income per capita rather real wages. We maintain however the classical assumption used in trade theory as the other would greatly complicate the analysis.
14. See, e.g. the recent analysis by Barba Navaretti (1994).
15. The reason why migration occurs at discrete intervals of time is that to migrate is generally costly and the decision requires some time.
16. As we argued (Chichilnisky and Di Matteo, 1992), in general we do not possess enough empirical information to know whether when the terms of trade equal $P_B^M$ the equalized real wage is negative: in this case a real wages gap could persist even after migration.
17. This outcome is in accord with a recent result (Chichilnisky and Di Matteo, 1992) where in a model with labour and capital we showed that for some values of the terms of trade it is possible that as one factor moves the reward differential for the other factor widens. In other words, we identified an interval for the terms of trade with the property that when equilibrium terms of trade belong to that interval the movement of one factor reduces its own price differential but increases the price differential of the other factor.
18. It has to be stressed that in (Di Matteo, 1993) Lerner's theorem does not hold. Also the reaction of the other country after the introduction of the tariff is not considered as it calls for different instruments of analysis.

# References

1. Barba Navaretti, G. (1994). *What Determines Intra-Industry Gaps in Technology?*, Milano, Fondazione ENI Enrico Mattei, Nota di lavoro.
2. Chichilnisky, G. (1981). "Terms of Trade and Domestic Distribution: Export Led Growth with Abundant Labor", *Journal of Development Economics* VIII, 163–192.
3. Chichilnisky, G. (1986). "A General Equilibrium Theory of North-South Trade", in *Equilibrium Analysis. Essays in Honour of K. Arrow*, W. Heller, R. Starr and D. Starrett (eds.), Cambridge, Cambridge University Press, pp. 3–56.
4. Chichilnisky, G. (1994). "North-South Trade and the Global Environment", *American Economic Review* LXXXIV, 851–874 (previously appeared as Technical Report No. 31, Stanford Institute for Theoretical Economics, 1991).
5. Chichilnisky, G. and M. Di Matteo (1992). "Migration of Labour and Capital in a General Equilibrium Model of North-South Trade", mimeo, revised July 1995.
6. Dasgupta, P. and G. M. Heal (1979). *Economic Theory and Exhaustible Resources*, Cambridge, Cambridge University Press.
7. Di Matteo, M. (1993). "Forms of Trade Control in an Equilibrium North-South Model: A Comparative Evaluation", *Rivista Internazionale di Scienze Economiche e Commerciali* XL, 63–74.
8. Myers, N. (1993). "Environmental Refugees in a Globally Warmed World", *BioScience* XLIII, 752–761.

GUIDO CAZZAVILLAN AND IGNAZIO MUSU*

# 2.4. A Simple Model of Optimal Sustainable Growth

## 1. Introduction

In a number of models studied by the contemporary literature, economic growth is obtained by endogenizing the productivity of labor services. This goal is typically achieved making the contribution to production due to the use of those factors depend upon the past accumulation of capital, be this physical, as in (Romer, 1986; Barro, 1990), or human, as in (Lucas, 1988). The purpose of this paper is to mimic such a technique to get sustainable growth in a simple model characterized by the presence of an environmental asset.

We shall consider environment as a stock which is valuable when preserved, but which provides production services when exploited. Emission flows constitute a clear example of these services. Sustainability, in this context, means that environmental production services must be equal to the regenerative capacity of the environmental asset so as to keep the stock of environment constant and, therefore, preserved at the level considered optimal from the intertemporal society's welfare point of view.

The rate of growth of the productivity of the environmental services is assumed to depend on the past accumulation of the physical capital stock. This assumption corresponds to the view that capital accumulation embodies new technologies requiring a decreasing emission coefficient per unit of output.

While the effect of the past capital accumulation on the productivity of the environmental services is a positive externality for each unit of production, and, therefore, treated as given at individual level, the stock of preserved environment provides utility to consumers and can be assimilated to a public good which delivers a non-marketed benefit. A rational environmental policy aiming at achieving a socially optimal sustainable growth path should internalize both external effects.

---

* The authors would like to thank financial support from NCR, under the contribution No. 93.04794.CT10.

In the next section we shall introduce the model, whereas in Section 3 we shall assess the issue of the existence and uniqueness of the sustainable balanced-growth path. In particular, we shall demonstrate that, when the assimilative capacity of environment depends on the environmental stock, the conditions that must be imposed on discounting to get sustainable growth are not independent of the stock of environment. It is, therefore, possible to establish a trade-off between the sustainable balanced growth rate and the sustainable environmental stock. In Section 4 we finally discuss the local stability properties of the balanced-growth path.

## 2. A Model of Optimal Sustainable Growth

We consider a continuous-time, infinite horizon economy which is endowed with two assets: a physical capital stock, $K$, and an environmental asset, $E$. Following (Becker, 1982), the stock of environmental resources is defined as the difference between a maximum tolerable pollution stock $\bar{P} > 0$ and the current pollution stock $P$:

$$E = \bar{P} - P, \tag{2.1}$$

that is

$$\dot{E} = -\dot{P}. \tag{2.2}$$

A constant proportion $m > 0$ of the pollution stock is assumed to be assimilated in each instant $t$ by the natural factors governing the environment. The pollution flow (emissions) $Z$ expresses, in this context, the rate at which the environmental asset is used as a source of productive services. It follows that the pollution stock changes according to the following rule

$$\dot{P} = Z - mP. \tag{2.3}$$

Using (2.3) and (2.1), Equation (2.2) can be rewritten as

$$\dot{E} = A(E) - Z, \tag{2.4}$$

where

$$A(E) = m(\bar{P} - E). \tag{2.5}$$

Equation (2.5), in other words, represents the assimilative capacity of the environment as a decreasing linear function of the environmental stock. The economy, which is also endowed with a large number of identical competitive firms, produces a unique consumption good using a standard aggregate Cobb–Douglas technology defined upon the fraction of the physical capital stock devoted to production, $K_1$, and labor in efficiency units, $hL$, i.e.

$$Y = BK_1^\alpha (hL)^{1-\alpha}, \tag{2.6}$$

where $B > 0$ is a scale parameter and $h$ represents the efficiency of the total labor force $L$ which is normalized and set to be equal to 1. $h$ acts as an externality for each individual firm and is assumed to depend on the past accumulation of the total capital stock used in production according to the following expression:

$$h = K_1. \tag{2.7}$$

Ex post, therefore, the aggregate production function is linear in $K_1$:

$$Y = BK_1. \tag{2.8}$$

The production process, however, entails polluting emissions $Z$ according to the emission function given by

$$Z = eY, \tag{2.9}$$

where the emission-output coefficient $e$ is supposed to be reduced through the exploitation of the remaining fraction $K_2$ of the total physical capital stock according to the function

$$e = \frac{1}{K_2}. \tag{2.10}$$

In view of (2.10), Equation (2.9) becomes

$$Z = \frac{Y}{K_2}. \tag{2.11}$$

Full factor employment requires, as usual,

$$K_1 + K_2 = K. \tag{2.12}$$

Hence, the whole economy's capital stock is completely utilized either to increase production, or to reduce the emission coefficient and, therefore, pollution.

Defining $u \equiv K_2/K$ and using (2.12), we can rewrite (2.11) as

$$Z = B\left(\frac{1}{u} - 1\right). \tag{2.13}$$

Assuming that capital lasts forever, the capital accumulation constraint is given by

$$\dot{K} = B(1-u)K - C, \tag{2.14}$$

where $C$ represents aggregate consumption.

A constant population of identical consumers endowed with an infinite lifetime profile is assumed to derive satisfaction from both consumption and the environment asset according to the following intertemporal utility function:

$$W(C, E) = \int_0^\infty e^{-\delta t} \frac{1}{1-\eta} (CE)^{1-\eta} \, dt, \tag{2.15}$$

where $\delta > 0$ is the standard subjective rate of time preference.

A benevolent central planner maximizes (2.15) subject to the constraints (2.4) and (2.14).

The Hamiltonian function associated with this program is

$$H = \frac{(CE)^{1-\eta}}{1-\eta} + v[BK(1-u) - C] + \lambda[A(E) - B(1/u - 1)]. \quad (2.16)$$

The first order necessary conditions for an optimum are

$$C^{-\eta} E^{1-\eta} = v, \quad (2.17)$$

$$vK = \lambda u^{-2}, \quad (2.18)$$

$$\frac{\dot{v}}{v} = \delta - (1-u)B, \quad (2.19)$$

$$\frac{\dot{\lambda}}{\lambda} = \delta + m - \frac{1}{\lambda} C^{1-\eta} E^{-\eta}, \quad (2.20)$$

whereas the transversality conditions at infinity are given by

$$\lim_{t \to \infty} e^{-\delta t} vK = 0, \quad (2.21)$$

$$\lim_{t \to \infty} e^{-\delta t} \lambda E = 0. \quad (2.22)$$

The variables $v$ and $\lambda$ designate the shadow prices of the capital and the environmental stocks, respectively. Conditions (2.17) and (2.18) are the temporary equilibrium requirements establishing the equality of the marginal utility of consumption and the marginal product of the environmental services to their respective prices. Condition (2.19) is the standard arbitrage condition which requires the rate of time preference to be equal to the marginal product of capital plus the capital gains. Finally, condition (2.20) is a modified version of the Hotelling rule requiring the rate of return from preserving the environmental stock to be equal to the rate of time preference.

Equations (2.17–2.20) constitute a four dimensional dynamical system which fully describes the equilibrium paths of the economy. Following a number of authors (Alogoskoufis and van der Ploeg, 1991; Buiter, 1992; Mulligan and Sala-i-Martin, 1991), that system can be studied appealing to the introduction of some auxiliary variables. If we introduce the notation $\tau \equiv \lambda/(vK)$, and $x \equiv C/K$, the original system can be reduced by one dimension. From Equation (2.18) one gets

$$u = \tau^{1/2} \quad (2.23)$$

and, substituting the latter expression in (2.13),

$$Z = B(\tau^{-1/2} - 1). \quad (2.24)$$

Inserting (2.23) in (2.19) yields

$$\frac{\dot{v}}{v} = \delta - B(1 - \tau^{1/2}). \qquad (2.25)$$

Using (2.17), Equation (2.20) can be expressed as

$$\frac{\dot{\lambda}}{\lambda} = \delta + m - \frac{1}{\tau}\frac{x}{E}. \qquad (2.26)$$

Differentiating (2.17) with respect to time and making use of (2.25) one obtains

$$\frac{\dot{C}}{C} = \frac{1-\eta}{\eta}\frac{\dot{E}}{E} + \frac{1}{\eta}[B(1 - \tau^{1/2}) - \delta]. \qquad (2.27)$$

Plugging again (2.23) in the accumulation equation (2.14) gives

$$\frac{\dot{K}}{K} = B(1 - \tau^{1/2}) - x, \qquad (2.28)$$

whereas substitution of (2.24) in (2.4) yields

$$\dot{E} = A(E) - B(\tau^{-1/2} - 1). \qquad (2.29)$$

Subtracting (2.28) from (2.27) and using (2.29) leads to

$$\frac{\dot{x}}{x} = \frac{1-\eta}{\eta}\frac{1}{E}[A(E) - B(\tau^{-1/2} - 1)]$$

$$+ \frac{1-\eta}{\eta}B(1 - \tau^{1/2}) - \frac{\delta}{\eta} + x. \qquad (2.30)$$

Taking into account that

$$\frac{\dot{\tau}}{\tau} = \frac{\dot{\lambda}}{\lambda} - \frac{\dot{v}}{v} - \frac{\dot{K}}{K}$$

and using (2.25), (2.26) and (2.28), one finally obtains

$$\frac{\dot{\tau}}{\tau} = m - \frac{1}{E}\frac{x}{\tau} + x. \qquad (2.31)$$

A sustainable balanced-growth path requires all the variables defining the dynamical system (2.29–2.31) to be constant in the long-run. This in turn implies that consumption, physical capital, and output all grow at the same positive growth rate, whereas the stock of environmental resources $E$ remains constant.

## 3. Existence and Uniqueness of the Sustainable Balanced-Growth Path

An (interior) optimal sustainable balanced-growth path is a positive triplet $(x^*, E^*, \tau^*)$ such that $\dot{x} = \dot{E} = \dot{\tau} = 0$, for all $t$, which satisfies, in addition, the transversality conditions (2.21) and (2.22). In view of the definition, it is clear that $(x^*, E^*, \tau^*)$, whenever it exists, must be a fixed point of the stationary system given by

$$E = \bar{P} - \frac{B}{m}(\tau^{-1/2} - 1) \tag{3.1}$$

$$x = \frac{1}{\eta}[\delta - (1-\eta)B(1-\tau^{1/2})] \equiv x(\tau), \tag{3.2}$$

$$E = \frac{x}{\tau(m+x)}. \tag{3.3}$$

Since each variable is defined only for non-negative values along the stationary loci (3.1–3.3), it is necessary to impose some restrictions on the structural parameters to ensure that $(x, E, \tau)$ is actually non-negative. Establishing existence and uniqueness through the choice of appropriate boundary conditions becomes relatively easy if one assumes that the state-variable $x$, i.e. $C/K$, is always non-negative for all $\tau$, where the domain of $\tau \equiv u^2$ is the open interval $(0, 1)$, as $0 < u < 1$ along each stationary locus. From Equation (3.2) one sees that, if $\eta \geq 1$, then $x(\tau) > 0$, for all $\tau$ in $(0, 1)$. When $\eta < 1$, however, $x(\tau)$ is strictly increasing when $\tau$ is increased from 0 to 1. As a result, $x(\tau) \geq 0$, for all $\tau$ in $(0, 1)$ if and only if $\delta \geq (1-\eta)B$. The following assumption, therefore, ensures that $x(\tau) \geq 0$, for all $\tau$ in $(0, 1)$.

ASSUMPTION. $\delta \geq (1-\eta)B$, i.e. $x(\tau)$ is non-negative for all $\tau$ in the open interval $(0, 1)$.

Consider now Equation (3.1). In that case, $E \geq 0$ if and only if

$$\bar{P} \geq \frac{B}{m}(\tau^{-1/2} - 1) \tag{3.4}$$

that is, if and only if

$$1 > \tau \geq [B/(\bar{P}m + B)]^2 \equiv \tau_1 > 0. \tag{3.5}$$

It follows that the domain of $E$ as a function of $\tau$ is restricted to the open interval $(\tau_1, 1)$. In view of the above assumption and after imposing the constraint in (3.5) to guarantee the non-negativity of $(x, E, \tau)$ along each stationary locus, we can now address the existence issue without incurring in ambiguities. Substituting Equations (3.1) and (3.2) in (3.3) yields

$$\tau\bar{P} - \frac{B}{m}(\tau^{1/2} - \tau) = \frac{x(\tau)}{m + x(\tau)}, \tag{3.6}$$

which is an equation in $\tau$ only. Finding the zeros of (3.6) is then equivalent to find the number of stationary solutions of the system (3.1–3.3). Let the left and the right-hand side of (3.6) be defined as $\Omega(\tau)$ and $\Gamma(\tau)$, respectively.

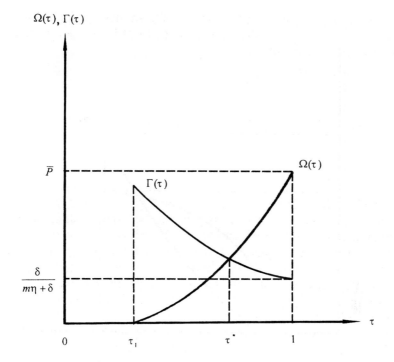

*Figure 1.* Case 1.

To determine the zeros of (3.6) we consider, first, the function $\Omega(\tau)$. Direct inspection shows that, as $\tau$ increases from $\tau_1$ to 1, $\Omega(\tau)$ increases monotonically from 0 to $\bar{P}$. Moreover, it is strictly convex. To study $\Gamma(\tau)$ we must distinguish two cases.

*Case 1*: $\eta \geq 1$. In such a case $\Gamma(\tau)$ decreases monotonically from $x(\tau_1)/[m+x(\tau_1)] > 0$ to $\delta/(\eta m + \delta) < 1$. A solution $\tau^*$ in $(\tau_1, 1)$ of Equation (3.6), whenever it exists, is then unique. To ensure existence, and consequently uniqueness, it is sufficient to choose the appropriate boundary condition. This reduces, in the present context, to setting $\bar{P} > \delta/(m\eta + \delta)$, as shown in Figure 1.

*Case 2*: $\eta < 1$, with $\delta \geq B(1 - \eta)$. In such a case, $\Gamma(\tau)$ increases monotonically from $x(\tau_1)/[m + x(\tau_1)] > 0$ to $\delta/(\eta m + \delta) < 1$. In addition, it is strictly concave. Once again, there exists a unique $\tau^*$ in $(\tau_1, 1)$ that solves (3.6) if and only if $\bar{P} > \delta/(m\eta + \delta)$, as shown in Figure 2.

The above argument can be now summarized in the following proposition.

PROPOSITION 1. *Assume that $\delta > B(1 - \eta)$. Then an interior solution $(x^*, E^*, \tau^*)$ for the system (3.1–3.3) exists and is also unique if and only if $\bar{P} > \delta/(\eta m + \delta)$.*

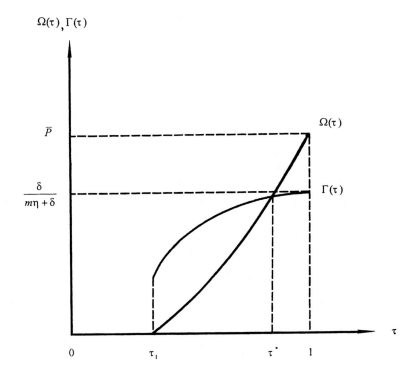

*Figure 2.* Case 2.

In light of the above proposition, it is possible to state that the unique solution $(x^*, E^*, \tau^*)$ of the stationary system (3.1–3.3) truly represents an interior optimal sustainable balanced-growth path if it also satisfies the transversality conditions (2.21) and (2.22), the requirement on the boundedness of the objective function (2.6), and the positive growth condition. Easy computations show that the integral in (2.6) is bounded if

$$\delta > (1-\eta)B(1-\tau^{*1/2}). \tag{3.7}$$

The condition in (3.7) also implies the fulfillment of (2.21) and (2.22). As far as positive steady-state growth is concerned, one obtains, from Equation (2.20),

$$g = \frac{\dot{C}}{C} = \frac{1}{\eta}[B(1-\tau^{*1/2}) - \delta]. \tag{3.8}$$

As a result, the long-run optimal growth rate is strictly positive if and only if

$$B(1-\tau^{*1/2}) > \delta. \tag{3.9}$$

Combining (3.7) and (3.9) gives

$$B(1-\tau^{*1/2}) > \delta > (1-\eta)B(1-\tau^{*1/2}), \tag{3.10}$$

where the second inequality is always fulfilled because of the assumption $\delta > B(1-\eta)$.

## 4. Local Dynamics

To investigate the local stability properties of the sustainable balanced-growth path, we shall, as usual, analyze the sign of the eigenvalues associated with the Jacobian of the three dimensional system (2.29–2.31) evaluated at the steady-state $(x^*, E^*, \tau^*)$. Since the dynamical system possesses one predetermined variable $(E)$ and two non-predetermined variables, $(\tau$ and $x)$, we conclude, in view of the Blanchard–Khan Theorem, that $(x^*, E^*, \tau^*)$ is locally unique if the Jacobian has two characteristic roots with positive real parts and one root with negative real part.

The Jacobian evaluated at the steady-state is given by

$$J = \begin{bmatrix} x^* & -\frac{1-\eta}{\eta}\frac{1}{E^*}mx^* & \frac{1-\eta}{\eta}\frac{1}{2}mF^* \\ 0 & -m & \frac{1}{2}\frac{F^*}{\tau^*} \\ \tau^* - \frac{1}{E^*} & x^* E^{*-2} & \frac{x^*}{E^*}\frac{1}{\tau^*} \end{bmatrix}, \quad (4.1)$$

where $F^* \equiv A(E^*) + B$. The trace and the determinant of J are, respectively,

$$\text{Tr}(J) = 2x^* > 0 \quad (4.2)$$

and

$$\text{Det}(J) = -m^2 x^* - mz^{*2} - \frac{1}{2}F^*\tau^*(m+x^*) + m^2\frac{1}{2}\tau^* F^* \frac{1-\eta}{\eta}. \quad (4.3)$$

Direct inspection of (4.3) shows that $\text{Det}(J) < 0$ if $\eta \geq 1$. When $\eta < 1$, on the other hand, to conclude that $\text{Det}(J) < 0$ is equivalent to prove that

$$-m^2 x^* + m^2 \frac{1}{2} \tau^* F^* \frac{1-\eta}{\eta} < 0, \quad (4.4)$$

that is

$$x^* > \frac{1-\eta}{\eta} \frac{B}{2} \tau^{*1/2}. \quad (4.5)$$

Plugging in (4.5) the expression of $x^*$ yields

$$\delta - (1-\eta)B + \frac{1}{2}(1-\eta)B\tau^{*1/2} > 0. \quad (4.6)$$

Since $\delta - (1-\eta)B > 0$ by assumption, one concludes that $\text{Det}(J) < 0$, and, therefore, that the sustainable balanced-growth path is always locally unique, i.e. there are two eigenvalues with positive real parts and one eigenvalue with negative real part. All this leads to the following result.

PROPOSITION 2. *Suppose that Proposition 1 holds. Then the sustainable balanced-growth path is locally saddle-point stable, i.e. given the initial condition $E_0 > 0$, there exists a unique choice of $\tau_0$ and $x_0$ in a neighborhood of $x^*, E^*, \tau^*$ that places the economy on the unique converging path.*

## 5. Conclusions

We have presented a simple model to achieve sustainable economic growth. This means that the model we have analyzed is able to explain both balanced persistent growth in national product, consumption and capital, and the possibility of a constant stock of the environmental asset at the steady-state. An intertemporal optimality concept is required to choose the level at which the environmental stock has to be maintained. A constant environmental stock, on the other hand, implies a constant pollution stock and, hence, a constant emission flow within the assimilative capacity of the environment itself. The only way to generate both economic growth and constant emissions in the long run consists of a continuously decreasing emission coefficient per unit of output; this in turn requires the firms to devote an appropriate share of capital to improve the environmental use of technologies. An optimal price of the environmental use is needed to obtain this appropriate share of capital. It is shown, indeed, that, along the optimal sustainable growth path, the optimal environmental price must grow at the balanced rate of growth. As a result, one gets a constant ratio of the value of the environment to national output.

We have finally showed that, under the very simple assumption made, the optimal sustainable growth equilibrium is locally saddle-point stable.

## References

1. Alogoskoufis, G. S. and F. van der Ploeg (1990). "Endogenous Growth and Overlapping Generations", Birkbeck College, University of London, Discussion Paper in Economics, No. 26–90.
2. Barro, R. (1990). "Government Spending in a Simple Model of Endogenous Growth", *Journal of Political Economy* 98, 103–125.
3. Barro, R. and X. Sala–i–Martin (1995). *Economic Growth*, New York, McGraw Hill.
4. Becker, R. (1982). "Intergenerational Equity: The Capital-Environment Trade-Off", *Journal of Environmental Economics and Management* 10, 165–185.
5. Buiter, W. (1991). "Saving and Endogenous Growth: A Survey of Theory and Policy", Yale University, mimeo.
6. Lucas, R. (1988). "The Mechanics of Economic Development", *Journal of Monetary Economics* 22, 3–42.
7. Mulligan, C. B. and X. Sala-i-Martin (1993). "Transitional Dynamics in Two-sector Models of Endogenous Growth", *Quarterly Journal of Economics* 108, 739–773.
8. Romer, P. (1986). "Increasing Returns and Long Run Growth", *Journal of Political Economy* 94, 1002–1037.

GIANCARLO MARINI AND PASQUALE SCARAMOZZINO

## 2.5. Environmental Externalities, Disconnected Generations and Policy

### 1. Introduction

Environmental resources can be depleted at a socially sub-optimal rate in a decentralised economy with incomplete markets. Pollution is an inevitable consequence of the production process: hence, when markets for tradable pollution rights are missing, there is in principle a clear *rôle* for government intervention. In particular, the welfare of unborn generations can be seriously impaired by the production decisions of optimising egoistic agents.

The central policy issue is to investigate what governments should do and which instruments they should use in order to achieve a socially equitable intertemporal distribution of natural resources and consumption (see Dasgupta and Heal, 1979; Pearce and Turner, 1992). A popular criterion is the so-called Solow–Hartwick rule, designed to preserve equal consumption opportunities over time. However, as argued by Solow (1986), the representative agent models typically employed do not appear to be adequate to investigate intergenerational equity issues. Overlapping generations models, by contrast, naturally lend themselves to analyse intertemporal externalities among heterogeneous agents.

Another important line of research has focussed on the choice of the discount rate that the planner should optimally set to achieve her social objectives (see, among others, Markandya and Pearce, 1988; van der Ploeg and Withagen, 1991; Musu, forthcoming). No clear-cut answer has been provided, since the long-run built-in trade-off between environment and consumption of physical assets cannot be eased by manipulation of the social discount rate alone. Intergenerational equity is not, in fact, a cost-benefit problem but depends on the intertemporal distribution of assets across disconnected generations, as clearly pointed out by Howarth and Norgaard (1992). The representative agent model is thus unsuitable, since it implicitly assumes away any form of heterogeneity across generations.

In the present paper we set out an overlapping generations (OLG) model in order to characterise the fiscal policy required to achieve an equitable use of environmental resources. The demand side of the model we develop is a variant of the Blanchard–Yaari–Weil–Buiter set-up,[1] where disconnected generations of individuals derive utility from consumption and from environmental quality. The supply sector is modelled as an aggregate constant returns to scale technology with labour, capital, and pollution as inputs. Pollution is in part endogenously assimilated by the environment. The absence of markets for pollution rights, which implies that the environmental resource has the nature of a public good, requires an active *rôle* for the government in enacting pollution abatement policies.

The structure of the paper is as follows. Section 2 outlines the model and discusses the steady state effects of government spending on pollution abatement. Section 3 addresses the social welfare issues and derives the optimal environmental tax. Section 4 concludes.

## 2. Disconnected Generations and Externalities

We consider a continuous-time overlapping generations framework in which individuals face a constant instantaneous death rate and a constant rate of (parthenogenetic) reproduction. There is a large number of agents who derive utility from consumption of a physical commodity and from the enjoyment of an environmental resource. The latter can, however, also be used directly as an input to production. This has a destructive impact on the remaining amount of the environmental resource. Since the environment available to each individual can be regarded as a public good, these externalities give rise to a socially suboptimal use of production inputs. Appropriate environmental taxes are required in order to correct such inefficiencies.

In addition to the above externalities, however, there are further market failures in the economy due to population heterogeneity and the disconnectedness across generations. Since no fully operative bequest motive is present, each generation will neglect the impact on the future generations of its own use of the environment. Hence, a fiscal policy directed at protecting the environment should be designed in such a way as to enact both the cross-sectional and the across-generations taxes and transfers which are required for achieving inter-generational equity and an optimal use of resources over time.

The objective function at time $t$ of agents born at time $s \leq t$ is defined as

$$\max_{\{\bar{c}(s,v)\}} \int_t^\infty [\gamma \ln \bar{c}(s,v) + (1-\gamma) \ln \bar{\eta}(s,v)] e^{-(\rho+\lambda)(v-t)} dv, \tag{1}$$

where $\bar{c}(s,v)$ and $\bar{\eta}(s,v)$ denote consumption of the physical commodity and of the environment, respectively, $\rho$ is the pure subjective rate of time preference, and $\lambda$ is the instantaneous death rate. The probability of death is constant over time and independent of age.[2] For simplicity, the instantaneous felicity function is assumed to be additively separable in its arguments.

The individual budget constraint on non-human wealth follows the differential equation

$$\frac{d}{dt}\bar{a}(s,t) = [r(t) + \lambda]\bar{a}(s,t) + \bar{w}(s,t) - \bar{c}(s,t), \qquad (2)$$

where $r(t)$ is the rate of interest and $\bar{w}(s,t)$ is labour income. In Equation (2), the term $\lambda\bar{a}(s,t)$ reflects the existence of a perfectly competitive market for annuities. Since generations are not interconnected by an operative bequest motive, the optimal insurance contract prescribes that each consumer's estate be appropriated by the insurance company upon the agent's death. Each individual thus receives the actuarially fair insurance premium, $\lambda\bar{a}(s,t)$, whilst alive. Human capital is defined as the present discounted value of expected future labour earnings:

$$\bar{h}(s,t) = \int_t^\infty w(s,v) e^{-\int_t^v [r(\mu)+\lambda]d\mu} dv. \qquad (3)$$

The appropriate discount rate must incorporate the instantaneous rate of death. The first-order conditions for an interior solution for consumption yield the usual Ramsey-type equation:

$$\frac{d\bar{c}(s,t)}{dt} = [r(t) - \rho]\bar{c}(s,t). \qquad (4)$$

It is important to note that in the objective function of the consumer, Equation (1), the path describing the use of the environmental resource, $\{\bar{\eta}(s,v) \mid v \geq t\}$, is not a control variable. Since at each moment in time there is a large number of individuals, and since the individual enjoyment of the environmental resource is given by total environment per head, each consumer's decision about the use of the natural resource is bound to have a negligible impact upon the amount of resources available for personal use. Thus, the path $\{\bar{\eta}(s,v) \mid v \geq t\}$ is taken as exogenously given by each individual consumer.

Subject to the usual condition that households are solvent, the consumption function takes the form

$$\bar{c}(s,t) = (\lambda + \rho)[\bar{a}(s,t) + \bar{h}(s,t)]. \qquad (5)$$

Since labour productivity is independent of the date of birth, wages are constant for all agents alive at time $t$, irrespective of their age: thus,

$$\bar{w}(s,t) = \bar{w}(t). \qquad (6)$$

It follows that human capital also is independent of age.

If we normalise population size by setting $L(0) = 1$, we obtain

$$L(t) = e^{nt} = \beta e^{-\lambda t} \int_{-\infty}^t e^{\beta s} ds, \qquad (7)$$

where $\beta$ is the instantaneous birth rate and $n \equiv \beta - \lambda$ is the population growth rate. The value of the other aggregate variables can be obtained in an analogous fashion (see, for instance, Buiter, 1988). Total human capital and assets are respectively given by

$$H(t) = \beta e^{-\lambda t} \int_{-\infty}^{t} \bar{h}(t) e^{\beta s} ds$$

$$= \bar{h}(t) e^{nt} \tag{8}$$

$$A(t) = \beta e^{-\lambda t} \int_{-\infty}^{t} \bar{a}(s,t) e^{\beta s} ds. \tag{9}$$

Upon aggregation of (5) and using (8) and (9), aggregate consumption is seen to be proportional to total wealth:

$$C(t) = (\lambda + \rho)[A(t) + H(t)]. \tag{10}$$

On the production side, output can be obtained by combining capital input, $K(t)$, a flow of environmental resources, $Z(t)$, and labour, $L(t)$.

$$Y(t) = F[K(t), Z(t), L(t)] = L(t) f[k(t), z(t)]. \tag{11}$$

The production function exhibits constants returns to scale and can, therefore, be written in the usual labour intensive form. We assume that $F_K, F_Z, F_L > 0$, $F_{KK}, F_{ZZ}, F_{LL} < 0$, $F_{KZ} > 0$, and $F_{ZZ} F_{KK} - F_{KZ}^2 > 0$. In particular, an increased use of the environmental resource raises the marginal product of capital. The use of natural resources in the production process directly adds to the cumulative stock of pollution, $P(t)$:

$$\frac{dP(t)}{dt} = -mP(t) + Z(t) - \psi[G(t)], \tag{12}$$

where $m$ is the assimilation rate at which the environment endogenously absorbs the stock of pollution, $G(t)$ is government spending on pollution abatement activities, and $\psi(\cdot)$ represents the impact of such expenditures. It is assumed that pollution abatement by the government exhibits decreasing returns: $\psi'(\cdot) > 0$, $\psi''(\cdot) < 0$. The formulation in (12) is consistent with the absolute effect model of pollution stock accumulation (see Ulph et al., 1991, for a motivation and a discussion). The stock of environment is given by

$$E(t) = \hat{E} - P(t), \tag{13}$$

where $\hat{E}$ is a constant. By combining (12) and (13) one obtains the evolution over time of the environmental resource:

$$\frac{dE(t)}{dt} = -mE(t) + m\hat{E} - Z(t) + \psi[G(t)]. \tag{14}$$

The government levies taxes on the use of the environment as a production input:

$$T(t) = \tau(t) Z(t), \tag{15}$$

where $\tau(t)$ is the (time-varying) tax rate. This form of taxation should be interpreted as a form of *carbon tax*, as discussed amongst others by Pearce (1991) and Bovenberg and van der Ploeg (forthcoming).[3] The entire tax revenue raised is devoted to curbing pollution. The government budget is thus always instantaneously balanced. For simplicity, we rule out the possibility of debt financing:

$$G(t) = T(t), \tag{16}$$

where $G(t)$ is public expenditure on pollution abatement. The dynamics of the system can be expressed in *pro capite* form as

$$\frac{dk(t)}{dt} = f[k(t), z(t)] - nk(t) - g(t) - c(t), \tag{17}$$

$$\frac{dc(t)}{dt} = \{f_k[k(t), z(t)] - \rho\}c(t) - (\lambda + \rho)\beta k(t), \tag{18}$$

$$\frac{d\eta(t)}{dt} = -(m+n)\eta(t) + m\hat{\eta} + \psi[g(t)] - z(t), \tag{19}$$

where small letters denote variables per head (we use the notation $\eta(t) = E(t)/L(t)$). Equation (17) requires that net investment in the economy be equal to total saving. Equation (18) is the usual Ramsey–Blanchard condition, and Equation (19) gives the dynamics of environment per head.

The conditions for the steady state of the economy are given by the following Equations (20–22):

$$f(k, z) = nk + g + c, \tag{20}$$

$$[f_k(k, z) - \rho]c = (\rho + \lambda)\beta k, \tag{21}$$

$$(m+n)\eta = m\hat{\eta} - z + \psi g, \tag{22}$$

together with

$$g = \tau z, \tag{23}$$

$$f_Z(k, z) = \alpha + \tau. \tag{24}$$

Equations (20–22) are obtained by setting $\dot{k} = \dot{c} = \dot{\eta} = 0$, and Equation (23) is the balanced budget requirement. Equation (24) is the first-order condition on the use of the environmental resource: the marginal product of the environment must be equal to its marginal private cost, which is here assumed to be given by the technological constant $\alpha$ plus the environmental tax, $\tau$. The system of steady state conditions is block recursive: Equations (20), (21), (23) and (24) determine $k, z, c$, and $g$, whilst Equation (22) determines $\eta$.

The steady state implications of an increase in government spending on pollution abatement can be analysed by log-linearising the sub-system formed of (20), (21), (23) and (24) in a neighbourhood of the steady state equilibrium. After substituting out government spending, $g$, one obtains in compact notation:

$$\begin{bmatrix} r-n & -1 & f_z - \tau \\ f_{kk}c - \nu & r-\rho & f_{kz}c \\ f_{kz} & 0 & f_{zz} \end{bmatrix} \begin{bmatrix} dk \\ dc \\ dz \end{bmatrix} = \begin{bmatrix} z \\ 0 \\ 1 \end{bmatrix} d\tau, \qquad (25)$$

where we have set $r = f_k$ and $\nu \equiv (\rho + \lambda)\beta$. There is one predetermined variable, $k$, and two jump variables: $c$ and $z$. The determinant of the system (25) is given by

$$\Delta = f_{kz}\Delta_1 + f_{zz}\Delta_2 < 0,$$

where

$$\Delta_1 \equiv -[f_{kz}c + \alpha(r-\rho)] < 0,$$
$$\Delta_2 \equiv f_{kk}c - \nu + (r-n)(r-\rho) \gtreqless 0,$$

and where the sign on $\Delta$ follows from assuming that the system is locally stable around its steady state equilibrium.[4] The main comparative statics results of interest are:

$$\frac{dc}{d\tau} = -\frac{1}{\Delta} [cz(f_{kk}f_{zz} - f_{kz}^2)$$
$$+ (r-n)cf_{kz} - \alpha(f_{kk}c - \nu) - \nu z f_{zz}] > 0, \qquad (26)$$

$$\frac{dk}{d\tau} = \frac{1}{\Delta} [\Delta_1 + z f_{zz}(r-\rho)] > 0, \qquad (27)$$

$$\frac{dz}{d\tau} = \frac{1}{\Delta} [\Delta_2 - z f_{kz}(r-\rho)] \lesseqgtr 0. \qquad (28)$$

An increase in public spending financed by the environmental tax leads to an increased use of capital input in production and to higher consumption per head. There is, therefore, a *trade-in* between pollution abatement and individual consumption. The reason for the positive impact on steady state capital stock is that an increase in the tax rate requires an increase in the marginal product of the environmental resource input. Because of the complementarity between capital and environmental inputs in production, this calls for an increased use of capital. On the other hand, the impact of the environmental tax $\tau$ on the use of the environmental resource is in principle ambiguous. If $f_{kz}$ is large, i.e. if an increase in $k$ is able to raise substantially the marginal product of the environmental resource, then a higher $\tau$ could be associated to a higher steady state value of $z$: the relevant condition at the margin, Equation (24), would still be met if *both $k$ and $z$ increase* as $\tau$ is raised. When $\Delta_2$ is negative, the balanced budget increase in the tax rate is associated with an increased use of $z$.[5] However, provided that $f_{kz} < \Delta_2/[z(r-\rho)]$ the environmental tax unambiguously brings about a reduction in the input of $z$ in production.

Government expenditure on pollution abatement increases with the tax rate if the elasticity of the environmental input with respect to the tax rate is either positive or, if negative, less than unity in absolute value.

The impact on the steady state stock of environment can be inferred by totally differentiating Equation (22): under balanced budget,

$$\frac{d\eta}{d\tau} = \frac{1}{m+n}\left[-\frac{dz}{d\tau} + \psi z\left(1 + \frac{dz}{d\tau}\frac{\tau}{z}\right)\right], \qquad (29)$$

which is certainly positive for $dz/d\tau < 0$ and if the tax elasticity of $z$ is less than unity in absolute value. When $dz/d\tau > 0$, steady state environment per head increases if and only if the effectiveness of pollution abatement dominates the negative impact of the increased environmental use.

## 3. Social Welfare and the Optimal Environmental Tax

Optimal setting of taxes and government expenditures requires that the welfare of both current and future generations be adequately taken into account. Since consumers alive at a given time are heterogeneous, equity considerations require that their individual utilities are appropriately weighted in the social welfare function. Calvo and Obstfeld (1988) have shown that, in the Blanchard–Yaari overlapping generations framework in which agents differ in their date of birth, the requirement that fiscal policy be time consistent prescribes that each consumer's welfare be discounted back to her birth date, rather than to the present. In accordance to this rule, the different generations would be treated in a perfectly symmetric fashion and the government would have no incentive to renege *ex post* on its *ex ante* transfer and spending commitments.

The appropriate objective functional for the social planner is given by[6]

$$\Omega(t) = \int_t^\infty \left\{\int_0^\infty u[\bar{c}(v-h,v), \bar{\eta}(v)]e^{[(\delta-n)-(\rho+\lambda)]h}\,dh\right\} e^{-(\delta-n)v}\,dv, \qquad (30)$$

where $\delta$ is the social rate of pure time preference and where the index $h$ denotes age. Time consistency of the fiscal policy programme requires that the utility of each generation be discounted back to its birth date. The functional (30) must be maximised subject to the balanced budget restriction (Equation (16)), the dynamic constraints on capital accumulation and consumption, and to the first-order condition on environmental use:

$$\frac{dK}{dt} = F[K(t), Z(t), L(t)] - G(t) - C(t), \qquad (31)$$

$$\frac{dC}{dt} = (F_K + n - \rho)C(t) - (\rho + \lambda)\beta K(t), \qquad (32)$$

$$F_Z[K(t), Z(t), L(t)] = \alpha + \tau(t). \tag{33}$$

In addition, the differential equation on the evolution of the environmental resource, Equation (14), must be met. The social planner can be thought of as seeking to achieve an optimal allocation of resources across all agents alive at a given time, and then maximising over time for the given cross-sectional allocations.[7] The problem, therefore, consists of maximising the following objective functional

$$\max \Omega(t) = \int_t^\infty U^*[C(\mu), E(\mu)] e^{-(\delta-n)\mu} d\mu, \tag{34}$$

where

$$U^*[C(\mu), E(\mu)] = U[C(\mu)] + V[E(\mu)]. \tag{35}$$

The functions $U[C(\cdot)]$ and $V[C(\cdot)]$ are respectively defined as

$$U[C(\mu)] = \max_{\{\bar{c}(\mu-h,\mu)\}_{h=0}^\infty} \int_0^\infty u[\bar{c}(\mu-h,\mu), \bar{\eta}(\mu)] e^{[(\delta-n)-(\rho+\lambda)]h} dh, \tag{36}$$

subject to

$$\beta e^{-\lambda\mu} \int_0^\infty \bar{c}(\mu-h,\mu) e^{\beta(\mu-h)} dh \leq C(\mu) \tag{37}$$

and

$$V[E(\mu)] = \frac{(1-\gamma)}{(\rho+\lambda)-(\delta-n)} \ln \bar{\eta}(\mu), \tag{38}$$

where (38) is obtained by integrating environment per head across all generations.

The first-order conditions for the optimal cross-sectional allocations yield

$$u_c[\bar{c}(t-h), \bar{\eta}(t)] e^{(\delta-n-\rho)h} = U'[C(t)], \tag{39}$$

that is, the age-weighted marginal utility of consumption must be equalised across all generations alive at a given time. For our choice of functional forms, Equation (39) can be expressed as

$$\frac{\gamma}{\bar{c}(t-h,t)} e^{(\delta-n-\rho)h} = U'[(C(t)]. \tag{40}$$

When $\delta = \rho + n$, i.e. when the social intertemporal discount rate is equal to the growth-augmented private discount rate, consumption must be the same for all generations irrespective of their age. When $\delta = \rho$ and $n > 0$, by contrast, consumption must be a decreasing function of age: if the social planner discounts the future at exactly the same rate as private individuals, then time consistency requires that the younger generations be allocated a greater amount of consumption *pro capite* that the older ones.[8]

The generalised Hamiltonian function for the dynamic programme,[9] which has an immediate interpretation as the net national product of the economy, can be written as

$$H = U[C(t)] + V[E(t)]$$
$$+ \mu_K(t)\{F[K(t), Z(t), L(t)] - \tau(t)Z(t) - C(t)\}$$
$$+ \mu_C(t)\{(F_K[K(t), Z(t), L(t)] + n - \rho)C(t) - (\rho + \lambda)\beta K(t)\}$$
$$+ \mu_E(t)\{-mE(t) + m\bar{E}(t) - Z(t) + \psi[\tau(t)Z(t)]\}$$
$$+ \lambda_Z(t)\{F_Z[K(t), Z(t), L(t)] - \alpha - \tau(t)\}, \qquad (41)$$

where $\mu_K(t)$, $\mu_C(t)$, and $\mu_E(t)$ are the dynamic co-state variables pertaining to $K(t)$, $C(t)$, and $E(t)$ respectively, and where $\lambda_Z(t)$ is the Lagrange multiplier associated to the constraint (33) on the use of the environmental resource in production. In our formulation of the planner's programme $Z(t)$ and $\tau(t)$ are the control variables, whereas $K(t), C(t)$, and $E(t)$ are the state variables.

Along the optimal path, the necessary Hamilton–Jacobi–Bellman conditions for an interior solution are:

$$\psi'(G)Z\mu_E = Z\mu_K + \lambda_Z, \qquad (42)$$

$$\alpha\mu_K + F_{ZZ}\lambda_Z + F_{KZ}C\mu_C = [1 - \tau\psi'(G)]\mu_E. \qquad (43)$$

Equation (42) prescribes that, at the margin, the benefit from an increase in abatement spending be equal to the loss from the displacement of private investment and foregone output due to the decreased use of environmental resource inputs. Equation (43) says that the marginal benefit on the environment from a reduced use of pollutant $Z$ must be balanced by the effects of a higher $Z$ on capital accumulation, on consumption and on the use of $Z$ in production.

The co-state equation associated with the stock of the environmental resource can be expressed as:

$$\dot{\mu}_E = (\delta - n + m)\mu_E - V'[E(t)]. \qquad (44)$$

If one integrates the differential equation (44) forward, one obtains the following solution for the dynamic multiplier pertaining to the environmental resource:

$$\mu_E(t) = \int_t^\infty e^{-(\delta+m-n)(s-t)} V'[E(s)]ds. \qquad (45)$$

Along the optimal path, the marginal social benefit of the environment must be equal to the present discounted value of marginal private utility. The growth-corrected discount rate must be augmented by the assimilation rate, $m$, which measures the capacity of the environment to absorb endogenously the stock of pollution.

In the above framework, the optimal Pigovian tax must equalise the marginal social benefit of the environment to the marginal private cost of pollution emissions. Thus, the government must set

$$\mu_E(t) = \alpha + \tau(t) = F_Z[K(t), Z(t), L(t)]. \tag{46}$$

By making use of (45) and (46) one obtains the optimal environmental tax as

$$\tau(t) = \int_t^\infty e^{-(\delta+m-n)(s-t)} V'[E(s)] ds - \alpha. \tag{47}$$

Equation (47) makes it clear that the optimal Pigovian tax must be set in a forward-looking fashion. The expected future marginal benefits from the environment must be discounted at the social discount rate, net of the rate of population growth and augmented by the endogenous assimilation rate. This is, therefore, the appropriate discount rate at which environmental projects should be assessed.

Finally, by rearranging Equation (42), the optimal level of public spending on pollution abatement is

$$G(t) = \Phi \left[ \frac{Z(t)\mu_K(t) + \lambda_Z(t)}{Z(t)\mu_E(t)} \right], \tag{48}$$

where $\Phi(\cdot) \equiv (\psi')^{-1}(\cdot)$, with $\Phi'(\cdot) < 0$ since $\psi'' < 0$. The optimal government expenditure on abatement is, therefore, an increasing function of the marginal social benefit of the environment and of the shadow value of environmental use in production, and a decreasing function of the marginal social benefit of physical capital accumulation.[10]

It is important to note that, if heterogeneity is assumed away – i.e. $\beta = \lambda = n = 0$ – then the problem of the social planner coincides with the maximisation of the individual objective function, Equation (1), where the discount factor is given by $\delta$ instead of $\rho$. It thus appears that the exclusive focus on the choice of the discount rate as the key policy decision is only justified in the restrictive case of perfect homogeneity across economic agents, that is in the representative consumer paradigm.

## 4. Conclusions

The present paper examines the issue of intergenerational redistribution in a general equilibrium model with disconnected generations and environmental externalities, where pollution directly enters a constant returns to scale production function. Extending the utilitarian criterion proposed by Calvo and Obstfeld (1988), and making use of the framework set out in (Marini and Scaramozzino, 1995), a social planner can achieve the optimal allocation of physical assets and environmental resources across generations. Social optimality requires, in particular, that the marginal social benefit of government spending on pollution abatement be equal to the marginal social loss from reduced private investment and foregone output due to the reduced environmental input. The optimal Pigovian tax must be set in order to equalise the marginal social benefit of the environment to the marginal private cost of pollution emissions. Furthermore, the optimal government spending on pollution abatement should be an increasing function of the ratio between the marginal social benefit of the environment and of physical capital accumulation.

Our analysis enables us to clarify the appropriate choice of the discount rate for environmental policy. In an infinitely-lived, representative agent framework, future benefits and costs should be discounted at the private intertemporal rate of time preference. By contrast, with heterogeneous agents and overlapping generations, the social discount rate is logically different from the private discount rate, since it reflects the social planner's system of weights over the different generations. The social discount rate must be augmented to incorporate the rate of population growth and the rate of endogenous assimilation of pollution. Hence, with heterogeneous agents and disconnected generations, discounting the future should reflect ethical considerations, rather than individual impatience.

## Acknowledgement

We wish to thank Andrea Beltratti and Alberto Bisin for useful comments.

## Notes

1. The original references are (Yaari, 1965; Blanchard, 1985; Weil, 1989; Buiter, 1988).
2. Blanchard and Fischer (1989, chapter 3) describe this set-up as the "perpetual youth" model.
3. Optimal environmental taxation in a representative agent model with endogenous growth is studied by Musu (1994).
4. Note that, if $f_{kz} = 0$, stability requires that $\Delta_2 > 0$ since $f_{zz} < 0$.
5. In this case, the system is less likely to meet the stability condition.
6. See Marini and Scaramozzino (1995) for a more extensive motivation and discussion of the planner's programme.
7. The two-stage optimisation procedure in a similar framework is described in detail in Marini and Scaramozzino (1995).
8. Howarth (1991) analyses the system of transfers across generations in a discrete time model with finite horizon.
9. See, for instance, Takayama (1985, chapter 8, section C).
10. Marini and Scaramozzino (1994) extend this model to analyse the conditions for ecological sustainability.

## References

1. Blanchard, O. J. (1985). "Debt, Deficits and Finite Horizons", *Journal of Political Economy* 93, 223–247.

2. Blanchard, O. J. and S. Fischer (1989). *Lectures on Macroeconomics*, Cambridge, MA, MIT Press.
3. Bovenberg, A. L. and F. van der Ploeg (forthcoming). "Environmental Policy, Public Finance and the Labour Market in a Second-Best World", *Journal of Public Economics*.
4. Buiter, W. H. (1988). "Death, Birth, Productivity Growth and Debt Neutrality", *Economic Journal* 98, 279–293.
5. Calvo, G. A. and M. Obstfeld (1988). "Optimal Time-Consistent Fiscal Policy with Finite Lifetimes", *Econometrica* 56(2), 411–432.
6. Dasgupta, P. S. and G. M. Heal (1979). *Economic Theory and Exhaustible Resources*, Cambridge, Cambridge University Press.
7. Howarth, R. B. (1991). "Intergenerational Competitive Equilibria under Technological Uncertainty and Exhaustible Resource Constraint", *Journal of Environmental Economics and Management* 21, 225–243.
8. Howarth, R. B. and R. B. Norgaard (1992). "Environmental Valuation under Sustainable Development", *American Economic Review* 80, 473–477.
9. Marini, G. and P. Scaramozzino (1994). "Intergenerational Equity, Fiscal Policy, and Environmental Sustainability", in *Modèles de Développement Soutenable. Des Approches Exclusive ou Complémentaires de la Soutenabilité?*, Conference Proceedings, Vol. 2, Paris, AFCET, pp. 937–948.
10. Marini, G. and P. Scaramozzino (1995). "Overlapping Generations and Environmental Control", *Journal of Environmental Economics and Management* 28 (forthcoming).
11. Markandya, A. and D. W. Pearce (1988). "Environmental Considerations and the Choice of the Discount Rate in Developing Countries", Washington, DC, World Bank.
12. Musu, I. (1994). "On Sustainable Endogenous Growth", in *Sustainable Growth and Uncertainty*, Conference Proceedings, Milan, Fondazione ENI Enrico Mattei.
13. Musu, I. (forthcoming). "Sustainable Economy and Time Preference", *Structural Change and Economic Dynamics*.
14. Pearce, D. W. (1991). "The Role of Carbon Taxes in Adjusting to Global Warming", *Economic Journal* 101(407), 938–948.
15. Pearce, D. W. and R. K. Turner (1990). *Economics of Natural Resources and the Environment*, Hertfordshire, Harvester Wheatsheaf.
16. Smith, S. (1992). "Taxation and the Environment: A Survey", *Fiscal Studies* 13(4), 21–57.
17. Solow, R. M. (1986). "On the Intergenerational Allocation of Natural Resources", *Scandinavian Journal of Economics* 88, 141–149.
18. Takayama, A. (1985). *Mathematical Economics*, 2nd ed., Cambridge, Cambridge University Press.
19. Ulph, A., D. Ulph and J. Pezzey (1991). "Should a Carbon Tax Rise or Fall over Time?", Department of Economics, University of Bristol, Discussion Paper No. 91/309.
20. van der Ploeg, F. and C. Withagen (1991). "Pollution Control and the Ramsey Problem", *Environmental and Resource Economics* 1(2), 215–236.
21. Weil, P. (1989). "Overlapping Families of Infinitely-Lived Agents", *Journal of Public Economics* 38, 183–198.
22. Yaari, M. (1965). "Uncertain Lifetime, Life Insurance and the Theory of the Consumer", *Review of Economic Studies* 32, 137–150.

MARCO P. TUCCI*

# 2.6. Stochastic Sustainability

## 1. Introduction

A lot of attention has recently been devoted to the concept of sustainable development or sustainable growth.[1] This is usually defined as development "that meets the needs of the present without compromising the ability of future generations to meet their own needs" (WCED, 1987, p. 43). Operationally it can be interpreted as: given a certain rate of time preference "a sustainable economy is ... one that provides the maximum level of social welfare over an infinite horizon maintaining both the optimal reproducible capital stock and the optimal stock of regenerable environmental stock" (Musu, 1991, p. 3). Consequently, sustainable development reduces to a constrained maximization of a social welfare function and "control theory ... (is the technique used) to examine sustainability in the context of renewables and non-renewables resources" (Pezzey, 1989, p. vi).[2]

The common tools are the calculus of variation and the 'maximum principle'.[3] The former is used when the control variables are the rates of change of the state variables, i.e. the rate of change of the stock of non-renewable resources, and they are unrestricted (Pezzey, 1989, pp. 72–75). The 'maximum principle', on the other hand, is applied when there are general constraints on the controls like those, on the accumulation of capital and deterioration of the environment, described in (Musu, 1991). In both cases the necessary and sufficient conditions for maximization are found and steady state solutions are obtained. Then comparative statics exercises are performed, in the range of the parameters compatible with certain conditions,[4] "to analyze the rational trade-offs between consumption and environmental quality at different stages of economic growth" (Pezzey, 1989, p. vi). Even though some authors realize that "risk and uncertainty (about the future) are perva-

---

* The author would like to thank A. Beltratti, D. Siniscalco and A. Vercelli for their comments on an earlier draft of this work. Any remaining errors are the sole responsibility of the author. Financial support from the Fondazione ENI Enrico Mattei is gratefully acknowledged.

sive on the time scales to which sustainable development concepts apply" (Pezzey, 1989, p. 54), these complications are usually ignored.[5]

The following pages analyze a simple model combining an economic system and a climate system and explicitly incorporating stochastic elements. The basic idea is that output affects pollution contemporaneously which in turn affects the environment, with a lag of one period. This ultimately influences next period's output. The environment has the nature of a public good and this requires the government to play an active role in enacting pollution abatement policies.[6] Both the functional forms and the parameters are treated as known. The only kind of uncertainty existing in the model is that associated with the actual realizations of the random variables. Furthermore, it is assumed that changes in the environment are irreversible. For this reason the attention is focused on the 'extreme consequences' rather than on the 'average consequences'.

Contrary to most of the literature in this area, which is interested in 'the optimal sustainable development' over an infinite horizon, the goal here is to find 'a stochastically sustainable development' for next period. Therefore, no maximization is needed and no assumptions about the existence of an intergenerational social welfare function and of an intergenerational social discount rate are required.[7] In the presence of irreversible changes all the maximizations need to be repeated every period to take into account the unanticipated changes. In Section 2 the model is introduced and the benchmark case, in which next period output is known with certainty but future environment is not, because of additive noise, is analyzed. Then, in Section 3, a stochastic element is introduced in the production side and the consequences are studied. In Section 4 a feedback between output and environment is introduced. A stochastic output becomes a function of a stochastic environment. The conclusions, together with suggestions for future research, are summarized in Section 5. The most tedious derivations are confined in the Appendices.

## 2. The Basic Model

The model proposed here combines an economic system and a climate system incorporating the greenhouse effect theory. Formally, it is specified as follows[8]

$$Y_{t+1} = f(K_{t+1}, L_{t+1}), \tag{2.1}$$

$$A_{t+1} = \bar{A}_{t+1}, \tag{2.2}$$

$$\Delta \mathcal{E}_{t+2} \equiv \mathcal{E}_{t+2} - \mathcal{E}_{t+1}$$
$$= h(Y_{t+1}, A_{t+1}) + \varepsilon_{t+2} \quad \text{with} \quad \varepsilon_{t+2} \sim Mom(0, \sigma_\varepsilon^2). \tag{2.3}$$

Equation (2.1) describes a deterministic production function relating the output of period '$t+1$' with the stock of labor and capital existing at the beginning of that period and is taken as exogenous by the decision maker.[9] The environmental asset $\mathcal{E}_{t+2}$ in (2.3) is regarded as a public good. As is well known, the 'private use' of a public good leads to inefficiencies which need to be corrected by the action of the government. This is achieved by allowing the decision maker to set, at the beginning of period '$t+1$', the level of the abatement pollution expenditure to its desired value, $\bar{A}_{t+1}$, in (2.2). This means that at the moment of deciding $A_{t+1}$, the actual mean temperature for '$t+1$' is unknown because the random shock occurs 'during' that period.[10] It is postulated that $A_{t+1}$ does not affect the marginal utility of consumption and has no direct consequences on the consumption/saving decision. To keep things simple, it is furthermore assumed that this kind of public expenditure, the only one in this model, is fully financed by taxes so it does not give rise to a public deficit.[11] The disposition of output implicit in (2.1–2.3) is

$$Y_{t+1} = C_{t+1} + I_{t+1} + A_{t+1},$$

that is produced output can be devoted to consumption, gross investment in new capital goods or to pollution abatement activities, and it deserves to point out that the only unknown, at the beginning of '$t+1$', is the environmental asset.

As in (Nordhaus, 1994) the environmental asset is represented by the global mean surface temperature.[12] Equation (2.3) states that the change in the mean temperature is a known function of output and abatement pollution expenditure plus some noise,[13] not necessarily white noise, with first and second moments 0 and $\sigma_\varepsilon^2$. It describes a situation in which the probability density function of the stochastic process is unknown and it seems consistent with the definition of "hard uncertainty" discussed in (Vercelli, 1994).[14] Moreover, the stochastic process in (2.3) does not have to be stationary. In the special case in which the greenhouse gas emissions generated by the economic process are exactly offset by the assimilative capacity allowed by the biogeochemical cycles, i.e. $h(Y_{t+1}, A_{t+1}) = 0$, the mean temperature follows a random walk.[15]

The production function in (2.1) possesses the usual neoclassical properties, therefore, $f_K > 0$ and $f_L > 0$, to indicate positive marginal productivity of the factors of production, and $f_{KK} < 0$ and $f_{LL} < 0$ to denote decreasing marginal productivity with $f_{KL} > 0$.[16] According to the greenhouse effect theory an increase in pollution, i.e. carbon dioxide and other trace gases, increases radiative forcing and consequently the committed temperature (Cline, 1991; Nordhaus, 1994), i.e. $h_Y > 0$. On the other hand, abatement pollution expenditures have a negative effect on pollution and, through radiative forcing, on next period temperature. The positive marginal effectiveness of $A$, the abatement pollution expenditure, on pollution is reflected in $h_A < 0$.[17] This implies that producing abatement pollution goods is as polluting as producing consumption or investment goods, but using them is beneficial from an environmental point of view.

The Arrhenius relationship between radiative forcing and the atmospheric concentration of carbon dioxide states that "as additional carbon dioxide is added in the atmosphere the blocking effect of infrared radiation rises less than linearly" (Cline, 1991, pp. 906–907). For this reason in the present situation, and indeed for levels of carbon dioxide much higher, the effect of production on the equilibrium mean surface temperature is positive but decreasing, i.e. $h_{YY} < 0$. Finally, it is assumed that $h_{AA} < 0$, to describe the decreasing marginal effectiveness of $A$, and $h_{YA} > 0$.[18] Summarizing the signs of the relevant (partial) derivatives of (2.1–2.3) are:

$$f_K > 0, \quad f_L > 0, \quad f_{KK} < 0, \quad f_{LL} < 0, \quad \text{and} \quad f_{KL} > 0;$$

$$h_Y > 0, \quad h_A < 0, \quad h_{YY} < 0, \quad h_{AA} < 0, \quad \text{and} \quad h_{YA} > 0. \quad (2.4)$$

One of the several definitions of sustainability reported in (Pezzey, 1989, p. 13) stresses the fact that sustainable development is characterized by non-declining outputs for all future periods.[19] Consequently, a decision maker concerned with achieving ex-post sustainable development with probability $\gamma$ (or a $\gamma$-sustainable development) will set abatement pollution expenditure at a level $\bar{A}_{t+1}$ such that, provided that the stock of capital at the end of period '$t+1$' is anticipated not lower than that existing at the beginning,[20]

$$Y_{t+1} > Y_t, \quad (2.5)$$

$$P\left[h(Y_{t+1}, \bar{A}_{t+1}) - r_\varepsilon \sqrt{\sigma_\varepsilon^2} < \Delta \mathcal{E}_{t+2}\right.$$

$$\left. < h(Y_{t+1}, \bar{A}_{t+1}) + r_\varepsilon \sqrt{\sigma_\varepsilon^2}\right] \geq \gamma, \quad (2.6)$$

with $E(\Delta \mathcal{E}_{t+2}) = h(Y_{t+1}, \bar{A}_{t+1})$, $\text{Var}(\Delta \mathcal{E}_{t+2}) = \sigma_\varepsilon^2$ and $r_\varepsilon > 1$[21] satisfying $[h(Y_{t+1}, \bar{A}_{t+1}) + r_\varepsilon \sqrt{\sigma_\varepsilon^2}] = T_\varepsilon$ and $\gamma = 1 - (1/r_\varepsilon^2)$.[22] $T_\varepsilon$ represents the decision maker warming threshold, i.e. the highest value of $\Delta \mathcal{E}_{t+2}$ considered bearable or whose consequences can be easily reversed.[23] When no warming is desired between period '$t+1$' and '$t+2$', $T_\varepsilon$ is zero. Equation (2.6) is one way to write Chebyshev's inequality.[24] Therefore, $\gamma$ represents the minimum probability, over all the possible distributions, that the actual value of the environmental variable in period '$t+2$' will be in the interval in (2.6), i.e. that development will be ex-post sustainable.[25] In this sense it is close in spirit to a maxmin rule.[26]

The introduction of a stochastic element in the environmental equation produces a meaningful result, graphically shown in Figure 1, where the origin of the axis is set to $T_\varepsilon$. It associates each single value of next period output to a set of values of the environmental variable (a line parallel to the horizontal axis) rather than to one single value as in the purely deterministic case. A certain level of future output, or equivalently a given growth rate,[27] is

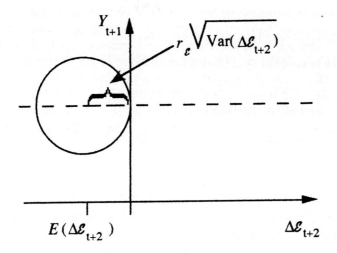

*Figure 1.* Representation of a $\gamma$-sustainable growth when no-warming is the desired threshold.

no longer sustainable or not sustainable, in the sense that causes the equilibrium global mean surface temperature to change below the given threshold or not, but becomes $\gamma$-sustainable. This means that it will be ex-post sustainable only with a probability equal to $\gamma$. The awareness of the stochastic nature of the environmental variable may induce to reject policies which, deterministically sustainable, are associated with a dangerously low $\gamma$. Differently put, the set of 'stochastically sustainable development' is included in the set of 'deterministically sustainable development'.

## 3. The Introduction of Multiplicative Uncertainty

In this section the assumption that $Y_{t+1}$ is deterministic is removed. More precisely, it is assumed that output is a known function of labor and capital stocks plus some noise, not necessarily white noise.[28] The new hypothesis introduces 'multiplicative uncertainty' in the environmental equation. Rewriting (2.1–2.3) in terms of growth rates with respect to a known base period yields

$$\mathcal{Y}_{t+1} = f(K_{t+1}, L_{t+1}) + \bar{\nu}_{t+1} \quad \text{with} \quad \bar{\nu}_{t+1} \sim \text{Mom}(0, \bar{\sigma}_\nu^2), \quad (3.1)$$

$$\mathcal{A}_{t+1} = \bar{\mathcal{A}}_{t+1} \quad (3.2)$$

$$\mathcal{X}_{t+2} = h(\mathcal{Y}_{t+1}, \mathcal{A}_{t+1}) + \bar{\varepsilon}_{t+2} \quad \text{with} \quad \bar{\varepsilon}_{t+2} \sim \text{Mom}(0, \bar{\sigma}_\varepsilon^2), \quad (3.3)$$

with the new variables defined as[29]

$$\mathcal{Y}_{t+1} = (Y_{t+1} - Y_t)/Y_t, \quad \mathcal{A}_{t+1} = (A_{t+1} - A_t)/A_t,$$

$$\bar{\mathcal{A}}_{t+1} = (\bar{A}_{t+1} - A_t)/A_t, \quad \mathcal{X}_{t+2} = (\mathcal{E}_{t+2} - \mathcal{E}_{t+1})/\mathcal{E}_t,$$

$$\bar{\nu}_{t+1} = \nu_{t+1}/Y_t, \quad \bar{\varepsilon}_{t+2} = \varepsilon_{t+2}/\mathcal{E}_t,$$

$$f(K_{t+1}, L_{t+1}) = [f(K_{t+1}, L_{t+1})/Y_t] - 1,$$

$$h(\mathcal{Y}_{t+1}, \mathcal{A}_{t+1}) = [h(Y_{t+1}, A_{t+1})/\mathcal{E}_t] - 1, \tag{3.4}$$

and the associated (partial) derivatives being[30]

$$f_K > 0, \quad f_L > 0, \quad f_{KK} < 0, \quad f_{LL} < 0, \quad \text{and} \quad f_{KL} > 0;$$

$$h_y > 0, \quad h_A < 0, \quad h_{yy} < 0, \quad h_{AA} < 0, \quad \text{and} \quad h_{yA} > 0. \tag{3.5}$$

The mean and variance of the growth rate are, respectively,

$$E(\mathcal{Y}_{t+1} \mid I_t) \equiv \bar{\mathcal{Y}}_{t+1} = f(K_{t+1}, L_{t+1}), \tag{3.6}$$

$$\text{Var}(\mathcal{Y}_{t+1} \mid I_t) = \bar{\sigma}_\nu^2. \tag{3.7}$$

Using a first order Taylor expansion[31] around the expected values of output and abatement pollution expenditure, the approximate mean and variance of the environmental variable are

$$E(\mathcal{X}_{t+2} \mid I_t) \equiv \bar{\mathcal{X}}_{t+2} \approx h(\bar{\mathcal{Y}}_{t+1}, \bar{\mathcal{A}}_{t+1}), \tag{3.8}$$

$$\text{Var}(\mathcal{X}_{t+2} \mid I_t) \approx h_y^2 \, \text{Var}(\mathcal{Y}) + \bar{\sigma}_\varepsilon^2. \tag{3.9}$$

In this situation a decision maker concerned with achieving a $\gamma$-sustainable development will set abatement pollution expenditure at a level $\bar{A}_{t+1}$ such that, assuming that the stock of capital at the end of '$t+1$' is anticipated not lower than the initial stock,[32] the following conditions are satisfied

$$E(\mathcal{Y}_{t+1} \mid I_t) \equiv \bar{\mathcal{Y}}_{t+1} > 0, \tag{3.10}$$

$$P\left[\bar{\mathcal{Y}}_{t+1} - r_y\sqrt{\text{Var}(\mathcal{Y}_{t+1} \mid I_t)} < \mathcal{Y}_{t+1}\right.$$

$$\left. < \bar{\mathcal{Y}}_{t+1} + r_y\sqrt{\text{Var}(\mathcal{Y}_{t+1} \mid I_t)}\right] \geq \alpha_0, \tag{3.11}$$

$$P\left[\bar{\mathcal{X}}_{t+2} - r_x\sqrt{\text{Var}(\mathcal{X}_{t+2} \mid I_t)} < \mathcal{X}_{t+2}\right.$$

$$\left. < \bar{\mathcal{X}}_{t+2} + r_x\sqrt{\text{Var}(\mathcal{X}_{t+2} \mid I_t)}\right] \geq \gamma, \tag{3.12}$$

with $r_y \geq r_y^{\min}$, $\alpha_0 = 1 - [1/(r_y^{\min})^2]$, $r_x > 1$ and $\gamma = 1 - (1/r_x^2)$. The constant $r_y$ is such that $[\bar{\mathcal{Y}}_{t+1} - r_y^{\min}\sqrt{\text{Var}(\mathcal{Y}_{t+1} \mid I_t)}] = T_y$, where $T_y$ represents a 'growth threshold' set by the planner, i.e. the minimum satisfactory growth rate of output for the next period.[33] If any increase in

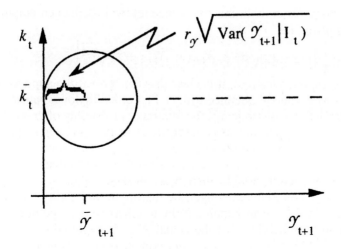

*Figure 2.* Representation of $\gamma$-sustainable output growth.

output is viewed as satisfactory $T_y$ is equal to some arbitrarily small positive rate of change whereas in other circumstances, for instance in the case of a developing country, the threshold may be 10/15%. Equation (3.11) states that only those growth rates above a certain threshold with a pre-set minimum probability of succeeding, for instance 90%, are considered relevant. This restricts considerably the number of alternatives desirable, or acceptable, from the point of view of the planner. In the case of a constant return to scale production function, with $k = K/L$, the situation is sketched in Figure 2 where the origin of the axis is set to $T_y$. Similarly, $r_x$ is set to satisfy the condition $[\bar{\mathcal{X}}_{t+2} + r_x \sqrt{\text{Var}(\mathcal{X}_{t+2} \mid I_t)}] = T_x$ where $T_x$ represents the critical warming threshold discussed in the previous section.

Combining the definition of $\gamma$-sustainability given by Equations (3.10–3.12) with (3.6–3.9) yields

$$f(K_{t+1}, L_{t+1}) > 0, \qquad (3.13)$$

$$P\left[f(K_{t+1}, L_{t+1}) - r_y\sqrt{\bar{\sigma}_\nu^2} < \mathcal{Y}_{t+1}\right.$$
$$\left. < f(K_{t+1}, L_{t+1}) + r_y\sqrt{\bar{\sigma}_\nu^2}\right] \geq \alpha_0, \qquad (3.14)$$

$$P\left[\bar{\mathcal{X}}_{t+2} - r_x\sqrt{h_y^2\bar{\sigma}_\nu^2 + \bar{\sigma}_\varepsilon^2} < \mathcal{X}_{t+2}\right.$$
$$\left. < \bar{\mathcal{X}}_{t+2} + r_x\sqrt{h_y^2\bar{\sigma}_\nu^2 + \bar{\sigma}_\varepsilon^2}\right] \geq \gamma. \qquad (3.15)$$

By comparing (3.15) with the confidence interval used when output growth is deterministic, i.e.

$$P\left[\bar{\mathcal{X}}_{t+2} - r_x\sqrt{\bar{\sigma}_\varepsilon^2} < \mathcal{X}_{t+2} < \bar{\mathcal{X}}_{t+2} + r_x\sqrt{\bar{\sigma}_\varepsilon^2}\right] \geq \gamma, \qquad (3.16)$$

which corresponds to (2.6), it is clear that the former, the approximate stochastic growth interval obtained using a first order Taylor expansion, always contain the latter. Consequently, the minimum probability of ex-post sustainability in the case of a stochastic production function is lower than in the case of a deterministic one. This means that anytime the deterministic confidence interval is mistakenly used, because output is assumed deterministic when indeed it is a random variable, there is an 'overestimation of sustainability'.

In (3.15) $\gamma$ represents no longer the minimum probability that the actual output growth will be sustainable from an environmental point of view, i.e. the minimum probability that the actual $\mathcal{X}_{t+2}$ is captured by the indicated confidence interval, but rather the 'approximate expected minimum probability' conditional on all the information available at time '$t$'. It is 'expected' in the sense that the interval in (3.15) is constructed using the expected value and the variance, $h_x^2 \text{Var}(Y)$, of the output growth rate. So it is based on results obtained from an infinite number of experiments. However the fact that changes are not reversible makes it interesting to know something closer to the minimum probability of ex-post sustainability, i.e. the probability of ex-post sustainability in the case that 'all the odds are against it'. From the practitioner view point, it is cold comfort knowing that he/she will miss the target with a chance of 5% if he/she could try 2 million times. It may be more relevant to know that 'if everything goes wrong' he/she will miss the chosen target with a probability of 20%.

Some interesting insights can be drawn by comparing two extreme cases. Namely, the case in which the actual output growth rate is equal to its expected value, $\mathcal{Y}_{t+1} = f(K_{t+1}, L_{t+1})$ in the present case, and the case in which it is equal to the least favorable 'of all the growth favorable cases' in terms of environment, i.e. $\mathcal{Y}_{t+1} \equiv \mathcal{Y}_{t+1}^{\max} = \bar{\mathcal{Y}}_{t+1} + r_y\sqrt{\text{Var}(\mathcal{Y}_{t+1} \mid I_t)}$.[34] It can be shown (Appendix 1) that the probability that the environmental variable is 'captured' by the desired interval in the latter case, $\gamma_x^e$, is always smaller than that associated with the former one, $\gamma_x^b$. In other words, the more one cares about output growth, which translates into the choice of higher $r_y$, the lower is the minimum probability that the actual growth rate will be environmentally sustainable.

Summarizing: the introduction of uncertainty in the output equation has significant consequences on the environmental variable. On one hand, condition (3.10–3.11) is stronger than (2.5) in the sense that it requires an $r_y$ associated with an $\alpha$ greater than, or equal to, $\alpha_0$. This $\alpha_0$ is the critical value arbitrarily chosen by the decision maker, for instance 90%, and can be interpreted as his/her degree of risk aversion toward 'slow growth'. On the other hand, by doing so it increases the probability that high growth rates will occur; this is desirable from a 'growth perspective' but detrimental from an environmental one. Therefore, the minimum probability that actual growth will be environmentally sustainable drops below its 'deterministic' value.

## 4. An Extension of the Basic Model

So far it has been assumed that current output is independent of the environment. However, there is no doubt that climate changes have an impact on economic activity (Nordhaus, 1994), for example agriculture. In this section the model is extended to take into account the effects of the contemporaneous environmental variable on output growth. The model, in terms of rates of change, becomes

$$\mathcal{Y}_{t+1} = f(K_{t+1}, L_{t+1}, \mathcal{X}_{t+1}) + \bar{\nu}_{t+1} \quad \text{with} \quad \bar{\nu}_{t+1} \sim Mom(0, \bar{\sigma}_\nu^2), \quad (4.1)$$

$$\mathcal{A}_{t+1} = \bar{\mathcal{A}}_{t+1}, \quad (4.2)$$

$$\mathcal{X}_{t+2} = h(\mathcal{Y}_{t+1}, \mathcal{A}_{t+1}) + \bar{\varepsilon}_{t+2} \quad \text{with} \quad \bar{\varepsilon}_{t+2} \sim Mom(0, \bar{\sigma}_\varepsilon^2), \quad (4.3)$$

where the variables are defined as in the previous section for Equations (4.2) and (4.3) and

$$\bar{\nu}_{t+1} = \nu_{t+1}/Y_t, \quad \text{and}$$

$$f(K_{t+1}, L_{t+1}, \mathcal{X}_{t+1}) = [f(K_{t+1}, L_{t+1}, \mathcal{E}_t(\mathcal{X}_{t+1}+1))/Y_t] - 1 \quad (4.4)$$

in (4.1). The signs of the new derivatives of the output growth rate with respect to the rate of change of the environmental variable need some discussion.[35] The marginal effect of environment on output, $f_\varepsilon$, is likely to be negative for the reasons spelled out by (Cline, 1991, p. 914) and for the reason that the present allocation of capital and human resources maximizes output given the present environment situation. The second derivative $f_{\varepsilon\varepsilon}$ is here assumed positive for the reasons reported in (Cline, 1991, pp. 914–915), namely that as the variations of the environment are more pronounced the economic consequences are 'far worse'.[36] Summarizing,

$$f_x = f_\varepsilon/Y_t < 0, \quad f_{xx} = f_{\varepsilon\varepsilon}/Y_t > 0. \quad (4.5)$$

From (4.3), it is clear that both the mean and the variance of the contemporaneous environmental variable are known, i.e.

$$E(\mathcal{X}_{t+1} \mid I_t) = h(\mathcal{Y}_t, \mathcal{A}_t), \quad (4.6)$$

$$\text{Var}(\mathcal{X}_{t+1} \mid I_t) = \bar{\sigma}_\varepsilon^2. \quad (4.7)$$

Given (4.6–4.7) a confidence interval capturing the true value of $\mathcal{X}_{t+1}$ with a probability higher than $\gamma_0$ can be constructed, namely

$$P\left[h(\mathcal{Y}_t, \mathcal{A}_t) - r_x^c\sqrt{\bar{\sigma}_\varepsilon^2} < \mathcal{X}_{t+1} < h(\mathcal{Y}_t, \mathcal{A}_t) + r_x^c\sqrt{\bar{\sigma}_\varepsilon^2}\right] \geq \gamma_x^c, \quad (4.8)$$

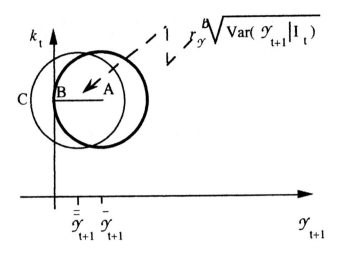

*Figure 3.* Change of the expected output growth due to changes in contemporaneous environmental variable.

with $r_x^c$ guaranteeing that $\gamma_x^c > \gamma_0$, for instance 90%. Differently from the previous section, $r_x^c$ is not chosen to satisfy a certain pre-set threshold. The reason is that $\mathcal{X}_{t+1}$ is not affected by current period decisions and the only goal is to construct a confidence interval capturing it with a high probability.

Similarly to the previous section, two scenarios are investigated: the case with $\mathcal{X}_{t+1} = E(\mathcal{X}_{t+1})$ which represents the case of perfect forecast, the best scenario, and the extreme scenario with

$$\mathcal{X}_{t+1} \equiv \mathcal{X}_{t+1}^{\max} = E(\mathcal{X}_{t+1}) + r_x^c \sqrt{\text{Var}(\mathcal{X}_{t+1})}. \tag{4.9}$$

In Appendix 2 it is shown that, keeping the lower bound of the confidence interval constant, the $r_y$ associated with the extreme scenario, $r_y^e$, is always smaller than that characterizing the 'best scenario', $r_y^b$. Therefore, the approximate minimum probability that there will be growth is smaller in the extreme case. As sketched in Figure 3 uncertainty about the actual value of this period environmental variable moves the expected output growth from $\bar{\mathcal{Y}}_{t+1}$ to $\bar{\bar{\mathcal{Y}}}_{t+1}$, which indicates the output growth associated with the extreme scenario. The larger is the probability attached to a certain confidence interval for this period environment, $r_x^c$, the lower will be the approximate minimum probability of output growth in the extreme scenario, $r_y^c$. In terms of Figure 3, a higher $r_x^c$ corresponds to an increase in the distance BC. As a result uncertainty about the actual 'value' of today's environment reduces further the set of stochastically feasible output growths in addition to the loss due to the stochastic nature of the output.

If a certain growth rate is desired the main consequence of this 'double uncertainty' on today's output is to generate some kind of overshooting and this will make environmental sustainability even less likely (Appendix 2). In other words the approximate minimum probability that this period output growth will be ex-post sustainable from an environmental point of view is negatively affected by the noise appearing in the output equation and by the presence of a stochastic environmental variable in the same equation. This leads to conclude that the impact of a certain desired output growth rate on the rate of change of the equilibrium mean surface temperature is stronger when stochastic elements are introduced and it is harder to combine stochastic development with stochastic sustainability.

## 5. Conclusions

Economists have started questioning the desirability of development (growth) as an end in itself. The concept of sustainable development (growth) has been introduced to stress the fact that development (growth) should not exploit natural resources beyond certain limits and should not hurt the opportunity set of future generations. Most of the models proposed in the literature use deterministic relationships and ignore uncertainty about the future and the imperfect knowledge of the present. A simple model combining the greenhouse effect theory with the usual economic assumptions, and explicitly incorporating stochastic elements, is analyzed. The main advantages of the approach proposed are its operational nature, is the elementary, but robust, analytical tools needed to implement it and the fact that it is independent of the probabilistic density function behind the stochastic processes. This seems to suggest that this approach can handle some types of 'hard uncertainty' as defined in (Vercelli, 1994). In addition it can easily accommodate irreversible changes.

First, the three equations model, composed of a production function, the definition of a policy variable and an environmental equation, is introduced. The benchmark case, in which the production function is deterministic but future environment is stochastic, is analyzed. A certain level of future output, or equivalently a given growth rate, is no longer sustainable or not sustainable but $\gamma$-sustainable, i.e. it will be ex-post sustainable only with a probability equal to $\gamma$. This may induce to reject growth paths which, deterministically sustainable, are associated with a dangerously low probability of ex-post sustainability. Consequently, the set of 'stochastically sustainable development' is included in the set of 'deterministically sustainable development'.

When noise is introduced in the production side (Section 3), an approximate expected confidence interval is constructed. The probability associated with this confidence interval represents no longer the minimum probability that the actual output growth will be sustainable from an environmental point of view, but rather the 'approximate expected minimum probability' conditional on all the information available at time '$t$'. This results in an 'overestimation of sustainability' when the deterministic interval is mistakenly used. Most of the times changes are not reversible and the probability of ex-post sustainability in the case that 'all the odds are against it' may be required. For this reason two extreme cases are compared: namely the case in which the actual value of output growth is perfectly forecasted and the case in which it is equal to the upper bound of the relevant interval. It turns out that the probability of ex-post sustainability in the latter case is always smaller than in the former one and the actual difference is shown to be a function of the 'eagerness for uncertain growth'.

Finally (Section 4), output becomes a function of the unknown contemporaneous environment. The new source of uncertainty is another possible cause of overshooting in the growth direction with detrimental consequences on the environment. Therefore, it makes harder to combine stochastic development with stochastic sustainability. The problem of choosing an economic policy which minimizes the uncertainty associated with the actual output growth and its effect on sustainability becomes fundamental. This is where future research should continue. The explicit introduction of stochastic policy variables needs to be done to select the 'optimal' (or 'acceptable') policy mix minimizing the uncertainty associated with output growth. Furthermore, the simplifying assumption of a known relationship between the level of output and the level of pollution should be removed and a more detailed description of the economic system and of the environment should be introduced. In addition the use of this approach in some numerical problems to test its validity and power and the specification of the functional forms are highly desirable. Both the functional forms and the parameters of the model have been treated as known in the previous pages. Even though extremely useful, as a first approximation, in simplifying the problem, these hypotheses are highly unrealistic. For this reason the analysis should be extended to cover the case in which both the functional forms and the parameters are unknown and have to be inferred from the data.

## Appendix 1

Assuming that the model of Section 3 holds and that the actual output growth rate is equal to its expected value $\mathcal{Y}_{t+1} = f(K_{t+1}, L_{t+1})$, i.e. the best scenario,

$$E(\mathcal{X}_{t+2} \mid I_t, \mathcal{Y}_{t+1} = f(K_{t+1}, L_{t+1})) \equiv \bar{\mathcal{X}}_{t+2}$$
$$= h(\bar{\mathcal{Y}}_{t+1}, \bar{\mathcal{A}}_{t+1}), \tag{A1.1}$$

$$\text{Var}(\mathcal{X}_{t+2} \mid I_t, \mathcal{Y}_{t+1} = f(K_{t+1}, L_{t+1})) = \bar{\sigma}_\varepsilon^2, \tag{A1.2}$$

and the confidence interval is

$$P\left[h(\bar{\mathcal{Y}}_{t+1}, \bar{A}_{t+1}) - r_x^b\sqrt{\bar{\sigma}_\varepsilon^2} < \mathcal{X}_{t+2}\right.$$
$$\left. < h(\bar{\mathcal{Y}}_{t+1}, \bar{A}_{t+1}) + r_x^b\sqrt{\bar{\sigma}_\varepsilon^2}\right] \geq \gamma_x^b, \tag{A1.3}$$

with $r_x^b > 1$ and such that $h(\bar{\mathcal{Y}}_{t+1}, \bar{A}_{t+1}) + r_x^b\sqrt{\bar{\sigma}_\varepsilon^2} = T_x$. Expressing $r_x^b$ in terms of the environment threshold it yields $r_x^b = [T_x - h(\bar{\mathcal{Y}}_{t+1}, \bar{A}_{t+1})]/\sqrt{\bar{\sigma}_\varepsilon^2}$, with $\gamma_x^b = 1 - [1/(r_x^b)^2]$ which represents the minimum probability of ex-post sustainability when the actual output growth rate is perfectly forecast.

In the least favorable 'of all the growth favorable cases' in terms of environment, i.e. $\mathcal{Y}_{t+1} \equiv \mathcal{Y}_{t+1}^{\max} = \bar{\mathcal{Y}}_{t+1} + +r_y\sqrt{\text{Var}(\mathcal{Y}_{t+1} \mid I_t)}$ or the extreme scenario,

$$E(\mathcal{X}_{t+2} \mid I_t, \mathcal{Y}_{t+1} = \mathcal{Y}_{t+1}^{\max}) = h(\bar{\mathcal{Y}}_{t+1}, \bar{A}_{t+1}) + \Phi_{t+1}^{\max}, \tag{A1.4}$$

$$\text{Var}(\mathcal{X}_{t+2} \mid I_t, \mathcal{Y}_{t+1} = \mathcal{Y}_{t+1}^{\max}) = \bar{\sigma}_\varepsilon^2, \tag{A1.5}$$

with

$$\Phi_{t+1}^{\max} = h_y[r_y\sqrt{\text{var}(\mathcal{Y}_{t+1} \mid I_t)}], \tag{A1.6}$$

and positive because of the assumptions on the function $h$, where $r_y$ is the value of $r$ satisfying the growth inequality. So the relevant interval is

$$h(\bar{\mathcal{Y}}_{t+1}, \bar{A}_{t+1}) + \Phi_{t+1}^{\max} - r_x^e\sqrt{\bar{\sigma}_\varepsilon^2} < \mathcal{X}_{t+2}$$
$$< h(\bar{\mathcal{Y}}_{t+1}, \bar{A}_{t+1}) + \Phi_{t+1}^{\max} + r_x^e\sqrt{\bar{\sigma}_\varepsilon^2}. \tag{A1.7}$$

If the upper bound of the confidence interval for the percentage mean surface temperature represents the crucial threshold for the decision maker then

$$r_x^e = [T_x - h(\bar{\mathcal{Y}}_{t+1}, \bar{A}_{t+1}) - \Phi_{t+1}^{\max}]/\sqrt{\bar{\sigma}_\varepsilon^2} = r_x^b - \Phi_{t+1}^{\max}/\sqrt{\bar{\sigma}_\varepsilon^2}, \tag{A1.8}$$

and the minimum probability of ex-post sustainability when output growth rate is $\mathcal{Y}_{t+1}^{\max}$ is equivalent to

$$P\left[h(\bar{\mathcal{Y}}_{t+1}, \bar{A}_{t+1}) - r_x^e\sqrt{\bar{\sigma}_\varepsilon^2} < \mathcal{X}_{t+2}\right.$$
$$\left. < h(\bar{\mathcal{Y}}_{t+1}, \bar{A}_{t+1}) + r_x^e\sqrt{\bar{\sigma}_\varepsilon^2}\right] \geq \gamma_x^e, \tag{A1.9}$$

where $\gamma_x^e = 1 - [1/(r_x^e)^2]$.

Given the positive sign of $\Phi_{t+1}^{\max}$, $r_x^e < r_x^b$ for any value of the deviation and consequently $\gamma_x^e$ is always smaller than $\gamma_x^b$.

## Appendix 2

Assuming that the model in Section 4 holds, two scenarios are investigated: the case with $\mathcal{X}_{t+1} = E(\mathcal{X}_{t+1})$ which represents the case of perfect forecast, the best scenario, and the extreme scenario with

$$\mathcal{X}_{t+1} = \mathcal{X}_{t+1}^{\max} = E(\mathcal{X}_{t+1}) + r_x^c \sqrt{\text{Var}(\mathcal{X}_{t+1})}. \tag{A2.1}$$

In the 'best scenario' the mean and variance of $\mathcal{Y}_{t+1}$ are simply

$$E(\mathcal{Y}_{t+1} \mid I_t, \mathcal{X}_{t+1} = E(\mathcal{X}_{t+1})) \equiv \bar{\mathcal{Y}}_{t+1}$$
$$= f(K_{t+1}, L_{t+1}, E(\mathcal{X}_{t+1})) \tag{A2.2}$$

$$\text{Var}(\mathcal{Y}_{t+1} \mid I_t, \mathcal{X}_{t+1} = E(\mathcal{X}_{t+1})) = \bar{\sigma}_\nu^2. \tag{A2.3}$$

In the extreme scenario, using a I order Taylor expansion around the deterministic mean of $\mathcal{Y}_{t+1}$, i.e. with $\mathcal{X}_{t+1}$ set at its mean value, yields

$$E(\mathcal{Y}_{t+1} \mid I_t, \mathcal{X}_{t+1} = \mathcal{X}_{t+1}^{\max})$$
$$\approx f(K_{t+1}, L_{t+1}, E(\mathcal{X}_{t+1})) + f_x r_x^e \sqrt{\text{Var}(\mathcal{X}_{t+1})}, \tag{A2.4}$$

$$\text{Var}(\mathcal{Y}_{t+1} \mid I_t, \mathcal{X}_{t+1} = \mathcal{X}_{t+1}^{\max}) = \bar{\sigma}_\nu^2. \tag{A2.5}$$

Given

$$P\left[E(\mathcal{Y}_{t+1} \mid I_t, \mathcal{X}_{t+1}) - r_y \sqrt{\bar{\sigma}_\nu^2} < \mathcal{Y}_{t+1}\right.$$
$$\left. < E(\mathcal{Y}_{t+1} \mid I_t, \mathcal{X}_{t+1}) + r_y \sqrt{\bar{\sigma}_\nu^2}\right] \geq \alpha, \tag{A2.6}$$

it can be shown that, keeping the lower bound of the confidence interval constant, the $r_y$ associated with the extreme scenario, $r_y^e$, can be expressed as a function of the $r_y$ characterizing the 'best scenario', $r_y^b$, namely

$$r_y^e = r_y^b + \left[\frac{f_x r_x^c \sqrt{\text{Var}(\mathcal{X}_{t+1})}}{\sqrt{\bar{\sigma}_\nu^2}}\right]. \tag{A2.7}$$

The bracketed term is negative because the assumptions on the $f$ function guarantee that the numerator is negative and the denominator, a standard deviation, is surely positive, therefore $r_y^e < r_y^b$. In Figure 3 the bracketed term in (A2.7) multiplied by the standard deviation of the output growth corresponds to the distance BC and $r_y^e$ times the square root of $\text{Var}(\mathcal{Y}_{t+1} \mid I_t, \mathcal{X}_{t+1})$ to AB minus BC.

Using (A2.7) to determine the mean and variance of the environmental variable in the extreme case, i.e. Equations (A1.4) and (A1.5), the relevant confidence interval becomes

$$h(\bar{\mathcal{Y}}_{t+1}, \bar{A}_{t+1}) + \Phi_{t+1}^{\max_1} - r_x^e \sqrt{\bar{\sigma}_\varepsilon^2} < \mathcal{X}_{t+2}$$
$$< h(\bar{\mathcal{Y}}_{t+1}, \bar{A}_{t+1}) + \Phi_{t+1}^{\max_1} + r_x^e \sqrt{\bar{\sigma}_\varepsilon^2}, \tag{A2.8}$$

where

$$\Phi_{t+1}^{\max_1} = h_y[r_y^e \sqrt{\text{Var}(\mathcal{Y}_{t+1} \mid I_t)}]. \tag{A2.9}$$

When the upper bound of the confidence interval is kept constant, $r_x^e$ in (A2.8) is selected such that

$$r_x^e = r_x^b - \left[\frac{h_y r_y^e \sqrt{\text{Var}(\mathcal{Y}_{t+1})}}{\sqrt{\bar{\sigma}_\varepsilon^2}}\right], \tag{A2.10}$$

where the bracketed term is positive and $r_x^e < r_x^b$ because of the assumptions on $h$. A superficial reading of (A2.10) may induce to think that this result is better than that obtainable with a known environment because, as previously noticed, $r_y^e$ is lower than $r_y^b$. However, if a certain growth with a given probability of sustainability is desired, the selected policies will be such that

$$(r_y^b)^* = r_y^b + \left|\left[\frac{f_x r_x^c \sqrt{\text{Var}(\mathcal{X}_{t+1})}}{\sqrt{\bar{\sigma}_\nu^2}}\right]\right| \tag{A2.11}$$

and some kind of overshooting will result because $(r_y^b)^* > r_y^b$. A larger confidence interval is equivalent to a higher growth threshold, i.e. $\alpha_1 \geq \alpha_0$, in (3.14) which means greater probability to achieve high values of output growth. Therefore, substituting $(r_y^b)^*$ for $r_y^b$ makes environmental sustainability less likely because

$$r_x^e = r_x^b - \left[\frac{h_y r_y^b \sqrt{\text{Var}(\mathcal{Y}_{t+1})}}{\sqrt{\bar{\sigma}_\varepsilon^2}}\right] - \left[\frac{h_y r_y^d \sqrt{\text{Var}(\mathcal{Y}_{t+1})}}{\sqrt{\bar{\sigma}_\varepsilon^2}}\right], \tag{A2.12}$$

where $r_y^d$ stands for the term in absolute value appearing in (A2.11), the first bracketed term reflects the noise appearing in the output equation and the second one the stochastic environmental variable in the same equation. When the two stochastic elements are eliminated (A2.12) reduces to $r_\varepsilon$ appearing in (2.6).

## Notes

1. For a brief account of the growing importance of sustainable development as a policy goal, with all the relevant references, see (Pezzey, 1989, p. 1). The distinction between sustainable growth and sustainable development is nicely sketched in (Pezzey, 1989, p. 14).
2. A relevant exception is represented by the models discussed in (Pezzey, 1989, pp. 76–80) in which, given the impossibility to provide a general analytical solution, only the "steady state solutions (of the models) which assume that all stocks and flows have constant, positive or negative, growth rates (are considered)" (Pezzey, 1989, p. 76). A nice survey of the major issues in environmental economics is contained in (Cropper and Oates, 1992).
3. See (Intrilligator, 1971) for an introduction to these techniques.
4. See (Musu, 1991, p. 6) for details.

5. Vercelli (1994) contains a very interesting discussion of the concept of uncertainty.
6. A similar hypothesis is used by Marini and Scaramozzino (1993) in an overlapping generation model.
7. The assumptions required to construct a social welfare function are discussed in (Deaton and Muellbauer, 1980, chapter 9), and the references therein cited, and some of the problems associated with the choice of an appropriate social discount rate are mentioned in (Cline, 1992; Broome, 1992; Heal, 1993). The necessary and sufficient conditions for the existence of a representative consumer, or of a representative agent born in time $t$, are spelled out in (Barnett, 1981, appendix B).
8. This model may be viewed as a stripped version of the DICE model (Nordhaus, 1994) in which both the economic system and the climate system are described by one equation and there is no explicit optimizing behavior.
9. There are no non-renewable resources such as metals and fossil fuels and no limits to growth due to the scarcity of resources in this model. For a similar assumption see (Musu, 1991; Nordhaus, 1994).
10. This is equivalent to imposing a time lag between the moment in which $\bar{A}_{t+1}$ is chosen by the decision maker and the moment in which it becomes reality however, given that

$$(\mathcal{E}_{t+2} - \mathcal{E}_t)^2 = [(\mathcal{E}_{t+2} - \mathcal{E}_{t+1}) + (\mathcal{E}_{t+1} - \mathcal{E}_t)]^2$$
$$= [(h(Y_{t+1}, A_{t+1}) + \varepsilon_{t+2} - \mathcal{E}_{t+1}) + (\mathcal{E}_{t+1} - \mathcal{E}_t)]^2,$$

minimizing the expected value of the left hand term with respect to $A_{t+1}$ is the same as minimizing the mean of the first term in the square bracket. Therefore, selecting a level of $A_{t+1}$ such that the actual value of (2.3) is below a certain threshold with a given probability is equivalent to choosing it such that the squared difference between $\mathcal{E}_{t+2}$ and $\mathcal{E}_t$ is below the corresponding threshold with the same probability.
11. When a lump sum tax is used, and the existence of a representative agent is accepted, the assumptions in the text guarantee that there is no effect of $\bar{A}_{t+1}$ on the level of output in the sense that only the proportion of output devoted to private use (consumption and investment) is affected. In an infinite horizon model, or an overlapping generation model with a bequest motive, only private consumption is affected (Blanchard and Fisher, 1989, p. 53). However, in general, the way of financing $A$, for instance through a carbon tax, will have consequences on the level of output because the agent's decisions will take into account the 'higher' cost of producing. The crucial assumption here is that the decision maker knows the way 'the form of taxation' will affect output. An alternative way of writing (2.1), which explicitates the relationship between output and the form of taxation, may be $Y_{t+1} = f(K_{t+1}, L_{t+1}, \tau)$ with $\tau$ the tax structure.
12. The climate variables considered relevant by the greenhouse theorists include also soil humidity, rainfalls and winds as pointed out by (Cline, 1991, p. 908). However, the change in the "mean temperature is chosen because it is a useful index of climate change" (Nordhaus, 1994, p. 25).
13. Given the known relationship between output (abatement pollution expenditure) and the level of pollution this is equivalent to assuming that the environmental variable is a known function of the last period level of pollution plus some noise.
14. Equation (2.3) does not cover the case of complete ignorance, when the mean and variance of the stochastic process are unknown, discussed in (Vercelli, 1994).
15. Equation (2.3) is very similar to the model discussed in (Nordhaus, 1994), i.e.

$$E_t = s_1 Y_t + s_2 A_t \qquad \text{where } s_1 > 0, \ s_2 < 0$$
$$M_t = c_1 E_t + (1 - \delta) M_{t-1} \qquad 0 < c_1, \ \delta < 1$$
$$\mathcal{E} = \mathcal{E}_{t-1} + c_2 (F_t - \lambda \mathcal{E}_{t-1}) \qquad c_2, \quad \lambda > 0$$
$$F_t = 4.1(\log M_t - \log 590)/\log(2)$$

with $E_t$ the amount of emissions, $M_t$ the atmospheric concentration of greenhouse gases,

$\mathcal{E}_t$ the equilibrium global mean surface temperature, $s_1$ the polluting effect of output and $s_2$ the unpolluting effect of $A$, $c_1$ the fraction of emissions which stays in the atmosphere, $c_2$ the inertial parameter, $\lambda$ the feedback parameter, $\delta$ the transportation rate between the atmosphere and the deep oceans and $F_t$ the radiative forcing variable.
Defining

$$h(Y_t, A_t, M_{t-1}, \mathcal{E}_{t-1}) = c_2(F_t - \lambda \mathcal{E}_{t-1}),$$

the temperature equation can be rewritten as

$$\mathcal{E}_t = \mathcal{E}_{t-1} + h(Y_t, A_t, M_{t-1}, \mathcal{E}_{t-1}) = \mathcal{E}_{t-1} + h_t(Y_t, A_t),$$

where the only differences with (2.3), except for the time subscript on $h$, are due to the absence of the stochastic term and to the fact that emissions affect the mean temperature immediately.

16. The actual process behind (2.1) may be the usual maximizing behavior of the economic agents and it is not necessarily static. For instance, in (Nordhaus, 1994) the economic agents maximize the discounted sum of per capita consumption, over an infinite time horizon, subject to, among the other things, a capital balance equation of the form

$$K_{t+1} = (1 - \delta_k)/K_t + I_{t+1}$$

with $\delta_k$ the rate of capital depreciation.

17. The total derivative of the environment with respect to pollution abatement expenditure is

$$dh/dA = h_Y(dY/dA) + h_A.$$

Consequently, the actual sign of $dh/dA$ depends upon the relative size of $h_Y$ and $h_A$ and the sign and size of $dY/dA$ which is closely related to the way pollution abatement expenditure is financed.

18. These signs of the partial derivatives are consistent with the climate system described in note 15.

19. For a discussion of the relationship between the definition of the text and general concepts such as "maintaining the stock of capital" or "ensuring non-declining utility" see (Pezzey, 1989, p. 19). It is opened to discussion the kind of restrictions implicit in the use of this apparently harmless assumption.

20. If there is uncertainty about this 'anticipation' a probability similar to that appearing in (2.6) may be computed and the joint probability should be used for sustainability purposes in place of $\gamma$. The interpretation of the forecast interval (2.6) is different from the classical definition of a confidence interval because $\Delta \mathcal{E}_{t+2}$ is a random variable and not a population parameter; it is similar in spirit to a Bayesian confidence interval. In the classical sense, (2.6) is a similar beta expectation tolerance interval (Hooper and Zellner, 1961).

21. If $A$ were absent from (2.3), any level of output above the assimilative capacity boundary would have been associated with a rising equilibrium global mean surface temperature.

22. In the case of an error term normally distributed the tables relative to the standard normal distribution should be used in place of the more general, but less precise, Chebyshev's inequality.

23. In this context it is irrelevant the way the warming threshold is selected. It may be taken as given from climate studies, such as General Circulation Models, or it may be the outcome of an optimization process in which the economic losses are minimized subject to the cost of reduction of greenhouse gases in the atmosphere (Nordhaus, 1994).

24. It provides the minimum probability that a variable will be in a certain interval, regardless of the probability density function as long as mean and variance exist (Mood et al., 1974, pp. 71–72).

25. $\gamma$ is related to the concept of reliability used in (Vercelli, 1994) and reflects the degree of risk aversion of the decision maker.

26. See, e.g., (Arrow and Hurwicz, 1972).
27. Equations (2.1–2.3) can be, and should be when a Taylor expansion is performed around a certain point, rewritten in terms of growth rates with respect to a known base period. All the results reported in this section hold also for the model expressed in terms of rates of change.
28. An alternative way to introduce uncertainty in the production equation would be through the factors of production. For instance the hypothesis that labor and capital services are some known function of the relative stocks existing at the beginning of the period plus some noise would equally generate a stochastic output.
29. The environmental variable is defined as the change in mean surface temperature between '$t+2$' and '$t+1$' expressed as percentage of that prevailing in '$t$'. Analogous to note 10, minimizing the expectation of the left hand term of Equation (3.3) with respect to $A$ is equivalent to minimizing the expectation of the squared rate of change between period '$t+2$' and '$t$'.
30. Using (3.1–3.3) and the definitions (3.4), it can be shown that $f_K = (f_K/Y_t)$, $f_L = (f_L/Y_t)$, $f_{KK} = (f_{KK}/Y_t)$, $f_{LL} = (f_{LL}/Y_t)$, $f_{KL} = (f_{KL}/Y_t)$, $h_y = (h_Y/\mathcal{E}_t)$, $h_A = (h_A/\mathcal{E}_t)$, $h_{yy} = (h_{YY}/\mathcal{E}_t)$, $h_{AA} = (h_{AA}/\mathcal{E}_t)$, $h_{yA} = (h_{YA}/\mathcal{E}_t)$.
31. A second order Taylor expansion, together with the implicit assumption that the third and fourth moments of the error term probability function are zero, is used in (Tucci, 1992).
32. See note 20 for the case in which this certainty does not exist.
33. It is irrelevant in this context if the growth threshold is arbitrarily set by the planner or reflects the preferences of the representative agent.
34. Another interesting comparison would be among the most and the least favorable cases in terms of the environmental variable.
35. The signs of the other derivatives are as reported in Equation (3.5).
36. Nordhaus (1994) uses the same assumptions for these two derivatives.

## References

1. Arrow, K. J. and L. Hurwicz (1972). "Optimality Criterion for Decision-Making under Ignorance", in *Uncertainty and Expectations in Economics: Essays in Honor of G. L. S. Shackle*, C. F. Carter and J. L. Ford (eds.), Oxford, Blackwell, pp. 1–11.
2. Barnett, W. A. (1981). *Consumer Demand and Labor Supply: Goods, Monetary Assets and Time*, Amsterdam, North-Holland.
3. Blanchard, O. J. and S. Fisher (1989). *Lectures on Macroeconomics*, Cambridge, MA, The MIT Press.
4. Broome, J. (1992). *Counting the Cost of Global Warming*, London, White Horse Press.
5. Cline, W. R. (1991). "Scientific Basis for the Greenhouse Effect", *The Economic Journal* 101, 904–919.
6. Cline, W. R. (1992). *The Economics of Global Warming*, Washington, D.C. Institute for International Economics.
7. Cropper, M. L. and W. E. Oates (1992). "Environmental Economics: A Survey", *Journal of Economic Literature* XXX, 675–740.
8. Deaton, A. and J. Muellbauer (1980). *Economics and Consumer Behavior*, Cambridge, Cambridge University Press.
9. Heal, G. M. (1993). "The Optimal Use of Exhaustible Resources", in *Handbook of Natural Resources and Energy Economics*, Vol. III, A. V. Kneese and J. L. Sweeney (eds.), Amsterdam, North-Holland, pp. 855–880.
10. Hooper, J. W. and A. Zellner (1961). "The Error Forecast for Multivariate Regression Models", *Econometrica* 29, 544–555.

11. Intriligator, M. D. (1971). *Mathematical Optimization and Economic Theory*, Englewood Cliffs, NJ, Prentice Hall.
12. Marini, G. and P. Scaramozzino (1993). "Environmental Externalities, Disconnected Generations and Policy", mimeo.
13. Mood, A. M., F. A. Graybill and D. C. Boes (1974). *Introduction to the Theory of Statistics*, 3rd ed., New York, McGraw Hill.
14. Musu, I. (1991). "Sustainable Growth and Time Preference", Università di Venezia, D.P. No. 91.08.
15. Nordhaus, W. D. (1994). *Managing the Global Commons: The Economics of the Greenhouse Effect*, Cambridge, MA, The MIT Press.
16. Pezzey, J. (1989). "Economic Analysis of Sustainable Growth and Sustainable Development", Environment Department, Working Paper No. 15, The World Bank Policy Planning and Research Staff, World Bank, Washington DC.
17. Tucci, M. P. (1992). "Sustainable Growth: A Stochastic Approach", Fondazione Eni Enrico Mattei, Via S. Sofia 27, 20122 Milano, Italy, Nota di Lavoro 10.92.
18. Vercelli, A. (1994). "Hard Uncertainty and the Environment", Fondazione Eni Enrico Mattei, Via S. Sofia 27, 20122 Milano, Italy, Nota di Lavoro 46.94.
19. World Commission on Environment and Development (1987). *Our Common Future*, Oxford, Oxford University Press.

ALESSANDRO VERCELLI

## 2.7. Sustainable Development and the Freedom of Future Generations*

### 1. Introduction

Since its introduction in the late 70s (see, e.g., Pirages, 1977; IUCN, 1980) the concept of sustainable development has suggested a synthesis between economic development and environmental preservation, as well as a possible compromise between the point of view of economists and that of environmentalists. Unfortunately, there is still no agreement on the precise meaning of the concept of sustainable development and, what is worse, none of the definitions suggested so far seems able to lead to a really operational measure, unless one is prepared to accept assumptions about the preferences of future generations which could be considered implausible and paternalistic. This is most unfortunate since the success of the idea of sustainable development is hardly 'sustainable' unless reliable measures of sustainability[1] are worked out.

This paper surveys the main definitions of sustainable development from the point of view of their adequacy to support operational measures of sustainability, and suggests a different approach which could turn out to be better suited to this end.

The structure of the paper is as follows. Section 2 argues that the main existing definitions of sustainable development are unable to lead to acceptable operational measures of sustainability. In Section 3 a new approach to the analysis of sustainability is suggested. The definition based on the preservation of the freedom[2] of future generations, and appears consistent with the ethical and juridical foundations of the concept of sustainable development. In Section 4 a few operational definitions of freedom are examined. In Section 5 an alternative measure of freedom, based on the degree of diversity of available options, is suggested. In Section 6 the preceding measure of freedom

---

* This paper is based on a contribution of the author to the final report of SUSTEE, a research promoted by EEC and co-ordinated by the OIKOS Foundation of Siena.

is applied to the definition of sustainable development. Concluding remarks follow in Section 7.

## 2. Shortcomings of the Existing Measures of Sustainability

The wide variety of existing definitions of sustainable development has been pointed out in many surveys (see, e.g., Pezzey, 1989; Pearce et al., 1989). The limited number of definitions that aim to give an operational criterion of sustainability have a common structure: economic development (or growth) is defined as sustainable whenever a certain crucial variable may be 'sustained', in the sense that it is not bound to diminish in the future as a consequence of development itself. The operational measures tentatively suggested in the literature may be grouped into three sets according to whether the crucial variable is welfare (or utility), consumption, or (man-made and/or natural) capital.[3] The choice of the crucial variable has far-reaching implications since its sustainability often implies the unsustainability of other plausible candidates for this role. For instance, Solow's condition of a constant capital stock (including non-renewable resources) is consistent with constant utility and consumption only because the implicit utility function ignores environmental amenity, and full substitution of man-made capital for natural capital is allowed by a Cobb–Douglas production function (Solow, 1986). With a different specification of the model, the sustainability of consumption is consistent with the unsustainability of utility (see, e.g., Heal, 1992), while the sustainability of capital (especially in the strong version referring separately to natural capital) very often implies unsustainability of welfare and consumption (see, e.g., Dasgupta and Heal, 1979). Chapters 1.1 and 2.1 of this book cover other operational definitions of the concept of sustainable growth which are not covered here.

Let us briefly consider the above measures of sustainability in order to discuss their chance of becoming really operational.

From the point of view of utilitarian mainstream economics it is natural to choose welfare (or utility) as the crucial variable to be sustained (see, e.g., Chichilnisky, 1996; Pezzey, 1989). The trouble is that the welfare of future generations can be measured only by making specific assumptions on their preferences. This approach raises two objections. First, this measure of sustainability could be considered paternalistic and therefore unacceptable from the ethical point of view, as it would imply a constraint on the freedom of future generations. Second, any assumption on the preferences of future generations is likely to appear out-of-date if not naive ex post, the more so the further they are projected into the future. The predictions on the preferences of the current generations made by projecting into the future the preferences of, say, Aristotle would appear today both as clumsy, since the structure of consumption has radically changed in a way which could not be predicted even by such a genius, and outrageous since he considered, e.g., piracy a noble occupation and manual work a debasing activity, according to the prevailing values of his generation. Moreover, the evolution of tastes and values has accelerated very much in the last centuries and it is further accelerating nowadays, while the most general concept of sustainable development must refer to the very long run (Chichilnisky, 1996).

The alternative choice of consumption as crucial variable (see, e.g., Solow, 1974, and Hartwick, 1977) does not surmount the above difficulties. The definition of consumption in aggregate terms presupposes the knowledge of prices which depend on the preferences of future generations. The definition in disaggregated physical terms does not avoid the reference to the preferences of future generations as the composition of the future baskets of consumption goods should be representative of the tastes of future generations.

A further criticism which may be raised against both the above approaches to the analysis of sustainability is that they rely on strictly utilitarian measures of quality of life which are liable to be considered as very reductionist (see, e.g., Sen, 1992). In principle, other magnitudes like the 'functionings' and 'capabilities' advocated by Sen (1987) or 'basic needs' as advocated by Chichilnisky (1977) would be a better choice for measuring and comparing the 'standard of living' of the present and future generations (see Section 3).

The third family of definitions, which focuses on the stock of capital as the crucial variable to be sustained, goes in what I believe to be the right direction. It is less liable to be considered paternalist as it rightly stresses the set of potential means to reach unspecified ends rather than the benefits of actual choices based on given preferences. However, specific assumptions on the preferences of future generations cannot be avoided for reasons similar to those already encountered with consumption. An aggregate index involves the knowledge of prices which depend on the tastes of future generations. A physical index requires precise assumptions on the composition of the capital stock which involve the preferences of future generations. An aggregate measure of the capital stock is particularly difficult to implement for well-known reasons extensively discussed in the economic literature. Moreover, in the case of natural capital, the value of externalities, which cannot be easily calculated especially for the future (see, e.g., Perrings, 1988), as well as such elusive magnitudes as existence and option values,[4] should also be taken into account. The choice of capital as crucial variable to be sustained is also virtually less reductionist than that of utility or consumption as it does not predetermine the criteria of its utilisation. However, the quality of life of present and future generations depends also on further conditions, e.g. social and institutional factors, ignored by this approach.

Summing up, the existing definitions of sustainable development are not satisfactory, first because they lead to reductionist measures of real welfare and quality of life, second and foremost because on their basis it seems impossible to work out a plausible and non-paternalist measure of sustainability.

## 3. A Suggested Approach to Sustainability

In order to avoid the paternalism and implausibility implied by arbitrary assumptions over the preferences of future generations, it is useful to start from the observation that what is crucial to preserve is just the extension of the option set available for future generations, without any need of specifying their preferences. Therefore, it is advisable to define development as sustainable whenever the extension of the option set available for future generations is not bound to diminish in the future. This condition guarantees, so to say, equal 'real' opportunities[5] to all generations. In other words, according to the approach here suggested, the crucial variable for assessing the sustainability of development is the freedom of future generations. In this view, the ultimate risk of economic development is that pollution and depletion of natural resources will constrain in an irreversible way our future freedom, as well as the freedom of future generations.

Natural resources are, so to say, common *property* of all, present and future, generations. The fact that the actual *possession* of natural resources belongs only to present generations does not authorise them to limit the property rights of future generations. Therefore, ethical and juridical considerations suggest that the freedom of future generations should be taken as the basic variable to be preserved through time by economic development.

This definition of sustainability is quite flexible and general since the elements of the option set may be specified in terms of vectors of goods, or more in general in terms of bundles of characteristics (Lancaster, 1971); or, even better, their definition may be enlarged beyond the strictly welfarist limits of standard economic analysis in order to consider what Sen defines 'functionings',[6] or more in general 'capabilities'[7] (see, e.g., Sen, 1992) and Chichilnisky defines as 'basic needs' (Chichilnisky, 1977).

From the purely conceptual point of view it would be advisable to reason in terms of capabilities which capture in the best possible way the dimensions of freedom; however, we should be aware that the broader the definition of the elements of the option set the more difficult it becomes to work out a really operational measure. In many contexts, a strictly welfarist point of view, based on vectors of goods or bundles of characteristics, can be sufficient for a first approximation to a satisfactory analysis. In any case, the approach here advocated is potentially less reductionist than the existing ones which focus on utility or consumption from an utilitarian, or welfarist, point of view.[8]

## 4. Operational Measures of Freedom

In order to make workable the above definition of sustainability it is necessary to define an operational ordering among option sets capable of providing a reasonable measure of degree of freedom. Unfortunately, as we are going to see, this is by no means a trivial matter.

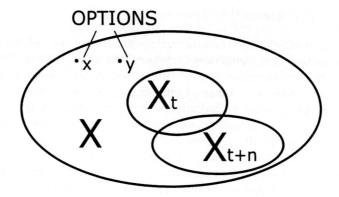

Figure 1. $x, y \in X$: options; $X$: universal set of options; $X_t$: feasible set of options.

Let us call $X$ the universal set of options, assumed to be finite, whose elements are denoted by lower-case letters, like $x$ and $y$. The elements may be interpreted as vectors of goods or bundles of characteristics, or better – when measurable – as $n$-tuples of functionings, or even better, of capabilities in the sense of Sen or basic needs in the sense of Chichilnisky (see the preceding section). Let $X'$ be the set of all non-empty subsets of $X$ which denote feasible option sets. $X_t$ is an element of $X'$ which denotes the feasible option set available to the generation living at time $t$ (see Figure 1).

Let us introduce $\succeq$, a reflexive and transitive binary relation defined over $X'$ as a measure of the degree of freedom of a certain generation. While $\succeq$ means 'offering a degree of freedom not inferior to', $\succ$ means 'offering a greater degree of freedom than', and $\sim$ means 'offering the same degree of freedom as'. Therefore, e.g., for every $X_{t+n}, 0 \leq n \leq \infty$, $X_{t+n} \succeq X_t$ means that 'the degree of freedom offered by the option set $X_{t+n}$ is not inferior to the degree of freedom offered by the option set $X_t$. In order to give an operational measure of freedom, as defined above, we have to find suitable properties of the option sets upon which to base it.

A first clue may be found by observing that, at least *prima facie*, freedom seems to be positively related to the range of the available option set. The usual ordering of the range of option sets utilised in the economic literature, e.g. about the determination of options and quasi-options values, is based on a criterion of inclusion between sets: the range of a set is not inferior to that of another set whenever the second is a subset of the first. This suggests the following ordering of degrees of freedom:

$$X_{t+n} \supseteq X_t \leftrightarrow X_{t+n} \succeq X_t. \tag{1}$$

At first sight, this definition is appealing since it seems reasonable to assume that the addition of a further option to a set cannot reduce the freedom of the agent. Unfortunately, this measure is applicable only to short-term sustainability problems, whenever it may be excluded that there will be a relevant loss of options within the time horizon considered: the range of two sets, neither of which may be considered as the subset of the other, cannot be compared according to the inclusion criterion.[9] No doubt, the sustainability of development must also be evaluated in the very long run. Biological evolution implies at the same time a loss of options due to natural selection and an increase of options due to mutations. Therefore, whatever the impact of human activity on the biosphere, biological evolution is characterised by an unavoidable loss of existing species accompanied by an addition of new forms of life. Analogously, as pointed out in particular by Schumpeter, a similar pattern of creative destruction is followed by economic development in the long run: continuous addition of new opportunities introduced by innovations and consequent obsolescence of old opportunities. The option set available to the present generations cannot thus be assumed to be a subset of the option set available to future generations.

What is required is a measure of the range of option sets capable of comparing option sets neither of which is a subset of the other. A simple way out seems to be, at first sight, an ordering based on the cardinality of the option sets compared, i.e. on the simple number of options contained in these sets. At a second inspection many difficulties arise:

(i) in any concrete situation the number of options faced by the decision maker is relative to a taxonomic criterion which may be more or less detailed. Any ordering is, therefore, relative to a well-specified taxonomy.

(ii) options referring to different values of the same continuous magnitude are infinite in any interval. However, it is possible to agree on some sort of discontinuous measure. Therefore, the ordering will be relative to an agreed-upon discontinuous grid.

(iii) some option may be redundant or irrelevant for the purposes of the analysis because it is dominated by another option in the set or because its specificity is useless in the given circumstances.

The first two problems are typical of many measures. The third one points out the specific inadequacy of this family of measures: a simple criterion based on the counting of the number of options does not take into account the degree of diversity among different options. The freedom of a decision maker is crucially influenced by the degree of diversity of the options available rather than by their number.

It is possible to go deeper into the analysis of the conditions of validity of this measure by analysing its axiomatic foundations as recently clarified by Pattanaik and Xu (1990). Let us denote by $|X_t|$ the cardinality of the set $X_t$; it is possible to prove that, for any subset $X_t$ of $X$, the relation

$$|X_{t+n}| \geq |X_t| \Rightarrow X_{t+n} \succeq X_t \tag{2}$$

## Sustainable Development and Freedom of Future Generations

is true iff the ordering $\succeq$, denoting as before a 'degree of freedom not inferior to', satisfies the three axioms:

*(INS) Indifference between no-choice situations*

For each subset of $X$ characterised by a unique option $x, y \in X$

$$\{x\} \sim \{y\},$$

i.e., sets characterised by different no-choice situations confer the same degree of freedom;

*(SM) Strict monotonicity*

for each single available option $x, y \in X$

$$\{x, y\} \succ \{x\},$$

i.e., a set with a further option added to those of another set gives strictly more freedom than the second one;

*(IND) Independence*

for each subset of $X$ and single option $x \in X - (X_t \cup X_{t+n})$,

$$X_{t+n} \succeq X_t \Rightarrow X_{t+n} \cup \{x\} \succeq X_t \cup \{x\},$$

i.e., the order between two option sets in terms of degree of freedom does not change if the same new option is added to both sets.

Closer inspection of these axioms reveals that the measure of freedom based on the cardinality of option sets exhibits strict limits of validity. The first axiom, INS, reveals a complete independence of the decision-maker's preferences, since e.g. $x$ could be a choice considered optimal and $y$ suboptimal and still this preference by definition would not affect the ordering between the two sets. Analogously, the second axiom, SM, reveals a complete irrelevance of the 'quality' of options; $y$ could be redundant, dominated or insignificant and still its presence would be decisive for the ordering. Finally, the third axiom, IND, reveals a complete irrelevance of the relations between options; the added option $x$ could, e.g., increase the diversity of set $X_t$ and not that of set $X_{t+n}$ and still this different impact would not be allowed to alter the ordering.

Pattanaik and Xu are aware that a measure of freedom based on the cardinality of the option sets is rather naive (Pattanaik and Xu, 1990, pp. 389–390). In their opinion the troubles arise with the axiom of independence, as is clearly shown through an example. Let us suppose that a train and a blue car are indifferent to the decision maker as alternative means of transport; now, if we add a red car as a second option to both sets, it is reasonable that a rational decision maker would prefer the first set {train, red car} to the second set {blue car, red car} because the first set offers a greater freedom in the sense that the available options are more diverse. According to Sen (1990, 1991, 1992), on the contrary, the basic reason why the option-counting measure of freedom is not satisfactory is different, and depends on the first two axioms which exclude any role for the preferences of the decision maker. In Sen's opinion a satisfactory measure of freedom cannot ignore the preferences of the decision maker. If this opinion were fully compelling we should abandon the search for a non-paternalistic measure of freedom. However, before giving up, I believe that alternative routes should be explored.

A clarification of the role of preferences in the measures of freedom comes from a recent work by Pattanaik and Xu (1993). They observe that the reference set of preferences does not need to be a singleton (the preferences of the decision maker). The opposite polarity, the universal set of all possible preferences, not surprisingly, leads back to the measure based on the cardinality of the sets of options compared. Intermediate choices would have the advantage of attenuating the paternalism and implausibility of a unique preference ordering. In particular, the authors advocate the choice of a reference set of 'reasonable' preferences. This is, no doubt, a step forward in what I believe to be the right direction. Still, the problems raised in this paper are not solved: the notion of what is, or is not, reasonable has changed radically many times in history. Therefore, the suggestion of Pattanaik and Xu, though appealing for the short run, is not fully convincing for the long run. However it is possible to explore a different way out.

## 5. Measures of Freedom Based on the Diversity of Options

Freedom of choice is not so much connected with the number of options but with their diversity. Generally speaking, a menu with 20 different kinds of pizza gives less freedom than a menu with 5 first courses, 5 second courses, and 5 different pizzas. The preferences may heavily affect the choice in the short run whenever they are fairly well known, but much less in the longer run and/or when they are uncertain. If I have to choose a menu for myself tonight and I am really sure that I want a pizza, I would appreciate the greater freedom offered by the first menu; but if I have to choose a menu for a guest whose tastes I do not know, or for myself in ten years time, I would rather appreciate the greater freedom offered by the second menu. Therefore, for a long-run horizon as that of sustainable development which refers to future generations with completely unknown preferences,[10] it is better to start by applying a measure of pure freedom based exclusively on the diversity of options, neglecting in the first stage of the analysis the degree of appreciation of such a liberty according to a given preference ordering.

I believe that this perspective is a promising one also because there is a long and consolidated tradition of measures of diversity applied to different fields

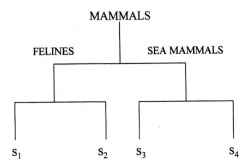

*Figure 2.* Biological taxonomy: example. $s_1$ = cat, $s_2$ = lynx, $s_3$ = dolphin, $s_4$ = whale.

(biodiversity measures, statistical indices of dispersion, entropic indices, etc.). I will explore in this paper only a limited track which starts from a cursory analysis of some measures of biodiversity and continues by drawing some insights from a recent contribution of Weitzman (1992).

The measures of biodiversity are particularly important for our purposes because the long-run sustainability of development depends on the preservation of biodiversity, and also because we can draw very important insights from their analysis.

Most measures of biodiversity start from a classification of biological species. In this case it is possible to take advantage from a very long tradition, beginning at least with Linneaus, which has led to consolidated taxonomies agreed by most scientists. Therefore, an index of diversity could be based on simple attributes of a taxonomy, such as the number of nodes which characterise it. According to a recent contribution by Vane-Wright et al. (1991), e.g., each species receives an index of diversity which is inversely proportional to the number of nodes associated with it; the diversity of a set of species is obtained by summing the values of each species in the set. Let us consider an elementary example of taxonomy which represents a subset of mammals characterised by two feline species ($s_1$ = cat, $s_2$ = lynx) and two marine mammals ($s_3$ = dolphin, $s_4$ = whale), and let us assume a simplistic index of diversity for each species $d = 1/n$, where $n$ designates the number of nodes in between the species and the root of the tree. Under these assumptions the set of species would have an index of diversity $d(s_1, s_2, s_3, s_4) = 1/2 + 1/2 + 1/2 + 1/2 = 2$.

A problem with this measure of diversity is that it is unable to take account of the distance between species, and this may lead to absurd results (see Solow et al., 1993, pp. 62–63). For instance, in our example of Figure 2, a subset characterised by $s_1$ (cat) and $s_2$ (lynx) would have the same diversity index of the subset characterised by $s_1$ (cat) and $s_3$ (dolphin): $d(s_1, s_2) = d(s_1, s_3) = 1$. This criticism suggests that in a satisfactory measure of diversity of a set the pairwise distances between the elements of the set must play a crucial role.

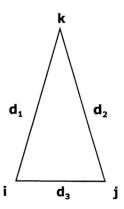

*Figure 3.* Ultrametric distances: example. $d_1 = d_2 > d_3$, $\max(d_1, d_2, d_3) = \mathrm{mid}(d_1, d_2, d_3)$.

This point has been confirmed in a recent contribution of Weitzman (1992) where the duality between a taxonomy of the elements of a set and a bundle of distances between couples of elements of the set has been thoroughly analysed.

Weitzman defines a cardinal measure $dij$ expressing the 'distance' between a couple of elements $i$ and $j$ of a set $X$ having the following basic properties:

$$d_{ij} \geq 0, \tag{3}$$

$$d_{ii} = 0, \tag{4}$$

$$d_{ij} = d_{ji}. \tag{5}$$

These properties are quite intuitive. A further property is less obvious but quite plausible; the distance between $X_t$ and an element $j$ not belonging to this set is equal to the difference between $j$ and its 'nearest neighbour' or 'closest relative' belonging to $X_t$:

$$d(j, X_t) = \min_{i \in X_t} d(j, i), \quad j \in X/X_t. \tag{6}$$

There is one particular case in which there is a perfect relation of duality between a taxonomy applied to the elements of a set and a complete collection of pairwise distances between the elements of the set. This occurs when the measure of pairwise distances is 'ultrametric' in the sense that it satisfies the following relation:

$$\max\{d(i,j), d(j,k), d(i,k)\} = \mathrm{mid}\{d(i,j), d(j,k), d(i,k)\}, \tag{7}$$

i.e., when for the three possible pairwise distances between any three points the two maximum pairwise distances are equal (see Figure 3).

In the case of ultrametric distances there is a perfect correspondence between a set of distances and a rooted directed tree (called 'perfect taxonomy': see Weitzman, 1992, pp. 369–370) having the following properties:

(i) the vertical distance between two species belonging to the same branch of the taxonomy is equal to their pairwise distance,
(ii) the pairwise distance between two species belonging to different branches of the tree is equal to the sum of the vertical branches of the taxonomy back to the closest common ancestor node,
(iii) the diversity function of the set is equal to the length of the associated taxonomic tree, i.e. equal to the sum of all its vertical branches, including the branch of the common ancestor back to some unspecified outgroup.

By exploiting the preceding properties, in the case of ultrametric distances it is possible to define a diversity function $V$:

$$V(X_t \cup j) - V(X_t) = d(j, X_t), \qquad (8)$$

which may be proved to be unique up to an additive constant of integration.

Unfortunately, in the general case of non-ultrametric distances, the relation (8) does not hold. In this case the diversity function is inductively defined by the solution of

$$V(X_t) = \max_{i \in X_t}(V(X_t/i) + d(i, X_t/i)). \qquad (9)$$

Weitzman proved that the solution of this dynamic programming equation is unique once the initial conditions,

$$V(i) = d_0, \quad \forall i, \qquad (10)$$

are specified (see Weitzman, 1992, p. 375). This function is considered by Weitzman as a suitable approximation to the 'exact' diversity function obtainable in the ultrametric case. It should be emphasised that Weitzman's measure of diversity of a set is strictly dependent on the assumption that it is possible to give operational cardinal measures of the degree of 'distance' between any pair of elements of the set. Pairwise distances may be derived as a weighted sum of distances between more fundamental micro-characteristics.[11] For the same set, it might be appropriate to use different measures of distance in different contexts, depending on the purposes of the analysis. Therefore Weitzman sensibly maintains that 'the focus of theoretical discussion must be about whether or not a particular set of distances is appropriate for the measurement of pairwise dissimilarity in a particular context, not about whether or not such distances exist in the first place' (Weitzman, 1992, p. 365).

A further obstacle to the application of Weitzman's approach is the number of pairwise measures of distance necessary to calculate the aggregate index for one set $X_t$. If $|X_t| = n$ there are $n(n-1)/2$ pairwise distance measures to be calculated as primitives for measuring the diversity of $X_t$. In addition, the aggregate distance measure is defined recursively, but an operational algorithm for its evaluation is not currently available unless the number of elements of $X_t$ is small.

The measures based on the function of diversity are applied by Weitzman to the case of biodiversity (1991, 1992). He also claims that an optimal policy of

182  A. Vercelli

conservation of biodiversity should maximise diversity as this would minimise the risk of negative uncertain consequences.

## 6. Diversity Measures of Freedom and Sustainability

The contribution by Weitzman is important for the purposes of this paper because in the case of sustainability, unlike that of biodiversity, a consolidated taxonomy is not available. The alternative foundations analysed by Weitzman in terms of pairwise distances suggest a possible solution. In this view, development may be defined as sustainable whenever the diversity of the option set available to future generations is not inferior to the diversity of the option set available to present generations:

$$V(X_{t+n}) \geq V(X_t) - X_{t+n} \succeq X_t. \tag{11}$$

The calculation of pairwise distances necessary to implement Weitzman's measure is of course very difficult to make operational. As we have seen, Weitzman himself recognises that his method is currently only applicable to small sets. The set of options available to current generations is certainly not a small set; the same is, hopefully, true for future generations.

However, there is a possible way out. For any practical purpose, what we are really interested in is to know whether a certain decision, or plan or intervention, is likely to reduce the diversity of options available to future generations. In order to find an answer, fortunately we do not need to calculate a diversity index of the option set available for future generations as compared with that of the option set available for present generations; it is enough to focus on the incremental loss and gain of options induced by the decision (or plan or intervention). In most cases the differential of options is very limited, and it is possible to measure the net effect on the basis of reasonable measures of pairwise distances between the lost or gained options and the closest option of the set before the addition or after the loss, according to the relation (6). To use a metaphor, in order to know whether the volume of water in a lake increases or decreases, it is not necessary to measure the volume of water itself but only to compare the inflow and outflow, a procedure which is certainly much easier to implement. Therefore, long-run sustainability imposes the following constraint on decisions:

$$\Delta V(X_t) = \sum_{i,j}[d(x_j, X_t) - d(x_i, X_{t+n})] \geq 0, \tag{12}$$

where the $x_i \in X_t/X_{t+n}$ denote the options lost and the $x_j \in X_{t+n}/X_t$ denote the options added in consequence of the decision. In plain words, any decision consistent with long-run sustainability must not reduce the degree of diversity of the option set.

The definition of sustainability here suggested should be taken as a very broad long-run constraint which, of course, does not exhaust the decision

# Sustainable Development and Freedom of Future Generations 183

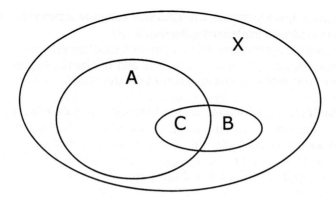

*Figure 4.* Two-stage criterion of sustainability. $X$: universal option set; $A$: set of options consistent with long-run sustainability; $B$: set of options consistent with short-run sustainability; $C$: $A \cap B$.

process, not even from the point of view of environmental conservation. It is a sort of minimal condition for an ethically sound decision. However, the diversity of the option set cannot be considered as the main argument of the objective function. On the contrary, even in order to achieve the optimal preservation policy of the natural environment, it is not advisable to maximise diversity, as suggested by Weitzman in reference to biodiversity, because further aspects of the interaction between economic development and the biosphere need to be taken into account. The value of environmental options itself depends in the short and medium run by other factors explored in the literature: the irreversibility of the consequences of alternative choices, the kind and degree of uncertainty, the potential for learning, etc. (see Basili and Vercelli, 1997). This suggests a two stage procedure for the analysis of sustainability. In the first stage, among the possible decisions, those that do not reduce the diversity of the option set available to future generations are selected, according to the criterion of long-run sustainability suggested above. In the second stage the selection of the optimal choice among those consistent with long-run sustainability can be based on a process of maximisation of the expected value of the decision which takes into account also the existence and option values of environmental goods. These values are relative to a reference set of preference orderings which therefore have to come back in the analysis following the suggestions of Sen (1990, 1991, 1992) and of Pattanaik and Xu (1993) mentioned in Section 3. However, there is no contradiction between the first stage, which avoids any reference to preferences, and the second stage which, on the contrary, is based on this crucial reference. In fact the first stage ensures that a very broad long-run ethical requirement is observed by all the economic decisions, while the second one selects the choice within the subset of ethically acceptable alternatives through an optimisation process which cannot neglect preferences (see Figure 4).

The objections against specific assumptions about the preferences of future generations, focusing on their paternalism and implausibility, are of course much more compelling for the long run. In the short run (time horizon of, say, one generation) it is much less questionable to make assumptions on future preferences, especially – as suggested by Pattanaik and Xu (1993) – if the set of possible preferences is not a singleton but a set characterised by a fairly large cardinality and diversity. In addition, the use of a short-run criterion of choice based on specific preferences is ethically sounder whenever the long-run criterion here suggested is satisfied.

## 7. Concluding Remarks

It is now time that the idea of sustainable development be translated into operational measures of sustainability to guide decision-making. Unfortunately, existing definitions of sustainable development have not succeeded so far in suggesting a satisfactory operational criterion of sustainability. The main reason for this failure lies in the fact that they are based on assumptions about the preferences of future generations which are bound to be implausible, the more so the further they are projected into the distant future. What is worse, specific assumptions about the preferences of future generations encounter the ethical objection of being paternalistic. This objection is particularly disturbing because the main motivation for ensuring long-run sustainability of economic development is an ethical one: intergenerational equity. Any effort to defend a fair share of resources for future generations without at the same time defending their freedom would be ethically questionable. It is, therefore, necessary to define the concept of sustainable development on the basis of an operational and non-paternalistic criterion.

A possible solution to the dilemma is indicated by the observation that the crucial variable to be preserved is indeed the freedom of future generations. Pollution and depletion of resources are a really serious problem for future generations to the extent that these phenomena will irreversibly limit their freedom. The criterion of intergenerational equity should therefore be applied to the effective freedom of future generations. Current generations should avoid any decision which could reduce the diversity of options available to future generations. This minimal ethical requirement of current economic decisions would ensure equal real opportunities to all the foreseeable generations which may live on earth. Natural resources are a common property of all, born and unborn, generations; present generations, that are only the present possessors of these resources are not authorised to damage this common property, nor to misuse their temporary power, in such a way as to limit the decision power of future generations.

## Sustainable Development and Freedom of Future Generations

Though the criterion of sustainability here suggested seems fully consistent with the fundamental ethical and juridical principles which lie at the foundations of the concept of sustainable development, its usefulness depends on the ability to translate its insights into operational measures. The preliminary explorations brought forward in this paper point out a line of research that could be promising. On the basis of a few suggestions recently put forward by Weitzmann, it is argueable that it is possible to apply to the problem of sustainability an operational measure of freedom based on the degree of diversity of the option set available to future generations. The hopes of empirical implementation of these measures lie in the observation that in our case, unlike in the cases explored by Weitzman, it is not necessary to measure the degree of diversity of the entire, current and future, option sets, but only the net differential effect of the options lost and gained on the diversity of the existing option set as a consequence of a certain decision. This assessment should in general be possible, as any concrete decision is unlikely to destroy or create many options. In addition, this measure does not need to utilise a rate of social discount, the determination of which is a vexed and unsolved question.

However, in order to implement the above measure in practice, it is necessary to find a reliable measure of pairwise distances between any option lost or gained and the closest option of the existing option set. The soundness and reliability of these measures can be judged only in each single practical application.

The research line pursued in this paper is not the only one which may eventually lead to fairly operational measures of sustainability based on the criterion of freedom of future generations. Chapters 1.1 and 2.1 propose alternative solutions. Entropic and statistic measures of diversity of the relevant option sets are also worth examining.

## Notes

1. For the sake of simplicity, throughout this paper the word 'sustainability' will mean 'environmental sustainability of economic development'.
2. For the sake of simplicity, the word 'freedom' will be used throughout the paper with the meaning of 'freedom of choice'.
3. As is well known, there are two different versions of the criterion of sustainability based on capital. The 'strong' version requires that the natural capital be preserved, while the weak version requires only that the global capital be preserved allowing for some degree of substitution of man-made capital for natural capital (see Pearce et al., 1989).
4. A recent survey of the literature on option and quasi option values with particular reference to environmental problems may be found in (Basili and Vercelli, 1997).
5. As has been rightly pointed out by Sen (1992, p. 7), 'equality of opportunity' has been routinely used in a restrictive way, being defined in terms of equal availability of particular means, or equal applicability of some specific constraints. The point of view here advocated defines equality of opportunities in the more basic sense of equality of options available to different individuals or sets of individuals; this approach is meant to capture the 'real'

equality of opportunities, particularly when the options are defined according to the more extensive meaning of 'capabilities' in the sense of Sen (see note 7).
6. The functionings are modes of being and doing constitutive of a person's achievement which define the quality of a person's life or his well-being (see, e.g., Sen, 1992, p. 39).
7. A capability represents the various combinations of functionings that a person can achieve and is represented by a set of vectors of functionings which reflect a person's freedom to choose one type of life or another (see, e.g., Sen, 1992, p. 40).
8. Following Sen (e.g., 1992, p. 43), utilitarianism may be factorised into three distinct components: (1) *consequentialism* according to which decisions have to be judged only by the consequences, (2) *welfarism*, according to which economic states must be judged only by the utilities achieved by the individuals in that state, (3) *linearity* of utility measures. Therefore, utilitarianism is more reductionist than welfarism because it imposes also consequentialism and linearity; welfarism is more reductionist than an approach in terms of functionings because it considers one of the possible functionings, 'being happy', exclusively, and judges it only from a subjective point of view (utility); an approach in terms of functionings is more reductive than one in terms of capabilities because, like utilitarianism and welfarism, it focuses exclusively on achievements without considering the degree of freedom to achieve.
9. Unfortunately, this is also true with more refined measures based on inclusion of sets (see Klemisch-Ahlert, 1993).
10. This is a case of what I called elsewhere 'hard uncertainty' (Vercelli, 1997).
11. Weitzman himself gives a few hints on the possible procedure in the case of architectural style, biodiversity, and linguistic diversity (Weitzman, 1992, p. 365) and fully develops an application to the case of intraspecific diversity of the species of cranes (Weitzman, 1991).

## References

1. Arrow, K. J. (1995). "A Note on Freedom and Flexibility", in *Choice Welfare, and Development*, K. Basu, P. Pattanaik and K. Suzumura (eds.), Oxford, Clarendon Press.
2. Basili, M. and A. Vercelli (1997). "Environmental Option Values, Uncertainty Aversion and Learning", this volume.
3. Chichilnisky, G. (1977). "Economic Development and Efficiency Criteria in the Satisfaction of Basic Needs", *Applied Mathematical Modeling* 1, 290–297.
4. Chichilnisky, G. (1996). "An Axiomatic Approach to Sustainable Development", *Social Choice and Welfare* 13(2), 231–257.
5. Dasgupta, P. and G. M. Heal (1979). *Economic Theory and Exhaustible Resources*, London, Nisbet/Cambridge University Press.
6. Grassle, J. F., G. P. Patil, W. Smith and C. Taillie (1979). *Ecological Diversity in Theory and Practice*, Fairland, International Co-operative Publishing House.
7. Hartwick, J. M. (1977). "Intergenerational Equity and the Investing of Rents from Exhaustible Resources", *American Economic Review* 67(5), 972–974.
8. Heal, G. (1992). "The Optimal Use of Exhaustible Resources", in *Handbook of Natural Resource Economics*, J. Sweeney (ed.), Amsterdam, North-Holland.
9. IUCN (1980). "World Conservation Strategy: Living Resource Conservation for Sustainable Development", IUCN-UNEP-WWF, Gland (Switzerland).
10. Jones, P. and R. Sugden (1982). "Evaluating Choice", *International Review of Law and Economics* 2, 47–65.
11. Klemisch-Ahlert, M. (1993). "Freedom of Choice. A Comparison of Different Rankings of Opportunity Sets", *Social Choice and Welfare* 10, 189–207.
12. Lancaster, K. J. (1971). *Consumer Demand: A New Approach*, New York, Columbia University Press.

13. Pattanaik, P. K. and Y. Xu (1990). "On Ranking Opportunity Sets in Terms of Freedom of Choice", *Recherches Économiques de Louvain* 56(3–4), 383–390.
14. Pattanaik, P. K. and Y. Xu (1993), "Rights and Freedom in Welfare Economics", mimeo.
15. Pattanaik, P. K. and Y. Xu (1995), "On Preference and Freedom", mimeo.
16. Pearce, D. W., A. Markandya and E. Barbier (1989). *Blueprint for a Green Economy*, London, Earthscan.
17. Perrings, C. (1988). *Economy and Environment*, Cambridge, Cambridge University Press.
18. Pezzey, J. (1989). "Economic Analysis of Sustainable Growth and Sustainable Development", Environment Department Working Paper No. 15, Washington DC, The World Bank.
19. Pielou, E. C. (1977). *Mathematical Ecology*, New York, Wiley.
20. Pirages, D. C. (1977). *The Sustainable Society – Implications for Limited Growth*, New York, Praeger.
21. Sen, A. (1987). "The Standard of Living (Lectures I and II)", in *The Standard of Living*, G. Hawthorn (ed.), Cambridge, Cambridge University Press.
22. Sen, A. (1990). "Welfare, Freedom and Social Choice: A Reply", *Recherches Économiques de Louvain*, 56(3–4), 451–485.
23. Sen, A. (1991). "Welfare, Preference and Freedom", *Journal of Econometrics* 50, 15–29.
24. Sen, A. (1992). *Inequality Reexamined*, Oxford, Clarendon Press.
25. Solow, R. M. (1974). "Intergenerational Equity and Exhaustible Resources", *Review of Economic Studies* 41, 29–45.
26. Solow, R. M. (1986). "On the Intergenerational Allocation of Natural Resources". *Scandinavian Journal of Economics* 88, 141–149.
27. Solow, A., S. Polasky and J. Broadus (1993). "On the Measurement of Biological Diversity", *Environmental and Resource Economics* 3, 171–181.
28. Vane-Wright, R. I., C. J. Humphries and P. H. Williams (1991). "What to Protect? – Systematics and the Agony of Choice", *Biological Conservation* 55, 235–254.
29. Vercelli, A. (1997). "Hard Uncertainty and Environmental Policy", this volume.
30. WCED – The World Commission on Environment and Development (1987). *Our Common Future*, ('The Bruntland Report'), Oxford, Oxford University Press.
31. Weitzman, M. (1991). "What to Preserve? An Application of Diversity Theory to Crane Conservation", HIER working paper.
32. Weitzman, M. (1992). "On Diversity", *Quarterly Journal of Economics* 107, 363–406.

# SECTION 3. UNCERTAINTY

ALESSANDRO VERCELLI

# 3.1. Hard Uncertainty and Environmental Policy*

## 1. Introduction

Games of chance provide the paradigmatic cases of 'soft'[1] uncertainty to which traditional decision theories naturally apply; environmental economics provides many paradigmatic cases of 'hard' uncertainty which cannot be properly analyzed under the present state of the art. This restricts the application of traditional decision theory to 'soft' risks which may be covered by traditional market instruments, such as commercial insurance and financial securities. These limits are fully admitted by frequentist (or objectivist) decision theories. On the contrary, Bayesian theory claims to be applicable to any kind of uncertainty. Unfortunately, as is argued in this paper, this is not the case. Even classic Bayesian theory is not really applicable to 'hard' risks such as those involved in many important environmental problems. This does not imply that hard uncertainty cannot be analyzed in scientific terms. Recent advances in decision theory have suggested various promising approaches to the analysis of hard uncertainty, which – to the best of my knowledge – have not yet been applied in environmental economics. This paper aims to survey the relevant literature on the subject and to draw some implications for environmental risk control.

The starting point of the following analysis is a distinction between different modalities of uncertainty with which various kinds of risk are associated. Such a distinction is crucial for decision theory and policy interventions, as this paper aims to show with reference to environmental uncertainty. This depends mainly on the observation that different modalities of uncertainty imply different kinds of risk, and that, in order to analyze and counter them, it is necessary to resort to different theories and policy approaches.[2]

In Section 2 of this paper the crucial distinction between first-order and second-order measures of uncertainty is introduced. In Section 3, two fundamental modalities of uncertainty are distinguished: 'soft' uncertainty, which

---

* A preliminary and shorter draft of this paper has been published in (Vercelli, 1995).

corresponds to the case analyzed by traditional probability theories, and 'hard' uncertainty, whose analysis requires innovative ideas, some of which have recently been put forward. Section 4 briefly surveys the main approaches to the analysis of decision under hard uncertainty. These theories are still basically static and have almost nothing to say about intertemporal decision problems. In Section 5 it is argued that the distinction between different modalities of uncertainty is admissible, notwithstanding strong contrary arguments put forward by Bayesian theory. Section 6 clarifies the relationship between uncertainty, ignorance, and unawareness. Section 7 examines some of the further complications raised by intertemporal decision theory under hard uncertainty, while in Section 8 it is briefly discussed how the learning process can be analyzed by different theories of decision under uncertainty. The main additional problem emerging in the intertemporal decision theory is irreversibility, and its consequences for decision theory are briefly discussed in Section 9. Some implications of the preceding discussion for the analysis and control of environmental risks are drawn in Section 10, and are followed by a few concluding remarks.

## 2. First-Order and Second-Order Measures of Uncertainty

Whenever certainty is assumed, it is not difficult to provide solid decision-theoretic foundations for microeconomics, and indirectly, for macroeconomics. These foundations work also for environmental economics, provided that the analysis is supplemented by well-established concepts which may be interpreted as natural extensions of the same theory (externalities, property rights, etc.).

The real trouble begins with uncertainty which is here understood as awareness of ignorance (see Section 7 for further clarifications to this point). We have to distinguish between first-order ignorance, i.e. ignorance about the characteristics of the empirical phenomena, and second-order ignorance, i.e. ignorance about characteristics of beliefs (about the characteristics of empirical phenomena). Therefore, we have to distinguish between first-order and second-order uncertainty (designating awareness of first-order or second-order ignorance, respectively). In a few cases, first-order and second-order ignorance may be measured. Probability is a first-order measure of uncertainty, as it refers directly to attributes of phenomena, and it represents first-order beliefs about phenomena; first-order beliefs have attributes (such as their reliability, or evidential weight, or variability) which may sometimes be measured by second-order measures of uncertainty. It is not always made clear that, as soon as different modalities of uncertainty are introduced, a second-order 'attribute' of uncertainty is also introduced. A measure of this second-order attribute of uncertain beliefs, when available, does not need to be a quantitative one; it may just be qualitative as an ordering or partial-ordering. Even

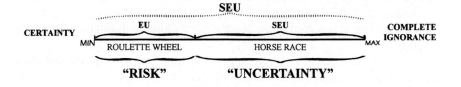

Figure 1. Standard terminology.

the simple dichotomy between known and unknown probabilities introduced by Luce and Raiffa (1957), developed by Anscombe and Aumann (1963) and almost universally accepted by contemporary theorists (see, e.g., Fishburn, 1988), may be interpreted as a second-order elementary ordering, since 'known' probabilities imply that second-order uncertainty is very low (or altogether absent, when the probability distribution is known for certain), while 'unknown' probabilities imply a higher (literally infinite) degree of second order uncertainty. According to the received view, the objectivist theory applies to the case of known probabilities (as in the 'roulette-wheel' games of chance) while the Bayesian theory applies to the case of 'unknown' probabilities (as in the horse-race bets). The received conceptualization may be expressed in a heuristic fashion by drawing a horizontal segment whose left boundary represents the minimum degree of second-order uncertainty (i.e. second-order certainty), and the right boundary represents the maximum degree of second-order uncertainty (complete second-order ignorance: see Figure 1).[3]

The standard conceptualization of the modalities of uncertainty and of the corresponding types of decision theory, as represented in Figure 1, is questionable. The scope of the objectivist theory is not easily extended far from the minimum value, while Bayesian theory pretends to span the entire segment (as suggested by the dashed line in Figure 1) claiming to be applicable to any second-order measure, and is not prepared to admit the superiority of the objectivist theory for known (or almost so) probabilities.

In recent years the dichotomy between known and unknown probabilities has been identified with the older dichotomy between risk and uncertainty introduced by Knight (1921) and further developed by an underground research line inspired also by Keynes (see, e.g., Hart, 1942; Shackle, 1952) which only recently has emerged in the mainstream literature (see next section). In this view the objectivist theory is defined as decision theory under risk and the Bayesian theory as decision theory under uncertainty. In my opinion this terminology should be avoided for a host of reasons; in particular:

(i) the traditional dichotomy between risk and uncertainty, as introduced by Knight and developed by the underground Knightian–Keynesian tra-

dition, cannot be identified with the more recent dichotomy between known and unknown probabilities,
(ii) in any case it is a confusing, if not intrinsically contradictory, terminology.

Let us see why. Knight's approach is based, as was usual with traditional probability theories, upon the concept of chance, i.e. the proportion of favorable cases over possible cases (Runde, 1996). He distinguished between risk which corresponds to a known chance, either because it is possible to apply an a priori reasoning or because there are stable and reliable frequencies, and uncertainty whenever neither a priori considerations nor stable frequencies permit a non-arbitrary assignment of probabilities (numerical measures of chances). In this view the assignment of numerical probabilities requires the homogeneity of the class of possible alternatives as well as the homogeneity of the class of favorable alternatives with that of possible alternatives, which is given either by a priori considerations or by stable frequencies (in the modern language, whenever we have stable and ergodic stochastic processes). We have uncertainty when the event considered is rare or irregular (i.e. it cannot be interpreted as the realization of a stationary and ergodic stochastic process). This is true in particular when the event is unique, e.g. because it is a genuine novelty.

Notwithstanding a completely different terminology and a different ontological view on probability, uncertainty and indeterminism, the Keynesian distinction between probability and uncertainty has similar, though sounder, foundations (Runde, 1996). In particular, it is much clearer that while probabilities are first-order measures of uncertainty, uncertainty proper involves a second-order measure concerning the confidence of the DM on the relevant first-order probability distribution(s). This second-order measure, dubbed by Keynes 'weight of argument', may be defined as the lack of relevant knowledge. Within the framework of CEU, the 'weight of argument' is negatively correlated with the degree of nonlinearity of the probability (or, better, capacity) distribution. Dow and Werlang (1992b) suggest a measure of the degree of nonlinearity of the capacity distribution dubbed 'uncertainty aversion'.[4] Whenever the weight of argument is less than compelling, (second-order) uncertainty is relevant in decision making. On the contrary, the distinction between known and unknown probabilities is only apparently similar to the Knightian–Keynesian distinction: it refers to the objective source of probabilistic beliefs (existence of stable frequencies), which is relevant for the objectivists but fully irrelevant for Bayesian theorists. In addition, this distinction is introduced in a way that is reminiscent of Knight but does not make explicit a second-order measure of uncertainty defined on the characteristics of the relevant probability distribution(s). Finally, also what is called 'uncertainty' in this view refers only to weak forms of uncertainty which characterize a 'familiar world' (see Section 3).

While the distinction between risk and uncertainty is still very controversial, the terminology itself could be misleading. In the ordinary language, uncertainty as awareness of ignorance generally implies risk, i.e. the possibility of an unfavorable contingency, while risk always presupposes uncertainty. Therefore, generally speaking, risk implies uncertainty and vice versa, which is in sharp contradiction with the dichotomic use of these terms. Their non-dichotomic use is so entrenched in the common conceptualization of uncertain situations that is generally found also when the dichotomic use is artificially introduced in the scientific discourse, so generating a great deal of confusion. Therefore, I think that the dichotomic use should be abandoned. This also permits the acknowledgment that to different modalities of uncertainty may correspond specific risks: e.g., the 'stronger' uncertainty characterizing an unfamiliar world clearly implies 'stronger' risks. In particular, whenever the specification of the states of the world and of the consequences is incomplete, the possibility of catastrophic consequences cannot be ruled out. Therefore, in this paper, I prefer to abandon this terminology in order to focus on what I believe to be the crucial divide between different modalities of uncertainty: the characteristics of the priors which are the object of the second-order measure of uncertainty and the limits of application implied by the axioms of the theory.

If we examine the axiomatic structure of the objectivist and subjectivist orthodox theories, we can appreciate how similar they are, notwithstanding the usual rhetoric opposition between known or unknown probabilities. The axioms are very similar, though this is clouded by a different terminology. E.g., the 'sure-thing' principle which plays a crucial role in the Bayesian theory by assuring the intertemporal coherence of decisions is virtually identical to the axiom of independence of the objectivist theory which plays there the same role (see Section 7). The point that I want to emphasize at this stage of the argument is that in both cases it is assumed that the DM represents her beliefs through a unique additive probability distribution. This literally implies that the DM knows the probability distribution for sure in the objectivist case, or that she behaves as if she had in mind a fully reliable prior in the Bayesian case. In both cases second-order uncertainty is altogether ruled out. This common feature of both orthodox theories suggests strict limitations in the scope of application of these theories. I maintain that they apply only to a 'familiar world'[5] characterized by:

(i) a closed world described by a complete set of possible states and consequences. Therefore, the admissibility of unforeseen contingencies is completely ruled out (Binmore, 1986; Smets, 1990; Kreps, 1992; Ghirardato 1994). In addition, the world is not only assumed to be closed but also very simple (see in particular points ii and iii);

(ii) 'Savage events' whose probability is independent of acts and consequences. This rules out the admissibility of 'endogenous uncertainty', see Chapter 1.2 of this book;

(iii) acts defined as a function from states to consequences ('crisp acts' as they are called by Ghirardato, 1994). This rules out the admissibility of more realistic acts defined as simple correspondences between states and consequences (Ghirardato, 1994).

It is important to stress that it is enough to relax one of these assumptions in order to fall in an 'unfamiliar world'. Therefore, we have to conclude that the hypothesis of an unfamiliar world is the general one, while the case of a familiar world must be taken as a special case corresponding to a restrictive set of particular assumptions. Finally, there are further, restrictive, conditions of applicability which are not intrinsic to the axiomatic system but are not less important (see the following sections).

In the light of the considerations discussed above, I maintain that the orthodox decision theories are unable to span the segment (or space) of possible uncertain situations, neither individually nor together. They apply only to a familiar world which is closed and particularly simple as far as the structure of states, consequences and acts is concerned. Therefore, whenever second-order uncertainty is relevant, we have to resort to a different decision theory which drops the assumption of a unique additive probability distribution jointly with at least one of the assumptions which define a familiar world. However, the hopes of extending decision theory beyond the confines of a familiar world as defined above are beginning to become concrete. In the last 15 years or so a wealth of new decision theories was suggested which aim to be applicable also to a somewhat less familiar world than that of orthodox theories. Some of them have a degree of rigor and sophistication comparable to that of orthodox theories and, already at this early stage of their development, are able to clarify many crucial issues concerning environmental uncertainty and risk-control policies.

## 3. A Taxonomy of Decision Theories

I am now in a position to suggest a different taxonomy of the principal modalities of uncertainty meant to replace the unsatisfactory traditional dichotomy between risk and uncertainty (or between known and unknown probabilities). I will distinguish between soft uncertainty, whenever the decision maker's (DM's) beliefs may be represented by a unique, fully reliable, additive probability distribution, and hard uncertainty whenever the DM's beliefs may only be represented in terms of a non-additive probability distribution or in terms of a plurality of (possibly linear) probability distributions, none of which is fully reliable. The decision theories under soft uncertainty (from now on SUDTs), apply only to a familiar world as defined above, while theories under hard uncertainty (from now on HUDTs) apply also to an unfamiliar, or at least to a less familiar, world (see a heuristic representation of this taxonomy in Figure 2 and compare it with the traditional one represented in Figure 1). SUDT has been characterized by three main competing points of view:

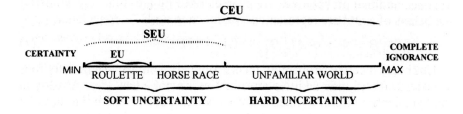

Figure 2. Suggested terminology.

(i) decision theory based on objective probabilities (Morgenstern and von Neumann, 1944), called objectivist or frequentist DT,
(ii) decision theory based on subjective probabilities (Savage, 1954), called subjectivist or personalist or Bayesian DT,
(iii) decision theory based on both subjective and objective probabilities (Anscombe and Aumann, 1963).

Each of these theories has received solid axiomatic foundations which guarantee their sophistication and rigor. We may wonder whether they are mutually exclusive or not. Anscombe and Aumann's (1963) theory maintains that the objectivist and subjectivist theories are mutually compatible in the sense that they are applicable under different modalities of uncertainty: the objectivist theory applies whenever probabilities are known as in games of chance of the roulette-wheel kind, while the subjectivist theory applies whenever probabilities are unknown, as in the case of horse-race gambling; their own theory is meant to accommodate both cases as well as the intermediate cases. However, this synthesis is not accepted neither by the adherents to the objectivist theory nor by the adherents to the subjectivist theory. According to the 'objectivists' only probabilities based on stable frequencies may provide a reliable support for rational decision-making. On the contrary, Bayesian theorists claim that their theory may be applied to any sort of uncertain situations, whether probabilities are considered 'known' or 'unknown'; in addition, they consider the distinction between 'known' and 'unknown' probabilities as completely meaningless: probabilities are revealed by the coherent behavior of a rational DM, in whatever situation she may happen to find herself. We have to conclude that the approach by Anscombe and Aumann attempts a synthesis between two approaches which consider themselves as mutually inconsistent, and reject the idea that such a synthesis is useful, or even viable.

We shall now suggest a classification of HUDTs. The definition of hard uncertainty suggests a basic distinction between theories based upon a non-additive prior and theories based upon multiple priors. Their reciprocal nexus must be spelled out in some detail.

Let us assume that $S$ is a set of possible states, $A$ and $B$ events (i.e. subsets of $S$), $\Sigma$ is an algebra of subsets of $S$, $R$ the set of real numbers.

Usual additive probabilities are characterized by the following property: the beliefs of a DM are represented by a function $v : \Sigma \to R$ such that

$$A \cap B = \emptyset \Rightarrow v(A \cup B) = v(A) + v(B). \tag{1}$$

Until very recently, probability theory routinely assumed that probabilities are additive. Still, non-additive probabilities are not a new idea. Already in the 18th century, Bernoulli and Lambert pursued this research line in order to represent uncertain subjective beliefs (Shafer, 1978). Unfortunately, these early attempts were interrupted by the sweeping success of the frequentist approach based upon additive probabilities. The twin contributions by Knight and Keynes, published in the same year (1921), revived the interest in measures of uncertainty not necessarily additive which was further developed by an underground stream of innovative scholars (Hart, 1942; Shackle, 1952; Dempster, 1967; Shafer, 1976; Zadeh, 1978; etc.). However, the recent success of non-additive probability theories began only when decision theorists discovered an important contribution by Choquet, a remarkable French mathematician who, as early as in 1955, suggested a rigorous and articulate generalization of probability by introducing the concept of capacity, a first-order measure of uncertainty which is not necessarily additive (Schmeidler, 1982; Quiggin, 1982). A normalized capacity is defined by Choquet as a measure which observes the following conditions:

$$v(\emptyset) = 0, \tag{2}$$

$$v(S) = 1 \quad \text{(condition of normalization)} \tag{3}$$

$$A \subseteq B \Rightarrow v(A) \leq v(B) \quad \forall A, B \in \Sigma, \tag{4}$$

Therefore, non-additive measures of uncertainty do not comply with condition (1), but only with the more general condition (4) which expresses the condition of monotonicity with respect to set inclusion. It is easy to realize that the usual additive probability is a special case of capacity which sets a thin boundary between the case of a convex or subadditive (or supermodular) capacity, when

$$v(A \cup B) \geq v(A) + v(B) - v(A \cap B) - v(A \cup B) + v(A \cap B)$$
$$\geq v(A) + v(B) \quad \forall A, B \in \Sigma, \tag{5}$$

and the case of a concave or superadditive (or submodular) capacity, when,

$$v(A \cup B) \leq v(A) + v(B) - v(A \cap B) - v(A \cup B) + v(A \cap B)$$
$$\leq v(A) + v(B) \quad \forall A, B \in \Sigma. \tag{6}$$

Most applications of capacity theory to economics refer to convex capacities which have a more intuitive interpretation.[6] The great strength of capacities theory resides in their integrability based upon a procedure suggested by

Choquet himself. The great obstacle to the development of nonlinear probability theory prior to Choquet was the lack of an integration procedure, since of course usual Riemann integrals do not apply in this case. The Choquet integral is the sum of two Riemann integrals with integrands ordered monotonously. The integrability of Choquet capacities allowed the elaboration of fully-fledged axiomatized theories of decision under hard uncertainty. They may be interpreted as generalizations of the theories of decision under soft uncertainty which apply also when probabilities are non-additive. There are versions which generalize the subjectivist framework (Gilboa, 1987), the mixed objectivist and subjectivist framework (Schmeidler, 1982), while it is mentioned by Schmeidler himself (1982) an objective version of non-additive probability theory suggested much earlier by a well-known physicist (Feynman, 1963).

The generalizations of the orthodox theories of expected utility (from now on EU) based upon Choquet theory of capacities are also called Choquet expected utility theories (from now on CEU). Though the formal modifications of EU theory operated by CEU are surprisingly limited, the conceptual implications are deep. The most popular modification of the axioms is the restriction of the independence axiom to comonotone acts, i.e. acts which do not reverse the order of preference of their consequences in the same state of nature:[7]

$$A > B - \alpha A + (1 - \alpha)C > \alpha B + (1 - \alpha)C. \tag{7}$$

This modification is quite plausible as it is consistent with the phenomenon of hedging, widespread practice in financial markets which remains unexplained within soft uncertainty decision theory.

An alternative formulation is based on the restriction of the independence axiom to unambiguous events, i.e. to events whose probability of occurrence may be represented by additive probabilities, while in all other cases (ambiguous events) the axiom of independence is substituted by the axiom of cumulative dominance which simply states that if an action $f$ gives a non-inferior payoff compared to $g$ for any possible consequence, then $f$ is preferred to $g$ (Sarin and Wakker, 1992).

In CEU theories the probabilities are weighted by means of the Choquet integral according to the EU of the consequences of each single act. In the case of a subadditive capacity the DM gives a higher weight to the probability of a state that for a given act leads to a worse consequence. The ensuing nonlinearity may be interpreted as the expression of aversion towards hard uncertainty (more on that later on).

The HUTD formalized in terms of Choquet capacities and integrals may also help one to classify other interesting HUTDs. An important alternative HUTD assumes that the DM is unable to express her beliefs by means of a unique, fully reliable, additive probability distribution and is bound to represent her beliefs by means of a plurality of additive probability distributions, none of which is considered fully reliable or completely unreliable.

Therefore, she expresses the probability of a certain event not by means of a point-probability but by means of a probability interval. The modern version of this plausible approach generally assumes a convex set of additive probability distributions (Ellsberg, 1961; Gärdenfors and Sahlin, 1982; Jones and Ostroy, 1984; Bewley, 1986). There is a strict link between a convex set of additive probability distributions and a convex Choquet capacity. As was proved by Schmeidler (1986), given a convex non-additive distribution $v$ on $\Sigma$, the CEU of a function relative to $v$ is equal to the minimum expected utility of the additive distributions belonging to the 'core' of $v$ (a convex set of finitely additive distributions such that the probability of the states is equal to the capacity of the states). On this basis, Gilboa and Schmeidler (1989) were able to give axiomatic foundations to an HUDT based on multiple (additive) priors. Not surprisingly, its structure and its results are very similar to those of HUDTs based on a unique Choquet capacity distribution.

Another interesting approach to HUDT is based on the definition of a belief function. The most interesting belief function has been suggested by Dempster (1967) and further extended by Shafer (1976). The Dempster–Shafer model defines two measures applicable in conditions of hard uncertainty: credibility and plausibility. It is possible to relate also this approach to the Choquet capacity approach by showing that credibility and plausibility are defined by a Möbius inversion (which Shafer calls a basic probability) of a Choquet capacity (see Chateauneuf and Jaffray, 1989; Billot, 1992; Ghirardato, 1984). More in general, a belief function in the sense of Dempster and Shafer is a capacity that in addition satisfies a property of total monotonicity, while for every belief function $\nu$ there is a probability measure $\varphi$ called 'Möbius transform' (see Shafer, 1976) such that:

$$v(X) = \sum_{A \subseteq X} \varphi(A). \tag{8}$$

Another approach to HUDT which I want to mention here is based on the theory of fuzzy sets introduced by Zadeh (1965) which originated a large stream of literature in different fields of science, including economics (for a brief but perceptive survey and assessment of the applications to economics and decision theory, see Billot, 1992). Zadeh himself utilized the theory of fuzzy sets in order to define two measures of uncertainty applicable in conditions of hard uncertainty: possibility and necessity (Zadeh, 1978). Later on it was proved that also possibility and necessity, as probability, are special cases of capacities (Dubois, 1980). A last approach is endogenous uncertainty, see also Chapter 1.2 of this book and (Chichilnisky, 1992; Hahn, 1992; Chichilnisky et al., 1992); Kurz (1991a, 1991b) studies the case of rational beliefs.

Table 1 represents a synoptic view of the classification of the DTU suggested so far.

Notice that the vertical order reproduces the heuristic representation of Figure 2, and that we have fully-fledged axiomatic theories for the case of soft

## TABLE 1
### Theories of decision under uncertainty.

| Measure of uncertainty | Axiomatic foundations | | |
|---|---|---|---|
| | Objective probabilities | Subjective probabilities | Objective & Subjective probabilities |
| **SOFT UNCERTAINTY** | | | |
| Additive probabilities | Morgenstern and von Neumann (1944) | De Finetti (1937), Savage (1954) | Anscombe and Aumann (1963) |
| **HARD UNCERTAINTY** | | | |
| Non-additive probabilities | Feynman (1963) | Gilboa (1987) | Schmeidler (1982) |
| Multiple probabilities | Elssberg (1961) | Gärdenfors and Sahlin (1982) | Schmeidler and Gilboa (1989) |
| Fuzzy measures | Zadeh (1965) | Ponsard (1986) | Wakker (1990) |
| Belief functions | Dempster (1967) | Shafer (1976) | Jaffray and Wakker (1994) |
| Endogenous uncertainty | | | Chichilnisky (1992); Hahn (1992); Chichilnisky et al. (1992) |
| **RADICAL UNCERTAINTY** | | | |
| Complete ignorance | Arrow and Hurwicz (1972) | Barret and Pattanaik (1986) | 'CBDT': Gilboa and Schmeidler (1992) |

uncertainty and for the case of a unique prior expressed in terms of Choquet capacities (not necessarily additive probabilities). As for the other HUTDs the names reported mention particularly important contributions which, generally speaking, are not axiomatized. An important exception is the paper by Gilboa and Schmeidler (1989) which has suggested an interesting attempt of axiomatization of a multiple-prior HUDT based on the correspondence mentioned above with the Choquet approach, and that of Wakker (1990) which has made a first attempt of axiomatization of an HUDT based upon the fuzzy set approach.

I still have to consider the extreme case of 'radical uncertainty', generally referred to as the case of 'complete ignorance', in which no conceivable probability distribution is reliable enough to be considered more plausible then the others. In this case probabilities (or capacities) are completely useless in guiding the choices of the DM, exactly because by definition they cannot perform their job of giving different existential weights to different prospective events. However, this symmetry of chances makes the analysis of decisions in a sense simpler than in the case of hard uncertainty. This explains why theories of decision under hard uncertainty abound and some of them have been suggested even before the new wave of rigorous theories of hard uncertainty. A few of them retain the state-consequences conceptual framework as the well-known theory suggested by Arrow and Hurwicz (1972). They conclude that rational decisions should rely on the maximum and minimum consequences, as for example in the maximin rule. A more radical set of models abandons even the state-consequences framework (see, e.g., Barret and Pattanaik, 1986). The normative conclusions are similar to those reached by the first set of models but, not surprisingly, the analysis turns out to be much more difficult to pursue (see, e.g., Fishburn, 1984).

An interesting axiomatically-based decision theory in conditions of complete[8] ignorance has been recently suggested by Gilboa and Schmeidler (1994) under the name of case-based decision theory (CBDT). A case is the combination of a decision problem, an act chosen as a solution of the problem, and its results; the cases experienced by a DM are stored, at least in part, in her memory. When a DM has to face a new decision problem she retrieves from her memory the most similar cases and bases her choice on the success (measured in terms of utility) of past acts in similar problems, giving more weight to the problems judged more similar to the current one. This theory is rooted in the Humean theory of induction and in Simon's theory of bounded rationality: in particular, a priori knowledge is not necessarily presupposed, while the decision criterion is strictly analogous to Simon's satisficing criterion.

In order to conclude this brief survey of recent developments in hard uncertainty analysis, it can be observed that they shed some light on the implications of environmental uncertainty. In many cases, even the opinion of the most respected experts is expressed in terms of probability intervals (the consequences of the hole in the ozone layer or of the greenhouse effect are good examples). In addition, since opinions of different experts may differ sizably, the DM must assess their reliability before making any decision based on them. Complete ignorance characterizes other cases (e.g., the environmental effects of a new biotechnological product or of the progressive reduction of biodiversity).

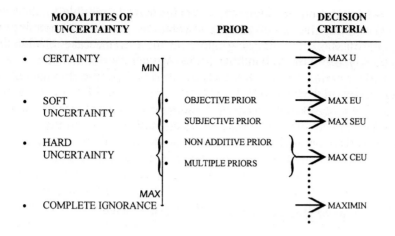

*Figure 3.* Decision criteria.

## 4. Decision Theories and Decision Criteria

In order to describe, explain, predict DMs choices (positive point of view) or to prescribe the right choice, any theory of decision requires a rationality criterion which may be intrinsic to the theory itself (the coherence of behavior in Bayesian theory) or extrinsic to it (in most other cases). When the rationality criterion is extrinsic, different rationality criteria may be associated to the same decision theory, giving different prescriptive indications. A decision theory, together with a rationality criterion, implies a decision criterion which describes (explains, predicts) or prescribes which decision is chosen, or should be chosen, by a rational DM among those available, given the structure of the choice problem. In most cases existing decision theories have assumed as rationality criterion the maximization of the utility function of the DM. This leads to a different decision criterion according to the decision theory utilized. In order to understand the different implications of different decision theories for the same rationality criterion we may resort again to the heuristic representation of different modalities of uncertainty in its vertical transposition and study how the decision criterion changes by going from one to the other extreme (see Figure 3).

The traditional utilitarian decision criterion of maximization of utility (Max U) translates into the decision criterion of the maximization of expected utility (Max EU) in the case of soft uncertainty. Before discussing the case of hard uncertainty, it is convenient to discuss the case of complete ignorance. In this case, the most popular decision criterion is the choice of the alternative which gives the best worst consequence (Maximin). In the case of hard uncertainty, not surprisingly, the decision criterion meant to maximize the Choquet expected utility (Max CEU) is in between the maximization of expected utility and the Maximin. In addition, it is possible to show that the less non-additive is the capacity distribution, the more it resembles the principle of Max EU collapsing into it in the extreme case of additivity; analogously, the more non-additive is the capacity distribution, the more the Max CEU criterion resembles the Maximin collapsing into it in the extreme case of complete ignorance.[9]

Figure 3 suggests that also from the normative point of view the approach based on Choquet capacities may be successfully applied to the gray zone between soft uncertainty and radical uncertainty and provides a general framework of analysis which includes the boundaries as limiting cases.

## 5. The Scope of Hard Uncertainty Decision Theory

Notwithstanding an early, and promising, start by Knight and Keynes, in this century hard uncertainty decision theory was inhibited in its development by powerful destructive arguments put forward by the leading decision theorists:

(i) Ramsey, the founding father of modern Bayesian theory, observed that 'someone whose degree of belief are not coherent "could have a book made against him by a cunning better" (Ramsay, 1988, p. 36) which would result in a certain loss' (Runde, 1994, p. 107). This argument has been developed in the form of a theorem, called 'Dutch book theorem', by de Finetti (1937) who also proved that only a DM behaving consistently with beliefs represented by a unique, additive, probability distribution may be considered rational. This has been interpreted until very recently as a conclusive impossibility theorem for hard uncertainty theories.

(ii) Savage (1954) accepted the Dutch Book theorem and added a further argument. He rightly observed that any hard uncertainty theory is bounded to introduce a second-order measure of uncertainty. He maintained that this first move would trigger an infinite regress of uncertainty measures of increasing order and suggested that this would constitute a further violation of sound logic. The great influence exerted by Savage theory on DT reinforced the conviction that any alternative to soft uncertainty theory was bound to be logically flawed.

However, SUDT was soon challenged in its descriptive power. Its prestige was so high that the counterexamples have been first presented in the form of 'paradoxes', such as the famous ones put forward by Allais (1953) and Ellsberg (1961). Then experimental research cumulated a formidable stock of evidence which has seriously undermined the faith in the descriptive power of these theories (for a summary, see Camerer and Weber, 1992). SUDT's exponents had to retreat by conceding that it is a basically normative theory whose descriptive power is bound by the limited rationality of actual agents. Symmetrically, the HUDTs came to be taken in consideration from the positive point of view as they were able to solve different 'paradoxes' or deviations from the SUDT (such as those of Allais and Ellsberg) but their normative viability has been, and still is, very controversial.

Contrary to the received view, I want to bring a few arguments in favor of the thesis that HUDT is not necessarily inconsistent with rationality, but that, on the contrary, it could take account of some aspects of a more comprehensive notion of rationality. In order to argue these theses I have first to clear the road from the impossibility arguments of Ramsay, de Finetti and Savage.

It is arguable that the Dutch book theorem is not as compelling as it was believed until recently. In fact its conclusions are based on a few premises which are now understood to be questionable. In particular, it is assumed that the DM is always prepared to bet in favor of or against a certain event at given odds, but this assumption is ungranted under hard uncertainty when the DM is adverse to second-order uncertainty and expects to learn more about the relevant probabilities (Shafer, 1976; Gärdenfors and Sahlin, 1982; Dow and Werlang, 1992b). In addition, second-order measures of uncertainty cannot be reduced to first-order measures by applying the compound-probability theorem in conditions of hard uncertainty because in this case second-order uncertainty could be partially resolved before the second-stage lottery is performed or, in any case, unforeseen contingencies could change its prospects. Finally, in this case the infinite-regress argument does not seem to have the status of a logical necessity but only of an obvious possibility whose relevance may be assessed in pragmatic terms. There are good reasons, e.g. coming from experimental evidence, for considering second-order measures, while no one found so far good reasons for considering higher-order measures. I feel allowed to conclude that the censorship on hard uncertainty decision theories may now be relieved also from the normative point of view.

## 6. Awareness of Ignorance and Rationality

I may now tentatively advance some affirmative argument in favor of the thesis that HUDTs are consistent with a more general notion of rationality. I start from the observation that the awareness of ignorance is to be considered a condition *sine qua non* of rationality. In particular, the awareness of structural ignorance implies hard uncertainty. In the case of soft uncertainty, the DM is aware of her ignorance about which event in the support of her probability distribution will actually occur but she believes that she knows for sure the systematic factors of the decision problem she faces (such as the structural parameters of the relevant probability distributions, the set of possible states and consequences as well as the functions connecting the states with the consequences). As soon as the DM becomes aware of her structural ignorance, in the sense specified above, she enters into the realm of hard uncertainty. This is a necessary condition for structural learning which seems to me a fundamental aspect of human rationality. Under soft uncertainty structural learning would be condemned to remain completely unintelligible (see Vercelli, 1996).

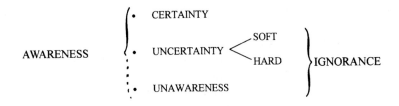

*Figure 4.* Uncertainty, ignorance, unawareness.

After the above informal introduction on the nexus between awareness and rationality, it is possible to hint at its formal treatment as recently developed by Modica and Rustichini. They contrast unawareness with certainty and uncertainty (Modica and Rustichini, 1994, p. 107):

> A subject is certain of something when he knows that thing; he is uncertain when he does not know it, but he knows he does not: he is consciously uncertain. On the other hand, he is *unaware* of something when he does not know it, and he does not know he does not know, and so on ad infinitum: he does not perceive, does not have in mind, the object of knowledge. The opposite of unawareness is awareness.

Therefore, awareness encompasses the cases of certainty and uncertainty (and, possibly, unawareness).[10] In the case of soft uncertainty the DM is aware that she does not know which state of the world will actually obtain but she knows which state of the world may obtain and she also knows the relevant probability distribution(s). In other words, the DM knows that, because of the (soft) ignorance of which she is aware, her predictions are liable to make stochastic mistakes but not systematic mistakes. In the case of hard uncertainty, the DM is aware not only that she is unable to forecast which state of the world will obtain, but also that her set of possible states may be incomplete, and that therefore she does not know the relevant distribution(s) of probability. In other words the DM knows that, because of the (hard) ignorance of which she is aware, her predictions are subject not only to stochastic mistakes but also to systematic mistakes.

The complex nexus between awareness, uncertainty and ignorance (see Figure 4) makes the process of learning much more complex than it was held to be by traditional decision theories (see Section 8).

I would like to emphasize that, in addition, the awareness of different modalities of uncertainty and of the different decision criteria associated to each of them seems consistent with a fully rational attitude of adaptation to different circumstances. Analogously, it is possible to argue that different modalities of uncertainty involve different categories of risks which are best countered by means of different policies.

## 7. Time and Rationality

In order to assess the applicability of different classes of decision theories to environmental problems a crucial, and very delicate, step concerns the possibility of extending their scope to dynamic or intertemporal problems involving in an essential way a succession of differently dated decisions. In fact environmental problems often concern long-run consequences on present and future generations. Unfortunately, it is widely recognized that orthodox decision theories are essentially static theories (see, e.g., Kreps, 1988). Their extension to intertemporal problems is strictly based on procedures which allow the telescoping of the future into the present. The basic idea is that the DM chooses at the initial point of time a complete intertemporal strategy which is contingent to the state of the world which will occur in the future periods. It is intuitive that this procedure of reduction strictly requires the assumptions which define a familiar world, and in particular a complete knowledge of the possible states which may occur in the future, i.e. that the world is closed and it will continue to be so in the future. The reduction of a temporal succession of choices to a unique first-period choice of a contingent strategy is possible only because time is assumed to by irrelevant from the structural point of view. The only role of time in intertemporal SUDT is, in consequence of the occurrence of a certain state of the world, the mechanic definition of the relevant branch of the decision tree which defines ex post the chosen contingent strategy. In other words, the only role assigned to chronological time is that of indexing ex ante the branching of the inertemporal decision tree and of defining ex post the actual realization of a stationary stochastic process whose structure is fully time-independent. We might say that, from the dynamic point of view, a familiar world is described by one or more stationary and ergodic stochastic processes which have persisted long enough for the DM to have learned its structural parameters (Lucas, 1986). Stationarity is explicitly recognized as a prerequisite for the application of the objectivist theory, otherwise the probabilities could not be derived by stable and reliable frequencies. On the contrary, most Bayesian theorists maintain that their theory is applicable to any conceivable situation; however the most rigorous representatives of this school of thought recognize that Bayesian theory is applicable only to exchangeable events, and it may be proved that this implies stationarity and ergodicity. In particular, the procedure of reduction of a sequence of decisions to a first-stage decision of a contingent strategy relies on the theorem of reduction of compound lotteries which allows to express a succession of lotteries in terms of a unique lottery which compounds the probability distributions which characterize each of them. It is intuitive that this theorem does not apply to HUDTs because in this case time is relevant from the structural point of view. Unforeseen contingencies or unforeseeable structural learning are liable to change the structure of the decision problem in a way that could not be considered, even hypothetically, ex ante. Therefore, it is impossible to define ex ante a complete intertemporal decision tree.

The fact that time is considered structurally irrelevant by SUDTs and crucially relevant by HUDTs suggests that, if it were possible to extend these theories also from the dynamic point of view, HUDTs would appear to be more general than SUDTs and this seems at first sight favorable to the acceptation of HUDTs. However, unfortunately, this generalization has proved to be very difficult and problematic so far. In particular, this generalization strictly depends upon the relaxation of the independence (or sure-thing) axiom which lies at the roots of SUDTs (see Section 3). Unfortunately, this relaxation has also the unpalatable consequence of allowing intertemporal incoherence in preferences and beliefs. According to most decision theorists this is an insurmountable obstacle for the viability of HUDTs, at least in the case of intertemporal problems and from the normative point of view. This argument has recently taken the particularly strong form of an impossibility theorem which adds itself to those already discussed in Section 6 and whose assessment is decisive for the future of HUDTs: according to Epstein and Le Breton (1993) intertemporal coherence implies the unrelaxed version of the independence axiom, which is the very hallmark of SUDTs (as well as the Bayesian rule for updating beliefs, which will be discussed in the next section). From this theorem most decision theorists draw the conclusion that HUDTs are inconsistent with (intertemporal) rationality. However, is it really this the case? Is it really plausible that in an open world characterized by unforeseen contingencies and structural learning a rational agent should not change preferences and beliefs? My own intuition suggests a negative answer: in an open world which changes its structural characteristics in an unforeseeable way a rational agent is likely to change her preferences and beliefs in order to adapt in the best possible way to the changing environment. The old (or young) people unable to update their beliefs and preferences to an increasingly changing world do not seem to provide a paradigmatic example of rationality. Of course this raises a crucial problem: not any change of preferences and beliefs can be considered rational unless we are prepared to dilute the concept of rationality in a tautological attribute of actual behavior. This problem can only be solved by defining a higher-order concept of coherence (based, e.g., on consistent procedures of revision of beliefs) and a more comprehensive concept of rationality, such as procedural or designing rationality (further considerations on these problems may be found in Vercelli, 1991, 1996). This is certainly not an easy task but a simple evasion of this crucial problem by avoiding HUDTs does not seem to be an appealing way out.

## 8. Learning

In the environmental field it is often unclear whether it is better to intervene immediately in order to avoid uncertain future damages or it is better to wait and learn more about the problem. In order to choose the best course of action, the DM should be able to assess the value of prospective learning. This raises the problem of how to model learning in decision theory. We have a clear and compelling answer only in the case of Bayesian theory: the principle of coherence of preferences and beliefs upon which Bayesian theory is built, through its intertemporal extension based on the sure-thing principle, implies the well-known procedure of Bayesian updating of beliefs:

$$p(A/B) = \frac{p(A \cap B)}{p(B)}. \tag{9}$$

This point which has always been, at least intuitively, perceived by Bayesian theorists, and which justifies the name itself given to the theory, has been recently confirmed by the theorem of Epstein and Le Breton (1993) mentioned above. Also in the case of the objectivist decision theory the modeling of the process of learning of stable frequencies can be pursued by well-known inductive methods developed by classical statistical inference theory.

On the contrary, in the case of HUDTs, how to model learning is an open problem. The application of the Bayesian rule implies a sort of intertemporal coherence which, as we have seen, is not necessarily granted in an unfamiliar world characterized by hard uncertainty. However, so far most attempts of modeling learning within a HUDT rely on generalizations of the Bayes' rule. In the case of multiple priors, two main approaches have been suggested. According to the 'convex Bayesian conditioning' rule all probability distributions must be conditioned to new information, while according to the 'maximum likelihood rule' (Gilboa and Schmeidler, 1993) Bayesian conditioning is applied only to the ex post maximum likelihood probability distribution. In the case of a nonlinear prior it has been suggested the application of the Dempster–Shafer rule (Shafer, 1976, pp. 66–67):

$$v(A/B) = \frac{v(A \cup B^c) - v(B^c)}{1 - v(B^c)}, \tag{10}$$

where $v$ is a non-necessarily additive distribution and the event $B^c$ is the complementary of $B$, i.e. $S \backslash B$. This rule was specifically designed to cope with situations described by belief functions and, therefore, characterized by hard uncertainty. However, Gilboa and Schmeidler have shown that in the case of uncertainty aversion, when the multiple prior may be reduced to a unique nonlinear convex prior, the application of the Dempster–Shafer rule to a unique nonlinear prior gives the same results than the application of the Bayesian rule to the corresponding multiple prior according to the 'maximum likelihood rule'.

We may conclude this section by observing that HUDTs still do not have a satisfactory theory of learning which is able to take account of their specificity. The rules suggested so far, being directly or indirectly founded upon the

210  *A. Vercelli*

Bayesian rule, or reducible to it, are consistent with the traditional notion of intertemporal coherence but are unable to analyze structural learning, the specific kind of learning associated with hard uncertainty.

## 9. Irreversibility and Intertemporal Flexibility

The intertemporal analysis of decisions in the face of uncertainty cannot ignore a dimension of the utmost importance for environmental economics: the degree of irreversibility which characterizes the consequences of decisions. It is irreversibility which makes uncertainty such an important issue in many fields including environmental economics. Any kind of uncertainty, even soft uncertainty, implies unavoidable ex-post mistakes even for the most rational decision maker. If these mistakes were easily remedied (promptly and at a low cost) the value of a normative theory of decision in the face of uncertainty would be invaluable for choosing the best ex-ante rule, but its practical implications would be strictly bounded. Irreversibility implies that the consequences of mistakes have a much higher value that may be virtually boundless (in the case of catastrophes) and that cannot be reliably evaluated in advance.

Unfortunately, while irreversibility greatly increases the practical importance of a normative decision theory in the face of uncertainty, it also prevents the use of SUDTs. Neither objectivist theories nor subjectivist SUDTs may be satisfactorily applied to irreversible events.

It is generally agreed that the objectivist theory put forward by Morgenstern and von Neumann (1944) applies only to stationary processes with stable frequencies. This is not very often the case in environmental economics which is characterized by irreversible structural changes. What is worse, it may be proved that whenever decision-makers believe that the economic system might be non-stationary, it becomes non-stationary even assuming that the exogenous environment is in fact stationary (Kurz, 1991b, p. 10). Stationarity is, therefore, not a very plausible assumption for the analysis of economic decisions that have to face structural change and irreversibility.

The limitations of Bayesian theory are less clear as its exponents claim that it is applicable to any kind of uncertain processes. But this claim is not really convincing. The main representatives of Bayesian theory admit that this approach may be applied only to exchangeable events, i.e. events the temporal order of occurrence of which does not affect the relevant probabilities. Events characterizing the realizations of an irreversible stochastic process cannot have the property of exchangeability,[11] because irreversibility implies, by definition, that the order of events is not random. Even the attempts to apply the Bayesian theory to learning are not fully convincing. As was rightly observed by Kurz (1993, p. 10) 'the idea that a decision maker will set out to use information in order to learn something about probabilities is intrinsically alien to Savage's vision: preferences are the primitives and probabilities emerge only as consequences'. The models of Bayesian learning developed subsequently by Bayesian statistics do not go beyond trivial conditioning, via the Bayes rule, of the information-free prior (Kurz, 1993). In addition, Bayesian learning involves unsolved problems of convergence and consistency even when observations are assumed to be i.i.d. or exchangeable (a good survey of these problems is contained in Diaconis and Freedman, 1986).

Though a fully-fledged rigorous normative decision theory in the face of uncertainty under the hypothesis of irreversibility is not currently available, there are fragments of analysis which may be used to clarify some important issues, such as that of the value of intertemporal flexibility. It may be argued that, under quite general assumptions, an increase in uncertainty determines the choice of a more rigid behavioral rule (because the DM takes account of a smaller set of possible actions), and of an action which is more intertemporally flexible in the sense that it keeps open a larger set of future options (see Vercelli, 1991, chapter 5 and literature cited therein). It is also possible, though only under more stringent conditions, to give a measure of the option value, i.e. the value of keeping an alternative available for a possible future choice (see Basili and Vercelli, 1997). Each of these measures focuses only on some particular aspect of uncertainty that affects environmental choices. For example, Chichilnisky, Beltratti and Heal give a measure of option value relative to a possible change of taste, see Chapter 3.4 of this book. However, even in the absence of any change in tastes, we would still give a positive value to options because we are also uncertain about future technologies, endowments of productive factors, consequences of our actions and the dynamics of exogenous variables. Since in each case, and for any measure suggested, the option value is generally positive (apart from some extreme assumptions) we should conclude that the existing measures sizably underestimate the actual measure of option values. This is important for environmental risk control because as soon as we take option values into account, we are induced to choose environmental policies much more concerned with the conservation of natural resources and the prevention of environmental risk.

## 10. Environmental Risk and Policy Strategies

As is well known, there are three main strategies to counter existing risks: *prevention*, or removal of the causes of risky events, *mitigation* or reduction of the probability of risk and *insurance* based on the redistribution of risk among a class of subjects (see, e.g., de Finetti and Emanuelli, 1967, p. 240). The word insurance is often used in two different senses which should not be confused. According to a broad definition, insurance encompasses the three strategies mentioned above, i.e. any action directed to counter the occurrence of risk or its effects. According to a strict definition, insurance refers only to the third strategy, i.e. to any strategy based on the redistribution of risk. To avoid confusions, not absent in the literature, the term insurance (without inverted commas) is used in this work only in the strict sense. Notice that the first two strategies may be defined as 'preventive' as they both reduce the intensity and probability of risk, while the insurance strategy may be defined as 'therapeutic' as it aims only to reduce the negative impact of bad contingencies. (On the contrary, if the insurance scheme is not well designed the intensity and probability of risk could even increase, as in the cases of adverse selection and moral hazard.)

In order to counter environmental risks both 'preventive' and 'therapeutic' policy instruments may be used, but the composition of the mix should change with the nature of the risk. Under certain conditions which will be discussed later, soft risk is properly met by 'therapeutic' instruments such as commercial insurance contracts and financial devices, while hard risk requires 'preventive' instruments, such as administrative regulation, Pigouvian taxes and subsidies, marketable permits, environmental bonds, etc. Under irreversibility, 'therapeutic' instruments may be insufficient even when risk is soft: in the case, say, of a 'Russian roulette', the risk is perfectly known but only prevention is effective. Unfortunately, many environmental problems are characterized by both irreversibility and hard uncertainty.

In any case the choice of the policy instruments best suited to control environmental risks must take into account the degree of irreversibility and the modality of uncertainty which characterize the problem faced. In order to illustrate this point I am going to discuss very briefly some of the advantages and disadvantages of the main policy instruments of environmental risk control in the light of the distinction between different modalities of uncertainty.

The traditional therapeutic system of risk control, commercial insurance, in principle also applies to environmental risks; however in this case, their applicability is rather limited. First, very often risks are collective as they depend on the quality and quantity of global commons, such as air, water, biodiversity, etc. In addition, very often environmental risks are hard risks and imply irreversibility (even in a strong 'physical' sense). The scope of insurance techniques may be somewhat extended by combining them with financial techniques. In a general equilibrium framework collective risks dependent on exogenous uncertainty may be 'insured' through 'Arrow securities'.[12] In the same framework, we can also 'insure' unknown risks by combining insurance contracts for individual risks and Arrow securities for collective risks (Chichilnisky and Heal, 1992). However, these devices do not apply to endogenous uncertainty.[13] In this case there is no way to complete the markets in an Arrow–Debreu framework (Chichilnisky, 1992; Hahn, 1992). Chichilnisky et al. (1992) show that in regular economies the introduction of successive levels of derivative securities is able to remove all the endogenous uncertainty in a finite number of steps and lead to a unique fully-insured and risk-free Pareto-efficient allocation. This is possible even when the agents do not know the set of possible equilibria but expect that one equilibrium will be selected randomly according to a probability distribution (Chichilnisky et al., 1992, p. 5). In general, however, risk control policies based on the general equilibrium framework are inconsistent with irreversibility. We, therefore, cannot rely exclusively on the therapeutic instruments to counter environmental risk. The more risk is irreducible to soft risks and irreversibility is compelling, the less we can rely on therapeutic instruments and the more we have to turn to preventive instruments. In Chapter 1.2 Chichilnisky and Heal suggest how therapeutic instruments can act as preventives.

A traditional preventive instrument is legal liability for damages caused to the environment. At first sight, this instrument could appear therapeutic as it imposes an ex-post payment on the victims. However, the imposition of such a liability is an incentive to avoid pollution and thus reduces the intensity and probability of risks, see Chapter 1.2. A recent case is that of Exxon–Valdez: Exxon agreed to pay about $900 million dollars over a period of several years. Whether or not this huge sum underestimates the actual damage to the Alaskan ecosystem, it is likely to be quite effective in avoiding this sort of pollution in the future. Legal liability can, in principle, fully internalize environmental externalities, as Pigouvian taxes do, apart from one fundamental feature: according to a sort of 'moral hazard' argument, payments to victims may reduce the defensive activity of potential victims (see, e.g., Cropper and Oates, 1992). In addition, the high costs and long delays of prosecution procedures, uncertainty about legal interpretation, discovery and proof of actual responsibility, make this instrument rather inefficient in its preventive role (the evidence confirms that the actual implementation of this instrument has worked rather imperfectly: see, e.g., Segerson, 1990).

Environmental taxes and subsidies are the classic preventive instruments advocated by economists since Pigou. In a competitive market model a well designed system of taxes or subsidies is deemed sufficient to permit a single-period optimal allocation of resources, notwithstanding the existence of externalities (see, e.g., Baumol and Oates, 1988, chapter 4). However, it is now clear that these two policy instruments have different implications in the long run, taking account of the entry-exit decisions of firms (Baumol and Oates, 1988, chapter 14). Taxes reduce profits and shift the supply curve to the left, reducing the size of industry; subsidies increase profits and shift the supply curve to the right, increasing the size of industry. All in all, in the case of subsidies the total amount of pollution decreases less than in the case of taxes and could even increase; moreover, subsidies worsen the budget. Despite this, they may still play a role as part of a mix of instruments.

On the contrary, in a world characterized by perfect foresight, marketable permits are considered a fully equivalent alternative to Pigouvian taxes. However, this equivalence breaks down under uncertainty and their comparative efficiency depends on the relative steepness of the marginal benefit and cost curves. If the marginal benefit curve has a greater absolute slope than the marginal cost curve, the social welfare is, so-to-say, more sensitive to quantity mistakes than to price mistakes; in this case, the regulator should therefore choose the marketable permits approach as it is a better guarantee of quantity targets, and vice versa (Weitzman, 1974). More generally, the main advantage of the marketable permit approach is that it focuses directly on the attainment of certain environmental standards, leaving to the market the burden of choosing the right prices and of adjusting them to different conditions produced by inflation, change in relative prices, etc. In the case of the Pigouvian taxes, on the contrary, the authority is bound to adjust the fees to assure that the environmental standard is attained, and continues to do so in changing conditions. This may imply high costs of monitoring and control and frequent unpopular revisions of fees. The main disadvantage of the marketable permits approach is that its effectiveness depends on the development of an efficient market in permits. This makes it particularly difficult to introduce this sort of instrument wherever it is still absent (as in Europe and Japan).

Notwithstanding the many unsolved problems raised by the actual use of economic instruments in a world of imperfect information, they have the important advantage of economizing on information gathering and monitoring, and on control costs. The empirical evidence suggests that the costs involved in the existing command-and-control regulatory programs are very high and often exceed several times the lowest cost levels attainable with economic instruments (Tietenberg, 1985, chapter 3).

In addition, many of the problems raised by the use of economic instruments may be solved by a suitable mix of instruments. Particularly promising is the set of deposit-refunds schemes. Any of these schemes is a sort of 'package of policy instruments with two components: (1) taxes (deposits) on certain kinds of transactions, such as purchases of particular commodities, and (2) subsidies (refunds) for particular forms of behavior with respect to consequences of the initial transactions' (Bohm, 1981, p. xiii). The best known example is the deposit on beverage containers connected with a refund if the containers are returned. However the deposit/refund scheme has a wide range of potential applications of which only some have actually been put into practice (for a survey, see Bohm, 1981). Deposit/refund systems applied to environmental targets are often called environmental bonds (Perrings, 1987, 1989; Costanza and Perrings, 1990). Their potential range of application is very wide:
- to prevent litter of containers, discarded autos, tires, etc., to prevent pollution from mercury cells, nickel-cadmium batteries, waste lubrication oil, or to encourage restoration of production, storage and dump sites after shut down, etc.;
- to encourage recycling of metals, paper, glass, lubrication oil, or to encourage efficiency in waste management by separating chemicals and toxic substances that would otherwise result in high treatment costs;

— to protect against unknown risk of pollution or waste of scarce resources when new products are launched on the market.

Environmental bonds may provide sizable incentives to prevent the occurrence of negative contingencies, and to introduce innovations favorable to the environment, particularly in cases of hard uncertainty, but many problems concerning their systematic implementation are still unsolved (see Torsello and Vercelli, 1997).

## 11. Concluding Remarks

Environmental uncertainty often cannot be reduced to soft uncertainty, i.e. to the kind of uncertainty which traditional decision theories are able to deal with. This does not imply that hard uncertainty, including that characterizing environmental problems, cannot be analyzed, at least partly, in precise scientific terms. The recent contributions briefly surveyed in this paper give promising hints in this direction.

The existing fragments of a decision theory under hard uncertainty have important implications for the choice of the optimal instruments of environmental risk control. In particular, we have seen that therapeutic instruments, such as traditional insurance and financial instruments, are insufficient. We have to turn to preventive instruments which must be evaluated according to the efficacy of the incentives induced in order to avoid the occurrence of negative contingencies. Command-and-control techniques are often inefficient and seem justified only when there is a sizable chance of catastrophic consequences in the short or medium period. Under hard uncertainty, preventive economic instruments should be chosen in such a way as to minimize the probability of unknown, or not well-known, risks. Taxes are preferable to subsidies because of their long-term preventive effects. The choice between taxes and marketable permits is more problematic, as it depends on the shape of the marginal benefit and marginal cost curves. Under hard uncertainty, marketable permits are preferable, ceteris paribus, whenever the attainment of a quantitative standard is important and enforceable; taxes are preferable when the main target is a change in the structure of relative prices in order to stimulate substitution and technical change. However, under hard uncertainty, the most promising approach to environmental risk control seems to involve the use of mixed instruments. In particular, deposit/refund schemes, such as environmental bonds seem able to combine the preventive efficiency of taxes and subsidies with fewer disadvantages than each of them taken separately.

In choosing the most appropriate set of risk control instruments for a given situation, it should be borne in mind that irreversibility and hard uncertainty determine a sizable intertemporal option value which encourages environmental conservation (see Basili and Vercelli, 1994, 1997). An appropriate measure of intertemporal option values is important in order to choose the best policy instruments.

## Notes

1. The distinction between 'soft' and 'hard' uncertainty is introduced in this paper in order to distinguish two basic modalities of uncertainty. Uncertainty is called 'soft' whenever the beliefs of the decision maker may be expressed by a unique, fully reliable, additive probability distribution; uncertainty is called 'hard' whenever the beliefs of the decision maker can be expressed only through a non-additive probability distribution or through a plurality of probability distributions, none of which is fully reliable (see Section 3).
2. This opinion has been recently expressed by many decision theorists (see, e.g., Machina, 1987, p. 149).
3. I warn the reader that such a representation is not fully rigorous. The distinction between known and unknown probabilities suggests a discontinuity between two situations described by two pointwise measures (in the extreme paradigmatic case designating zero and infinite second-order uncertainty); however, it is generally admitted that the two theories can be applied to situations sufficiently close to the paradigmatic case: this authorizes a 'heuristic' representation such as that of Figure 1 even in the absence of a continuous second-order measure of uncertainty (though we will see in the next section that it is possible to define a measure of this kind).
4. The trouble with this measure is that it is unable to separate the rational component (awareness of structural ignorance) from the psychological component (optimism or pessimism). A way to separate the two components is suggested by Ghirardato (1994), while a more general measure of uncertainty aversion is suggested by Montesano (1993).
5. Notwithstanding a certain terminological kinship, a 'familiar world' should not be confused with a 'small world' in the sense of Savage. He is aware that in the real world states and consequences must necessarily be described at some limited level of detail so that his DT can work only with regard to a 'small world' (as opposed to a 'grand world' which describes the world in a complete and fully detailed way). In this sense a familiar world is certainly a small world, but the vice versa is not necessarily true. Indeed the 'problem of small worlds' as discussed by Savage is completely different from the 'problem of familiar worlds' as discussed in this work. The trouble with a small world according to Savage is that a subjective expected utility analysis of a decision problem may give different results in different small worlds which may be in their turn different from the results we would get in a 'grand world'. In other words, through the problem of small worlds the problem of which is the 'true' representation' of the decision problem expelled from the main door in the Bayesian approach comes back from the window. The concept of 'familiar world', on the contrary, is meant to make explicit the intrinsic limits of applications of Bayesian DT, i.e. the limits which derive directly from the axioms of the theory. An insightful discussion of the problem of small worlds is provided by Shafer (1988).
6. An exception are the works by Chateauneuf et al. (1992a, 1992b) which apply superadditive capacities in order to interpret a few anomalies observed in the behavior of investors in financial markets.
7. Two acts $A$ and $B$ are comonotone if it never happens that $A(s) \succ A(t)$ and $B(t) \succ B(s)$ for states of nature $s$ and $t$, where '$\succ$' means 'is strictly preferred to'.
8. Gilboa and Schmeidler (1994) claim that this theory may be conveniently applied also to roulette-wheel problems giving a possible explanation of the genesis of rule-based behavior. However, in this case the probability distribution may be considered given so that SUDTs may be successfully applied.
9. Of course, by taking account of the equivalence discussed above (Section 3) between a subadditive capacity distribution and a convex set of additive probability distributions, the decision criterion for hard uncertainty may be rephrased in terms of multiple priors. The smaller the number of probability distributions, the more the decision criterion resembles the Max EU collapsing into it when just one probability distribution is retained; the higher the number of probability distributions, the more the decision criterion resembles the

Maximin collapsing into it when the convex set comprises all conceivable probability distributions.
10. The DM could be aware of not being aware of possible contingencies. However, a formal characterization of 'awareness of unawareness' is still lacking.
11. Exchangeable events are events that occur in a random sequence, such that the order of their occurrence does not affect the probabilities we are interested in. The most profound Bayesian theorists recognize that this is the fundamental notion on which Bayesian theory rests. According to Kyburg and Smokler (1963, p. 12) 'until this notion was introduced by de Finetti in 1931, the subjectivist theory of probability remained pretty much of a philosophical curiosity ... with the introduction of the concept of ... exchangeability ... a way was discovered to connect the notion of subjective probability with the classical procedures of statistical inference'. Kreps regards de Finetti's theorem as the 'fundamental theorem of (most) statistics' (1988, p. 159), as it justifies from a subjectivist point of view the usual assumption of statistical induction that the samples are 'independent and identically distributed with unknown distribution function'. Notice that it may be shown that the conditions for exchangeability are practically the same as those for ergodicity.
12. 'Arrow securities' are securities payable in money, the amount depending on the state which has actually occurred (Arrow, 1970, p. 124). As Arrow maintains, 'when the state s occurs, the money transfers determined by the securities take place, and then the allocation of commodities takes place through the market in the ordinary way, without further risk-bearing.' (Arrow, 1970, p. 124).
13. Endogenous uncertainty depends on the behavior of economic agents. Its importance for economic analysis was first stressed by Kurz (1974).

## References

1. Allais, M. (1953). "Le comportement de l'homme rationnel devant le risque: Critique des postulats et axiomes de l'école americaine", *Econometrica* 21, 503–546.
2. Anscombe, F. J. and R. Aumann (1963). "A Definition of Subjective Probability", *Annals of Mathematical Statistics* 34, 199–205.
3. Arrow, K. (1970). *Essays in the Theory of Risk Bearing*, Amsterdam, North-Holland.
4. Arrow, K. J. and L. Hurwicz (1972). "Optimality Criterion for Decision-Making under Ignorance", in *Uncertainty and Expectations in Economics*, C. F. Carter and J. L. Ford (eds.), Oxford, Basil Blackwell, pp. 1–11.
5. Barret, C. R. and P. K. Pattanaik (1986). "Decision Making under Complete Uncertainty: The Ordinal Framework", in *Uncertainty in Economic Life*, S. Sen (ed.), Elgar, Aldershot, U.K.
6. Basili, M. and A. Vercelli (1994). "Option Value and Environment: A Survey", Working Paper F.E.E.M., Milano.
7. Basili, M. and A. Vercelli (1997). "Environmental Option Values: Uncertainty Aversion and Learning", this volume.
8. Baumol, W. J. and W. E. Oates (1988). *The Theory of Environmental Policy*, Second Edition, Cambridge, Cambridge University Press.
9. Bell, D. E., H. Raiffa and A. Tversky (eds.) (1988). *Decision Making: Descriptive, Normative and Prescriptive Interactions*, Cambridge, Cambridge University Press.
10. Beltratti, A., G. Chichilnisky and G. Heal (1992). "Option and Non-Use Values of Environmental Assets", manuscript.
11. Bewley, T. F. (1986). "Knightian Decision Theory: Part I", Cowles Foundation Discussion Paper No. 807, New Haven, CT.
12. Billot, A. (1992). "From Fuzzy Set Theory to Non-Additive Probabilities: How Have Economists Reacted?", *Fuzzy Sets and Systems* 49, 75–90.

13. Binmore, K. G. (1986). "Remodeled Rational Players", Discussion Paper, London School of Economics, London.
14. Bohm, P. (1981). *Deposit-Refund Systems: Theory and Applications to Environmental, Conservation, and Consumer Policy*", Washington, DC, Johns Hopkins University Press for Resources for the Future.
15. Camerer, C. and M. Weber (1992). "Recent Developments in Modeling Preferences: Uncertainty and Ambiguity", *Journal of Risk and Uncertainty* 5, 325–370.
16. Chateauneuf, A. and J. Y. Jaffray (1989). "Some Characterizations of Lower Probabilities and Other Monotone Capacities through the Use of Möbius Inversion", *Math. Social Sciences* 17, 263–283.
17. Chateauneuf, A., R. Kast and A. Lapied (1992a). "Choquet Pricing for Financial Markets with Frictions", mimeo.
18. Chateauneuf, A., R. Kast and A. Lapied (1992b). "Pricing in Slack Markets", Document de Travail GREQE, No. 92A05.
19. Chichilnisky, G. (1992). "Layers of Uncertainty and Price Risks", Discussion Paper, Columbia University, forthcoming in *Market Risks*, Springer-Verlag.
20. Chichilnisky, G. and G. Heal (1992). "Financial Markets for Unknown Risks", Chapter 3.5 of this book.
21. Chichilnisky, G., J. Dutta and G. M. Heal (1992). "Price Uncertainty and Derivative Securities in a General Equilibrium Model", manuscript, forthcoming in *Market Risks*, Springer-Verlag.
22. Chichilnisky, G. (1996). "Markets with Endogenous Uncertainty; Theory and Policy". *Theory and Decision* 41, 99–131.
23. Chichilnisky, G. and G. M. Heal (1997). "Managing Unknown Risks: The Future of Global Reinsurance". *Journal of Portfolio Management* Spring 1998.
24. Choquet, G. (1955). "Theory of Capacities", *Annales Institut Fourier* 5, 131–295.
25. Costanza, R. (1991). "Assuring Sustainability of Ecological Economic Systems", in *Ecological Economics*, R. Costanza (ed.), New York, Columbia University Press.
26. Costanza, R. and C. Perrings (1990). "A Flexible Assurance Bonding System for Improved Environmental Management", *Ecological Economics* 3, 231–245.
27. Cropper, M. L. and W. E. Oates (1992). "Environmental Economics: A Survey", *Journal of Economic Literature* 30(2), 675–740.
28. De Finetti, B. (1937). "La Prévision: Ses Lois Logiques, Ses Sources Subjectives", *Annales de l'Institute Henry Poincaré* 7, 1–68. English translation: "Foresight: Its Logical Laws, Its Subjective Sources", in *Studies in Subjective Probability* H. E. Kyburg and H. E. Smokler (eds.), New York, Wiley and Sons, 1964, pp. 93–158.
29. De Finetti, B. and F. Emanuelli (1967). *Economia delle Assicurazioni*, Torino, Utet.
30. Dempster, A. P. (1967). "Upper and Lower Probabilities Induced by a Multivalued Mapping", *Ann. Math. Statist.* 38, 325–339.
31. Diaconis, P. and D. Freedman (1986). "On the Consistency of Bayes Estimates", *The Annals of Statistics* 14(1), 1–26.
32. Dow, J. and S. R. C. Werlang (1992a). "Excess Volatility of Stock Prices and Knightian Uncertainty", *European Economic Review* 36, 631–638.
33. Dow, J. and S. R. C. Werlang (1992b). "Uncertainty Aversion, Risk Aversion, and the Optimal Choice of Portfolio", *Econometrica* 60, 197–204.
34. Dow, J. and S. R. C. Werlang (1992c). "The Ex-Ante Non-Optimality of the Dempster–Shafer Rule for Ambiguous Beliefs", EPGE-Fundacao Getulio Vagas, Working Paper No. 185.
35. Dubois, D. (1980). "Un économiste précurseur de la théorie des possibilités: G. L. S. Shackle", *BUSEFAL* 2, 70–73.
36. Ellsberg, D. (1961). "Risk, Ambiguity, and the Savage Axioms", *Quarterly Journal of Economics* 75, 643–669.

37. Epstein, L. and M. Le Breton (1993). "Dynamically Consistent Beliefs Must Be Bayesian", *Journal of Economic Theory* 61, 1–22.
38. Farber, S. (1991). "Regulatory Schemes and Self-Protective Environmental Risk Control: A Comparison of Insurance Liability and Deposit-Refund Systems", *Ecological Economics* 3, 231–245.
39. Feynman, R. P. (ed.) (1963). *The Feynman Lectures on Physics*, Vol. 1, pp. 643–669.
40. Fishburn, P. C. (1984). "Comment on the Kannai–Peleg Impossibility Theorem for Extending Orders", *Journal of Economic Theory* 32, 176–179.
41. Fishburn, P. C. (1988). *Nonlinar Preferences and Utility Theory*, Baltimore, Johns Hopkins University Press.
42. Freedman, D. A. and R. A. Purves (1969). "Bayes' Method for Bookies", *Annals of Mathematical Statistics* 40, 1177–1186.
43. Gärdenfors, P. and N.-E. Sahlin (1982). "Unreliable Probabilities, Risk Taking, and Decision Making", *Synthèse* 53, 361–386.
44. Ghirardato, P. (1994). "Coping with Ignorance: Unforeseen Contingencies and Non-Additive Uncertainty", Discussion Paper, Department of Economics, Berkeley.
45. Gilboa, I. (1987). "Expected Utility with Purely Subjective Non-Additive Probabilities", *Journal of Mathematical Economics* 16(1), 65–88.
46. Gilboa, I. (1989). "Additivizations of Nonadditive Measures", *Mathematics of Operation Research* 4, 1–17.
47. Gilboa, I. and D. Schmeidler (1989). "Maximin Expected Utility with a Non-Unique Prior", *Journal of Mathematical Economics* 18, 141–153.
48. Gilboa, I. and D. Schmeidler (1993). "Updating Ambiguous Beliefs", *Journal of Economic Theory* 59, 33–49.
49. Gilboa, I. and D. Schmeidler (1994). "Case-Based Decision Theory", mimeo.
50. Hahn, F. (1992). "A Remark on Incomplete Market Equilibrium', Working Paper.
51. Hart, A. G. (1942). "Risk, Uncertainty, and the Unprofitability of Compounding Probabilities", in *Studies in Mathematical Economics and Econometrics*, O. Lange, F. McIntyre and T. O. Yntema (eds.), Chicago, Chicago University Press.
52. Heal, G. (1991). "Risk Management and Global Change", Paper presented at the First Nordic Conference on the Greenhouse Effect in Copenhagen, September, 1991.
53. Jones, R. and J. Ostroy (1984). "Flexibility and Uncertainty", *Review of Economic Studies* 51, 13–32.
54. Kelsey, D. and J. Quiggin (1992). "Theories of Choice under Ignorance and Uncertainty", *Journal of Economic Surveys* 6(2), 133–153.
55. Keynes, J.M. (1921). *A Treatise on Probability*, London, Macmillan.
56. Knight, F. (1921). *Risk, Uncertainty and Profit*, New York, Houghton Mifflin.
57. Kreps, D. M. (1988). *Notes on the Theory of Choice*, Boulder, CO, Westview Press.
58. Kreps, D. M. (1992). "Static Choice in the Presence of Unforeseen Contingencies", in *Economic Analysis of Markets and Games*, P. Dasgupta, D. Gale, O. Hart and E. Maskin (eds.), Cambridge, MA, MIT Press, pp. 258–281.
59. Kurz, M. (1974). "The Kesten–Stigum Model and the Treatment of Uncertainty in Equilibrium Theory", in *Essays in Economic Behaviour Under Uncertainty*, M. C. Balch, D. M. McFadden and S. Wu (eds.), Amsterdam, North-Holland.
60. Kurz, M. (1991a). "On Rational Belief Equilibria", Discussion Paper, Stanford University, CA.
61. Kurz, M. (1991b). "On the Structure and Diversity of Rational Beliefs", Discussion Paper, Stanford University, CA.
62. Kurz, M. (1993). "Rational Preferences and Rational Beliefs", manuscript.
63. Kyburg, H. E., Jr. and H. E. Smokler (eds.) (1964). *Studies in Subjective Probability*, New York, Wiley and Sons.

64. Lucas, R. E. (1986). "Adaptive Behavior and Economic Theory", *Journal of Business* 59 (Supplement), 5401–5426.
65. Luce, R. D. and H. Raiffa (1957). *Games and Decisions. Introduction and Critical Survey*, London, Wiley.
66. Machina, M. J. (1982). "'Expected Utility' Analysis without the Independence Axiom", *Econometrica* 50(2), 277–323.
67. Machina, M. J. (1987). "Choice under Uncertainty: Problems Solved and Unsolved, *Economic Perspectives* 1, 121–154.
68. Machina, M. J. and D. Schmeidler (1992). "A More Robust Definition of Subjective Probability", *Econometrica* 60(4), 745–780.
69. Modica, A. and A. Rustichini (1994). "Awareness and Partitional Information Structures", *Theory and Decision* 37, 107–124.
70. Montesano, A. (1991). "Measures of Risk Aversion with Expected and Nonexpected Utility", *Journal of Risk and Uncertainty* 4, 271–283.
71. Montesano, A. (1993). "Non-Additive Probabilities and the Measure of Uncertainty and Risk Aversion", mimeo.
72. Morgenstern, O. and J. von Neumann (1944). *Theory of Games and Economic Behaviour*, Princeton, NJ, Princeton University Press.
73. Perrings, C. (1987). *Economy and Environment*, Cambridge, Cambridge University Press.
74. Perrings, C. (1989). "Environmental Bonds and Environmental Research in Innovative Activity", *Ecological Economics* 1, 95–110.
75. Quiggin, J. (1982). "A Theory of Anticipated Utility", *Journal of Economic Behavior and Organization* 3(4), 323–343.
76. Ramsey, F. P. (1988). "Truth and Probability", in *Decision, Probability and Utility: Selected Readings*, P. Gärdenfors and N.-E. Sahlin (eds.), Cambridge, Cambridge University Press, pp. 19–47.
77. Runde, J. (1994). "Keynes after Ramsay: In Defense of *A Treatise on Probability*", *Studies in History and Philosophy of Science* 25(1), 97–121.
78. Runde, J. (1996). "Chances and Choices. Notes on Probability and Belief in Economic Theory", in *The Metaphysics of Economics*, U. Maki (ed.), Cambridge, Cambridge University Press (forthcoming).
79. Sarin, R. and P. Wakker (1992). "A Simple Axiomatization of Nonadditive Expected Utility", *Econometrica* 60, 1255–1272.
80. Savage, L. J. (1954). *The Foundations of Statistics*, New York, John Wiley and Sons. Revised and enlarged edition, Dover, New York, 1972.
81. Schmeidler, D. (1982). "Subjective Probability without Additivity", Working Paper, Foerder Institute for Economic Research, Tel Aviv University.
82. Schmeidler, D. (1986). "Integral Representation without Additivity", *Proceedings of the American Mathematical Society* 97(2), 255–261.
83. Schmeidler, D. (1989). "Subjective Probability and Expected Utility without Additivity", *Econometrica* 57, 571–587.
84. Segal, U. (1987). "The Ellsberg Paradox and Risk Aversion: An Anticipated Utility Approach", *International Economic Review* 28(1), 175–202.
85. Segerson, K. (1990). "'Institutional Markets': The Role of Liability in Allocating Environmental Resources", in *Proceedings of the AERE Workshop on Natural Resource Market Mechanisms*, Association of Environmental and Resource Economists.
86. Shackle, G. L. S. (1952). *Expectations in Economics*, Cambridge, Cambridge University Press.
87. Shafer, G. (1976). *A Mathematical Theory of Evidence*, Princeton, NJ, Princeton University Press.

88. Shafer, G. (1978). "Non-Additive Probabilities in the Works of Bernoulli and Lambert", *Arch. Hist. Exact. Sci.* 19, 309–370.
89. Shafer, G. (1988). "Savage Revisited", in *Decision Making: Descriptive, Normative and Prescriptive Interactions*, D. F. Bell, H. Raiffa and A. Tversky (eds.), Cambridge, Cambridge University Press, pp. 193–234.
90. Smets, P. (1990). "The Combination of Evidence in the Transferable Belief Model", *IEEE Transactions on Pattern Analysis and Machine Intelligence* 12, 447–458.
91. Tietenberg, T. H. (1985). *Emissions Trading: An Exercise in Reforming Pollution Policy*, Washington DC, Resources for the Future.
92. Torsello, L. and A. Vercelli (1993). "The Environmental Bonds: A Critical Assessment", Working Paper F.E.E.M., Milano.
93. Vercelli, A. (1991). *Methodological Foundations of Macroeconomics. Keynes and Lucas*, Cambridge, Cambridge University Press.
94. Vercelli, A. (1995). "From Soft Uncertainty to Hard Environmental Uncertainty", *Economie Appliquée* 48, 251–269.
95. Vercelli, A. (1996). "Uncertainty, Rationality and Learning: A Keynesian Perspective", mimeo.
96. Wakker, P. (1990). "A Behavioural Foundation for Fuzzy Measures", *Fuzzy Sets and Systems* 37, 327–350.
97. Weitzman, M. (1974). "Prices vs Quantities", *Review of Economic Studies* 41(4), 477–491.
98. Yaari, M. (1987). "The Dual Theory of Choice under Risk", *Econometrica* 55(1), 95–115.
99. Zadeh, L. A. (1965). "Fuzzy Sets", *Information and Control* 8, 338–353.
100. Zadeh, L.A. (1978). "Fuzzy Sets as a Basis for a Theory of Possibility", *Fuzzy Sets and Systems* 1, 3–28.

MARCELO BASILI AND ALESSANDRO VERCELLI

# 3.2. Environmental Option Values, Uncertainty Aversion and Learning*

## 1. Introduction

The concept of option value, originated in finance, has long since found interesting applications in environmental economics. Environmental goods may be considered as (at least in part) irreplaceable assets, the preservation of which has an option value as it leaves open options of consumption (as in the case of a park) and production (as in the case of medicinal plants). The option value of environmental goods is a function of their perceived degree of substitutibility by alternative goods, which in turn may change in time with change of tastes, knowledge concerning their current and potential uses, and availability of new goods.

A reliable measurement of the magnitudes of relevant option values would be invaluable for environmental policy because the costs and benefits of decisions having an environmental impact would be heavily distorted without considering them. However, the models worked out in order to give a quantitative characterization of option values often give different results, also because they are focused on different aspects of option value. In particular, they show that environmental option values basically depend on two different causes: a psychological attitude of aversion towards risk and uncertainty, and the prospects of learning about the potential benefits of options.

The environmental literature has clearly distinguished between the (plain) option value which depends on risk aversion and the so-called 'quasi-option value' which is independent of risk aversion and depends on the prospects of learning within an intertemporal decision problem characterized by a certain degree of irreversibility of some of the available choices (Arrow and Fisher, 1974). It has also been noticed that different degrees of perceived uncertainty generally affect the magnitude of option values, while the influence of

---

* Though this paper was jointly written by the authors, Marcello Basili takes responsibility for Section 3, and Alessandro Vercelli for the rest of the paper.

different modalities of uncertainty on them has been almost completely overlooked. In this paper we intend to emphasise the importance of this neglected influence and we begin to examine some of its implications. In order to do so, we have to distinguish four concepts of environmental option value, which taken together give the magnitude of the global value of a certain option.

The structure of this work is very simple. After a brief critical survey of the literature (Section 2) we proceed to distinguish and define four basic concepts of environmental option value hinting at some of their properties and at some of their implications for environmental policy (Section 3). The concluding remarks summarize the main findings of the paper.

## 2. A Taxonomy of Option Values[1]

The economic aspects of environmental conservation under uncertainty have recently been studied in terms of option values and quasi-option values. Weisbrod (1964) was the first to relate environmental conservation to option value. Considering, for example, the possible closure of a national park, he argued that many people would be willing to pay a significant sum of money to preserve the option of visiting the park in the future. Under uncertainty and risk aversion, it is generally rational to keep open an option which could turn out to be useful in the future. The concept of option value Weisbrod has in mind is the standard concept of option value based on risk aversion. In addition, the greater is the degree of risk aversion, the higher is the value attached to the conservation of existing options.

A few years later, Arrow and Fisher (1974) and Henry (1974a, 1974b) independently pointed out that under uncertainty, when a given decision may (at least in part) have irreversible effects and learning is possible before future decisions have to be made, it is generally valuable to keep open an option, even in the case of risk neutrality. Arrow and Fisher called 'quasi-option value' the extra value attached to the preservation of an option in order to stress the crucial role played in this case by irreversibility and learning (neglected in the preceding analysis of option value), and stressed its independence of risk aversion. The theory of environmental quasi-option values is of quite general applicability to problems of environmental conservation under uncertainty, since it is relevant whenever there are at least two options the consequences of which have different degrees of irreversibility (perfect temporal symmetry would obviously be an extreme case), and whenever learning is possible before future choices have to be made (the impossibility of learning would be a very extreme hypothesis).

In order to avoid confusion, not absent in the literature even after the above mentioned contributions, we have to distinguish sharply between the two different concepts of option value. Although all of them refer to rational behaviour under conditions of uncertainty and assume different degrees of reversibility of the consequences of available choices, the conceptual differences are quite radical.

The (plain) option value depends exclusively on 'risk' aversion. Though 'risk' refers to possible unfavourable events which may occur in the future, the (plain) option value is an essentially static concept since time is altogether irrelevant for determining its magnitude. On the contrary, the intertemporal option value (or 'quasi-option value') is independent of risk aversion and it depends exclusively upon factors which are strictly related to time, such as the degree of time irreversibility of the consequences of choices, and the prospects of learning between successive decisions. This second concept of option value is defined as intertemporal because, unlike in the first case, the intertemporal decision problem cannot be reduced to the choice of the optimal contingent strategy in the first period. In this second case, possibility of learning before a subsequent choice is to be made is the crucial factor.

The (plain) option value is a sort of 'risk premium' the value of which is mainly precautionary and related to different adjustment costs (e.g., transaction costs). On the contrary, the value of an intertemporal option is mainly strategic and reveals a preference for intertemporal flexibility which is related to the reversal costs of a given strategy and is the higher the larger the choice set available for the future.[2]

The main results of the contributions of Arrow and Fisher (1974) and Henry (1974a, 1974b) were the following:
(a) the sign of the intertemporal option (or 'quasi-option') value is positive under quite general assumptions;
(b) an increase in the perceived degree of 'risk' induces an increase in the intertemporal option value and, therefore, encourages environmental conservation.

Both these conclusions were challenged in the ensuing debate. The debate on the importance and the sign of the quasi-option value clarified the dependence of the intertemporal option value on the shape of the benefit function and on different degrees of uncertainty.

As for the sign of intertemporal option value, Schmalensee (1972) and Bohm (1975) claimed that the sign of the option value is undetermined as it depends on the particular shape of the utility function. Plummer and Hartmann (1986) found an undetermined sign when uncertainty is related to a change of preference, but were able to prove that when uncertainty is relative to the quality of an environmental good, the sign of option value is generally positive. As soon as we consider irreversibility, neglected by the preceding models, a positive quasi-option value becomes likely (Smith, 1983). However, also in this case, it has been maintained (notably by Freeman, 1984) that the sign of quasi-option value need not be positive. On the contrary, Fisher and Hanemann (1987, p. 189) proved that if information about future benefits and costs of development is independent of the current development decisions, the quasi-option value of preservation must be positive. Contrary assertions are based on the confusion of the quasi-option value with the net benefits of preservation which need not be positive.

As for the effects of an increase in uncertainty on the intertemporal option value, Arrow and Fisher (1974) and Henry (1974a, 1974b) proved that, generally speaking, an increase in 'risk' tends to increase the intertemporal option value, inducing a more conservationist environmental policy. However, this statement is quite sensitive to different assumptions on the nature of prospective information and viable learning processes. Generally speaking, the more it is possible to learn in subsequent periods, the more it is rational to increase intertemporal flexibility, which allows the exploitation of expected learning (Epstein, 1980). However, if prospective learning depends on the choice made in the first period, the above conclusions may be altered (Viscusi and Zeckauser, 1976). If uncertainty refers to the benefits of development, learning might depend on the effective implementation of the development project, so that the desirability of a policy of environmental conservation would be weakened. If uncertainty refers to the conservation benefits, learning is fostered by a conservaton policy. In addition, when information is dependent on development, a very slow and cautious process of development could be sufficient to make learning possible (Fisher and Hanemann, 1987, p. 190).

It is important to stress that both plain option value and quasi-option value, as defined in the literature, refer to rational behaviour under *soft uncertainty*.[3] This is altogether clear in the case of (plain) option value, where uncertain beliefs are invariably represented by a unique, fully reliable, additive probability distribution. This is less clear in the case of quasi-option value where the crucial role played by time irreversibility and learning often invites a verbal description which goes beyond soft uncertainty and evokes what we call *hard uncertainty* (Fisher and Hanemann, 1987); however, the formal treatment of quasi-option value always assumes that the probability of future structural changes (such as a change in tastes) may be represented by a known additive probability distribution, which implies also in this case soft uncertainty. Unfortunately, notwithstanding some sparse hints (Keynes, 1936; Jones and Ostroy, 1984; Vercelli, 1991), a satisfactory theory of option values under hard uncertainty has not yet been developed (see Section 3 for a first step in this direction). As in the case of soft uncertainty considered in the literature, when uncertainty is hard we have to distinguish between an option value which depends on (hard) uncertainty aversion,[4] from now on called the *h-option value*, and an intertemporal option value which depends on prospective learning, from now on called the *intertemporal h-option value* (see Table 1).

As soon as we assume uncertainty aversion, an increase in uncertainty generally increases the intertemporal option values (Caballero, 1991). In addition, given a certain degree of uncertainty aversion, the intertemporal h-option values are sensitive to the extent and to the characteristics of expected learning which depends not only on the amount of missing information, but also on the actual viability and timing of learning and its dependence on

TABLE 1

Taxonomy of option values.

|  | 'Risk' and 'Uncertainty' aversion | Prospective learning |
| --- | --- | --- |
| Soft uncertainty | (Plain) option value | (Quasi-option value) intertemporal option value |
| Hard uncertainty | h-option value | Intertemporal h-option value |

different categories of actions. The analogy with the relationship between quasi-option value and prospective learning is evident; however, prospective learning is much more relevant in the case of hard uncertainty, since only hard uncertainty is consistent with the existence of systematic mistakes and structural learning (Vercelli, 1997a).

We cannot say much a priori about the degree of 'uncertainty' aversion (as is usual with individual tastes), however, psychological considerations and experimental research provide some interesting insights. A few authors have observed that ignorance of relevant information that could be possessed by someone else is particularly upsetting. This may explain why hard uncertainty may restrain people from betting, particularly when they feel incompetent in the field to which the bet relates (Heath and Tversky, 1991; Frisch and Baron, 1988). Further insights come from experimental economics. Generally speaking, economic agents are (hard) uncertainty averse, though a limited degree of (hard) uncertainty preference may emerge for very low gain probability or for very high loss probability (Hogart and Einhorn, 1990; Camerer and Weber, 1992). It is also confirmed that agents prefer to bet on events in which they feel fairly competent (Fellner, 1961, p. 687; Keppe and Weber, 1991), or on events whose occurrence is affected by their ability rather than on purely random events (Langer, 1975). Similarly, they prefer to bet on future events rather than on past events which might be known to others (Brun and Teigen, 1990). These experimental results also depend on the fact that competence affects the social attitude towards the choices of an agent: competent people may be praised for having chosen the right bet, while incompetent people may be only blamed for having chosen the wrong bet (Heath and Tversky, 1991).

Summarizing, the recent literature suggests that the value of an intertemporal h-option is generally positive because decision-makers are in general (hard) uncertainty averse. This value crucially depends on the value attributed by the decision-maker to prospective learning and on the awareness of ignorance which is affected by past learning and competence. However, notwithstanding its potential relevance for environmental economics and finance, a fully-fledged theory of h-option values has not yet been developed. Some hints at such a theory are tentatively suggested in the next section.

## 3. Measures of Option Value

In the preceding section we have identified two basic concepts of option value, the plain option value and the intertemporal option value, and we have stressed that they assume different characterizations according to whether we assume either soft or hard uncertainty.

The aim of the decision-maker is to choose a possible strategy, that is a sequence of choices over time, so as to maximize the expected net present value of the payoffs. The decision-maker faces a scalar binary variable, the value of which is zero if he waits and one if he invests. In the first period, the decision-maker is uncertain on future states of the world. Let us assume that: the passage of time brings significant new information; learning does not depend on the decision-maker's choices; uncertainty is resolved in the second period; and the decision-maker can make a choice at the beginning of both periods, but his second period choice depends on the degree of irreversibility of his first period act. The irreversible act is possible in both periods, that is investment is not a 'now or never' opportunity, but a 'now or next period' one.

Let $\Omega = \{A, B, C, D\}$ be a non-empty set composed of 'environmental' states of the world, $S = 2^\Omega$ the set of all events, $x$ an act with $x \in X$, the set of all acts, $x : \Omega \to R_+$, $n_i^x$, a consequence, such that $n_i^x \in N \subseteq R_+$ with $i = A, B, C, D$, $p$ and $s$ probability measures on $\Omega$, $F_1$ and $F_2$ partitions of $\Omega$, so that $F_2$ is finer than $F_1$.

On the basis of the taxonomy represented in Table 1, we consider two different cases of decision process, the first affected by decision-maker's risk and uncertainty attitude and the second by the possibility of prospective learning.

### 3.1. Risk and Uncertainty Attitude

In this section we consider two different definitions of option value which crucially depend on the risk and uncertainty attitude of the decision-maker: plain option value and h-option value.

The notion of plain option value assumes (either explicitly or implicitly) that the decision-maker's description of the environmental states of the world is exhaustive. The decision-maker attaches additive subjective probabilities[5] to uncertain future events and chooses the optimal act by Savage Expected Utility (SEU).

# Environmental Option Values, Uncertainty Aversion and Learning 229

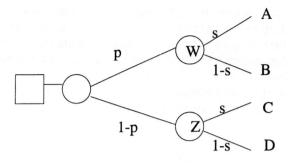

Figure 1. Two-stage lottery.

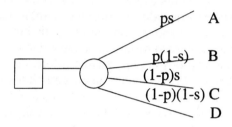

Figure 2. Single-stage lottery.

The notion of h-option value is defined when the decision-maker has a non-additive measure of uncertainty on the set of future events, either because the space of states is mis-specified or because it is incomplete.

Both these definitions of option value consider the asymmetry between reversible and irreversible acts, but they disregard the possibility of receiving additional news. The decision-maker's behavior is modeled by using preferences over single-stage or two-stage money lotteries,[6] that is acts will result in money lotteries and the consequence space $N$ is the set of money lotteries $L$. In this decision process the decision-maker's strategy is defined by one choice node (represented by a square in Figures 1–6), three chance nodes (represented by a circle in Figures 1–6) and four terminal nodes $(A, B, C, D)$. At the beginning of each period the decision-maker can choose either act $x$ (reversible) or act $y$ (irreversible). In the first period an event occurs as a result of a 'horse lottery', in the second period the consequences of that act are derived by an objective mechanism such as roulette, coins, or dice (Figure 1).

Let $L_1$ be a set of single-stage lotteries, $V : L_1 \to R$ (Figure 2) and let us assume that the decision-maker has preferences over $L_1$.[7] The decision-maker also has preferences over the set of the two-stage lotteries, $U : L_2 \to R$ (Figure 1). In the two-stage lotteries each stage is clearly distinct and they are separated by a time interval. The decision-maker's expected utility function $U$

is continuous and monotone. The expected utility representation is standard: the choices faced by the decision-maker are in $L_2$ and it is assumed that the utility of a lottery is just the expected utility of its prizes.

The decision-maker's risk attitude involves curvature properties of the utility function on degenerated lotteries and its consequences for expected utility maximization with monetary outcomes (prizes). He selects the optimal feasible act defined on the set of uncertain environmental states.

### 3.1.1. *Plain Option Value*

In (Freeman, 1984), a plain option value is defined as the difference between the maximum option price and the expected consumer surplus. The maximum option price measures the maximum willingness to pay for an option contract that covers the supply uncertainty of a natural resource.[8] The expected consumer surplus is the mean value of consumer surplus over states of nature that can occur with a known and unique additive probability. The plain option value depends on the functional form and on the parameters of the decision-maker's utility function and it may be positive, negative or null, depending on supply-side (price) or demand-side (income or preferences) uncertainty. Freeman's two-period model consists of a first period (present), followed by a second period (all future periods are collapsed); furthermore, the risk averse decision-maker[9] has a utility function which is separable in income and state variables.

Consider the case of a park which can be either preserved (act $x$) or destroyed by industrial development (act $y$), while the benefits are a linear function of an (indivisible)[10] act. The risk averse decision-maker assigns a 'subjective' additive probability (unique prior) to the first period environmental (symmetric and complementary) events. These two events are named $W = A \cup B$ and $Z = C \cup D$, thus each event occurs with probability $1/2$ on $F_1 = \{\{A, B\}, \{C, D\}\}$. In the second period he faces the set of sublotteries of a compound lottery. In both sublotteries, complementary and symmetric events occur with probability $1/2$ (Figure 3). The decision-maker has to evaluate the contribution of each sublottery to the expected utility of the compound lottery:

$$\{p[(n_A)s + (n_B)(1-s)]; (1-p)[(n_C)s + (n_D)(1-s)]\},$$

where $n_A$ is the payoff at node $A$, etc. Because of the Reduction of Compound Lotteries Axiom (RCLA), the decision-maker is characterized by *time neutrality* and *indifference* between single and two-stage lotteries that are *probabilistically equivalent*.[11] He evaluates the expected utility with respect to a single-stage lottery:

$$\{n_A, ps; n_B, p(1-s); n_C, (1-p)s; n_D, (1-p)(1-s)\}.$$

The risk averse decision-maker has preferences either on the reversible or the irreversible act fully defined by prizes, conditional probability, future

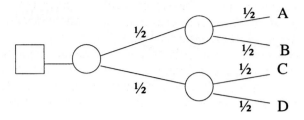

*Figure 3.* Two-stage lottery: an example.

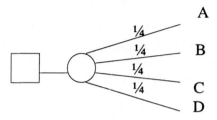

*Figure 4.* Single-stage lottery: an example.

income and prices, disregarding the possibility of receiving additional information[12] in the future (Figure 4).

Freeman's model describes a timeless world, where the "*probabilistically sophisticated expected utility maximizer*" (Machina and Schmeidler, 1992) can always transform a multistage dynamic decision process in a simple static process.[13] By the RCLA, all decisions are made at the beginning and there is no real learning.

PROPOSITION 1. *By the Reduction of Compound Lotteries Axiom, we obtain:*

$$L_2(W, p; Z, (1-p))$$
$$\sim L_1[n_A, ps; n_B, p(1-s); n_C, (1-p)s; n_D, (1-p)(1-s)].$$

The decision-maker evaluates the plain option value by comparing the expected value of a two-stage lottery and a single-stage lottery to a given certainty equivalent[14] (CE), that is he values the expression $L_2(W, p; Z, (1-p)) - L_1(CE, 1)$. The sign of the plain option value depends only on the risk attitude of the decision-maker.

An investment decision under uncertainty with a certain degree of irreversibility (due to, e.g., sunk costs) can be represented as a problem of evaluation of a perpetual call option.

Dixit and Pindyck (1994) apply an option value approach over a broad range of investment problems, for instance when "there is uncertainty over

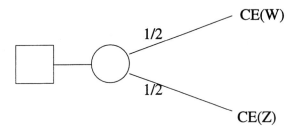

*Figure 5.* Certainty Equivalent lottery.

future fuel prices, over future demand for electricity, over the future environmental regulations that will constrain the utility, and over the costs of alternative technologies to comply with those regulations" (Dixit and Pindyck, 1994, p. 395). As a result, this method can be used to solve environmental problems that involve uncertainty, irreversibility and waiting for new information. In a simple model, "the problem to find a rule for policy adoption that maximizes the net present value function ... is an optimal stopping problem" (Dixit and Pindyck, 1994, p. 414), given the stochastic dependence among arguments in the functional and boundary conditions.

In a process with continuous time and Wiener or generalized Brownian processes, the decision-maker has to choose either a reversible or an irreversible act (scalar binary choice) by using only current information. According to the Bellman's Principle of Optimality, the decision process is split in two parts, the present decision and all future decisions. Then, the additive expected utility is a recursive stochastic adapted process in which an aggregator and a conditional certainty equivalent are the primitives. This recursive utility function is time invariant "with calendar times irrelevant and suppressed" (Epstein, 1995, p. 158). Since "diffusion processes are Markov processes ... they can be regarded as limits of random walks in discrete time as the length of each time period and of each step of the walk both become small in a suitable way" (Dixit and Pindyck, 1994, p. 98). A multistage process is the generalized form of the two-period decision process. The decision-maker faces the sublotteries $W = [n_A, s; n_B, (1 - s)]$ and $Z = [n_C, s; n_D, (1 - s)]$ and by the Certainty Equivalent Mechanism he substitutes both sublotteries with their Certainty Equivalent $CE(W)$ and $CE(Z)$[15] (see Figures 3 and 5). The decision-maker evaluates the degenerate lotteries $d_W$ and $d_Z$ that yield $CE(W)$ and $CE(Z)$ with probability one and solves the $\max\{p[CE(W), 1]; (1 - p)[CE(Z), 1]\}$ problem at the beginning, in a single-stage lottery (Figure 5). This approach which is compatible with the compound independence and time neutrality axioms, proves "that time neutrality does not imply the reduction axiom" (Segal, 1990, p. 356). There is neither effective learning nor a genuine sequential decision process.[16]

According to Dixit and Pindyck's approach, the plain option value depends on the decision-maker's attitude towards risk. From the equality $L(CE(W), 1) = d_W$, when the decision-maker is risk-averse (lover), by Jensen's inequality $U[E(W)] > (<)E[U(d_W)]$, the plain option value is equal to

$$L_2(W, p; Z, (1-p)) - L_1\{[(CE(W), 1), p]; [(CE(Z), 1), (1-p)]\}$$
$$= L_2(W, p; Z, (1-p)) - L_1[CE(W), p; CE(Z), (1-p)]$$
$$= E[(W, p); (Z, (1-p))] - \{p[CE(W), 1]; (1-p)[CE(Z), 1]\} > (<)0.$$

PROPOSITION 2. *By the Certainty Equivalent Mechanism, a two-stage lottery can be reduced to a single-stage lottery. When the decision-maker is risk-neutral the two approaches are equivalent, thus $L_2[W, p; Z, (1-p)] \sim L_1\{[(CE(W), 1), p]; [(CE(Z), 1), (1-p)]\}$ or $L_2[W, p; Z, (1-p)] \sim L_1[CE(W), p; CE(Z), (1-p)]$ and the plain option value is null.*

### 3.1.2. H-Option Value

The previous framework, used to describe the plain option value, assumes that the environmental states of the world have an additive probability of occurring.

Consider now a decision problem in which the "states of the world included in the model do not exhaust the actual ones" (Gilboa and Schmeidler, 1992, p. 13). In this situation that involves hard uncertainty rather than soft uncertainty, the decision-maker has a non-additive prior probability. A non-additive measure is defined on the set of future events and it is possible to represent a preference relation on the set of the decision-maker feasible acts by an utility function, unique up to a positive linear transformation. Given this utility function and a non-additive probability, the Choquet integral[17] (Choquet, 1954) permits the evaluation of the expected utility (Choquet Expected Utility) of an act. The decision-maker expresses hard uncertainty aversion (preference) if his non-additive measure is convex (concave)[18]

Consider the two-stage approach where the decision-maker faces comonotonic acts.[19] If the decision-maker is strictly hard-uncertainty averse, he assigns a subjective non-additive measure (non-additive probability[20]), in the first stage. The probability $m$ attached to both uncertain symmetric events $W$ and $Z$ is less than $1/2$, but their union occurs with probability one, that is $m'(W \cup Z) = m'(\{A, B\} \cup \{C, D\}) = 1$ and $m'(AUB) = m'(CUD) < 1/2$. At the end of the first period uncertainty is resolved and an event in $\{\{A, B\}, \{C, D\}\}$ occurs. The consequence is derived by flipping an unbiased coin. Probabilities $s$ are symmetric and complementary, then $s'(A) = s'(B) = 1/2$ and $s'(C) = s'(D) = 1/2$. Given the set $S$ of events in $\Omega$, let $m' = 1/3$ and $s'(A) = s'(B) = 1/2$ and $s'(C) = s'(D) = 1/2$ be the

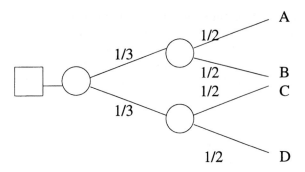

Figure 6. Non-additive two-stage lottery.

probabilities and $n_A = 1$, $n_B = (-1)$, $n_C = 0$, $n_D = 0$ the consequences. The decision-maker faces a two-stage lottery (Figure 6).

By Choquet Expected Utility (CEU), the two-stage approach yields $\text{CEU}^T(W) = 0$ and $\text{CEU}^T(Z) = 0$, then $W$ can be considered indifferent to a constant act with consequence 0. In this one-stage formulation, it is assumed that the measures are $v(A) = 1/6$ and $v(Z) = 1/3$, for consistency with the two-stage approach. The Choquet Expected Utility of the one-stage lottery is

$$\begin{aligned}\text{CEU}^\circ &= 1/6(1) + (1 - (1/3 + (1 - 1/3)1/2))(-1) \\ &= 1/6 + (1 - (1/3 + 1/3)) = 1/6 - 1/3 \\ &= (-1/6) < 0.\end{aligned}$$

Because of the decision-maker's hard uncertainty aversion expressed by a convex non-additive probability, a two-stage lottery cannot be reduced to a simple one-stage lottery by the RCLA.[21] The difference between the single and the two-stage approach measures the h-option value and it only depends on the decision-maker's attitude towards hard uncertainty.

PROPOSITION 3. *When the decision-maker is hard-uncertainty averse and has convex non-additive probability, a two-stage lottery cannot be reduced to a probabilistically equivalent single-stage lottery by the RCLA. The positive difference between the two-stage and the single-stage lotteries is the h-option value.*

### 3.2. Prospective Learning

When a decision-maker faces a dynamic choice situation,[22] and he has to consider the possibility of receiving new information before choosing an irreversible or reversible act, and he faces asymmetric acts with respect to the reversibility of their effects, two different notions of option value can be described: the intertemporal option value (quasi-option value) and the intertemporal h-option value. The intertemporal option value arises in a decision process in which the decision-maker has an additive prior on states of the world. The intertemporal h-option value depends on the updating process for a non-additive prior. In this case learning can be represented as a process of additivization, i.e. the replacement of a non-additive probability measure by an additive one.

### 3.2.1. *Intertemporal Option Value (Quasi-Option Value)*
Arrow and Fisher argued that whenever uncertainty is assumed, "even where it is not appropriate to postulate risk aversion in evaluating an activity, something of the feel of risk aversion is produced by a restriction on reversibility of decision" (Arrow and Fisher, 1974, p. 318).

Also with risk neutrality, they are able to identify "a quasi-option value having an effect in the same direction as risk aversion, namely, a reduction in net benefits from development" (Arrow and Fisher, 1974, p. 315). In Arrow and Fisher's model there are two periods (present and future) and the decision-maker has to choose either preservation or development. This formulation of the decision process is sufficient to produce the quasi-option value. Assuming that the decision-maker replaces the uncertain variables with their expected values, Arrow and Fisher find that "the expected value of benefits under uncertainty is seen to be less then the value of benefits under certainty" (Arrow and Fisher, 1974, p. 317). The value of this difference is named quasi-option value and is related to the possibility of acquiring and exploiting the potential information in the second period.

In the same year, but independently of Arrow and Fisher, Henry published two seminal articles (1974a, 1974b) which further clarified what Arrow and Fisher had called quasi-option value. Henry proved (1974b) that the coexistence of uncertainty and irreversibility prevents the use of the certainty equivalence methods to solve decision problems, even if the payoff function is quadratic. He clarified that only the reversible act allows one to exploit additional information in the future and this asymmetry between reversible and irreversible acts encourages a more conservative choice.

When there is asymmetry between acts and $x$ is considered,[23] the decision-maker has to value the prospect of getting better information in each period. When the decision-maker disregards the prospect of additional information, he replaces uncertain outcomes with their certainty equivalents. The decision-maker evaluates the expected value of choices and chooses $\max[E(n_A, s; n_B, (1 - s)); E(n_C, s; n_D, (1 - s))]$, that is $\max[CE(W); CE(Z)]$. When he takes into account that an event will occur in the second period, that is the acquisition of news, he considers the dynamic problem $\{\max[n_A, s, n_B, (1-s)]; \max[n_C, s; n_D, (1-s)]\}$. It follows, by the convexity of the maximum operator and Jensen (in-)equality, that:

$$E\{\max[n_A, s; n_B, (1-s)]; \max[n_C, s; n_D, (1-s)]\}$$
$$- \max[\mathrm{CE}(W); \mathrm{CE}(Z)] \geq 0.$$

This positive difference[24] is the intertemporal (quasi-)option value and it has an effect similar to risk aversion, even if the decision-maker is risk neutral. This approach to option value considers the possibility of learning and the irreversibility of acts in an intertemporal decision problem, and it shows that under these conditions a dynamic process cannot be reduced to a timeless one.

PROPOSITION 4. *Because of asymmetry between reversible and irreversible acts and the prospect of additional information, the risk neutral decision-maker faces also a sort of risk premium which is called the intertemporal option value and is always positive.*

### 3.2.2. Intertemporal H-Option Value

If the possibility of learning is introduced under the hypothesis of hard uncertainty, we have to consider a further concept of option value which we call the intertemporal h-option value. Also in this case, as in the case of the intertemporal option value (quasi-option value), given a certain first-period attitude towards uncertainty (optimism and pessimism) on the part of the decision-maker, the possibility of learning produces a specific intertemporal option value which depends on the possible future resolution of uncertainty.

A fully-fledged characterization of this magnitude would require a complex intertemporal model which goes beyond the purpose of this paper. Here we confine ourselves to a very simple example under the assumption of a two-period model in which hard uncertainty is fully resolved at the beginning of the second period. In this framework learning, in the sense of resolution of hard uncertainty, is represented by a process of additivization of the prior, i.e. by "the replacement of non-additive probability measure by additive one. This process will be named *additivization* ... [which] is defined as an operator from a Banach space of non-additive measure into a subspace of additive ones satisfying some axiomatic requirements" (Gilboa, 1989, p. 1). Additivization may be obtained by applying the Dempster and Shafer rule, the Gilboa rule, or some pseudo-Bayesian rule. Hence, the decision-maker has a non-additive probability in the first period and additive probability on events in the second period. Under the above assumption, we get the following result which extends that of Arrow and Fisher and defines intertemporal h-option value as the difference $E\{[\max(n_A, s; n_B, (1-s))], m; [\max(n_C, s; n_D, (1-s))], m\} - \max[CE(W), m; CE(Z), m]$.

This result is independent from the decision-maker's attitude towards risk but it crucially depends on the convexity of the maximum operator, the Jensen (in-)equality,[25] the Choquet integral and the additivization process.

The Choquet integral requires that the environmental states of the world are ranked from most to least favorable with respect to their utility, that is the decision-maker has to realize a bijection (permutation).[26] The Choquet integral with respect to a non-additive measure $m$ is a generalization of the Lebesgue integral and the capacities (or non-additive signed measures) are non-additive generalizations of the additive probability. That is the Choquet integral is a generalization of mathematical expectation with respect to a capacity. The Choquet integral is concave if and only if the non-additive measure is superadditive and convex if and only if the non-additive measure is subadditive.[27] By the Choquet integral it is possible to evaluate the CEU of acts and generalize the Arrow and Fisher result, which is obtained by evaluating the SEU of acts by the Lebesgue integral. With an additive probability the Choquet integral coincides with the Lebesgue integral and the Choquet Expected Utility is equal to the Savage Expected Utility. The intertemporal h-option value also depends on the extent of the additivization, which is obtained by updating (conditioning) a capacity by the Dempster and Shafer rule, when the non-additive measure is convex (pessimism) or by the Gilboa and Schmeidler rule,[28] when the non-additive measure is concave (optimism). These rules generalize the Bayes rule.

When the risk neutral decision-maker is hard uncertainty averse and takes into account prospective learning, the intertemporal h-option value is positive and increases with the degree of uncertainty aversion,[29] by conditioning rule and Choquet integral. The intertemporal h-option value is a sort of positive '*uncertainty premium*' derived from asymmetry between acts and the additivization process. The presence of an intertemporal h-option value prevents the possibility of reducing a dynamic decision process to a timeless one.

PROPOSITION 5. *When the decision-maker is averse to uncertainty and takes into account irreversibility and learning, a further correction factor, called intertemporal h-option value, has to be introduced into the evaluation of feasible acts. This factor increases the net benefits of a more conservative choice which allows the decision-maker to exploit more efficiently the possibility of learning, in the specific sense of additivization of the prior.*

## 4. Concluding Remarks

Environmental option values play an important role in any assessment of environmental values for both theoretical and pratical purposes, and provide the ultimate foundations for a rational policy directed towards the conservation of environmental resources.

We have pointed out that the traditional dichotomy between plain option value and quasi-option value (or intertemporal option value) implicitly assumes a very restrictive modality of uncertainty which we called soft uncertainty. Since environmental problems are often characterized by hard uncertainty, in order to take account of the implications of this modality of uncertainty on option values we have crossed with them the dichotomy between plain and intertemporal option value in a two-entry table, so obtaining four concepts of option value.

The two concepts in the first row of the table are relevant when uncertainty is soft and markets complete. In this case a more flexible choice commands a sort of 'risk' premium for a 'risk' averse decision-maker because it is a safer store of values (plain option value); moreover it makes possible the exploitation of prospective learning in order to make better decisions in the future (intertemporal option value).

The two concepts in the second row, which have been completely neglected in the literature, are relevant when markets are incomplete, uncertainty is hard, and the decision problem is intertemporal. In this second case, a more flexible choice involves a sort of 'hard risk' premium for a decision-maker averse to (hard) uncertainty (h-option value); in addition, it makes possible the exploitation of prospective strucural learning before subsequent decisions have to be made (intertemporal h-option value).

In the environmental field, intertemporal h-option values are particularly important because the uncertainty faced is typically hard, and irreversibility is very serious, involving very delicate intertemporal decision problems. Unfortunately, while fairly precise measures may be assigned to (plain) and intertemporal environmental option values, particularly through the methods developed in financial theory for financial options, h-option values and intertemporal h-option values cannot be easily measured. The available measures are only ordinal and, what is worse, the ordering of choices according to intertemporal flexibility, which gives the ordering of intertemporal option values, is very sensitive to the specification of the model. However, new decision theories in conditions of hard uncertainty offer promising analytical tools for developing a satisfactory theory of option values under hard uncertainty.

Notwithstanding all the shortcomings emphasized in this paper, the theory of option values here sketched points out a few qualitative results which are relevant for the evaluation and conservation of environmental goods. First, whenever intertemporal options have a positive value, the traditional techniques for selecting the optimum choice on the basis of the certainty equivalent are generally incorrect because they underestimate the value of environmental resources. Second, it was observed that the methods developed in financial theory to evaluate derivatives work only under soft uncertainty and only permit the evaluation of plain option value. Third, it was argued that the intertemporal h-option value is positive under quite general conditions, whenever hard uncertainty and irreversibility coexist and learning is possible before future choices have to be made. Fourth, the intertemporal h-option value increases, under quite general conditions, with the degree of (hard) uncertainty. Fifth, the value of an intertemporal h-option, given a certain degree of hard uncertainty, depends basically on the characteristics of prospective learning, and on the degree of irreversibility (irreversibility effect). Therefore, we may conclude that the growing awareness of our deep ignorance about the long-term effects of the interaction between economic development and environment, as well as of their irreversibility, should induce more cautious environmental policies.

## Notes

1. This section partially overlaps with Section 2.1 of (Basili and Vercelli, 1994.)
2. In monetary theory the distinction was already quite clear with Keynes (1936) who distinguished between precautionary liquidity related to probability (risk in the Knightian sense) and speculative liquidity related to the weight of evidence (uncertainty in the Knightian sense). In this view, precautionary liquidity plays the role of a risk premium, while speculative liquidity is best interpreted in terms of preference for intertemporal flexibility (Hicks, 1974). A similar dichotomy was emphasised by Makower and Marschak (1938) who distinguished between two properties of liquidity: safety and plasticity.
3. It has been argued elsewhere (Vercelli, 1997a) that decision theory under uncertainty is deeply affected by the distinction between different modalities of uncertainty. In particular, it is important to distinguish between 'soft' uncertainty, when the beliefs of the decision-maker can be represented by a unique and additive probability distribution which is considered fully reliable, and 'hard' uncertainty when the beliefs of the decision-maker can be represented by a non-additive probability distribution or a plurality of probability distributions (Vercelli, 1997a).
4. The literature on hard uncertainty has suggested different methods to give separate measures of 'risk' aversion and (hard) uncertainty aversion (see, e.g., Montesano, 1993).
5. A function $m : \Omega \to R$ is a *capacity* or a *non-additive measure* if it has the following characteristics: $m(\phi) = 0, m(\Omega) = 1, m(A) \geq 0$ and for every $A \subseteq B$, where $A, B \in S$, $m(A) \leq m(B)$. If $m(A \cup B) = m(A) + m(B)$ for every $A, B \in S$ and $A \cap B = \phi$, then $m$ is *additive*.
6. A money lottery is a probability distribution with finite support over $R$ and it is possible to identify money lotteries with constant acts.
7. Then $V : L_1 \to R$ represents a weak preference relation, over money lotteries, if for every $l^*, l^{**} \in L_1$, it is $l^* \geq_1 l^{**}$ if and only if $V(l^*) \geq V(l^{**})$.
8. It is interesting to observe that "paying the option price does not eliminate supply uncertainty ... rather it changes the individual's conditions of access to the good or service from a certainty of no access to a certainty of complete access" (Smith, 1985, p. 303).
9. When the decision-maker is risk averse the utility function is concave.
10. The actual decision can always be thought of as a convex combination of $x$ and $y$. In fact, if benefits from preserving or developing are linear functions of the amount of the park preserved or developed during that time, a corner solution with either full preservation or development generally prevails.
11. In Savage's expected utility theory a two-stage lottery is equivalent in preference to a single-stage lottery with the same prizes and probability derived from the compound lottery by probability calculus.
12. See (Freeman, 1984, p. 6).
13. In this class are also Schmalensee (1972), Bishop (1982), Graham (1981), etc.
14. Under Expected Utility it is simple to show that the Certainty Equivalent Mechanism is equivalent to the Reduction of Compound Lotteries Axiom (see Segal, 1990).

15. The equivalence between a two-stage lottery and a set of lotteries the "outcomes of which are degenerate" in a set of simple lotteries is proved in (Segal, 1990).
16. There is a close analogy between dynamic programming and contingent claims valuation. The Bellman equation and the definition of the replicating portfolio or the use of spanning assets leads to similar valuation. The contingent claim approach requires "the existence of a sufficient rich set of markets in risky assets [and] not only that the stochastic components obey the same probability law, but also that they are perfectly correlated, namely that each and every path (realization) of one process is replicated by the other" (Dixit and Pindyck, 1994, p. 121).
17. For a capacity $m : 2^\Omega \to [0, 1]$ and a function $f : \Omega \to R$, the Choquet integral of $f$ with respect to $m$ is

$$\int f dm = \int_0^\infty m(\{m \mid f(m) \geq t\}) dt + \int_{-\infty}^0 [m(\{m \mid f(m) \geq t\}) - m(\Omega)] dt.$$

The Choquet integral is well-defined and for non-negative $f$ the second part disappears. When a capacity is additive, that is when is a probability, the Choquet integral coincides with the usual integral. The Choquet Expected Utility can be represented like a weighted average, where the weights are not given by prior probability (non-additive probability distribution) but are derived from cumulate distributions induced by the bijection.
18. A non-additive measure $m$ is convex (concave) if, all pairs of events $A, B \in 2^\Omega$, $m(A \cup B) + m(A \cap B) \geq (\leq) m(A) + m(B)$. It is superadditive (subadditive) if $m(A \cup B) \geq (\leq) m(A) + m(B)$, all pairs of events so that $(A \cap B) = \phi$.
19. Two acts $x, y \in X$ are comonotonic if and only if there are no $s, t \in \Omega$, so that $x(s) > x(t)$ and $y(s) < y(t)$. The axiom of comonotonic independence is a less restrictive condition than the sure-thing principle (see Gilboa, 1987 and Schmeidler, 1989).
20. The informal expression non-additive probability is used instead of the formal one non-additive signed measure or capacity.
21. Sarin and Wakker (1992) show that a two-stage lottery and a single-stage lottery yield different and irreconcilable results.
22. "A situation is said to involve dynamic choice if it involves decisions that are made after the resolution of some uncertainty. This could occur for a couple of reasons. One is simply that the individual may not have to commit to a decision until after some uncertainty is resolved. Another reason might be that the available set of choice depends upon the outcome of uncertainty. In any event, a dynamic choice situation will include at least some choices that the individual can (or must) postpone until after nature has made at least some of her moves" (Machina, 1989, p. 1623).
23. With irreversible act in the first period, the two strategies must provide the same value.
24. Inequality follows from the fact that the maximum is a convex function and for any convex function $f$: $Ef(v) \geq f(E(v))$ (Fisher and Hanemann, 1990).
25. See Section 3.2.1.
26. Two acts are comonotonic when they induce the same favorable ordering of states, that is when they induce the same permutation.
27. With a convex capacity the Choquet integral is the *minimum* among Lebesgue integrals with respect to an additive probability $p \in P$, the core $(m)$ so that $p(A) \geq m(A)$ for every $A \in 2^\Omega$, with a concave capacity the Choquet integral is the *maximum* among Lebesgue integrals with respect to a probability $p \in P$, so that $p(A) \leq m(A)$.
28. This updating rule is defined as $m_{A|B} = m(A \cap B)/m(B)$ for every $A, B \in 2^\Omega$ (Gilboa and Schmeidler, 1993).
29. The degree of uncertainty aversion is defined as $1 - m(A) - m(A)^C$, for every $A \in 2^\Omega$.

# References

1. Arrow, K. J. and A. Fisher (1974). "Environmental Preservation, Uncertainty and Irreversibility", *Quarterly Journal of Economics* 89, 312–319.
2. Basili, M. (1995). "Valore di opzione intertemporale ed apprendimento", *Note Economiche* 1, 23–38.
3. Basili, M. and A. Vercelli (1994). "Environmental Option Values: A Survey", Nota di Lavoro 47.94, FEEM, Milano.
4. Bishop, R. (1982). "Option Value: An Exposition and Extension", *Land Economics* 58, 1–15.
5. Bohm, P. (1975). "Option Demand and Consumer's Surplus: Comment", *American Economic Review* 65, 733–737.
6. Brun, W. and K. Teigen (1990). "Prediction and Postdiction Inferences in Guessing", *Journal of Behavioural Decision Making* 3, 17–28.
7. Caballero, R. (1991). "On the Sign of the Investment-Uncertainty Relationship", *American Economic Review* 81, 279–288.
8. Camerer, C. and M. Weber (1992). "Recent Developments in Modeling Preferences: Uncertainty and Ambiguity", *Journal of Risk and Uncertainty* 5, 325–370.
9. Choquet, G. (1954). "Theory of Capacity", *Annales de l'Institute Fourier* 5, 131–295.
10. Dixit, A. and R. Pindyck (1994). *Investment under Uncertainty*, Princeton, NJ, Princeton University Press.
11. Epstein, L. (1980). "Decision Making and Temporal Resolution of Uncertainty", *International Economic Review* 21, 269–283.
12. Epstein, L. (1995). "Consumption, Saving and Asset Returns with Non-Expected Utility", International School of Economic research, Siena (Italy).
13. Fellner, W. (1961). "Distortion of Subjective Probabilities as a Reaction to Uncertainty", *Quarterly Journal of Economics* 75, 670–694.
14. Fisher, A. and M. Hanemann (1987). "Quasi-Option Value: Some Misconceptions Dispelled", *Journal of Environmental Economics and Management* 14, 183–190.
15. Fisher, A. and M. Hanemann (1990). "Option Value: Theory and Measurement", *European Review of Agricultural Economics* 17, 167–180.
16. Freeman, A. M. (1984). "Supply Uncertainty, Option Price, and Option Value", *Land Economics* 61(2), 176–181.
17. Frisch, D. and J. Baron (1988). "Ambiguity and Rationality", *Journal of Behavioural Decision Making* 1, 149–157.
18. Gilboa, I. (1989). "Additivization of Non-Additive Measures", *Mathematics of Operations Research* 14, 1–17.
19. Gilboa, I. and D. Schmeidler (1992). "Additive Representation of Non-Additive Measures and the Choquet Integral", Discussion Paper No. 985.
20. Gilboa, I. and D. Schmeidler (1993). "Updating Ambiguous Beliefs", *Journal of Economic Theory* 59, 31–49.
21. Graham, A. (1981). "Cost-Benefit Analysis under Uncertainty", *American Economic Review* 71, 715–725.
22. Heath, C. and A. Tversky (1991). "Preference and Belief: Ambiguity and Competence in Choice under Uncertainty", *Journal of Risk and Uncertainty* 4, 5–28.
23. Henry, C. (1974a). "Option Values in the Economics of Irreplaceable Assets", *Review of Economic Studies* 41, 89–104.
24. Henry, C. (1974b). "Investment Decision under Uncertainty the Irreversible Effect", *American Economic Review* 64, 1006–1012.
25. Hicks, J. (1974). *The Crisis in Keynesian Economics*, New York, Basic Books.
26. Hogart, M. and H. J. Einhorn (1990). "Venture Theory: A Model of Decision Weights", *Management Science* 36, 780–803.

27. Jones, R. and J. Ostroy (1984). "Flexibility and Uncertainty", *Review of Economic Studies* 51, 13–32.
28. Keppe, H. J. and M. Weber (1991). "Judged Knowledge and Ambiguity Aversion", Working Paper No. 277, Christian-Albrechts Universität, Kiel, Germany.
29. Keynes, J.M. (1936). *The General Theory of Employment, Interest and Money*, London, MacMillan.
30. Knight, F. H. (1921). *Risk, Uncertainty and Profit*, Boston, Houghton Mifflin.
31. Langer, E. J. (1975). "The Illusion of Control", *Journal of Personality and Social Psychology* 32, 311–328.
32. Machina, M. J. (1989). "Dynamic Consistency and Non-Expected Utility Models of Choice under Uncertainty", *Journal of Economic Literature* 27, 1622–1668.
33. Machina, M. J. and D. Schmeidler (1992). "A More Robust Definition of Subjective Probability", *Econometrica* 60, 745–780.
34. Makower, H. and T. Marschak (1938). "Assets, Prices and Monetary Theory", *Economica* 5, 261–288.
35. Montesano, A. (1993). "Non-Additive Probabilities and the Measure of Uncertainty and Risk Aversion", mimeo.
36. Plummer, M. L. and R. C. Hartman (1986). "Option Value: A General Approach", *Economic Inquiry* 24, 455–470.
37. Sarin, R. and P. Wakker (1992). "A Simple Axiomatization of Non-Additive Expected Utility", *Econometrica* 60, 1255–1272.
38. Schmalensee, R. (1972). "Option Demand and Consumer's Surplus: Valuing Price Changes, under Uncertainty", *American Economic Review* 62, 813–824.
39. Schmeidler, D. (1989). "Subjective Probability and Expected Utility without Additivity", *Econometrica* 57, 571–587.
40. Segal, U. (1990). "The Two-Stage Lotteries without the Reduction Axiom", *Econometrica* 58, 349–377.
41. Smith, V. K. (1983). "Option Value: A Conceptual Overview", *Southern Econ. J.* 49, 654–668.
42. Smith, V. K. (1985). "Supply Uncertainty, Option Price, and Indirect Benefit Extimation", *Land Economics* 61(3), 303–307.
43. Vercelli, A. (1991). *Methodological Foundations of Macroeconomics. Keynes and Lucas*, Cambridge, Cambridge University Press.
44. Vercelli, A. (1997a). "Hard Uncertainty and Environment Policy", this volume.
45. Vercelli, A. (1997b). "The Sustainability of Development and the Freedom of Future Generations", this volume.
46. Viscusi, W. K. and R. Zeckhauser (1976). "Environmental Policy Choice under Uncertainty", *Journal of Environmental Economics and Management* 3, 97–112.
47. Weisbrod, B. (1964). "Collective-Consumption Services of Individual-Consumption Goods", *Quarterly Journal of Economics* 78, 471–477.

LOREDANA TORSELLO AND ALESSANDRO VERCELLI

## 3.3. Environmental Bonds: A Critical Assessment*

### 1. Introduction

This paper aims to clarify the meaning, or meanings, and the applicability of the environmental bond (from now on *e-bond*), an interesting instrument of environmental risk control recently advocated by Perrings and Costanza.[1] The e-bond is a compulsory deposit which must be paid by anyone who wants to utilize certain natural resources the disposal of which is potentially polluting or, more in general, who wants to undertake an activity which may damage the environment. The amount of the deposit is conceived as a function of the possible environmental consequences of the relevant activity: according to the prevailing opinion it should cover the maximum potential damage to the environment so that society is insured against any possible damage produced by the activity. The deposit is refundable, in whole or in part, to the extent that the holder of the bond is able to prove to the environmental agency managing the e-bond scheme that she was able to avoid the anticipated environmental damage. The deposits paid are kept in an interest-earning escrow account which may be partially utilized, provided the social insurance role of the fund is not jeopardized, by the agency in order to pay the management costs of the e-bond schemes and to encourage research and innovations meant to reduce environmental risks.

The e-bond is regarded by its supporters as a potentially efficient instrument of environmental risk control, particularly in cases of hard (or Knightian) uncertainty (see Vercelli, 1997), when other forms of insurance are not available. On the other hand, the definition of its characteristics and the procedures of its implementation are still rather confused and problematic. This fact may help to explain why e-bond schemes have not yet been implemented in a systematic way, notwithstanding the interest voiced by a few scholars and policy makers.

---

* Though this paper was jointly written by the authors, Loredana Torsello takes responsibility for Sections 1, and 2, and Alessandro Vercelli for Sections 3, 4, and 5. We would like to thank Charles Perrings for helpful comments.

Section 2 traces the genesis of the idea of the e-bond, starting from a few seminal proposals and experiences up to the recent contributions. Section 3 discusses in some detail analogies and differences with alternative instruments of environmental risk control, briefly comparing some of their advantages and disadvantages. Section 4 discusses some of the open problems which hamper the implementation of an e-bond scheme. Finally, in the concluding section, we argue that the debate on the viability and efficiency of e-bond schemes is blurred by a basic confusion in the literature between two different conceptions of the e-bond and of its role in environmental risk control.

## 2. Genesis

The first to use the expression 'environmental bond', and to clarify its basic features, was Perrings in his book *Economy and Environment* published in 1987. However, he correctly refers back to the *material disposal tax* suggested earlier by Mills (1972) and Solow (1971).

According to Mills, the use of any potentially polluting material should be liable to a tax meant to cover the potential damage should the material be disposed of in an incorrect way. On the other hand, if the real damage is less than hypothesized, he suggests that the tax should be partially refunded. Moreover, in his opinion, recycled materials should be exempted from the tax in order to encourage their use.

A similar proposal was suggested by Solow (1971),[2] who underlined the economic advantages of incentives induced by a material disposal tax, which is seen as a device for correcting the divergence between social and private costs. Nevertheless, Solow did not neglect the problems that such a scheme could encounter. In particular, he stressed that in order to implement a scheme of material disposal taxes, it would be necessary to possess much more information than is currently available.

The tax scheme conceived by Solow and Mills to meet situations in which the observation and discovery of environmental damage is impossible, or very difficult, is taken up and appropriately modified by Baumol and Oates (1979). They advocate the introduction of instruments of environmental risk control based on refundable deposits managed by an international agency. Such an organization would manage the funds as if they were loans and would pay back the capital plus interest. Baumol and Oates maintain that the purpose of using such a system is to render unprofitable, or socially undesirable, inappropriate waste disposal by encouraging, in particular, recycling and reuse of materials. In their opinion, such an instrument has the advantage of being politically more attractive than other fiscal methods, particularly when a determinate activity cannot be reliably monitored.

A few years later, Bohm (1981) published a book which is so far the most complete analysis of deposit-refund systems. He argues that they would stimulate environmentally sound behavior at very low social cost, as have many existing applications: mandatory deposits on beverage containers, waste lubricant oil, junked cars, refrigerant use of CFM, etc. He also advocated the systematic introduction of producer-orientated deposit-refund systems, called 'performance bonds' (direct ancestors of the e-bonds), in order to guarantee the restoration of production sites after shut-down (even in the case of intentional or unintentional bankruptcies), or to protect society against unknown environmental effects of new products or new production processes.

In a following contribution, Bohm and Russell (1985) stress that a system of refundable deposits may have the following advantages: firstly, it can work even when the detection of activities that risk harming the environment is hampered by concrete difficulties; secondly, it is sometimes possible to simplify the problem of the burden of proof; thirdly, as far as single tax payers are concerned, the maximum economic consequences of an activity which pollutes the environment are known in advance; fourthly, all possible damage is covered by payments; and finally, it is possible to include in this mechanism people who are not directly interested but who can intervene to reduce the effects of harmful activities. Bohm and Russell maintain that the refundable deposit system is also politically more attractive than the imposition of taxes and subsidies. The deposit does not burden state funds and it is not subject to the distortions of the classical systems of economic incentives. However, the feasibility of this instrument is closely linked to the condition that it is technically and economically possible to prove to what extent environmental pollution has been avoided, otherwise the deposit simply becomes a tax.

Among the deposit-refund systems, "security deposits on dangerous substances" (Huppes, 1988) can also be included. They involve a deposit to be paid for every kilogram of dangerous substance contained in materials or products. The deposit is paid when goods containing dangerous substances are imported and refunded when they are exported or treated so as to be no longer dangerous. According to Huppes, administrative costs are excessively high if the substances subject to a security deposit are dispersed in very small quantities in a myriad of goods; on the other hand, it would be sufficient to control the payment of deposits as goods enter a country and determine repayment when they go out. The larger the size of the jurisdiction of the controlling authority, the lower the incidence of such costs.

Recently, Perrings (1987) suggested a generalization of the deposit-refund systems which he has christened 'environmental bond', and has emphasized in particular their potential role of social assurance against environmental risks. He thinks that this instrument is particularly attractive under hard (or 'Knightian') uncertainty[3] when most other instruments of environmental-risk control cannot be applied. In this case, there is no algorithm to determine the 'social insurance' premium against the loss derived from such environmental effects. The maximin criterion suggested by Perrings maintains that this 'premium' should be related to the greatest hypothetical damage caused by the environmental effects of a given activity.[4] The loss linked to a certain activity (if concave and continually differentiating functions are hypothesized) depends upon the function of social welfare that reflects the society's level of risk aversion. Further, the e-bond could cover the social risks of uncertain external effects of productive activities. As for the value of the e-bond, Perrings suggests a sequential process according to which the initial deposit (based on the maximum hypothetical damage relative to a certain resource) can be modified according to greater information obtained as a result of further efforts of research.

Perrings (1989) links the use of e-bonds to innovative activities about the consequences of which we do not possess reliable information; this undermines the possibility of covering the risks through commercial insurance contracts. An e-bond on these activities would lead to a private incentive to increase research investments and consequently the stock of available information with the hope that increased information will bring about a decrease in the e-bond value. Perrings reaches the conclusion that the value of an e-bond is a function of the costs of private research in preceding periods. In fact, a profit-maximizing firm increases its research expenditure to the point where marginal research costs equalize the marginal reduction expected from the cost sustained in paying the e-bond. In addition, by setting a high deposit price, the environmental authority can avoid or postpone the development of new activities which may have negative effects upon the environment.

Perrings and Costanza (1990) subsequently define the e-bond as a necessary instrument for the correction of distortions in the signals which guide the private use of resources that may cause 'social traps.'[5] Perrings and Costanza also clarify a few aspects of the procedures of implementation of the e-bond schemes. They suggest that the responsibility for the management of the e-bond should be given to an independent environmental agency. The determination of the deposit should be based upon a 'worst case analysis' according to information and advice furnished by a consulting scientific committee. This committee should also have the responsibility of judging the applications for refund according to equity and justice. Furthermore, the committee would have the responsibility of diffusing information gathered on potential environmental damage and the associated level of uncertainty. The e-bonds paid would be deposited in a trust fund which would produce interest to maintain the real value of the deposits, to cover the administration costs and to provide research incentives for innovative technologies more benign to the environment.

This flexible assurance bonding system, as defined by Costanza and Perrings, is in their opinion a useful incentive-based instrument of environmental risk control, particularly in cases of hard uncertainty (Costanza, 1992). Admittedly, this system could discriminate between bigger firms which can financially afford even high cost e-bonds, and firms which cannot sustain such a burden and consequently find themselves forced out of the market.

However, according to Costanza, firms which cannot sustain the financial burden of e-bonds should not necessarily be eliminated from the market; rather, they should transfer production towards sectors which do not involve environmental damage; or else they may enter into a partnership with the intention of dividing the financial responsibility of the bond and restoring the original environmental conditions.

## 3. E-Bonds vis-à-vis Other Instruments of Environmental Risk Control

The concept of e-bond is strategically located at the intersection of different policy instruments. Unfortunately, its definition has been somewhat fluctuating and fuzzy. This is at the same time consequence and cause of the fact that it has not yet been implemented in a systematic way, notwithstanding the appreciation, at least in principle, of a few scholars and experts. We intend to contribute to clarify the concept by analyzing how it overlaps with, and is distinguished from, other existing instruments of environmental risk control.

The best way to look at an e-bond is to consider it as a particular kind of deposit-refund scheme applied to environmental risk control. Deposit-refund systems have been widely applied in the past, generally with excellent results, especially for encouraging recycling and appropriate waste behavior (for a comprehensive survey, see Bohm, 1981). The basic idea underlying the e-bond proposal is that a generalization of the deposit-refund schemes could be systematically employed in many situations which are characterized by environmental risks, particularly when they are induced by hard (or Knightian) uncertainty, in order to mitigate them.

As in any deposit-refund scheme, we may regard the e-bond as an environmental tax (the initial price of the e-bond) coupled with a potential subsidy (the value of the refund). This is the way in which the idea of e-bond has been introduced (the 'material disposal tax' of Mills, 1972) and analyzed in many papers (see, e.g., Bohm and Russel, 1985). The coordination of a tax and a subsidy may have remarkable advantages over the separate use of each of them. The subsidies (refunds) would be fully financed by the taxes (deposits) previously paid and would be only received by agents who really deserve them. Similarly, taxes would be proportional to effective pollution according to the 'polluter pays principle' (see Section 4 for further comments on this point).

The e-bond is an *ex-ante* risk control mechanism which is meant to fill the gap between privately and socially optimum risk control levels. *Ex-ante* mechanisms impose upon private agents behavioral restrictions and/or financial or insurance obligations before knowing what state of the world will occur. On the contrary, *ex-post* mechanisms impose obligations on the agents which are a function of the state of the world actually occurred; instances are direct regulation with enforcement, as well as legal sanctions and tort rules which impose liability after the fact. The *ex-post* risk control methods have been criticized as inefficient incentive mechanisms having a dubious impact due to high legal and monitoring costs and difficulties in defining the amount of tort liabilities (Farber, 1991, p. 232). In addition, in cases of irreversible damage, any *ex-post* mechanism is bound to come too late, unless the *ex-ante* disincentive effect of potential sanctions is designed and enforced in such a way as to be very effective. On the contrary, *ex-ante* mechanisms provide much more efficiently the right incentives in order to avoid or at least mitigate environmental risks. Admittedly the *ex-ante* incentives may turn out to be not fully adequate for a satisfactory control of environmental risks. However, in the case of *ex-ante* mechanisms, distortions in the incentives may be detected and corrected before the worst events occur. In any case, the comparative assessment of risk control instruments should analyze in detail the consequences of their implementation on the structure of incentives, which affect economic behavior, taking into account the institutional characteristics of the country or region to which the instruments are to be applied.

As an *ex-ante* regulatory device, the e-bond is, in a sense, symmetrical to the marketable permit. In the case of marketable permits, the environmental authority fixes the global quantity of a certain resource which may be used, or the degree of pollution which may be tolerated, while the price of these permits is left to decentralized market decisions. In the case of e-bonds what is fixed is a sort of price, or risk premium, of the use of natural resources involving possible damage to the environment, while the quantities are left to decentralized market decisions. In both cases, the market may have a role, though only in the framework of a centralized administrative mechanism. The basic idea is exactly that of exploiting in a coordinated way the advantages of regulation and those of the market, avoiding at the same time their disadvantages. However, the apparent symmetry between marketable permits and e-bonds is somewhat illusory, due to the fact that e-bonds are not easily negotiable since, according to the prevailing view, their contents are strictly related to the specific characteristics of the (first) buyer. Still this obstacle could be removed, at least in part. The e-bond could be defined, as far as possible, in standard impersonal terms. The 'deposit' could even be conceived as a sort of negotiable permit. In this case (marketable e-bonds), the main difference with respect to marketable permits would be the determination of an issue price rather than an issue quantity, coupled with the possibility of obtaining a refund based on the issue price (not on the subsequent market price which might change). Refund would be obtained by the final owner who would provide evidence of actual resource use or pollution by all the owners of the e-bond since its first purchase. However, in this case transactions would be limited by the increasing costs that the final owner would incur to prove that the damage was inferior to that expected by the authority. On the other hand, if the final owner is a firm specialized in these specific activities, and therefore capable of reducing the effects of harmful consequences for the environment, the costs of implementing a market system could be reduced.

Though many authors have insisted on the insurance role of the e-bond, this role can be considered effective only in a limited sense. From the point of view of the owner, it has an insurance value only to the extent that it posits an upper limit to her liabilities (generally based on the 'polluter pays principle'). In this case, a derivative title could be devised, a sort of insurance against the risk of not having the price of the bond refunded. However, such a derivative instrument could weaken the incentive contents of the e-bond for moral-hazard reasons (see, e.g., Bohm, 1981, p. 88).

It is also claimed that the introduction of an e-bond scheme would have an insurance value for society, since possible environmental damage would be covered *ex-ante* by the price of e-bonds. If the risk affects particular subjects, this peculiar sort of 'social insurance' is obtained not through the usual technique of spreading the burden of risk bearing, but through its concentration on the potential polluters. However, the most important environmental risks are collective risks, which – as is well known – cannot be safely insured. The e-bonds set incentives for limiting or reducing the risk of damaging the environment, differently from insurance contracts which typically do not act on the risks themselves but on their consequences. Risks are not necessarily reduced in the case of commercial insurance; on the contrary, if the contract is not well designed they may increase (e.g., in the case of moral hazard or adverse selection). In the case of e-bonds, polluters are stimulated by effective incentives to avoid damage in order to recover their deposits.

From the point of view of incentives directed towards the elimination or reduction of environmental risks, the e-bond is not very different from the 'polluters-pays' liability principle. In the case of an e-bond, the incentive for the polluters could be slightly inferior whenever the maximum liability were fixed *ex-ante*. However, since the payment precedes the refund, the polluter cannot hope that he will not be identified and enforcement of the sanction is much more effective than in the case of the *ex-post* mechanisms of liability.

E-bonds cannot be considered a genuine financial instrument. As we have seen, they are not easily negotiable, though this shortcoming could be remedied in part. In addition, the expected cash flows are very uncertain and conditional to the effective success of the action taken to avoid the risks and their acknowledgment by the environmental agency. Finally, the e-bond fund cannot be regarded as a genuine financial fund since it is committed to covering the risks and paying the administrative costs of e-bond management. We should therefore not expect a significant contribution from this fund to finance environmental research and projects as maintained by Costanza and Perrings (1990). The social insurance role of this fund is inconsistent with a significant financial role.

Finally, it should be kept in mind that the ranking of different instruments of environmental risk control may be relative to the structural features of a certain sector or a certain economy. In particular, it depends on the degree of risk aversion (or uncertainty aversion) and on the private discount rates. Whenever the degree of risk aversion is particularly low, or the rate of private discount particularly high, the e-bond seems especially suitable for inducing a degree of environmental risk control exceeding that of other instruments and close to the social optimum. This is apparently the case of highly competitive sectors (Farber, 1991, p. 236) or of small firms sectors (Farber, 1991, p. 244). Generally speaking, this is also the case of the USA as compared to most European countries (Heal, 1991).

## 4. Open Problems and Critical Remarks

The e-bond is an attractive risk control instrument because of its peculiar combination of efficient prevention incentives and political palatability. If we look at this instrument, in the most abstract terms, as a combination of a tax and a subsidy, we have in principle an integration of the incentives typical of taxes with those typical of subsidies. Of course, this integration of incentives is not fully additive. Activities constrained by the purchase of e-bonds of a certain value discourage pollution and/or waste of natural resources with respect to those not constrained in such a way, but less than in the case of taxes of the same amount in proportion to the prospects of reimbursement. On the other hand, incentives to save resources and/or to reduce pollution provided by the refund policy should not be inferior to those of subsidies of equal amount, provided that their uncertain nature is taken into account.

In addition, the introduction of e-bonds appears to be more politically palatable than alternative measures having the same target. Environmental taxes are very unpopular as they are perceived as undiscriminatingly 'punitive'; the perspective of a refund could make them more acceptable to the public, as the 'punishment' would be proportional to the environmental damage effectively produced. Furthermore, while subsidies imply an additional burden to the public budget, e-bond refunds are self-financed by the 'deposits' provided by the e-bond schemes.

Though the basic idea underlying the proposition of an e-bond scheme seems very attractive, its implementation raises a host of delicate problems. First, how should we fix the value of the deposit? If we think of the deposit in terms of Pigouvian taxes, the usual answer should apply, taking uncertainty into due account. Therefore, deposits should internalize negative expected externalities according to a rational criterion. The one suggested in the literature here surveyed is the maximin criterion which should guarantee a sufficient indemnity to society even in the worst expected contingency. However, the use of this criterion is questionable since it could quite often destroy the viability of the e-bond idea. In many cases of unknown externalities we are unable to rule out the possibility of catastrophic consequences. In this hypothesis the price of the deposit would become infinite, or in any case too high to be paid. In addition, even a payable but excessive deposit could raise liquidity problems and hinder economic activities which would otherwise be beneficial. This may be consistent with Perrings's 'precautionary principle' (1991) but would reduce the political attractiveness of an e-bond scheme. These critical remarks are confirmed by recent advances in decision theory under hard uncertainty which show that the maximin criterion should not always be considered the best one. It is often better to choose a criterion which takes into account not only the worst possible contingencies, but all possible contingencies, though with different weights (Kelsay and Quiggin, 1992; Vercelli, 1997). In any case, when the chance of a catastrophic event within the e-bond time horizon is quite sizable, it is not clear which is the advantage *vis-à-vis* plain prohibition. The same is true with irreversible damage, when the reversal costs can be only partially covered by the e-bond. These observations might limit the potential scope of e-bonds. On the contrary, if we rule out these extreme cases, an attractive feature of e-bonds is the possibility of correcting the value of the deposit as new information flows in, even before the feared contingencies occur. In any case, this evaluation also reflects the degree of risk and uncertainty aversion characterizing a society. (A thorough discussion of alternative measures of risk and uncertainty aversion under hypotheses of expected and non-expected utility, additive and non-additive probabilities, may be found in Montesano, 1991 and 1992.)

The initial determination of the e-bond value should consider the user and non-user benefits and costs of the relevant activity. In the absence of sound theories and data, a useful approach to estimate these values is furnished by 'Contingent Valuation Methods'[6] although their reliability is dubious (for a good survey on this argument see, e.g., Cropper and Oates, 1992).

Delicate problems could also arise when it is difficult to attribute the responsibility for a certain damage to a potential polluter, because it is too expensive to efficiently monitor the emissions (due to the existence of asymmetric information, uncertainty, non-point sources, etc.). In this case, the e-bond could set proper incentives to have information about the environmental performance of each firm.[7] A policy based on e-bonds would probably be inefficient at first, but if policy-makers give firms the right incentives to monitor their effective contribution to environmental damage, efficiency could rapidly be attained.

Another unsolved problem is the choice of the optimum refund policy. A low level would reduce the possible advantages of e-bonds with respect to Pigouvian taxation; a high level could reduce the intensity of control (Farber, 1991, p. 243). Political viability and budgetary rigor would also suggest that the sum of expected reimbursements and management costs of the scheme should, in principle, not exceed the total amount of deposits. This constraint is difficult to comply with in the first stage of implementation of an e-bond scheme due to fixed costs of monitoring and management. However, these problems should attenuate as e-bonds become increasingly widespread.

Any risk control instrument implies monitoring and management costs. It has been claimed that an attractive feature of the e-bond scheme is the absence of monitoring costs, as the burden of proof that the negative externality has actually been inferior to that expected falls on the holder (Perrings, 1987; Perrings and Costanza, 1991). This opinion is not fully convincing, since the evidence brought forward by the holders has to be evaluated by a board of experts or by a specialized court, and this may imply sizable costs. However, the incremental costs could be low if the board of experts or the specialized court have a wider jurisdiction. The same is true for the incremental costs of the environmental agency (management of the e-bond fund, fixing and revision of the price of deposits, etc.). In some cases, it could be impossible, or very difficult, to give sound proofs of having caused a damage inferior to that expected. Thus the holder of the e-bond would not be able to receive a reimbursement, notwithstanding the fact that her activities had not caused negative external effects. Therefore, in order to make the refund possible, the burden of proof should not be very expensive or problematical.

The incentive and disincentive role of the e-bond is crucial but quite ambiguous. Firms could either modify the price or the quality of their products, or both. If they prefer to change the price to absorb the cost of the initial deposit, ignoring the possibility of a refund, the e-bond would merely play the role of discouraging demand for these products, like a simple tax. On the other hand, if the firm is interested in the refund, it may try to improve its environmental performance by improving the environmental quality of products and production processes. In this case, the incentives typical of subsidies would have more effect on supply conditions.

However, notwithstanding the widespread belief that a tax on potentially dangerous activities coupled with the possibility of a reimbursement represents an incentive to avoid pollution (see, e.g., Bohm, 1981, p. 45), this is not necessarily true. The final effect on incentives of the interaction between the tax (deposit) and subsidy (reimbursement) is quite uncertain. A fully rigorous analysis of these issues has not yet been developed.

## 5. Concluding Remarks

The e-bond may eventually prove to be a useful instrument of environmental risk control. Unfortunately its implementation is not easy to design. It would be useful to initiate some pilot scheme in order to test its efficiency as an environmental-risk control instrument, and begin to solve the problems in practice. In the meantime the issues should be thoroughly clarified. However, the debate on the scope and conditions of application of e-bonds is blurred by the confusion between two possible types of this instrument.

The first type, that could be called 'soft e-bond', applies whenever uncertainty is soft and the worst possible damage, which in this case is by definition quite well known, is not too high. This is, e.g., the idea of e-bond that Shogren et al. (1993) have in mind in their critical contribution.[8] They have pointed out a few strict conditions for a safe application of this kind of e-bond: in particular, observability and reversibility of the damage, easy identification of the source of environmental damages, limited time horizon of the bond. However, in the case of soft uncertainty, particularly under the further restrictive conditions mentioned above, other instruments of environmental risk control apply, such as commercial insurance and financial instruments (Vercelli, 1997). The specific advantages of a soft e-bond scheme should therefore be carefully discussed in each case. Generally speaking, the comparative advantage of soft e-bonds over alternative risk control instruments rests on its greater efficiency in providing incentives to reduce environmental risks, and/or to promptly restore the environment in an adequate way. A case in point is that of bonding in surface mining. In the USA, the Surface Mining Control and Reclamation Act (SMCRA) of 1977 requires the operator to post a bond as a condition to mine coal. The value of the bond is fixed according to the 'worst case method' so as to ensure full environmental restoration at the end of mining operations. The bond is usually forfeited in terms of dollars per acre of disturbed land, and is released after mining and reclamation operations have been inspected by the regulatory authority. The application of this scheme has had moderate success so far (see Shogren et al., 1993, pp. 120–121). In particular, the social insurance role was performed only in part, as the value of the bonds proved insufficient to reclaim the disturbed land, so that the state had to intervene with supplementary funds to reclaim the land. In addition, a shift in the burden of proof was not attempted in this case. Nevertheless, this example suggests the viability of the soft e-bond idea, at least under the restricted conditions mentioned above; by extending the applications the idea could be progressively refined.

The second type of e-bond, which could be called 'hard e-bond', is applicable in cases of hard uncertainty. Its systematic introduction is more appealing, as in this case most other instruments of risk control do not apply. This is the case that Perrings and Costanza have in mind when they argue the virtues of the e-bond, but not all the problems raised by their application have been fully solved so far. Hard uncertainty generally makes it impossible to exclude huge worst-possible damage to the environment (even in a 'focus loss' sense). The price of the e-bond would be so high to amount to an implicit prohibition, or it should be based on a different criterion: the most likely damage, or simply a reasonable amount which provides some limited social insurance without thwarting the activity more than is desired by the policy authorities. Of course, in the second case, asymmetry of information between policy authorities and holders of e-bonds could raise problems of moral hazard. In order to avoid these problems, the holder of the bond could be considered liable to pay the excess value of the damage. However, this provision would fully eliminate the insurance value for the bond holder.

In either case, the e-bond fund is unlikely to play a very significant role in financing activities benign to the environment. Under soft uncertainty, taking into account the fixed costs of the management of the scheme and its insurance role, the value of the bond is likely to be too low to provide a sizable surplus for financial purposes. In the second case, notwithstanding the larger size of the fund, a free surplus is unlikely because of the much higher reserve ratios required for insurance purposes under hard uncertainty.

## Notes

1. The main references are: (Perrings, 1987, 1989, 1991; Perrings and Costanza, 1990; Costanza, 1991, 1992).
2. Solow (1971) refers to the draft of Mills (1972).
3. In this paper uncertainty is defined as 'soft' whenever the beliefs of the decision-maker can be expressed in terms of a unique, fully reliable, additive probability distribution; uncertainty is defined as 'hard' whenever the beliefs of the decision maker cannot be expressed in that way (Vercelli, 1997).
4. Perrings and Costanza (1990) clarify that the conjectured worst case outcome recommended as the basis of the bond should not be identified with the worst case 'imaginable', but with the 'focus loss' of the activity, i.e. with 'the least unbelievable of those costs of an activity to which the decision-maker's attention has been drawn for whatever reason – publicity or public sentiment included' (p. 67).
5. We find ourselves in a social trap when private rational decisions inevitably lead to results which are not optimal from a social point of view; such situations are determined by distorted signals within the information parameters (Costanza and Perrings, 1990).
6. The contingent valuation methods allow one to infer how common people estimate the total value of a certain public good (use value and non-use value). As is well known, these methods are based on the results of questionnaires, submitted to a sample of people, investigating the amount that they are willing to pay to conserve environmental goods.
7. "The deposit-refund system introduces a shift in liability of a kind that creates economic incentives for the party that normally has a monopoly on the best available information about risk" (Bohm, 1981, p. 86)
8. Perrings, on the contrary, prefers to reserve the name of environmental bond to what is here called hard e-bond, and to call 'performance bond' what is here called soft e-bond (private communication).

## References

1. Basili, M. and A. Vercelli (1997). "Environmental Option Values: A Survey", this volume.
2. Baumol, W. and W. Oates (1979). *Economics, Environmental Policy and Quality of Life*, Englewood Cliffs, NJ, Prentice Hall.
3. Baumol, W. and W. Oates (1988). *The Theory of Environmental Policy*, Cambridge, Cambridge University Press.
4. Bohm, P. (1981). *Deposit-Refund Systems*, Baltimore, MD, Johns Hopkins University Press.
5. Bohm, P. and C. S. Russel (1985). "Comparative Analysis of Alternative Policy Instruments", in *Handbook of Natural Resources and Energy Economics*, A. V. Kneese and J. L. Sweeney (eds.), New York, North-Holland, pp. 395–455.

6. Costanza, R. (1991). "Assuring Sustainability of Ecological Economic System, in *Ecological Economics*, R. Costanza (ed.), New York, Columbia University Press, pp. 331–343.
7. Costanza, R. (1992). "Three Things We Can Do to Achieve Sustainability", Paper presented to the Second Conference of the ISEE, Stockholm.
8. Costanza, R. and C. Perrings (1990). "A Flexible Assurance Bonding System for Improved Environmental Management", *Ecological Economics* 2, 57–75.
9. Cropper, M. and W. Oates (1992). "Environmental Economics: A Survey", *Journal of Economic Literature* 30, 675–740.
10. Farber, S. (1991). "Regulatory Schemes and Self-Protective Environmental Risk Control: A Comparison of Insurance Liability and Deposit/Refund System", *Ecological Economics* 3, 231–245.
11. Heal, G. (1991). "Risk Management and Global Change", Paper presented at the first Nordic Conference on the Greenhouse Effect in Copenhagen, September 1991.
12. Huppes, G. (1988). "New Instruments for Environmental Policy: A Perspective", *International Journal of Social Economics* 15(3/4), 42–51.
13. Kelsay, D. and J. Quiggin (1992). "Theories of Choice under Ignorance and Uncertainty", *Journal of Economic Surveys* 6(2), 133–153.
14. Mäler, K. G. (1974). *Environmental Economics: A Theoretical Inquiry*, Baltimore, MD, Johns Hopkins University Press.
15. Mills, E. S. (1972). *Urban Economics*, Glenview, Scott Foresman.
16. Montesano, A. (1991). "Measures of Risk Aversion with Expected and Nonexpected Utility", *Journal of Risk and Uncertainty* 4, 271–283.
17. Montesano, A. (1992). "Non-Additive Probabilities and the Measure of Uncertainty and Risk Aversion", mimeo.
18. Perrings, C. (1987). *Economy and Environment*, Cambridge, Cambridge University Press.
19. Perrings, C. (1989). "Environmental Bonds and Environmental Research in Innovative Activity", *Ecological Economics* 1, 95–110.
20. Perrings, C. (1991). "Reserved Rationality and the Precautionary Principle: Technological Change, Time and Uncertainty in Environmental Decision Making", in *Ecological Economics*, R. Costanza (ed.), New York, Columbia University Press, pp. 153–166.
21. Shogren, J. F., J. A. Herriges and R. Govindasamy (1993). "Limits to Environmental Bonds", *Ecological Economics* 8, 109–133.
22. Solow, R. M. (1971). "The Economist's Approach to Pollution Control", *Science* 173, 498–503.
23. Swierzbinski, J. E. (1994). "Guilty until Proven Innocent – Regulation with Costly and Limited Enforcement", *Journal of Environmental Economics and Management* 27, 127–146.
24. Vercelli, A. (1997). "Hard Uncertainty and Environmental Policy", this volume.
25. Xepapadeas, A. P. (1991). "Environmental Policy under Imperfect Information: Incentive and Moral Hazard", *Journal of Environmental Economics and Management* 20, 113–126.

ANDREA BELTRATTI, GRACIELA CHICHILNISKY AND GEOFFREY HEAL

## 3.4. Uncertain Future Preferences and Conservation

### 1. Introduction

An important problem in environmental economics arises from the irreversibility of consuming or destroying certain resources. Extractive resources like oil are a clear example. Even for environmental resources the same seems to be true in a number of important cases, for example biodiversity, current climate conditions, or complex ecological systems. Irreversibility imposes a severe externality across different generations; future generations will suffer from the destruction of a unique asset like Amazonia, and it is not clear how such a loss could be compensated in terms of other goods. If such an asset is destroyed, then it is not possible subsequently to restore it. In contrast, if the asset is preserved, then it is possible to "use" the asset at a subsequent date. If there is uncertainty about future preferences or valuations, then preservation provides a type of insurance which is not available if the irreversible decision is carried out.

Such an intuitive form of insurance policy has been related to the concept of option value. Amongst the earliest studies of these issues were [1, 7, 17, 18, 20, 26]. Subsequent works that built on these contributions include [4, 5, 11, 12, 21, 23, 24, 27, 28]. An extensive survey of the concept and the meaning of option value is provided in other chapters of this book (those by Chichilnisky and Heal and Vercelli) to which we refer the reader.

None of the previous papers, however, take into account the fact that generations yet to be borne may value natural resources and environmental assets quite differently from us. They may value them more because of an enhanced appreciation of the relationship between humanity and the rest of nature: they may value them less because their world may be more synthetic and created than ours, and they may be pleased with that. Casual empiricism suggests that in fact over the last few decades, the citizens of industrial countries have rediscovered the importance of environmental assets such as clean air and water, biodiversity, rain forests, and many others. The value placed on these appears to have increased substantially, suggesting the possibility of further changes in the future. The possibility of such changes has important implications for our current decisions about environmental preservation: many of the most difficult preservation decisions today concern very long-run issues such as climate change, species conservation and nuclear waste disposal. In all of these cases, most of the benefits and costs will fall on future generations: their valuations of environmental assets should therefore be central to our decisions, and uncertainty about their valuations, inevitable because they are not yet borne, must be explicitly recognized and modeled in our evaluations. This is the agenda of this paper. Solow [25] has argued that such uncertainty must be at the center of any analysis of sustainability. Asheim [2] has also made uncertainty, albeit of a different type, central to a theory of sustainability, as has Tucci in his papers in this volume.

We develop a simple continuous-time stochastic dynamic framework within which we can analyze the optimal preservation of an asset whose consumption is irreversible, in the face of uncertainty about future preferences. This framework is derived from that introduced by Dasgupta and Heal [8], who analyze optimal depletion of a fixed stock of an environmental resource. In a first version of the model utility depends only on the flow of consumption, so that the stock of the resource can be interpreted as an extractive resource which is used in production such as oil or gas. In a second version of the model, utility also depends directly on the stock of the resource, which can therefore be interpreted as an environmental asset such as a forest, a landscape or the biodiversity of a region. As the resource is available in a fixed total supply, its consumption is irreversible: any consumption today leads ineluctably to a reduction in the amount available for future consumption.

The innovation with respect to [8] lies in our using a dynamic optimization model in which current planners are uncertain about the preferences of future generations, and wish to respect the possibility of their having a stronger preference for an environmental good. We compare the optimal depletion paths and associated shadow prices for two cases, one where preferences for the consumption of the resource are known with certainty to be the same at all dates, and a second in which there is a possibility of a change in preferences in the future. We study the difference in optimal depletion (or, equivalently, conservation) policies, and their associated shadow prices, resulting from the introduction of the possible alteration in preferences.

The effect of uncertainty about future preferences on conservation decisions depends, naturally, on the probability distribution governing the evolution of preferences; the exact nature of this effect depends on whether the stock represents an extractive resource or an environmental asset, i.e. whether utility depends on the flow only or on stock and flow. In case of utility depending only on the flow, we show that the possibility of an increase in the intensity of preference for the consumption flow need not on its own have any effect on the optimal conservation policy. There is an impact on conservation policy if and only if the probability distribution is not neutral in a certain very intuitive sense. Roughly speaking, this non-neutrality means that the introduction of uncertainty is not mean-preserving in the sense of Rothschild and Stiglitz [22]: there is not only pure uncertainty about future preferences but also an expected drift.

In the case of an environmental asset valued both as a stock and as a flow, the optimal consumption policy will in general involve the preservation of a positive stock in perpetuity (see Heal's paper "Interpreting Sustainability", Chapter 1.1 of this book). In this case, we study the impact of uncertainty about future preferences on the size of the stock conserved. We take as a benchmark the stock which would be conserved if there were no uncertainty and it was known with certainty that preferences would continue for ever in their initial form. We show that whether preference uncertainty leads to the conservation of a greater or a lesser stock, depends in an intuitive way on the parameters describing the uncertainty. Although this problem is very complex, it is possible to give a complete characterization of how uncertainty affects the desirability of conserving the asset in the long run.

We conclude this introduction with some remarks about the relationship between our formulation and earlier papers (referenced above) which address the concepts of option and quasi-option value. Clearly, all the papers share a common motivation: that it is important, in present decisions, to recognize that the valuation of environmental assets may change over time and so has to be seen as uncertain. Our framework seems rather more general than that of most studies of option values, in that we consider an infinite horizon continuous time problem in which the choice variable is also continuous. The standard, though not uniform, paradigm for the option value literature is two periods and a zero-one choice variable, "conserve" or "don't conserve". We also work within a framework which is now standard in dynamic welfare economics, namely within the framework of a simple optimal growth model. In spite of the increased generality, we are able to obtain results which are at least comparable with earlier results in terms of their degree of detail.

The plan of the paper is as follows: in Section 2 we describe the model and its solution, while in Section 3 we describe a particular specification of the change in preferences and show that in this case pure uncertainty about the valuation of the flow of consumption of a resource requires consumption policies that do not deviate from those under certainty. In Section 4 we study a simpler version of the model involving uncertainty about the direction, but not about the timing, of the change in preferences. Section 5 extends the analysis to the case where uncertainty is about the relative importance of the flow and the stock in the utility function. Section 6 considers option values and the relationship to the previous literature. Section 7 concludes.

## 2. Conservation with Uncertain Future Preferences

### 2.1. *Modelling Uncertain Future Preferences*

Our aim is to model a situation where there is irreversible consumption of an asset in fixed supply. This could happen for example in the case of oil consumption. In order to keep the model as simple as possible we abstract from problems related to the production side of the economy, and imagine that consumption takes place directly by depletion of the asset.

The most natural counterpart to this kind of structure is a variant of the cake-eating problem, described, for example, in [9]. We consider an environmental good of which there is at time $t$ a stock $S_t$. This good may be consumed at a rate $c_t$, so that the rate of change of the stock is given by

$$\frac{dS_t}{dt} \equiv \dot{S}_t = -c_t. \tag{1}$$

Feasibility requires that $S_t \geq 0 \, \forall t$. At time zero society derives utility from the consumption of this good according to the function $u(c_t)$ which is assumed to be increasing, twice continuously differentiable and strictly concave. There is a possibility that at a random future date which we shall denote $T$ the utility of consuming this good will change according to a multiplicative factor. For simplicity it is assumed that the function $u(c_t)$ will become equal to $(1 + \alpha)u(c_t)$ with probability $q$ or to $(1 - \beta)u(c_t)$ with probability $(1 - q)$, for $\alpha, \beta \geq 0$. The date $T$ at which there is a switch of preferences is a random variable with marginal density $\omega_t$. We also assume that the change in preferences is a once-for-all phenomenon. We can think of the change in preferences as representing a change of tastes from one generation to another: the current generation is uncertain about the preferences of its successors and wishes to allow for the fact that they may value more highly the environmental good. Alternatively, it might be the discovery that some aspect of the environment is medically important in ways not previously recognized, leading to an increase in its valuation.

We begin by formulating an ancillary problem. Following Dasgupta and Heal [8] we define a state valuation function $W_F(S_T)$ which values the stock $S_T$ remaining at time $T$ at which the change in preferences occurs. The valuation is according to the utility function $F(c_t)$, where $F$ stands for the utility function that applies after $T$.

$$W_F(S_T) = \max \int_T^\infty F(c_t) e^{-\delta(t-T)} dt \text{ subject to } \int_T^\infty c_t dt = S_T. \tag{2}$$

$\delta$ is of course a discount rate applied to future utilities: for a discussion of the appropriateness of discounting in this context, see [16]. Let $W_F$ be denoted $W_1(S_T)$ when $F(c) = (1 + \alpha)u(c)$ and $W_2(S_T)$ when $F(c) = (1 - \beta)u(c)$. Define

$$EW_F(S_T) = qW_1(S_T) + (1-q)W_2(S_T) \tag{3}$$

as the expected valuation of the stock at time $T$.

Given this, we may now define an overall problem as:

$$\max \int_0^\infty w_T \left\{ \int_0^T u(c_t)e^{-\delta t} dt + e^{-\delta T} EW_F(S_T) \right\} dT$$

$$\text{subject to } \dot{S}_t = -c_t \text{ and } S_t \geq 0 \ \forall t. \tag{4}$$

The interpretation of this problem is as follows. The date $T$ at which preferences may change is a random variable. For any particular $T$, the expected utility of a consumption path is given by the expression in the parentheses { }. We then take as the maximand the expectation of this over all possible values of $T$. In other words, we maximize the expected discounted value of utility derived from consuming the environmental good, where the expectation is taken with respect to the probability distributions governing changes in preference for the environmental good. By integrating by parts, the maximand in (4) can be reformulated as

$$\int_0^\infty e^{-\delta t} \{u(c_t)\Omega_t + w_t EW_F(S_t)\} dt, \tag{5}$$

where $\Omega_t = \int_t^\infty w_\tau d\tau$.

## 2.2. Stochastic and Deterministic Solutions

When solving the actual problem (4), it will be useful to consider as a standard of comparison the solution of a problem where a decision maker consumes a fixed stock of resources but ignores uncertainty about future preferences altogether, and assumes that the utility function is never going to change. Under these assumptions we face a standard cake-eating problem whose solution requires that consumption decline over time at a rate depending on the discount rate and the elasticity of the marginal utility of consumption. The problem can be formulated as

$$\max \int_0^\infty u(c_t)e^{-\delta t} dt \text{ subject to } \int_0^\infty c_t dt \leq S_0. \tag{6}$$

The solution to (6) is:

$$\frac{\dot{c}_t}{c_t} = \frac{\delta}{\eta}, \tag{7}$$

where $\eta$ is the elasticity of the marginal utility of the function $u$ with respect to consumption, i.e., $\eta = (u''c)/u' < 0$ and the single prime denotes the first and the double prime denotes the second derivative of $u$ with respect to its argument. In the rest of the paper, we denote by $c_t(7)$ the consumption path that satisfies (7), and by $g_{ct}(7)$ the corresponding rate of growth.

In order to solve the general problem (4) we now introduce a shadow price or adjoint variable on the stock $S_t$, denoted $p_t$. Then a necessary condition for a consumption path and a shadow price path to solve (4) is that $c_t$ and $p_t$ satisfy the following equations:[1]

$$u'(c_t)\Omega_t = p_t,$$
$$\dot{p}_t - \delta p_t = -\omega_t EW'_F. \tag{8}$$

A little manipulation allows us to condense these into the intuitive single equation

$$\frac{\dot{c}_t}{c_t} = \frac{\delta}{\eta} + \left\{\frac{u' - EW'_F}{u'}\right\} \frac{\omega_t}{\eta \Omega_t}. \tag{9}$$

According to Equation (9) the rate of growth of consumption is time-varying, and depends in a complicated way on the probabilities and on the marginal utilities that are in turn a function of the past consumption policy. In the rest of the paper we will denote by $c_t(9)$ the time path of consumption which satisfies (9), and by $g_{ct}(9)$ the corresponding rate of growth.

Equation (9) tells us that the rate of change of consumption depends on the discount rate, the elasticity of the marginal utility of consumption and the expectation of the increase in the marginal valuation of consumption conditional on the change in preferences not having yet occurred.[2] For a given elasticity of marginal utility, the rate of change of consumption depends negatively on the rate of time preference. The effect of the second term on the right-hand side of (9) is ambiguous, and depends on the difference between the immediate marginal utility of consumption at time $t$, and the expected marginal valuation of the remaining stock of the asset; for a given ratio $\omega/\Omega$, the larger is the marginal valuation of the remaining stock, the faster is its rate of depletion falls.

If the utility function is scaled up by $(1+\alpha)$ from $T$ onwards, then $F(c) = (1+\alpha)u(c)$ and the appropriate state valuation function is $(1+\alpha)W(S_T)$, and if it is scaled down by $(1-\beta)$, then the state valuation function is $(1-\beta)W(S_T)$. Therefore, in this case the function (3) assumes the simple form:

$$EW_F(S_T) = q(1+\alpha)W(S_T) + (1-q)(1-\beta)W(S_T) = \Gamma W(S_T), \tag{10}$$

where $\Gamma = q(1+\alpha) + (1-q)(1-\beta)$.

By using such a description of uncertainty and the proposition proven in the Appendix, according to which the marginal valuation of the stock is equal to the marginal utility of consumption after the change in preferences, it is possible to rewrite Equation (9) as:

$$g_{ct}(9) = g_{ct}(7) + \left\{\frac{u'(c_t(9)) - \Gamma u'(c_t^*(7))}{u'(c_t(9))}\right\} \frac{\omega_t}{\eta \Omega_t}, \tag{11}$$

where $c_t^*(7)$ is optimal consumption after preferences have changed. Such a consumption level is different from the consumption which would hold under the solution to a standard cake-eating problem, which we have denoted by

$c_t(7)$; $c_t^*(7)$ applies at time $t$ if a solution to a certainty problem is followed from time $t$ on, but not before time $t$, while $c_t(7)$ is the time t consumption that holds when the solution to the certainty problem has been followed since the very beginning. Formally:

$$c_t(7) = -\frac{\delta}{\eta} S_0 e^{\frac{\delta}{\eta}t},$$

$$c_t^*(7) = -\frac{\delta}{\eta}\left[S_0 - \int_0^t c_t(9)dt\right].$$

Clearly, $c_t^*(7) < c_t(7)$ whenever the actual policy prescribes an integral of consumption from time 0 to time $t$ that is larger than the one required by the solution to the deterministic problem.

## 3. Specific Cases

Two specific cases of the general framework will be helpful in obtaining clearer results and building up intuition.

### 3.1. Symmetric Uncertainty

$\Gamma = 1$ provides an interesting benchmark, as in this case the probabilities of the states of nature compound with the magnitudes of the change in utility in such a way as to make the mathematical expectation of the future utility equal to the current utility; we describe this as symmetric uncertainty. In this case we can show that the decision maker may optimally ignore uncertainty about future preferences, and adopt the policy suggested by the certain problem. In this case, uncertainty about future preferences has no impact at all on optimal current consumption levels: it is not appropriate to consume more conservatively (with respect to the model that ignores uncertainty) in the face of a possible increase in future preferences for the good, if this is balanced by a possible decrease. So uncertainty about future preferences alone does not give rise to a conservation motive: the uncertainty has to be asymmetric, in the sense that the possibility of an increase in preferences outweighs that of a decrease.

Formally:

PROPOSITION 1. *The optimal consumption policy for the uncertain problems (4) with symmetric uncertainty about future preferences is identical to that for the certain problem (6) with unchanging preferences.*

*Proof.* In the case of symmetric uncertainty $EW_F(S_T) = W(S_T)$ and the maximand becomes:

$$\int_0^\infty \omega_T \left\{\int_0^T u(c_t)e^{-\delta t}dt + e^{-\delta T}W(S_T)\right\}dT$$

$$= \int_0^\infty \omega_T \left\{ \int_0^\infty u(c_t) e^{-\delta t} dt \right\} dT$$

and the two problems are obviously identical. □

Intuitively, the result is due to the fact that risk aversion by itself does not necessarily imply aversion to uncertainty about future preferences. In our model the agent is risk averse for each given preference structure, but is risk neutral with respect to uncertainty about the structure of preferences. So for a risk averse decision maker who follows the standard paradigm of expected utility maximization, we obtain the strong result that uncertainty about preferences alone does not give rise to a more conservative policy for the use of the resource: there needs to be an asymmetry in the distribution of possible outcomes as well. This is also true of the earlier formulation of option value as in [1, 17]: this aspect of those results is reviewed by Chichilnisky and Heal in Chapter 1.2 of this volume.

### 3.2. Preference Uncertainty Alone

We now eliminate one source of uncertainty, the one due to timing shocks, and consider a decision-maker who knows that at a given time $T$ her preferences will change, although in an uncertain way. Formally, the problem is now:

$$\max \int_0^T u(c_t) e^{-\delta t} dt + e^{-\delta T} EW_F(S_T) \text{ subject to} \dot{S}_t = -c_t, S_t \geq 0 \ \forall t, \quad (12)$$

where $EW_F(S_T)$ is given by Equation (10). Using the expression given in Equation (10), the maximand can be rewritten as:

$$\max \int_0^T u(c_t) e^{-\delta t} dt + e^{-\delta T} \Gamma W(S_T), \quad (13)$$

which shows that the particular specification we have chosen for the change in the utility function makes the problem with preference uncertainty only exactly equivalent from a formal point of view to a problem with a known change in preferences.

The necessary conditions of problem (12) are, apart from a transversality condition, the same as those of an infinite horizon problem:

$$u'(c_t) = p_t, \dot{p}_t - \delta p_t = 0, p_T = \Gamma W'(S_T).$$

The solution from time zero to $T$ is:

$$c_T = -\frac{\delta}{\eta} S_T,$$

$$\frac{\dot{c}}{c} = \frac{\delta}{\eta}, \quad \frac{\dot{p}}{p} = \delta$$

Together with the transversality condition:

$$p_T = \Gamma W'(S_T), \quad (14)$$

this yields an expression for the marginal utility of consumption at time 0:

$$u'(c_0) = e^{-\delta T}\Gamma W'(S_T). \tag{15}$$

Such an expression is useful in understanding the effect of uncertainty about future preferences on the optimal policy, as clearly it shows that *in the case of preference uncertainty and certain timing, initial consumption is larger than, less than, or equal to that obtaining under certainty according to whether $\Gamma$ is less than, greater than, or equal to 1.*

## 4. The Stock as Source of Utility

It is now assumed that society derives utility both from the consumption of this good according to the function $u(c_t)$ and also from the stock according to the function $v(S_t)$. This extended specification is particularly useful when studying environmental resources, see, for example, [19]. Uncertainty in this case may be interpreted in terms of the relative valuation of consumption goods and the environmental asset. The scenario that will be described here is that at some future date society may increase its valuation of environmental assets relative to the flow of consumption which can be obtained by depleting the assets. Both utility functions $u(c)$ and $v(S)$ are assumed to be increasing, twice continuously differentiable and strictly concave. In order to consider a model with a steady state we assume that marginal utility of consumption evaluated at zero consumption is finite, $u'(0) < \infty$.

While at the beginning of the planning horizon the flow of consumption provides a certain utility $u(c_t)$ and the stock of the asset provides a certain utility of $v(S_t)$, there is a possibility that at a random future date $T$, the utility function is affected by an exogenous shock. The utility of the flow will not be affected, but the utility directly provided by the stock will change to either $(1+\alpha)v(S)$ (with probability $q$) or to $(1-\beta)v(S)$ (with probability $1-q$), for $\alpha, \beta \geq 0$. As before, the date $T$ at which there is a switch of preferences is a random variable with marginal density $\omega_t$.

The state valuation function $W(S_T)$ which values the stock $S_T$ remaining at the time $T$ at which the change in preferences occurs is now:

$$W_\alpha(S_T) = \max \int_T^\infty \left[u(c_t) + (1+\alpha)v(S_t)\right] e^{-\delta(t-T)} dt$$

$$\text{subject to } \int_T^\infty c_t dt = S_T, \tag{16}$$

$$W_\beta(S_T) = \max \int_T^\infty \left[u(c_t) + (1-\beta)v(S_t)\right] e^{-\delta(t-T)} dt$$

$$\text{subject to } \int_T^\infty c_t dt = S_T. \tag{17}$$

The overall problem can be written as the maximization of:

$$E\left\{\int_0^T e^{-\delta t}\left[u(c_t)+v(S_t)\right]dt + e^{-\delta T}\left[qW_\alpha(S_T)+(1-q)W_\beta(S_T)\right]\right\}$$

given the standard resource constraint. By integrating by parts, the maximand can be reformulated as:

$$\int_0^\infty e^{-\delta t}\left\{(u(c_t)+v(S_t))\Omega_t + \omega_t\left[qW_\alpha(S_t)+(1-q)W_\beta(S_t)\right]\right\}dt, \quad (18)$$

where $\Omega_t = \int_t^\infty \omega_\tau d\tau$. Necessary conditions for a consumption path and a shadow price path to solve (18) are:

$$u'(c_t)\Omega_t = p_t,$$

$$\dot{p}_t - \delta p_t = -\Omega_t v'(S_t) - \omega_t\left[qW'_\alpha(S_t)+(1-q)W'_\beta(S_t)\right], \quad (19)$$

which can be used to derive:

$$\eta\frac{\dot{c}_t}{c_t} = \delta - \frac{v'(S_t)}{u'(c_t)} + \lambda\left\{\frac{u'(c_t) - qW'_\alpha(S_t) - (1-q)W'_\beta(S_t)}{u'(c_t)}\right\}, \quad (20)$$

where $\lambda = \omega/\Omega$.

Equation (20) admits a steady state at which consumption is constant. At any stationary state, the consumption of the flow must be zero and the stock must be constant. Hence at a stationary state of (20):

$$\delta u'(0) = v'(S) - [u'(0) - qW'_\alpha(S) - (1-q)W'_\beta(S)].$$

We shall consider three different steady states, each corresponding to a problem with no uncertainty about preferences. In one case the utility of the stock is constant at $v(S)$: this leads to stationary state value of the stock of $S_D$. In the other cases the utility of the stock is constant at $(1+\alpha)v(S)$ or $(1-\beta)v(S)$: these cases lead respectively to stationary states with stock levels $S_\alpha$ and $S_\beta$. Note that if preferences never change, $\lambda = 0\ \forall t$. Hence:

PROPOSITION 2. *The steady state corresponding to the original preference structure of the agent is characterized by a level of the stock $S_D$ such that $\delta u'(0) = v'(S_D)$, while the steady state corresponding to an increase (decrease) in preferences is characterized by a level of the stock $S_\alpha$ ($S_\beta$) such that $\delta u'(0) = (1+\alpha)v'(S_\alpha)$ ($\delta u'(0) = (1-\beta)v'(S_\beta)$).*

It is easy, simply by concavity of the valuation function, to relate the three stocks:

*Remark 1.* $S_\alpha > S_D > S_\beta$.

We now locate the level of the stock corresponding to a point of rest of the system before uncertainty is resolved, and compare it with the steady state which holds after resolution of uncertainty, which will be $S_\alpha$ or $S_\beta$.

Equation (20) can be used to characterize a steady state of the system before uncertainty is resolved ($S_S$) by evaluating it at zero consumption and setting it equal to 0, while not setting $\lambda$ to zero:

$$\delta - \frac{v'(S_S)}{u'(0)} + \lambda \left\{ \frac{u'(0) - qW'_\alpha(S_S) - (1-q)W'_\beta(S_S)}{u'(0)} \right\} = 0. \quad (21)$$

To evaluate the general properties of such a function we define:

$$A_t \equiv \delta - \frac{v'(S_t)}{u'(c_t)} \equiv A(S_t, c_t)$$

and

$$B_t \equiv \lambda \left\{ \frac{u'(c_t) - qW'_\alpha - (1-q)W'_\beta}{u'(c_t)} \right\} \equiv B(S_t, c_t)$$

and analyze these two components as a function of various values of the stock, for zero consumption, in order to find the equilibrium point.

The following remark, which derives directly from the very definition of the term $S_D$, takes care of the first term.

Remark 2. $A(S_D, 0) = 0$, $A(S, 0) > 0$ for $S > S_D$, $A(S, 0) < 0$ for $S < S_D$.

It follows that the function $A(.,.)$ is positive (negative) for large (small) values of the stock, and equals zero when the actual stock coincides with the stock representing the equilibrium of the deterministic system with the initial stock utility function $v(S)$.

The term $B_t$ is more complicated to analyze. We now characterize the sign of $B(S_t, 0)$ at the stationary states $S_\alpha$ and $S_\beta$. The following lemma is used in this characterization:

LEMMA 3. $W'_\alpha(S_\alpha) = W'_\beta(S_\beta) = u'(0)$, $W'_\alpha(S_\beta) = ((1+\alpha)/(1-\beta))u'(0)$, $W'_\beta(S_\alpha) > ((1-\beta)/(1+\alpha))u'(0)$.

Proof. The first two equalities follow from the definition of the steady state, which implies a marginal valuation of the stock equal to the marginal utility of consumption. The third equality comes from noting that if an extra unit of stock is given to an economy whose stock is currently $S_\beta$ with utility of the stock $(1 + \alpha)v(S)$ then this unit will be preserved, as with these preferences a stock equal to $S_\beta$ implies a corner solution with a marginal valuation of the stock larger than the marginal utility of consumption. Therefore, the utility value of an extra unit is equal to $((1 + \alpha)v'(S_\beta))/\delta$, which equals $((1 + \alpha)/(1 - \beta))u'(0)$ from using the definition of $v'(S_\beta)$ given in Proposition 2. Finally, the inequality describes the case where an extra unit of the stock is assigned to the decision maker in the case where he is already depleting the stock in order to reach a steady state with a lower stock level. Suppose that preferences are described by $(1 - \beta)v(S)$ but the stock is $S_\alpha$. Given an extra unit of the stock $\Delta S$ if such extra unit is added to the stock $S_\alpha$ and maintained forever, the increment in total utility is $((1-\beta)v'(S_\alpha))/\delta$. But since the economy is not at the stationary state where $u'(c) = ((1-\beta)v'(S))/\delta$ then it is possible to increase utility by more than that so $W'_\beta(S_\alpha) > ((1-\beta)v'(S_\alpha))/\delta$. Using $v'(S_\alpha) = (\delta u'(0)/1 + \alpha)$ one obtains $W'_\beta(S_\alpha) > ((1-\beta)u'(0)/1 + \alpha)$, and this gives the inequality. □

We are now ready to show:

PROPOSITION 4. *There exists a positive stock preserved at the stochastic steady state defined by (21), which we denote $S_S$.*

*Proof.* Equation (21) defines a stochastic steady state. Multiplying both sides by $u'(0)$ and using Proposition 2 this can be rewritten as:

$$v'(S_D) - v'(S_S) = -\lambda \left[u'(0) - W'_\beta(S_S) - q\left(W'_\alpha(S_S) - W'_\beta(S_S)\right)\right],$$

according to which the difference in the marginal utility of the stock between the deterministic and the stochastic steady state is always positive. To see this, note that:

$$v'(S_D) - v'(S_S) = -u'(0)B(S_S, 0)$$

so that the sign of $v'(S_D) - v'(S_S)$ depends on the sign of $B(S_S, 0)$. To evaluate such a sign note that:

$$B(S, 0) = u'(0) - qW'_\alpha(S) + qW'_\beta(S) - W'_\beta(S)$$
$$= u'(0) - W'_\beta(S) + q\left[W'_\beta(S) - W'_\alpha(S)\right].$$

The second term $W'_\beta(S) - W'_\alpha(S)$ is always negative. The term $u'(0) - W'_\beta(S)$ is equal to zero if $S = S_\beta$, is positive if $S > S_\beta$ and negative if $S < S_\beta$. Therefore at $S_\beta$ $B(S_\beta, 0)$ is negative. At $S = S_\alpha$ instead $B(S_\alpha, 0) = u'(0) - W'_\beta(S_\alpha) + q\left[W'_\beta(S_\alpha) - u'(0)\right] = (1-q)\left[u'(0) - W'_\beta(S_\alpha)\right]$. To give a definite sign we need to show that $u'(0) - W'_\beta(S_\alpha) > 0$. We need therefore an upper bound for $W'_\beta(S_\alpha)$. To obtain such a bound, suppose that preferences are such that the utility function of the stock is $(1-\beta)v(S)$ and the stock is $S_\alpha$. It follows that the best use is consumption, i.e. $W'_\beta(S_\alpha) = u'(\hat{c})$ where $\hat{c}$ is current consumption. But $u'(\hat{c}) \leq u'(0)$ by concavity of the utility function. Therefore, $W'_\beta(S_\alpha) \leq u'(0)$. Hence $u'(0) - W'_\beta(S_\alpha) \geq 0$. Therefore the function $B(S_t, c_t)$ is non-negative at $S_\alpha$ and the function $A(S_t, c_t) + B(S_t, c_t)$ is negative at $S_\beta$ and positive at $S_\alpha$ and it has to change sign in the interval. □

The previous proposition also allows us to characterize the connection between the level of the stock in the stochastic steady state and the level of the stock in the deterministic steady state. In fact:

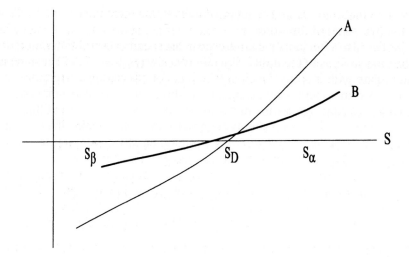

Figure 1. A is negative below $S_D$, zero at $S_D$ and positive above. B is negative at $S_\beta$ and non-negative at $S_\alpha$, so the sum must equal zero somewhere between $S_\alpha$ and $S_\beta$.

PROPOSITION 5. *The level of the stock in the stochastic steady state, $S_S$ may be larger than, equal to or smaller than the level of the stock in the deterministic steady state, $S_D$. For a small probability of a preference increase it is less than $S_D$, and vice versa.*

*Proof.* The figure shows that the function $A(S,0)$ is equal to zero for $S = S_D$, positive for $S > S_D$ and negative for $S < S_D$. The function $B(S,0)$ instead may be either larger or smaller than zero when evaluated at $S = S_D$. For example, when $q = 0$ one has $u'(0) = W'_\beta(S_\beta) > W'_\beta(S_D)$. It follows that when $q = 0$ at $S = S_D$ one has $A(S_D,0) + B(S_D,0) > 0$ so that the intersection with the horizontal axis, which defines the level of the stock corresponding to the stochastic steady state, is to the left of $S_D$. □

### 4.1. *A Comparison between the Two Models*

In the model with environmental assets as source of utility, uncertainty about future preferences may give rise to a path of consumption of resources which implies an increase or a decrease in the total use of resources with respect to the total consumption under the certainty of no change. No equivalent result could be obtained in the previous model, where all the stock was eventually consumed due to the absence of a steady state.

Note that with utility depending on the stock it is difficult to analyze the consequences of symmetric uncertainty, which can again be defined as the constancy of the expected utility of wealth. In the model with the stock in the utility function in fact the two marginal valuation functions do not have a simple relation to each other given that the total use of the stock is different in the two states of the world.

Notice also a fundamental difference in the specification of the two models: when the stock is in the utility function it is always possible to consume at a future date with a utility function which is not affected by uncertainty, as it is assumed that there is no change in the direct utility of consumption. This provides a hedge against the bad state of the world, to the extent that a low utility of the stock in itself simply suggests to the policy-maker the optimality of consuming a larger fraction of the remaining stock, deriving from this a utility that has not been affected by the change. Our conjecture, which cannot be proven formally at this stage, is that this characteristic promotes a more conservative usage policy, in the same way as the introduction of a riskless asset always increases savings on the part of a risk-averse agent.

## 5. Shadow Prices and Option Values

This section discusses the connections of our model with the definitions of option value given in the environmental resources literature.[3] Such definitions involve both taxes aimed at inducing a myopic decision-maker to take an optimal decision and comparisons of value functions of optimal and suboptimal problems.

The effects of uncertainty about preferences on the consumption policies are reflected in the effects on the shadow prices associated with consumption. The first order conditions can be evaluated at the equilibrium quantities in order to find the market price that would induce the agent to follow a policy leading exactly to those quantities. It follows that at each point of the planning horizon one can compare the market price for the case where the change in preferences is ignored with the market price for the case where the possibility of new preferences is taken into account.

In the specification where uncertainty about future preferences only involves the flow of utility, there may or may not be any effects on competitive prices. It has been shown that there are no effects in the case of symmetric uncertainty, as the optimal solution under uncertainty corresponds to that under certainty, with no change in shadow prices. In the case of uncertain preferences but certain timing instead it was observed that the optimal policy changes in an intuitive way, depending on the direction of the shift in preferences, anticipating (postponing) consumption in the case that a worsening (improving) of utility is anticipated. In this case the shadow price is also different from the one holding under certainty.

The difference in the prices can then be interpreted as a tax that should be imposed on the myopic decision-maker in order to induce him to adopt the optimal policy which takes into account the possibility of a change in preferences. A way to interpret such a change is in terms of the price that a benevolent and fully-informed dictator should impose on myopic private agents in order to induce them to internalize the possibility of a change in preferences.

Consider as an example a case of asymmetric uncertainty in the model for the environmental asset, where the optimal stochastic policy deviates from the optimal deterministic policy assuming no change of preferences. Assume, for the sake of the argument, that it is optimal to decrease current (time 0) consumption so as to reach a stochastic steady state with a stock which is larger than the stock which would obtain in the deterministic case. Then the (positive) difference in the prices of the stochastic and the deterministic problems may be considered a tax that must be imposed on the private agents in order to take into account the dynamic externality when deciding their consumption path. A positive tax should be put on consumption of environmental assets to induce myopic decision-makers to slow down the rate of deletion of the stock. Such a tax resembles the "development tax" that is sometimes suggested in the environmental literature in cases of irreversible consumption.

The difference in the shadow prices between the solution which ignores and the solution which takes into account uncertainty is also connected with the definition of option value given in the environmental literature. This literature, as was pointed out in the introduction, has largely been based on very simple two-period discrete choice models. In the context of such a models there is a one-to-one relationship between the value function of the problem and the shadow prices of the problem. In fact, in these models the tax on development is also the measure which equates the value functions of a problem under full information and a problem with less information.

For example, Henry [17] defines the option value, for the case of a discrete control variable, as the amount of consumption good that a person would pay to have the possibility of making decisions taking into account all the information. Paying this amount and then making the decision with full information would leave her as well off as in the case where she has to make all the decisions at the beginning of the planning period, before the uncertainty is resolved. He shows that considering the value of information in this sense tilts the decision towards a more conservative policy. Likewise, omitting this value leads to under-conservation. As another example, Hanemann interprets the option value as the difference between the value of the problem when this is solved with a closed loop (CL) policy and the value of the problem solved with an open loop policy, which may be a simple open loop (OL) policy or a feedback open loop (FOL). He shows that in cases of discrete control variables, such a value is always positive, because a CL policy takes into account the state of the system while the OL policy does not. An OL policy is therefore in general a sub-optimal policy when compared with a CL policy.

The common characteristics of these examples are: (1) a comparison between a model with full information and a model with partial information;

(2) a comparison between the value functions of such problems; and (3) a comparison between the shadow prices so as to induce a myopic decision-maker to take a rational solution. In the more general models we have worked with, (1) and (2) are still closely connected: we can compare optimal and sub-optimal decision structures and then evaluate the value functions. However, (3) is not the same as (2): the change in the shadow prices at each point in time is in general different from the difference in the value functions. It is, therefore, necessary to distinguish more clearly what is meant by option value. We believe (see also [13] for a similar opinion) that the definition of option value connected with the difference in shadow prices is the most relevant, at least from the point of view of environmental policy, because affecting market prices is an important instrument for promoting sustainable policies.

The relevance of shadow prices for environmental policy is well described by the following example proposed by Graham-Tomasi [13]: "A resource problem that illustrates most of the issues is the depletion of moist tropical rainforest. The resource stock has value both for its timber and the agricultural land (or other uses) it may be converted to, as well as for the ecosystem services it provides and the biodiversity it contains. The values of the goods and services provided by a tropical forest in its natural state are not well known in comparison with our understanding of the value of harvested timber and agricultural products... The basic idea of quasi-option value, then, is that the mere prospect of improved research programs on the value of moist tropic forest ecosystems, even allowing for the possibility that they may find that such forests are less valuable than we now believe, should lead to greater conservation of such forests".

## 6. Conclusions

We have analyzed the problem of making irreversible decisions in a situation where preferences may change in the future, after the irreversible decision has been made. Following [1, 7, 20, 26], we have used this as a framework for thinking about the conservation of environmental assets and deriving an option value. Contrary to most of the papers in the literature, we have worked with a general model in which there is a possibility of a quantum increase in the intensity of preference for environmental goods at an unknown future date. The present generation does not know the preferences of its successors and wishes to allow for the possibility of them having a greater valuation of the environmental good. We have studied the change in the shadow price of the environmental asset as a result of the possibility of a preference change.

Perhaps the most interesting conclusion is that in the present framework uncertainty about future preferences, including the possibility of an increase in the strength of the preference for the environmental good, is not on its own a source of a conservation motive. It is only asymmetric uncertainty that leads to these conclusions. In other words, it is not sufficient for a positive option value that we believe that future generations may have a stronger preference for environmental goods: we have to believe that on average they will do so.

## A. Appendix

### A.1. *Marginal Utility of Wealth*

In the next Proposition we establish a simple identity that was used in earlier computations. It shows that the derivative of the state valuation function with respect to the remaining stock at time $T$, is equal to the marginal utility of consumption at time $T$ along a path which is optimal according to the utility function which applies from $T$ on.

PROPOSITION 6. *Let $W_C(S_T)$ be defined as in (6). Then $(dW/dS_T) = (du(c_T^*)/dc_T^*) = p_T$, where $c_T^*$ is the optimal consumption path from time $T$ onwards and $p_T$ is the shadow price of the stock $S_T$ at time $T$.*

*Proof.* Without any loss of generality we shall set $T = 0$ and $W_C = W(S_0)$.

$$\frac{dW}{dS_0} = \frac{d}{dS_0}\left\{\max \int_0^\infty u(c_t)e^{-\delta t}dt \text{ subject to } \int_0^\infty c_t \leq S_0\right\}$$

$$= \frac{d}{dS_0}\left\{\int_0^\infty u(c_t)e^{-\delta t}dt \text{ where } \frac{\dot{c}}{c} = \frac{\delta}{\eta} \text{ and } c_0 = \frac{-S_0\delta}{\eta} \text{ by (7)}\right\}$$

$$= \frac{d}{dS_0}\left\{\int_0^\infty u\left(\frac{-S_0\delta}{\eta}e^{(\delta/\eta)t}\right)e^{-\delta t}dt\right\}$$

$$= -\int_0^\infty \frac{du(c_t)}{dc}e^{-\delta t+(\delta/\eta)t}\frac{\delta}{\eta}dt$$

$$= \frac{du(c_0)}{dc}\frac{\delta}{\eta}\int_0^\infty e^{(\delta/\eta)t}dt \text{ using (9) for the problem in (6).}$$

The equality with $p_T$ follows from the first order condition (9), applied to the problem (4). This completes the proof. □

## Notes

1. For mathematical details, see [9].
2. $\omega/\Omega$ is of course the probability of the change in preferences occurring at t given that it has not previously occurred.
3. See [13] for a general discussion of this point.

## References

1. Arrow, K. J. and A. C. Fisher. "Environmental Preservation, Uncertainty and Irreversibility", *Quarterly Journal of Economics* 88, 1974, 312–319.
2. Asheim, G. "Sustainability When Resource Management Has Stochastic Consequences", Discussion Paper, Norges Handelshøyskole, 1193.
3. Beltratti, A., G. Chichilnisky and G. Heal. "Sustainable Growth and the Green Golden Rule", in *Approaches to Sustainable Economic Development*, I. Goldin and A. Winters (eds.), Paris, OECD, pp. 147–156.
4. Bishop, R. "Option Value: An Exposition and Extension", *Land Economics* 58, 1982, 1–15.
5. Bohm, P. "Option Demand and Consumers' Surplus: Comment", *American Economic Review* 65(4), 1975, 733–736.
6. Chichilnisky G. and G. M. Heal. "Global Environmental Risks", *Journal of Economic Perspectives* 7, 1993, 65–86.
7. Cicchetti, C. J. and A. M. Freeman. "Option Demand and Consumer Surplus: Further Comment", *Quarterly Journal of Economics* 85, 1971, 528–539.
8. Dasgupta, P. S. and G. M. Heal. "The Optimal Depletion of Exhaustible Resources", *Review of Economic Studies*, Special Issue on Symposium on the Economics of Exhaustible Resources, 1974, 3–28.
9. Dasgupta, P. S. and G. M. Heal. *Economic Theory and Exhaustible Resources*, Cambridge, U.K., Cambridge University Press, 1979.
10. Fisher, A. C. and W. M. Hanemann. "Quasi-Option Value: Some Misconceptions Dispelled", *Journal of Environmental Economics and Management* 15, 1987, 183–190.
11. Fisher, A. C. and W. M. Hanemann. "Option Value and the Extinction of Species", in *Advances in Applied Microeconomics*, Vol. 4, V. K. Smith (ed.), Greenwich, CT, JAI Press, 1979.
12. Fisher, A. C., J. V. Krutilla and C. J. Cicchetti. "The Economics of Environmental Preservation: A Theoretical and Empirical Perspective", *American Economic Review* 57, 1972, 605–619.
13. Graham-Tomasi, T., "Quasi-Option Value", in *Handbook of Environmental Economics*, D. W. Bromley (ed.), Oxford (U.K.) and Cambridge (U.S.A.), Blackwell, 1995.
14. Hanemann, W. M. "Information and the Concept of Option Value", *Journal of Environmental Economics and Management* 16, 1989, 23–37.
15. Heal, G. M. "Uncertainty and the Optimal Supply Policy for an Exhaustible Resource", in *Advances in the Economics of Energy and Resources*, Vol. 2, R. Pindyck (ed.), Greenwich, CT, JAI Press, 1979, pp. 119–147.
16. Heal, G. M. "Depletion and Discounting", in *Proceedings of Symposia in Applied Mathematics*, Vol. 32, R. McKelvey (ed.), American Mathematical Society, 1985, pp. 33–43.
17. Henry, C. "Option Values in the Economics of Irreplaceable Assets", *Review of Economic Studies*, Special Issue on Symposium on the Economics of Exhaustible Resources, 1974, 89–104.
18. Henry, C. "Investment Decisions under Uncertainty: The Irreversibility Effect", *American Economic Review* 64, 1974, 1006–1012.
19. Krautkraemer, J. A. "Optimal Growth, Resource Amenities and the Preservation of Natural Environments", *Review of Economic Studies* LII, 1985, 153–170.
20. Krutilla, J. V. "Conservation Reconsidered", *American Economic Review* 57, 1967, 777–786.
21. Mitchell, R. C. and R. Carson, *Using Surveys to Value Public Goods: the Contingent Valuation Method*, Washington DC, Resources for the Future, 1989.
22. Rothschild, M. and J. E. Stiglitz. "Increasing Risk 1: A Definition", *Journal of Economic Theory* 2(3), 1970, 225–243.

23. Schmalensee, R. "Option Demand and Consumers' Surplus: Valuing Price Changes under Uncertainty", *American Economic Review* 62, 1972, 813–824.
24. Smith, V. K. "A Bound for Option Value", *Land Economics* 60(3), 1984, 292–296.
25. Solow, R. M. "Sustainability: An Economist's Perspective", The Eighteenth J. Seward Johnson Lecture, Woods Hole Oceanographic Institution, Woods Hole, MA, 1992.
26. Weisbrod, B. A. "Collective Consumption Services of Individual Consumption Goods", *Quarterly Journal of Economics* 77, 1964, 71–77.
27. Viscusi, W. K. "Environmental Policy Choice with an Uncertain Chance of Irreversibility", *Journal of Environmental Economics and Management* 12, 1985, 28–44.
28. Viscusi, W. K. "Irreversible Environmental Investments with Uncertain Benefit Levels", *Journal of Environmental Economics and Management* 15, 1988, 147–157.
29. World Commission on Environment and Development. *Our Common Future*, (the "Brundtland Report"), Oxford University Press, 1987.

GRACIELA CHICHILNISKY AND GEOFFREY HEAL

## 3.5. Financial Markets for Unknown Risks *

### 1. Introduction

New risks seem to be an unavoidable in a period of rapid change. The last few decades have brought us the risks of global warming, nuclear meltdown, ozone depletion, failure of satellite launcher rockets, collision of supertankers, AIDS and Ebola.[1] A key feature of a new risk, as opposed to an old and familiar one, is that one knows little about it. In particular, one knows little about the chances or the costs of its occurrence. This makes it hard to manage these risks: existing paradigms for the rational management of risks require that we associate probabilities to various levels of losses. This poses particular challenges for the insurance industry, which is at the leading edge of risk management. Misestimation of new risks has lead to several bankruptcies in the insurance and reinsurance businesses.[2] In this paper we propose a novel framework for providing insurance cover against risks whose parameters are unknown. In fact many of the risks at issue may be not just unknown but also unknowable: it is difficult to imagine repetition of the events leading to global warming or ozone depletion, and, therefore, difficult to devise a relative frequency associated with repeated experiments.

A systematic and rational way of hedging unknown risks is proposed here, one which involves the use of securities markets as well as the more traditional insurance techniques. This model is quite consistent with the current evolution of the insurance and reinsurance industries, which are beginning to explore the securitization of some aspects of insurance contracts via Act of God bonds, contingent drawing facilities, catastrophe futures and similar innovations. In fact, our model provides a formal framework within which such moves can be evaluated. An earlier version of this framework was presented in [6]; Chichilnisky [3] gives a more industry-oriented analysis.

This merging of insurance and securities market is not surprising: traditionally economists have recognized two ways of managing risks. One is risk

---

* We are grateful to Peter Bernstein, David Cass and Frank Hahn for valuable comments on an earlier version of this paper.

pooling, or insurance, invoking the law of large numbers for independent and identically distributed (IID) events to ensure that the insurer's loss rate is proportional to the population loss rate. This will not work if the population loss rate is unknown. The second approach is the use of securities markets, and of negatively correlated events. This does not require knowledge of the population loss rate, and so can be applied to risks which are unknown or not independent. In fact, securities markets alone could provide a mechanism for hedging unknown risks by the appropriate definition of states, but as we shall see below this approach requires an unreasonable proliferation of markets. Using a mix of the two approaches can economize greatly on the number of markets needed and on the complexity of the institutional framework. In the process of showing this, we also show that under certain conditions the market equilibrium is anonymous in the sense that it depends only on the distribution of individuals across possible states, and not on who is in which state.

The reason for using two types of instrument is simple. Agents face two types of uncertainty: uncertainty about the overall incidence of a peril, i.e., how many people overall will be affected by a disease, and then given an overall distribution of the peril, they face uncertainty about whether they will be one of those who are affected. Securities contingent on the distribution of the peril hedge the former type of uncertainty: contingent insurance contracts hedge the latter.

Our analysis implies that insurance companies should issue insurance contracts which depend on the frequency of the peril, which we call a statistical state. The insurance companies should offer individuals an array of insurance contracts, one valid in each possible statistical state. Insurance contracts are, therefore, contingent on statistical states. Within each statistical state, of course, probabilities are known. Therefore, companies are writing insurance only on known risks, something which is actuarially manageable. Individuals then buy the insurance that they want between different statistical states via the markets for securities that are contingent on statistical states. The following is an illustration for purchasing insurance against AIDS, if the actuarial risks of the disease are unknown. One would buy insurance against AIDS by (1) purchasing a set of AIDS insurance contracts each of which pays off only for a specified incidence of AIDS in the population as a whole, and (2) making bets via statistical securities on the incidence of AIDS in the population. Likewise, one would obtain cover against an effect of climate change by (1) buying insurance policies specific to the risks faced at particular levels of climate change, and (2) making bets on the level of climate change, again using statistical securities. The opportunity to place such bets is currently provided in a limited way by catastrophe futures markets which pay an amount depending on the incidence of hurricane damage.

The present paper draws on recent findings of Chichilnisky and Wu [5] and Cass et al. [4], both of which study resource allocation with individual risks.

Both of these papers develop further Malinvaud's [15, 16] original formulation of general equilibrium with individual risks, and Arrow's [1] formulation of the role of securities in the optimal allocation of risk-bearing. Our results are valid for large but finite economies with agents who face unknown risks and who have diverse opinions about these risks: in contrast, Malinvaud's results are asymptotic, valid for a limiting economy with an infinite population, and deal only with a known distribution of risks. Our results use the formulation of incomplete asset markets for individual risks used to study default in [5, section 5.c]. The risks considered here are unknown and possibly unknowable, and each individual has potentially a different opinion about these risks, while Chichilnisky and Wu [5] and Cass et al. [4] assume that all risk is known.

## 2. Notation and Definitions

Denote the set of possible states for an individual by $S$, indexed by $s = 1, 2, \ldots, S$. Let there be $H$ individuals, indexed by $h = 1, 2, \ldots, H$. All households have the same state-dependent endowments: endowments depend solely on the household's individual state $s$, and this dependence is the same for all households. The probability of any agent being in any state is unknown, and the distribution of states over the population as a whole is also unknown. A complete description of the state of the economy, called a *social state*, is a list of the states of each agent. There are $S^H$ possible social states. A social state is denoted $\sigma$ : it is an $H$-vector. The set of possible social states is denoted $\Omega$ and has $S^H$ elements. A statistical description of the economy, called a *statistical state*, is a statement of the fraction of the population in each state: it is an $S$-vector. There are $\binom{H+S-1}{S-1}$ statistical states. Clearly many social states map into a given statistical state. For example, if in one social state you are well and I am sick and in another, I am well and you are sick, then these two social states give rise to the same statistical state. Intuitively, we would not expect the equilibrium prices of the economy to differ in these two social states. One of our results shows that under certain conditions, the characteristics of the equilibrium are in fact dependent only on the statistical state.

How does the distinction between social and statistical states contribute to risk management? Using the traditional approach, we could in principle trade securities contingent on each of the $S^H$ social states. Clearly this would require a large number of markets, a number which grows rapidly with the number of agents. The institutional requirements can be greatly simplified. When the characteristics of the equilibrium depend only on the statistical state, one can trade securities which are contingent on statistical states, i.e., contingent on the distribution of individual states within the population, and still attain efficient allocations. We will trade securities contingent on whether

4 or 8% of the population are in state 5, but not on which people are in this state. Such securities, which we will call *statistical securities*, plus mutual insurance contracts also contingent on the statistical state, lead (under the appropriate conditions) to an efficient allocation of risks. A mutual insurance contract contingent on a statistical state pays an individual a certain amount in a given individual state if and only if the economy as a whole is in a given statistical state.

Let $z_{jh\sigma}$ denote the quantity of good $j$ consumed by household $h$ in social state $\sigma$: $z_{h\sigma}$ is an $N$-dimensional vector of *all* goods consumed by $h$ in social state $\sigma$, $z_{h\sigma} = z_{jh\sigma}$, $j = 1, \ldots, N$ and $z_h$ is an $NS^H$-dimensional vector of *all goods consumed in all social states* by $h$, $z_h = z_{h\sigma}, \sigma \in \Omega$.[3]

Let $s(h, \sigma)$ be the state of individual $h$ in the social state $\sigma$, and $r_s(\sigma)$ be the proportion of all households for whom $s(h, \sigma) = s$. Let $r(\sigma) = r_1(\sigma), \ldots, r_S(\sigma)$ be the distribution of households among individual states within the social state $\sigma$, i.e., the proportion of all individuals in state $s$ for each $s$. $r(\sigma)$ is a statistical state. Let $R$ be the set statistical states, i.e., of vectors $r(\sigma)$ when $\sigma$ runs over $\Omega$. $R$ is contained in $S^I$, the product of $I$ $S$-dimensional simplices, and has $\binom{H+S-1}{S-1}$ elements.

$\Pi^h$ is household $h$'s probability distribution over the set of social states $\Omega$, and $\Pi^h_\sigma$ denotes the probability of state $\sigma$. Although we take social states as the primitive concept, we in fact work largely with statistical states. We, therefore, relate preferences, beliefs and endowments to statistical states. This is done in the next section: clearly any distribution over social states implies a distribution over statistical states.

The following *anonymity assumption* is required:

$$r(\sigma) = r(\sigma') \rightarrow \Pi^h_\sigma = \Pi^h_{\sigma'}.$$

This means that two overall distributions $\sigma$ and $\sigma'$ which have the same statistical characteristics are equally likely. Then $\Pi^h_\sigma$ defines a probability distribution $\Pi^h_r$ on the space of statistical states $R$. $\Pi^h_r$ can be interpreted, as remarked above, as $h$'s distribution over possible distributions of impacts in the population as a whole. The probability that a statistical state $r$ obtains and that simultaneously, for a given household $h$ a particular state $s$ also obtains, $\Pi^h_{sr}$, is[4]

$$\Pi^h_{sr} = \Pi^h_r r_s \quad \text{with} \quad \sum_s \Pi^h_{sr} = \Pi^h_r. \tag{1}$$

The probability $\Pi^h_s$ that, for a given $h$, a particular individual state $s$ obtains is, therefore, given by

$$\Pi^h_s = \sum_{r \in R} \Pi^h_r r_s,$$

where $r_s$ is the proportion of people in individual state $s$ in statistical state $r$. Note that we denote by $\Pi^h_{s|r}$ the conditional probability of household $h$ being in individual state $s$, conditional on the economy being in statistical state $r$. Clearly $\sum_s \Pi^h_{s|r} = 1$. Anonymity implies that

$$\Pi^h_{s|r} = r_s,$$

i.e., that the probability of anyone being in individual state $s$ contingent on the economy being in statistical state $r$ is the relative frequency of state $s$ contingent on statistical state $r$.

## 3. The Behavior of Households

Let $e^h_s$ be the endowment of household $h$ when the individual state is $s$. We assume that household $h$ always has the same endowment in the individual state $s$, whatever the social state. We also assume that all households have the same endowment if they are in the same individual state: endowments differ, therefore, only because of differences in individual states. This describes the risks faced by individuals.

Individuals have von Neumann–Morgenstern utilities:

$$W^h(z_h) = \sum_\sigma \Pi^h_\sigma U^h(z_{h\sigma}).$$

This definition indicates that household $h$ has preferences on consumption which may be represented by a "state separated" utility function $W^h$ defined from elementary state-dependent utility functions.

We assume like Malinvaud [15] that *preferences are separable over statistical states*. This means that the utility of household $h$ depends on $\sigma$ only through the statistical state $r(\sigma)$. If we assume further that in state $\sigma$ household $h$ takes into account only its individual consumption, and what overall frequency distribution $r(\sigma)$ appears, and nothing else, then its consumption plan can be expressed as $z^h_\sigma = z_{hsr}$: its consumption depends only on its individual state $s$ and the statistical state $r$. Summation with respect to social states $\sigma$ in the expected utility function can now be made first within each statistical state. Hence we can express individuals' utility functions as:

$$W^h(z_{h\sigma}) = \sum_{r,s} \Pi^h_{sr} U^h(z_{hsr}), \qquad (2)$$

which expresses the utility of a household in terms of its consumption at individual state $s$ within a statistical state $r$, summed over statistical states. This expression is important in the following results, because it allows us to represent the utility of consumption across social states $\sigma$ as a function of statistical states $r$ and individual states $s$ only. The functions $U^h_s$ are assumed to be $C^2$, strictly increasing, strictly quasiconcave, and the closure of the indifference surfaces $\{U^h_s\}^{-1}(x) \subset \text{int}(R^{N+})$ for all $x \in R^+$. The probabilities $\Pi^h_\sigma$ are in principle different over households.

## 4. Efficient Allocations

Let $p^*$ be a competitive equilibrium price vector of the Arrow–Debreu economy $E$ with markets contingent on all social states[5] and let $z^*$ be the associated allocation. We will as usual say that $z^*$ is *Pareto efficient* if it is impossible to find an alternative feasible allocation which is preferred by at least one agent and to which no agent prefers $z^*$. Let $p_\sigma^*$ and $z_\sigma^*$ be the components of $p^*$ and $z^*$, respectively, which refer to goods contingent on state $\sigma$.

We now define an Arrow–Debreu economy $E$, where markets exists contingent on an exhaustive description of all states in the economy, i.e. for all social states $\sigma \in \Omega$. We, therefore, have $NS^H$ contingent markets. An *Arrow–Debreu equilibrium* is a price vector $p^* = (p_\sigma), p_\sigma \in R^{N+}, \sigma \in \Omega$, and an allocation $z^*$ consisting of vectors $z_h^* = (z_{h\sigma}^*), z_{h\sigma}^* \in R^{N+}, \sigma \in \Omega, h = 1, \ldots, H$ such that for all $h$, $z_h^*$ maximizes

$$W^h(z_h^*) = \sum_\sigma \Pi_\sigma^h U^h(z_{h\sigma}^*) \tag{3}$$

subject to a budget constraint

$$p(z_h^* - e_h) = 0 \tag{4}$$

and all markets clear:

$$\sum_h (z_h^* - e_h) = 0. \tag{5}$$

Proposition 1 considers the case when households agree on the probability distribution over social states, this common probability being denoted by $\Pi$. It follows that they agree on the distribution over statistical states. It shows that in this case, the competitive equilibrium prices $p^*$ and allocations $z^*$ are the same across all social states $\sigma$ leading to the same statistical state $r$.[6]

PROPOSITION 1. *When agents have common probabilities, i.e., $\Pi^h = \Pi^j$ $\forall h, j$, then equilibrium prices depend only on statistical states. Consider an Arrow–Debreu equilibrium of the economy $E$, $p^* = (p_\sigma^*)$, $z^* = (z_\sigma^*)$, $\sigma \in \Omega$. For every state $\sigma$ leading to a given statistical state $r$, i.e., such that $r(\sigma) = r$, equilibrium prices and consumption allocations are the same, i.e., there exists a price vector $p_r^*$ and an allocation $z_r^*$ such that $\forall \sigma : r(\sigma) = r$, $p_\sigma^* = p_r^*$ and $z_\sigma^* = z_r^*$, where $p_r^* \in R^{N+}$ and $z_r^* \in R^{NI}$ depend solely on $r$.*

*Proof.* In the Appendix.

DEFINITION. An economy $E$ is *regular* if at all equilibrium prices in $E$ the Jacobian matrix of first partial derivatives of its excess demand function has full rank [11]. Regularity is a generic property [10, 11].

We now consider the general case, which allows for $\Pi^h \neq \Pi^j$ if $h \neq j$. Proposition 1 no longer holds: the reason is that households may not achieve full insurance at an equilibrium. However, Proposition 2 states that if the economy is *regular, if all households have the same preferences* and if there are two individual states, there is always one equilibrium at which prices are the same at all social states leading to the same statistical state. This confirms the intuition that the characteristics of an equilibrium should not be changed by a permutation of individuals: if I am changed to your state, and you to mine, everyone else remaining constant, then provided you and I have the same preferences, the equilibrium will not change.

PROPOSITION 2. *An Arrow–Debreu equilibrium allocation of the economy $E(p^*, z^*)$ is not fully insured if $\Pi^h \neq \Pi^k$ for some households $h, k$ with $U^h \neq U^k$ in (2). In particular, household $h$ has a different equilibrium allocation across social states $\sigma_1$ and $\sigma_2$ with $r(\sigma_1) = r(\sigma_2)$. When $E$ is a regular economy, all agents have the same utilities,[7] and there are two individual states, then one of the equilibrium prices $p^*$ must satisfy $p^*_{\sigma_1} = p^*_{\sigma_2}$ for all $\sigma_1, \sigma_2$ with $r(\sigma_1) = r(\sigma_2)$.*

*Proof.* In the Appendix.

## 5. Equilibrium in Incomplete Markets for Unknown Risks

Consider first the case where *there are no assets to hedge against risk*, so that the economy has incomplete asset markets. Individuals cannot transfer income to the unfavorable states. Examples are cases when individuals are not able to purchase hurricane insurance, as in some parts of the south eastern United States and in the Caribbean. Market allocations are typically inefficient in this case, since individuals cannot transfer income from one state to another to equalize welfare across states. Which households will be in each individual state is unknown. Each individual has a certain probability distribution over all possible social states $\sigma$, $\Pi^h$. In each social state $\sigma$ each individual is constrained in the value of her/his expenditures by her/his endowment (which depends on the individual state $s(h, \sigma)$ in that social state). In this context, a *general equilibrium of the economy with incomplete markets $E_I$* consists of a price vector $p^*$ with $NS^H$ components and $H$ consumption plans $z^*_h$ with $NS^H$ components each, such that $z^*_h$ maximizes $W^h(z_h)$:

$$W^h(z_h) = \sum_\sigma \Pi^h_\sigma U^h(z_{h\sigma}) \tag{6}$$

subject to

$$p_\sigma(z_{h\sigma} - e_{h\sigma}) = 0 \quad \text{for each} \quad \sigma \in \Omega \tag{7}$$

and

$$\sum_{h=1}^H (z_h - e_h) = 0. \tag{8}$$

The above economy $E_I$ is an extreme version of an economy with incomplete asset markets (see, e.g., [13]) because there are no markets to hedge against risks: there are $S^H$ budget constraints in (7).

## 6. Efficient Allocations, Mutual Insurance and Securities

In this section we study the possibility of supporting Arrow–Debreu equilibria by combinations of statistical securities and insurance contracts, rather than by using state contingent contracts. As already observed, this leads to a very significant economy in the number of markets needed. In an economy with no asset markets at all, such as $E_I$, the difficulty in supporting an Arrow–Debreu equilibrium arises because income cannot be transferred between states. On the basis of Propositions 1 and 2, we show that households can use securities defined on statistical states to transfer into each such state an amount of income equal to the expected difference between the value of Arrow–Debreu equilibrium consumption and the value of endowments in that state. The expectation here is over individual states conditional on being in a given statistical state. The difference between the actual consumption-income gap given a particular individual state and its expected value is then covered by insurance contracts. Recall that $A$ is the binomial number $A = \binom{H+S-1}{S-1}$.

THEOREM 1. *Assume that all households in $E$ have the same probability $\Pi$ over the distribution of risks in the population. Then any Arrow–Debreu equilibrium allocation $(p^*, z^*)$ of $E$ (and, therefore, any Pareto Optimum) can be achieved within the general equilibrium economy with incomplete markets $E_I$ by introducing a total of $I.A$ mutual insurance contracts to hedge against individual risk, and $A$ statistical securities to hedge against social risk. In a regular economy with two individual states and identical preferences, even if agents have different probabilities, there is always an Arrow–Debreu equilibrium $(p^*, z^*)$ in $E$ which is achievable within the incomplete economy $E_I$ with the introduction of $I.A$ mutual insurance contracts and $A$ statistical securities.*

*Proof.* In the Appendix.

### 6.1. Market Complexity

We can now formalize a statement made before about the efficiency of the institutional structure proposed in Theorem 1 by comparison with the standard Arrow–Debreu structure of a complete set of state-contingent markets. We use here complexity theory, and in particular the concept of *NP-completeness*. The key consideration in this approach to studying problem complexity is how fast the number of operations required to solve a problem increases with the size of the problem.

DEFINITION. If the number of operations required to solve a problem must increase exponentially for any possible way of solving the problem, then the problem is called *"intractable"* or more formally, *NP-complete*. If this number increases polynomially, the problem is *tractable*. Further definitions are in [12].

The motivation for this distinction is of course that if the number of operations needed to solve the problem increases exponentially with some measure of the size of the problem, then there will be examples of the problem that no computer can or ever could solve. Hence there is no possibility of ever designing a general efficient algorithm for solving these problems. However, if the number of operations rises only polynomially then it is in principle possible to devise a general and efficient algorithm for the problem.

Theorem 2 investigates the complexity of the resource allocation problem in the Arrow–Debreu framework and compares this with the framework of Theorem 1. We focus on how the problem changes as the economy grows in the sense that the number of households increases, and consider a very simple aspect of the allocation problem, which is as follows. Suppose that the excess demand of the economy $Z(p)$ is known. A particular price vector $p^*$ is proposed as a market clearing price. We wish to check whether or not it is a market clearing price. This involves computing each of the coordinates of $Z(p)$ and then comparing with zero. This involves a number of operations proportional to the number of components of $Z(p)$; we, therefore, take the rate at which the dimension of $Z(p)$ increases with the number of agents to be a measure of the complexity of the resource allocation problem. In summary: we ask how the difficulty of verifying market clearing increases as the number of households in the economy rises. We show that in the Arrow–Debreu framework this difficulty rises exponentially, whereas in the framework of Theorem 1 it rises only polynomially.

THEOREM 2. *Verifying market clearing is an intractable problem in an Arrow–Debreu economy, i.e., the number of operations required to check if a proposed price is market clearing increases exponentially with the number of households $H$. However, under the assumptions of Theorem 1, in the economy $E_I$ supplemented by $I.A$ mutual insurance contracts and $A$ statistical securities, verifying market clearing is a tractable problem, i.e., the number of operations needed to check for market clearing increases only polynomially with the number of households.*

*Proof.* The number of operations required to check that a price is market clearing is proportional to the number of market clearing conditions. In $E$ we have $NS^H$ markets. Hence the number of operations needed to check if a proposed price is market clearing must rise exponentially with the number of households $H$. Consider now the case of $E_I$ supplemented by $I.A$ mutual insurance contracts and A securities. Under the assumptions of Theorem 1, by Propositions 1 and 2, we need only check for market clearing in one social state associated with any statistical state, as if markets clear in one social state leading to a certain statistical state they will clear in all social states leading to the same statistical state. Hence we need to check a number of goods markets equal to $N.A$, plus markets for mutual insurance contracts and securities. Now

$$A = \binom{H+S+1}{S-1} = \Phi(H, S),$$

where $\Phi(H, S)$ is a polynomial in $H$ of order $(S-1)$. Hence $A$ itself is a polynomial in $H$ whose highest order term depends on $H^{S-1}$, completing the proof. □

## 7. Catastrophe Futures and Bundles

We mentioned in the introduction that securities contingent on statistical states are already traded as "catastrophe futures" on the Chicago Board of Trade, where they were introduced in 1994. Recently, hurricane bonds and earthquake bonds have been introduced, additional examples of statistical securities. (The concept was discussed by Chichilnisky and Heal in 1993 [6].) Catastrophe futures are securities which pay an amount that depends on the value of an index of insurance claims paid during a year. One such index measures the value of hurricane damage claims: others measure claims stemming from different types of natural disasters. The value of hurricane damage claims depends on the overall incidence of hurricane damage in the population, but is not of course affected by whether any particular individual is harmed. It, therefore, depends, in our terminology, on the statistical state, on the distribution of damage in the population, but not on the social state. Catastrophe futures are thus financial instruments whose payoffs are conditional on statistical state of the economy: they are statistical securities. According to our theory, a summary version of which appeared in [6] in 1993, they are a crucial prerequisite to the efficient allocation of unknown risks. And as the incidence and extent of natural disaster claims in the U.S. has increased greatly in recent years, risks such as hurricane risks are in effect unknown risks: insurers are concerned that the incidence of storms may be related to trends in the composition of the atmosphere and incipient greenhouse warming. However, catastrophe futures are not on their own sufficient for this: they do not complete the market. Mutual insurance contracts, as described above, are also needed. These provide insurance conditional on the value of the catastrophe index. The two can be combined into "catastrophe bundles", see [3].

## 8. Conclusions

We have defined an economy with unknown individual risks, and established that a combination of statistical securities and mutual insurance contracts can be used to obtain an efficient allocation of risk-bearing. Furthermore, we have shown that this institutional structure is efficient in the sense that it requires exponentially fewer markets that the standard approach via state-contingent commodities. In fact, the state-contingent problem is "intractable" with individual risks (formally, NP-complete) in the language of computational complexity, whereas our approach gives a formulation that is polynomially complex. This greatly increases the economy's ability to achieve efficient allocations. Another interesting feature of this institutional structure is the interplay of insurance and securities markets involved. Its simplicity leads to successful hedging of unknown risks and predicts some convergence between the insurance and securities industries.

## 9. Appendix

PROPOSITION 1. *When agents have common probabilities, i.e., $\Pi^h = \Pi^j$ $\forall h, j$, then equilibrium prices depend only on statistical states. Consider an Arrow–Debreu equilibrium of the economy $E, p^* = (p^*_\sigma), z^* = (z^*_\sigma), \sigma \in \Omega$. For every state $\sigma$ leading to a given statistical state $r$, i.e., such that $r(\sigma) = r$, equilibrium prices and consumption allocations are the same, i.e., there exists a price vector $p^*_r$ and an allocation $z^*_r$ such that $\forall \sigma : r(\sigma) = r, p^*_\sigma = p^*_r$ and $z^*_\sigma = z^*_r$, where $p^*_r \in R^{N+}$ and $z^*_r \in R^{NI}$ depend solely on $r$.*

*Proof.* Consider $\sigma_1$ and $\sigma_2$ with $r(\sigma_1) = r(\sigma_2) = r$. Note that the total endowments of the economy are the same in $\sigma_1$ and $\sigma_2$, both equal to $s_r = Hr_s e_{hs}$ (recall that $e_{hs} = e_s$ as endowments depend only on individual states and not on household identities). Also, by the anonymity assumption, $\Pi_{\sigma_1} = \Pi_{\sigma_2} = \Pi_r$, where $\Pi_r$ is the common probability of any social state in the statistical state $r$. Let $\Pi_{\sigma|r}$ be the probability of being in social state $\sigma$ given statistical state $r$. By the anonymity assumption on probabilities this is just $1/\#\Omega_r$. We now show that for every household $h$, $z^*_{h\sigma_1} = z^*_{h\sigma_2}$, due to the Pareto efficiency of Arrow–Debreu equilibria. Let $\Omega_r = \{\sigma : r(\sigma) = \sigma\}$. Let $z^* = (z^*_{h\sigma})$, and assume in contradiction to the proposition that there are $\sigma_1$ and $\sigma_2 \in \Omega_r$ such that $z^*_{h\sigma_1} \neq z^*_{h\sigma_2}$ for some $h$. Define $Ez_{hr} = \sum_{\sigma \in \Omega_r} z^*_{h\sigma} \Pi_{\sigma|r} = (1/\#\Omega_r) \sum_{\sigma \in \Omega_r} z^*_{h\sigma}$. This is the expected value of $(z^*_{h\sigma})$ given that the economy is in the statistical state $r$. Now

$$\sum_h E z_{hr} = \sum_h \frac{1}{\#\Omega_r} \sum_{\sigma \in \Omega_r} z^*_{h\sigma} = \sum_h z^*_{h\sigma},$$

so that $Ez_{h\sigma}$ is a feasible consumption vector for each $h$ in the statistical state $r$. Next we show that by strict concavity, moving for each $h$ and each $\sigma$ from

$z_{h\sigma}^*$ (which depends on $\sigma$) to $Ez_{hr}$ (which is the same for all $\sigma \in \Omega$), is a strict Pareto improvement. This is because

$$W^h(z_{h\sigma}^*) = \sum_\sigma \Pi_\sigma U^h(z_{h\sigma}^*) = \sum_r \Pi_r \sum_{\sigma \in \Omega} \Pi_{\sigma|r} U^h(z_{h\sigma}^*).$$

By strict concavity of preferences,

$$\sum_r \Pi_r \sum_{\sigma \in \Omega_r} \Pi_{\sigma|r} U^h(z_{h\sigma}^*)$$

$$< \sum_r \Pi_r \sum_{\sigma \in \Omega_r} U^h \left( \sum_{\sigma \in \Omega} z_{h\sigma}^* \Pi_{\sigma|r} \right) = \sum_r \Pi_r \sum_{\sigma \in \Omega} U^h(Ez_{h\sigma}).$$

Since $Ez_{h\sigma}$ is Pareto superior to $z^*$ with $z_{h\sigma_1}^* \neq z_{h\sigma_2}^*$, such a $z^*$ cannot be an equilibrium allocation. Hence $z_{h\sigma_1}^* = z_{h\sigma_2}^* = z_{hr}^*$ for all $h = 1, \ldots, H$. Note that this implies that in an equilibrium, household $h$ consumes the same allocation $z_{hr}^*$ across all individual states $s$ in a given statistical state, i.e. it achieves full insurance. Since $p^*$ supports the equilibrium allocation $z^*$, and $z_{h\sigma_1}^* = z_{h\sigma_2}^*$ it follows that $p_{\sigma_1}^* = p_{\sigma_2}^*$ when $r(\sigma_1) = r(\sigma_2)$, because utilities are assumed to be $C^2$ and, in particular, to have a unique gradient at each point which, by optimality, must be collinear both with $p_{\sigma_1}^*$ and with $p_{\sigma_2}^*$, i.e. $p_{\sigma_1}^* = p_{\sigma_2}^* = p_r^*$. This implies that at an equilibrium, household $h$ faces the same prices $p_r^*$ at any $\sigma$ with $r(\sigma) = r$. □

PROPOSITION 2. *An Arrow–Debreu equilibrium allocation of the economy $E(p^*, z^*)$ is not fully insured if $\Pi^h \neq \Pi^k$ for some households $h, k$ with $U^h \neq U^k$. In particular, household $h$ has a different equilibrium allocation across social states $\sigma_1$ and $\sigma_2$ with $r(\sigma_1) = r(\sigma_2)$. When $E$ is a regular economy, all agents have the same utilities,[8] and there are two individual states, one of the equilibrium prices $p^*$ must satisfy $p_{\sigma_1}^* = p_{\sigma_2}^*$ for all $\sigma_1, \sigma_2$ with $r(\sigma_1) = r(\sigma_2)$.*

*Proof.* Suppose that household $h$ is in fact fully insured so that $z_{h\sigma_1}^* = z_{h\sigma_2}^*$ for all $\sigma^1$ and $\sigma_2$ with $r(\sigma_1) = r(\sigma_2)$. Household $h$'s consumption levels are $y_{s_1r}^i$ and $y_{s_2r}^i$ where $s_1 = s(h, \sigma_1)$ and $s_2 = s(h, \sigma_2)$. By assumption we have $y_{s_1r}^i = y_{s_2r}^i$. Now from (2) household $h$'s marginal rate of substitution between consumption in states $\sigma_1$ and $\sigma_2$ is $\Pi_{s_1|r}^h / \Pi_{s_2|r}^h$. Suppose also that household $k, k \neq h$, is fully insured. Then by the same argument $k$'s marginal rate of substitution between consumption in states $\sigma_1$ and $\sigma_2$ is $\Pi_{s_1|r}^k / \Pi_{s_2|r}^k$. But if different households have different probability distributions this is a contradiction as both face the same price vector.

Assume now that $E$ is regular, that all agents have the same preferences, and that $S = 2$. Consider two social states $\sigma_1$ and $\sigma_2$ with $r(\sigma_1) = r(\sigma_2)$, and such that $\sigma_1$ differs from $\sigma_2$ only on the individual states of the two households $h_1$ and $h_2$ which are permuted, i.e., $s(h_1, \sigma_1) = s(h_2, \sigma_2)$ and

$s(h_2, \sigma_1) = s(h_1, \sigma_2)$. Assume that there exists an equilibrium price for $E$, $p^* \in R^{NS^H}$, such that its components in states $\sigma_1$ and $\sigma_2$ are different, i.e. $p^*_{\sigma_1} \neq p^*_{\sigma_2}$. Define now a new price $p^*_c \in R^{NS^H}$, called a "conjugate" of $p^*$, which differs from $p^*$ only in its coordinates in states $\sigma_1$ and $\sigma_2$, which are permuted as follows: $\forall \sigma \neq \sigma_1, \sigma_2, \overline{p}^*_\sigma = p^*_\sigma, \overline{p}^*_{\sigma_1} = p^*_{\sigma_2}$, and $\overline{p}^*_{\sigma_2} = p^*_{\sigma_1}$. We shall now show that $\overline{p}^*$ is also an equilibrium price for the economy $E$. At $\overline{p}^*$, household $h_1$ has the same endowments and faces the same prices in states $\sigma_1$ and $\sigma_2$ as it did at states $\sigma_2$ and $\sigma_1$ respectively at price $p^*$; at all other states $\sigma \in \Omega$, $h_1$ faces the same prices and has the same endowments facing $p^*$ and facing $\overline{p}^*$. The same is true of household $h_2$. Furthermore, $h_1$ and $h_2$ have the same utilities and probabilities at $\sigma_1$ and $\sigma_2$ because $r(\sigma_1) = r(\sigma_2)$ and probabilities are anonymous. Therefore, the excess demand vectors of $h_1$ in states $\sigma_1$ and $\sigma_2$ at prices $p^*$ equal the excess demand vectors of $h_2$ in $\sigma_2$ and $\sigma_1$ respectively, at prices $\overline{p}^*$, and at all other states $\sigma \in \Omega$ the excess demand vectors of $h_1$ are the same at prices $p^*$ and $\overline{p}^*$. Reciprocally: the excess demand vectors of $h_2$ in $\sigma_1$ and $\sigma_2$ at prices $p^*$ equal the excess demand vectors of $h_1$ in $\sigma_2$ and $\sigma_1$ respectively at prices $\overline{p}^*$, and in all other states $\sigma$, the excess demand vectors of $h_2$ are the same as they are with prices $p^*$. Formally:

$$z_{h_1\sigma_1}(\overline{p}^*) = z_{h_2\sigma_2}(p^*), z_{h_1\sigma_2}(\overline{p}^*) = z_{h_2\sigma_1}(p^*)$$
$$z_{h_2\sigma_1}(\overline{p}^*) = z_{h_1\sigma_2}(p^*), z_{h_2\sigma_2}(\overline{p}^*) = z_{h_1\sigma_1}(p^*)$$

and $\forall \sigma \in \Omega, \sigma \neq \sigma_1, \sigma_2$:

$$z_{h_1\sigma}(p^*) = z_{h_1\sigma}(\overline{p}^*), z_{h_2\sigma}(p^*) = z_{h_2\sigma}(\overline{p}^*).$$

The excess demand vectors of all other households $h \neq h_1, h_2$ are the same for $p^*$ and $\overline{p}^*$. Therefore, at $\overline{p}^*$ the aggregate excess demand vector of the economy is zero, so that $\overline{p}^*$ is an equilibrium. The same argument shows that permuting the two components $p^*_{\sigma_1}, p^*_{\sigma_2}$ of a price $p^*$ at any two social states $\sigma_1, \sigma_2$ leading to the same statistical state $r(\sigma_1)$ leads from an equilibrium price $p^*$ to another equilibrium price $\overline{p}^*$. This is because if two social states $\sigma_1$ and $\sigma_2$ lead to the same statistical state and there are two individual states $s_1$ and $s_2$ then there is a number $k > 0$ such that $k$ households who are in $s_1$ in $\sigma_1$ are in $s_2$ in $\sigma_2$ and another $k$ households who were in $s_1$ in $\sigma_2$ are in $s_2$ in $\sigma_1$, while remaining in the same individual states otherwise. These two sets of $k$ households can be paired. For every pair of households, the above argument applies. Hence it applies to the sum of the demands, so that the new price $\overline{p}^*$ is an equilibrium.

Now consider any regular economy $E$ with a finite number of equilibrium prices denoted $p^*_1, \ldots, p^*_k$. We shall show that there exists a $j \leq k$ s.t. $p^*_j$ assigns the same price vector to all social states $\sigma_1, \sigma_2$ with $r(\sigma_1) = r(\sigma_2)$. Start with $p^*_1$: if $p^*_1$ does not have this property, consider the first two social states $\sigma_1, \sigma_2$ with $r(\sigma_1) = r(\sigma_2)$ and $p^*_{1\sigma_1} \neq p^*_{1\sigma_2}$. Define $\overline{p}^*_1$ as the conjugate of $p^*_1$ constructed by permuting the prices of the social states $\sigma_1$ and $\sigma_2$. If

$\forall j > 1, p_j^* = \bar{p}_1^*$, then there are two price equilibria, i.e. $k = 2$; however, since the number of price equilibria must be odd,[9] there must exist $p_{j_1}^*$ with $j_1 > 1$, and $p_{j_1}^* \neq \bar{p}_1^*$. Consider now the conjugate of $p_{j_1}^*$ with respect to the first two social states $\sigma_1, \sigma_2$ which correspond to the same statistical state and have different components in $p_{j_1}^*$, and denote this conjugate $\bar{p}_{j_1}^*$. Repeat the procedure until all equilibria are exhausted. In each step of this procedure, two different price equilibria are found. Since the number of equilibria must be odd, it follows that there must exist a $j \leq k$ for which all conjugates of $p_j^*$ equal $p_j^*$: this is the required equilibrium which assigns the same equilibrium prices $p_{\sigma_1}^* = p_{\sigma_2}^*$ to all $\sigma_1, \sigma_2$ with $r(\sigma_1) = r(\sigma_2)$, completing the proof. □

THEOREM 1. *Assume that all households in E have the same probability $\Pi$ over the distribution of risks in the population. Then any Arrow–Debreu equilibrium allocation $(p^*, z^*)$ of $E$ (and, therefore, any Pareto Optimum) can be achieved within the general equilibrium economy with incomplete markets $E_I$ by introducing a total of $I.A$ mutual insurance contracts to hedge against individual risk, and $A$ statistical securities to hedge against social risk. In a regular economy with two individual states and identical preferences, even if agents have different probabilities, there is always an Arrow–Debreu equilibrium $(p^*, z^*)$ in $E$ which is achievable within the incomplete economy $E_I$ with the introduction of $I.A$ mutual insurance contracts and $A$ statistical securities.*

*Proof.* Consider first the case where all households have the same probabilities, i.e., $\Pi^h = \Pi^j = \Pi$. By Proposition 1, an Arrow–Debreu equilibrium of $E$ has the same prices $p_\sigma^* = p_r^*$ and the same consumption vectors $z_{h\sigma}^* = z_{hr}^*$ for each $h$, at each social state $\sigma$ with $r(\sigma) = r$. Define $\Omega(r)$ as the set of social states mapping to a given statistical state $r$, i.e. $\Omega(r) = \{\sigma \in \Omega : r(\sigma) = r\}$. The budget constraint (4) is

$$p^* (z_h^* - e_h) = \sum_\sigma p_\sigma^* \left(z_{h,\sigma}^* - e_{h\sigma}\right) = \sum_r p_r^* \sum_{\sigma \in \Omega(r)} (z_{h\sigma}^* - e_{h\sigma}) = 0.$$

Individual endowments depend on individual states and not on social states, so that $e_{h\sigma} = e_{hs(\sigma)} = e_{hs}$; furthermore, by Proposition 1 equilibrium prices depend on $r$ and not on $\sigma$, so that for each $r$ the equilibrium consumption vector $z_{h\sigma}$ can be written as $z_{hs}$. The individual budget constraint is, therefore, $\sum_r p_r^* \sum_{s(r)} (z_{hs} - e_{hs})$, where summation over $s(r)$ indicates summation over all individual states $s$ that occur in any social state leading to $r$, i.e. that are in the set $\Omega(r)$. Let $\#\Omega(r)$ be the number of social states in $\Omega(r)$. As $\Pi_{s|r} = r_s$ is the proportion of households in state $s$ within the statistical state $r$, we can finally rewrite the budget constraint (4) of the household $h$ as:

$$\#\Omega(r) \sum_r p_r^* \sum_s \#\Omega(r) \Pi_{s|r} (z_{hs} - e_{hs}) = 0. \tag{9}$$

Using (2), the household's maximization problem can, therefore, be expressed as:

$$\max \sum_{s,r} \Pi_{sr} U^h(z_{hsr}) \text{ subject to (9)}$$

and the equilibrium allocation $z_h^*$ by definition solves this problem. Similarly, we may rewrite the market clearing condition (5) as follows:

$$\sum_h (z_h^* - e_h) = \sum_h (z_{h\sigma}^* - e_{hs(\sigma)}) = 0, \quad \forall \sigma \in \Omega.$$

Rewriting the market clearing condition (5) in terms of statistical states $r$, and within each $r$, individual states $s$, we obtain:

$$\sum_s r_s H\left(z_{hr}^* - e_{sr}^h\right) = 0, \quad \forall r \in R \tag{10}$$

or equivalently:

$$\sum_s \Pi_{s|r} H\left(z_{hr}^* - e_{sr}^h\right) = 0, \quad \forall r \in R.$$

Using these relations, we now show that any Arrow–Debreu equilibrium allocation $z^* = (z_{hr}^*)$ is within the budget constraints (7) of the economy $E_I$ for each $\sigma \in \Omega$, *provided that* for each $\sigma \in \Omega$ we add the income derived from a statistical security $A_r, r = r(\sigma)$, and, given $r(\sigma)$, the income derived from mutual insurance contracts $m_{sr}^h = m_{s(\sigma)r(\sigma)}^h$, $s = 1, \ldots, S$. We introduce $A$ statistical securities and $I.A$ mutual insurance contracts in the general equilibrium economy with incomplete markets $E_I$. The quantity of the security $A_r$ purchased by household $h$ in statistical state $r$, when equilibrium prices are $p^*$, is:

$$a_r^{h*} = \sum_s \Pi_{s|r} p_r^* (z_{hr}^* - e_{hs}). \tag{11}$$

The quantity $a_r^{h*}$ has a very intuitive interpretation. It is the expected amount by which the value of equilibrium consumption exceeds the value of endowments, conditional on being in statistical state $r$. So *on average*, the statistical securities purchased deliver enough to balance a household's budget in each statistical state. Differences between the average and each individual state are taken care of by the mutual insurance contracts. Note that (10) implies that the total amount of each security supplied is zero, i.e., $\sum_h a_r^{h*} = 0$ for all $r$, so that this corresponds to the initial endowments of the incomplete economy $E_I$. Furthermore, $\sum_r a_r^{h*} = 0$ by (9), so that each household $h$ is within her/his budget in $E_I$.

We now introduce a mutual insurance contract as follows. The transfer made by individual $h$ in statistical state $r$ and individual state $s$, when prices are $p_r^*$, is:

$$m_{sr}^{h*} = p_r^*(z_{hr}^* - e_{hr}) - a_r^{h*}. \tag{12}$$

Note that, as remarked above, $m_{sr}^{h*}$ is just the difference between the actual income-expenditure gap, given that individual state $s$ is realized, and the expected income-expenditure gap $a_r^{h*}$ in statistical state $r$, which is covered by statistical securities. In each statistical state $r$, the sum over all $h$ and $s$ of all transfers $m_{sr}^{h*}$ equals zero, i.e. the insurance premia match exactly the payments: for any given $r$,

$$\sum_{h,s} H\Pi_{s|r} m_{sr}^{h*} = \sum_{h,s} H\Pi_{s|r} p_r^* (z_{hr}^* - e_{hs}) - \sum_h H a_r^{h*} \sum_s \Pi_{s|r}$$

$$= 0 \tag{13}$$

because $\sum_s \Pi_{s|r} = 1$. Therefore, the $\{m_{sr}^{h*}\}$ meet the definition of mutual insurance contracts. Finally, note that with $N$ spot markets, $A$ statistical securities $\{a_r\}$ and $I$ mutual insurance contracts $\{m_{sr}^h\}$

$$p_r^* \left( z_{hr}^* - e_s^h \right) = m_{sr}^{i*} + a_r^{i*}, \quad \forall \sigma \in \Omega \text{ with } r(\sigma) = r, s = s(\sigma) \tag{14}$$

so that (7) is satisfied for each $\sigma \in \Omega$. This establishes that when all households have the same probabilities over social states, all Arrow–Debreu equilibrium allocation $z^*$ of $E$ can be achieved within the incomplete markets economy $E_I$ when $A$ securities and $I.A$ mutual insurance contracts are introduced into $E_I$, and completes the proof of the first part of the proposition dealing with common probabilities.

Consider now the case where the economy $E$ is regular, different households in $E$ have different probabilities over social states but have the same preferences, and $S = 2$. By Proposition 2, we know that within the set of equilibrium prices there is one $p^*$ in which at all social states $\sigma \in \Omega(r)$ for a given $r$, the equilibrium prices are the same, i.e. $p_\sigma^* = p_r^*$. In particular, if $E$ has a unique equilibrium $(p^*, z^*)$, it must have this property. It follows from the above arguments that the equilibrium $(p^*, z^*)$ must maximize (2) subject to (9). Now define the quantity of the security $A_r$ purchased by a household in the statistical state $r$ by

$$a_r^{h*} = \sum_s \Pi_{s|r}^h p_r^* \left( z_{hsr}^* - e_s^h \right) \tag{15}$$

and the mutual insurance transfer made by a household in statistical state $r$ and individual state $s$, by

$$m_{sr}^{h*} = p_r^* \left( z_{hsr}^* - e_s^h \right) - a_r^{h*}. \tag{16}$$

As before, $\sum_r a_r^{h*} = 0$ and for any given $r$, $\sum_{h,s} \Pi_{s|r}^h H m_{sr}^{h*} = \sum_{h,s} r_s H m_{sr}^{h*} = 0$, so that the securities purchased correspond to the initial endowments of the economy $E_I$ and at any statistical state the sum of the premia and the sum of the payments of the mutual insurance contracts match, completing the proof. □

## Notes

1. A dealy viral disease.
2. Many were associated with hurricane Andrew which at $18 billion in losses was the most expensive catastrophe ever recorded. Some of the problems which beset Lloyds of London arose from underestimating environmental risks.
3. All consumption vectors are assumed to be non-negative.
4. See [16, p. 387, para. 1].
5. Defined formally below.
6. Related propositions were established by Malinvaud in an economy where all agents are identical, and risks are known.
7. The condition that all agents have the same preferences is not needed for this result. However, it simplifies that notation and the argument considerably. The general case is treated in the working papers from which this article derives.
8. The condition that all agents have the same preferences is not needed for this result, but simplifies the notation and the proof considerably. In the working papers from which this article derives, the general case was covered.
9. This follows from Dierker [11, p. 807] noting that his condition D is implied by our assumption that preferences are strictly increasing (see Dierker's remark following the statement of property D on p. 799).

## References

1. Arrow, K. J. "The Role of Securities in an Optimal Allocation of Risk-Bearing", in *Econometrie, Proceedings of the Colloque sur les Fondements et Applications de la Theorie du Risque en Econometrie*, Paris, Centre National de la Recherche Scientifique, 1953, pp. 41–48. English translation in *Review of Economic Studies* 31, 1964, 91–96.
2. Arrow, K. J. and R. C. Lind. "Uncertainty and the Evaluation of Public Investments", *American Economic Review* 60, 1970, 364–378.
3. Chichilnisky, G. "Catastrophe Bundles Can Deal with Unknown Risks", *Bests' Review*, February 1996, 1–3.
4. Cass, D., G. Chichilnisky and H. M. Wu. "Individual Risks and Mutual Insurance", CARESS Working Paper No. 91-27, Department of Economics, University of Pennsylvania, 1991.
5. Chichilnisky, G. and H. M. Wu. "Individual Risk and Endogenous Uncertainty in Incomplete Asset Markets", Working Paper, Columbia University and Discussion Paper, Stanford Institute for Theoretical Economics, 1991.
6. Chichilnisky, G. and G. M. Heal. "Global Environmental Risks", *Journal of Economics Perspectives* 7(4), 1993, 65–86.
7. Chichilnisky G., J. Dutta and G. M. Heal. "Price Uncertainty and Derivative Securities in General Equilibrium", Working Paper, Columbia Business School, 1991.
8. Chichilnisky, G., G. M. Heal, P. Streufert and J. Swinkels. "Believing in Multiple Equilibria", Working Paper, Columbia Business School, 1992.
9. Debreu, G. *The Theory of Value*, New York, Wiley, 1959.
10. Debreu, G. "Economies with a Finite Set of Equilibria", *Econometrica* 38, 1970, 387–392.
11. Dierker, E. "Regular Economies", in *Handbook of Mathematical Economics*, Vol. II, Chapter 17, K. J. Arrow and M. D. Intrilligator, eds., Amsterdam, North-Holland, 1982, pp. 759–830.
12. Gary, M. R. and D. S. Johnson. *Computers and Intractability: A Guide to NP-Completeness*, New York, W.H. Freeman and Company, 1979.

13. Geanakoplos, J. "An Introduction to General Equilibrium with Incomplete Asset Markets", *Journal of Mathematical Economics* 19, 1990, 1–38.
14. Heal, G. M. "Risk Management and Global Change", Paper presented at the *First Nordic Conference on the Greenhouse Effect*, Copenhagen, 1992.
15. Malinvaud, E. "The Allocation of Individual Risk in Large Markets", *Journal of Economic Theory* 4, 1972, 312–328.
16. Malinvaud, E. "Markets for an Exchange Economy with Individual Risk", *Econometrica* 3, 1973, 383–409.

MARCO P. TUCCI*

## 3.6. Stochastic Sustainability in the Presence of Unknown Parameters

### 1. Introduction

"Clearly, global warming is rife with uncertainty – about future emissions paths, GHGs (Green House Gases)-climate linkage, about the timing of the climate change, about the impacts of climate upon flora and fauna (and human economic activity), about the costs of slowing climate change and even about the speed with which we can reduce the uncertainties. How should we proceed in the face of uncertainty?" (Nordhaus, 1991, p. 58).[1] Most of the times a certain functional form is assumed and the "certainty equivalence" analysis is applied simply ignoring uncertainty. Even conceding that the assumed functional form is the correct one, uncertainty about the unknown parameters remains. As is well known "when the point estimator ... (has) a probability density function, the probability (that the estimate is equal to) the parameter being estimated (is) 0" (Mood et al., 1974, p. 372). For this reason "the potential consumer of the applied ... model must be reasonably convinced of the reliability ... of the model and its parameters before he can have any degree of confidence in its results" (Lau, 1984, p. 135). Hence the need to consider both the parameter estimates and the measures of their reliability.

Sometimes parameters are estimated using the econometric approach (Jorgenson and Wilcoxen, 1992). The number of unknown parameters in the utility and production functions is limited only by the number of observations, and no particular year's data has a predominant effect on the estimated parameters.[2] A measure of their reliability is the covariance matrix whose estimate is readily available. The use of parameter estimates and their covariances allows the construction of intervals, for the parameters and/or the forecasted values, associated with a known, or approximately known, probability.[3]

---

* The author would like to thank A. Vercelli for his steadfast encouragement and suggestions, during the various stages of the research, and G. Heal for reading and carefully commenting on an earlier draft of this work. The usual disclaimers apply.

In many cases "however the likelihood (may not be) well defined ... (and,) ... with a moderate sample size, for most applied general equilibrium models the number of independent parameters to be estimated will exceed the number of observations" (Mansur and Whalley, 1984, p. 74).[4] This induces many authors to prefer the calibration procedure which requires only one observation. It is assumed "that the economy is in equilibrium in a particular year (called benchmark and) ... the parameter values are obtained in a nonstochastic manner by solving the equations that represent the equilibrium conditions of the model using the data on prices and quantities that characterize the benchmark" (Mansur and Whalley, 1984, p. 100). When utility and production functions are Cobb-Douglas or Leontief, the observed equilibrium is sufficient to determine uniquely the unknown parameters. If more flexible forms such as CES are assumed, literature search for key model parameters, whose values are required before calibration can proceed, plays a crucial role. A measure of the reliability of the model and its parameters is obtained from "sensitivity analysis in which alternative values of the key variables (pivotal to results) are tried and model findings are crudely evaluated for their robustness" (Mansur and Whalley, 1984, p. 86).[5]

In a famous example, Mansur and Whalley (1984) show that under certain circumstances parameter estimates obtained from calibration are similar to those produced by econometric estimation.[6] One question is, however, left open: do the two different procedures generate the same, or approximately the same, intervals for the dependent variables? Or alternatively, what can be said about the numerical results of a sensitivity analysis exercise? In the following pages the relationship between the numerical results associated with sensitivity analysis and the usual econometric confidence regions is investigated. In the process the relevant econometric literature on the standard theory of simultaneous confidence intervals is reviewed. In Section 2, a model combining an economic and a climate system is introduced and the simplest case, with only one unknown parameter, is considered. Special attention is paid to the difference between this case and that in which all the parameters are known. Then the presence of two unknown parameters in one equation is analyzed (Section 3). If they appear in different equations the discussion of Section 4 applies. The general case with several unknown parameters in a system of simultaneous equations is considered in Section 5. Finally, Section 6, an empirical example using Nordhaus' (1994) model and data is provided. This is not intended to provide new empirical evidence about global warming but rather to show how the concepts discussed in the previous sections apply in empirical work. The main results are summarized in the conclusions.

## 2. One Unknown Parameter

Consider a simple model combining an economic system and a climate system incorporating the greenhouse effect theory, i.e.[7]

$$Y_n = f(K_n, L_n) \tag{2.1}$$

$$\Delta \mathcal{E}_n \equiv \mathcal{E}_n - \mathcal{E}_{n-1} = h(Y_n, A_n) + \varepsilon_n \quad \text{with} \quad \varepsilon_n \sim \mathcal{N}(0, \sigma_\varepsilon^2). \tag{2.2}$$

Equation (2.1) describes a deterministic production function relating output with the stock of labor and capital. As in (Nordhaus, 1994) the environmental asset is represented by the equilibrium global mean surface temperature,[8] and (2.2) states that its dynamics is a known function of current output and A plus some white noise with variance $\sigma$.[9] This is consistent with a variety of models. Variable A may be modelled as a control (Tucci, 1997) in the hands of a decision maker minimizing the probability that the environmental variable exceeds a certain threshold.[10] Alternatively, (2.2) can be used to summarize an "emissions-carbon cycle-climate" model (Nordhaus, 1994).[11]

Assuming that $h$ is a known function, linear in the parameters and strongly separable in the arguments,[12] (2.2) can be rewritten as

$$\Delta \mathcal{E}_n = \beta_0 + \beta_1 h_1(Y_n) + \beta_2 h_2(A_n) + \varepsilon_n \tag{2.2a}$$

and, under more stringent restrictions, as

$$y_n = \beta_2 x_n + \varepsilon_n, \quad n = 1, \ldots, N \tag{2.3}$$

with $y_n = \Delta \mathcal{E}_n - \beta_0 - \beta_1 Y_n$, $x_n = A_n$ and $N$ the number of observations.[13] This reduces to the usual econometric model with no intercept when $\beta_2$ is unknown. The best, Least Squares (LS), estimator is

$$\hat{\beta}_2 = \left( \sum_{n=1}^{N} y_n x_n / \sum_{n=1}^{N} x_n^2 \right) \tag{2.4}$$

normally distributed with $E(\hat{\beta}_2) = \beta_2$ and $V(\hat{\beta}_2) = (1/\sum_{n=1}^{N} x_n^2)\sigma_\varepsilon^2$.[14] Therefore, a $(1-\alpha)$ confidence interval for the parameter looks like

$$\beta_2 = \hat{\beta}_2 \pm z_{\alpha/2} \sqrt{V(\hat{\beta}_2)} \tag{2.5}$$

with $z_{\alpha/2}$ the upper-$\alpha/2$ percentile of the standard normal distribution.

The actual value of $y$ at time $N+1$, given $x_{N+1}$, can be forecasted by[15]

$$\hat{y}_{N+1} = \hat{\beta}_2 x_{N+1} \tag{2.6}$$

and the associated forecast interval is[16]

$$y_{N+1} = \hat{y}_{N+1} \pm z_{\alpha/2} \sqrt{\sigma_\varepsilon^2 + x_{N+1}^2 V(\hat{\beta}_2)} \tag{2.7}$$

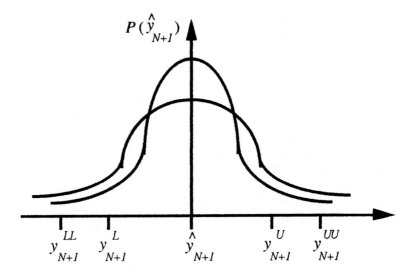

*Figure 1.* Confidence intervals with known and unknown parameters.

with $z_{\alpha/2}$ replaced by $t_{N-1;\alpha/2}$, the appropriate critical value of a $t$-distribution with $N-1$ degrees of freedom, when $\sigma_\varepsilon^2$ is unknown and its estimate

$$\hat{\sigma}_\varepsilon^2 = \sum_{n=1}^{N}(y_n - \hat{y}_n)^2/(N-1)$$

is used.[17]

The prediction interval generated by (2.7) when the parameter is known, i.e. $V(\hat{\beta}_2) = 0$, and when it is not are compared in Figure 1.[18] The interval with extremes $y_{N+1}^L$ and $y_{N+1}^U$ captures with probability $(1-\alpha)$, say 95%, the future change in the environmental variable when $\beta_2$ is known. If it is estimated the same probability is achieved only by the wider interval $y_{N+1}^{LL}$ and $y_{N+1}^{UU}$.

When the extremes of a $(1-\alpha)$ confidence interval for the parameter are plugged into (2.6), or equivalently when sensitivity analysis on $\beta_2$ is performed, it yields

$$y_{N+1} = \left[\hat{\beta}_2 \pm z_{\alpha/2}\sqrt{V(\hat{\beta}_2)}\right]x_{N+1}$$
$$= \hat{y}_{N+1} \pm z_{\alpha/2}\sqrt{x_{N+1}^2 V(\hat{\beta}_2)}. \qquad (2.8)$$

Consequently, the researcher simulating his/her "one-unknown-parameter" model with the extremes of the confidence interval for the parameter ends up with an interval for the expected value of tomorrow's environmental variable, rather than for its actual value.[19] In other words, the process generating the dependent variable is implicitly assumed deterministic.

If $A$ is set by a decision maker minimizing the probability that the environmental variable exceeds a certain threshold (Tucci, 1997), uncertainty about the parameter determines a more cautious behavior. The reason is that the extreme $y_{N+1}^{UU}$, rather than $y_{N+1}^{U}$, is now required to be below, or at, the preset limit.[20] For example, if the threshold is at $y_{N+1}^{U}$, the level of $A$ associated with $\hat{y}_{N+1}$, acceptable when $\beta_2$ is known because the extreme lies on the boundary, is rejected when the parameter is estimated. In a Nordhaus (1994) type of model with $A$ identical to $\mathcal{E}_n$, as shown in Section 6, $\beta_2$ is proportional to the feedback parameter. The fact that it is unknown may not affect the main results of the agent's maximization process based on expected values, when climate change is assumed reversible and a symmetric probability density function is used. However, the introduction of irreversibility, or of probabilistic asymmetries, may produce far reaching consequences on the optimizing process not fully analyzed yet. Furthermore, the expected value of the dependent variable does not necessarily equal the deterministic one.[21]

## 3. Two Unknown Parameters in One Equation

Alternatively, Equation (2.3) can take the form of the usual linear statistical model

$$y_n = \beta_0 + \beta_2 x_n + \varepsilon_n, \quad n = 1, \ldots, N \tag{3.1}$$

with $y_n = \Delta\mathcal{E}_n - \beta_1 Y_n$, $x_n = A_n$ and $\varepsilon_n$ defined as in (2.2). When $\beta_0$ and $\beta_1$ are unknown, LS estimators should be used, i.e.[22]

$$\hat{\beta}_0 = \bar{y} - \hat{\beta}_2 \bar{x},$$

$$\hat{\beta}_2 = \sum_{n=1}^{N}(x_n - \bar{x})(y_n - \bar{y}) / \sum_{n=1}^{N}(x_n - \bar{x})^2 \tag{3.2}$$

with $\bar{y}$ and $\bar{x}$ denoting the sample mean of $y$ and $x$, respectively. These estimators are normally distributed with mean $\beta_0$ and $\beta_2$, respectively,

$$V(\hat{\beta}_0) = \left(\sum_{n=1}^{N} x_n^2 / N\right) V(\hat{\beta}_2),$$

$$V(\hat{\beta}_2) = \left[1 / \sum_{n=1}^{N}(x_n - \bar{x})^2\right] \sigma_\varepsilon^2$$

and

$$\text{Cov}(\hat{\beta}_0, \hat{\beta}_2) = -\bar{x} V(\hat{\beta}_2),\text{[23]}$$

As before the confidence interval of each parameter is given by (2.5), with $z_{\alpha/2}$ replaced by $t_{N-2;\alpha/2}$ when the estimate $\hat{\sigma}_\varepsilon^2$, with $N-2$ as divisor, is needed. However, using the individual intervals to construct a confidence region gives rise to two problems. Firstly, the probability associated to the former is different from that associated to the latter.[24] Secondly, the derived region is not the smallest one with that probability. The correct joint confidence intervals for $\beta_0$ and $\beta_2$ are obtained from the following probability statement[25]

$$P\left\{\left(\frac{1}{2\hat{\sigma}_\varepsilon^2}\right)\left[N(\hat{\beta}_0-\beta_0)^2+2N\bar{x}(\hat{\beta}_0-\beta_0)(\hat{\beta}_2-\beta_2)+(\hat{\beta}_2-\beta_2)^2\sum_{n=1}^N x_n^2\right]\right.$$
$$\left.\leq F_{2,N-2;\alpha}\right\} = 1-\alpha \qquad (3.3)$$

with $F_{2,N-2;\alpha}$ the upper-$\alpha$ percentile of an $F$ distribution with 2 and $N-2$ degrees of freedom.[26] The term in braces indicates an ellipse with center $\hat{\beta}_0$ and $\hat{\beta}_2$ and is the smallest confidence region with probability $1-\alpha$ for all possible values of $x_n$ and $N$.[27]

The forecast for the expected value of $y_{N+1}$, given $x_{N+1}$, is

$$E(\hat{y}_{N+1} \mid x_{N+1}) = \hat{\beta}_0 + \hat{\beta}_2 x_{N+1} \qquad (3.4)$$

and the associated interval has the form

$$E(y_{N+1} \mid x_{N+1}) = E(\hat{y}_{N+1} \mid x_{N+1})$$
$$\pm t_{N-2;\alpha/2}\sqrt{V(\hat{y}_{N+1} \mid x_{N+1})} \qquad (3.5)$$

with $V(\hat{y}_{N+1} \mid x_{N+1}) = V(\hat{\beta}_0) + x_{N+1}^2 V(\hat{\beta}_2) + 2x_{N+1}\text{Cov}(\hat{\beta}_0,\hat{\beta}_2)$. As is well known, the forecast variance increases as the exogenous variable get farther from its sample mean. When an infinite number of future expected values are considered, the $t$ critical value is replaced by $(2F_{2,N-2;\alpha})^{1/2}$ and a $(1-\alpha)$ forecast band is obtained.[28] It should be noticed that this band is derived using all the $\beta_0$ and $\beta_2$ included in the ellipsoid centered on the estimated values of the parameters, i.e. the confidence region for all future $E(y_{N+i} \mid x_{N+i})$ is based on the ellipse for the parameters. Furthermore, if $1-\alpha$ is the confidence level used for the parameters, $1-\alpha$ will be the level associated to the relative forecast band.[29]

Equation (3.4) can be used to forecast also the actual value of $y_{N+1}$, given $x_{N+1}$. In this case the correct interval is [30]

$$y_{N+1} = E(\hat{y}_{N+1} \mid x_{N+1}) \pm t_{N-2;\alpha/2}\sqrt{\hat{\sigma}_\varepsilon^2 + V(\hat{y}_{N+1} \mid x_{N+1})}, \quad (3.6)$$

where the first term under the square root takes into account the variability of $y_{N+1}$ around its expected value and the second is due to the presence of

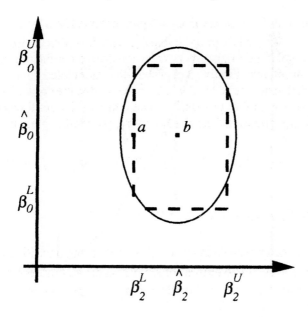

*Figure 2.* Confidence regions for $\beta_0$ and $\beta_2$ based on individual intervals given by (2.5), rectangle, and on (3.3) with zero covariance, ellipse.

unknown parameters.[31] A confidence region for $l$ future observations is given by[32]

$$y_{N+i} = E(\hat{y}_{N+i} \mid x_{N+i}) \pm \sqrt{lF_{l,N-2;\alpha}} \sqrt{\hat{\sigma}_\varepsilon^2 + V(\hat{y}_{N+1} \mid x_{N+1})}$$
$$\text{for} \quad i = 1,\ldots,l. \tag{3.7}$$

The main problem with this forecast band is that as the number of predictions, $l$, increases the term $(lF_{l,N-K;\alpha})^{1/2}$ grows without limit. This combined with the increasing forecast variance may generate nonsensible confidence intervals over very long periods. It may be useful then to concentrate only on a limited number of forecasts, for instance, in a time series predicting only every 25 or 50 years.[33]

In the previous section it was found that performing sensitivity analysis in a "one-unknown-parameter" yields the extremes of a confidence interval for the expected value of the environmental variable. It is time to check if this is true also in a "two-unknown-parameters" model. Point $a$ in Figure 2 indicates the combination of parameters used by a researcher assuming $\beta_0$ known and setting $\beta_2$ at its lower bound, i.e. performing sensitivity analysis on $\beta_2$. It is on the boundary of a rectangle, with probability $(1-\alpha)^2$, derived from two individual confidence intervals given by (2.5). When the covariance between $\hat{\beta}_0$ and $\hat{\beta}_2$ is zero, as in Figure 2, point $a$ is inside the ellipse associated with

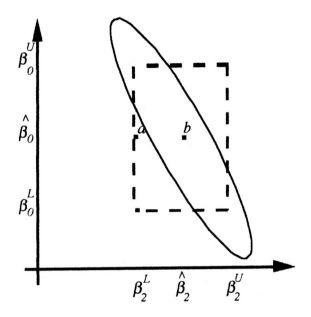

*Figure 3.* Confidence regions for $\beta_0$ and $\beta_2$ based on individual intervals given by (2.5), rectangle, and on (3.3) with a negative covariance, ellipse.

a $1 - \alpha$ confidence region.[34] By using this combination of parameters the researcher ends up with a forecast interval for the mean equal to

$$E(y_{N+1} \mid x_{N+1}) = E(\hat{y}_{N+1} \mid x_{N+1}) \pm t_{N-2;\alpha/2}\sqrt{x_{N+1}^2 V(\hat{\beta}_2)} \quad (3.8)$$

when the correct one, for one single forecast, is[35]

$$E(y_{N+1} \mid x_{N+1}) = E(\hat{y}_{N+1} \mid x_{N+1})$$
$$\pm t_{N-2;\alpha/2}\sqrt{V(\hat{\beta}_0) + x_{N+1}^2 V(\hat{\beta}_2)}. \quad (3.9)$$

Consequently, the computed interval, (3.8), is smaller than the true one, (3.9), and the stated probability larger than the true one. If the covariance between the unknown parameters is negative point $a$ is outside the ellipse, Figure 3, and the situation is ambiguous in terms of the size of the different intervals obtained. In any case the probability associated to the confidence interval used is different from the stated one.[36]

## 4. Two Unknown Parameters in Two Equations

Consider the case in which the two unknown parameters appear in different equations and the system (2.1–2.2) can be rewritten as

$$Y_n = \beta_{11} + \beta_{21} K_n + \beta_{31} L_n + \nu_n, \quad n = 1, \ldots, N \quad (4.1)$$

$$\Delta \mathcal{E}_n = \beta_{12} + \gamma_{12} Y_n + \beta_{42} A_n + \varepsilon_n, \quad n = 1, \ldots, N \quad (4.2)$$

with the error terms $\nu_n$ and $\varepsilon_n$ independently and normally distributed with zero mean and variance $\sigma_\nu^2$ and $\sigma_\varepsilon^2$, respectively. Assuming $\beta_{21}$ and $\beta_{42}$ unknown, it yields

$$\tilde{Y}_n = \beta_{21} K_n + \nu_n, \quad n = 1, \ldots, N \quad (4.1a)$$

$$\widetilde{\Delta \mathcal{E}}_n = \beta_{42} A_n + \varepsilon_n, \quad n = 1, \ldots, N \quad (4.2a)$$

with $\tilde{Y}_n = Y_n - \beta_{11} - \beta_{31} L_n$ and $\widetilde{\Delta \mathcal{E}} = \Delta \mathcal{E}_n - \beta_{12} - \gamma_{12}(\beta_{11} + \beta_{31} L_n + \tilde{Y}_n)$. In matrix form, (4.1a–4.2a) reduce to

$$\mathbf{y} = \mathbf{X}\boldsymbol{\beta} + \mathbf{e} \quad (4.3)$$

with $\mathbf{y} = [\tilde{\mathbf{Y}}' \ \widetilde{\Delta \mathcal{E}}']'$ and $\mathbf{e} = [\boldsymbol{\nu}' \ \boldsymbol{\varepsilon}']'$ $2N$-vectors, $\mathbf{e} \sim \mathcal{N}(\mathbf{0}, \boldsymbol{\Sigma} \otimes \mathbf{I}_N)$ where $\boldsymbol{\Sigma}$ is a $2 \times 2$ matrix with $\sigma_\nu^2$ and $\sigma_\varepsilon^2$ on the diagonal, $\mathbf{X}$ a partitioned matrix with $\mathbf{K}$ and $\mathbf{A}$ as diagonal blocks and zeroes elsewhere, $\boldsymbol{\beta}' = [\beta_{21} \ \beta_{42}]'$ and $\tilde{\mathbf{Y}}, \widetilde{\Delta \mathcal{E}}, \boldsymbol{\nu}, \boldsymbol{\varepsilon}, \mathbf{K}$ and $\mathbf{A}$ vectors of dimension $N$ containing the relative components. Applying LS separately to each equation produces efficient estimators and a confidence region can be derived from the usual[37]

$$(\mathbf{R}\hat{\boldsymbol{\beta}} - \mathbf{r})'\{\mathbf{R}[\mathbf{X}'(\boldsymbol{\Sigma}^{-1} \otimes \mathbf{I}_N)\mathbf{X}]^{-1}\mathbf{R}'\}^{-1}(\mathbf{R}\hat{\boldsymbol{\beta}}' - \mathbf{r}) \sim \chi_J^2. \quad (4.4)$$

Setting $\mathbf{R} = \mathbf{I}_2$, $\mathbf{r} = \boldsymbol{\beta}$ and $J = 2$ with $\hat{\boldsymbol{\beta}}$ the estimated parameter vector, (4.4) is equal to[38]

$$P\left\{\left[(\hat{\beta}_{21} - \beta_{21})\sum_{n=1}^N \frac{K_n^2}{\sigma_\nu^2} + (\hat{\beta}_{42} - \beta_{42})^2 \sum_{n=1}^N \frac{A_n^2}{\sigma_\varepsilon^2}\right] \geq \chi_{2;\alpha}^2\right\} = 1 - \alpha. \quad (4.5)$$

If the error terms in (4.1) and (4.2) have a contemporaneous correlation, $\boldsymbol{\Sigma}$ is not diagonal and the model belongs to the class of Seemingly Unrelated Regression (SUR) models (Zellner, 1962). The correct estimator is then (Judge et al., 1988, pp. 450–452)

$$\hat{\boldsymbol{\beta}} = [\mathbf{X}'(\boldsymbol{\Sigma}^{-1} \otimes \mathbf{I}_N)\mathbf{X}]^{-1}\mathbf{X}'(\boldsymbol{\Sigma}^{-1} \otimes \mathbf{I}_N)\mathbf{y} \quad (4.6)$$

and (4.4) still applies. When the covariance matrix $\boldsymbol{\Sigma}$ is unknown, it is replaced by a consistent estimator.[39] Then Equations (4.4) and (4.5) are valid only asymptotically.[40]

Sometimes forecasts for the expected values of the dependent variables for $l$ future periods are needed. Equation (4.4), with $J = l$ and $\mathbf{R}$ containing the future values of exogenous variables, can be used to derive the relative simultaneous confidence intervals. If interest centers on the construction of a confidence region for $l$ future actual values[41]

$$(\mathbf{R}\hat{\boldsymbol{\beta}} - \mathbf{r})'\{\mathbf{R}[\mathbf{X}'(\boldsymbol{\Sigma}^{-1} \otimes \mathbf{I}_N)\mathbf{X}]^{-1}\mathbf{R}' + (\boldsymbol{\Sigma} \otimes \mathbf{I})N)\}^{-1}(\mathbf{R}\hat{\boldsymbol{\beta}} - \mathbf{r}) \sim \chi_l^2 \quad (4.7)$$

is appropriate. As before, $\boldsymbol{\Sigma}$ is unknown a consistent estimator is required and (4.7) holds asymptotically.

## 5. The General Case

To examine the general case with several unknown parameters appearing in different equations, consider

$$\gamma_{11} Y_n + \gamma_{21} \Delta \mathcal{E} = \beta_{11} + \beta_{21} K_n + \beta_{31} L_n + \beta_{41} A_n + \nu_n \tag{5.1}$$

$$\gamma_{12} Y_n + \gamma_{22} \Delta \mathcal{E}_n = \beta_{12} + \beta_{22} K_n + \beta_{32} L_n + \beta_{42} A_n + \varepsilon_n \tag{5.2}$$

with the error terms $\nu_n$ and $\varepsilon_n$ normally, but not necessarily independently, distributed with mean 0 and variance $\sigma_\nu^2$ and $\sigma_\varepsilon^2$, respectively. In matrix form (5.1–5.2) look like

$$\underset{N\times 2}{\mathbf{Y}} \underset{2\times 2}{\mathbf{\Gamma}} + \underset{N\times 4}{\mathbf{X}} \underset{4\times 2}{\mathbf{B}} = \underset{N\times 2}{\mathbf{E}} \tag{5.3}$$

where $\mathbf{Y}$ and $\mathbf{X}$ contain the observations on the endogenous and exogenous variables, respectively, $\mathbf{\Gamma}$ and $\mathbf{B}$ the coefficients of current endogenous and exogenous variables, respectively, and $\mathbf{E}$ is the matrix of error terms with each row identically and independently distributed normal with mean zero and covariance $\mathbf{\Sigma}$.[42]

Under certain functional hypothesis, and assuming that $\mathbf{\Sigma}$ is diagonal and

$$\gamma_{11} = \gamma_{22} = 1, \quad \gamma_{21} = 0, \quad \beta_{41} = \beta_{22} = \beta_{32} = 0, \tag{5.4}$$

system (5.3) reduces to (2.1–2.2). This is a fully recursive model and estimating each equation separately by LS yields Maximum Likelihood (ML) estimators which are unbiased and, conditional on $Y_n$, efficient (Johnston, 1972, pp. 30–32).[43] A joint confidence region for the unknown parameters can be constructed exploiting the fact that $\mathbf{\Sigma}$ is diagonal.[44] Two ellipses, similar to those discussed earlier, can be derived and given their independence the probability that both of them include the appropriate unknown parameters is the product of the two individual probabilities.

However, the covariance matrix does not have to be diagonal and $\mathbf{\Gamma}$ need not be triangular for a system of simultaneous equations to be identified.[45] It is useful then to consider the reduced form of (5.3), i.e.

$$\mathbf{Y} = \mathbf{X}\mathbf{\Pi} + \mathbf{V}, \tag{5.5}$$

where $\mathbf{\Pi} = -\mathbf{B}\mathbf{\Gamma}^{-1}$ is the matrix of reduced form parameters and $\mathbf{V} = \mathbf{E}\mathbf{\Gamma}^{-1}$ contains the reduced form error terms with each row identically and independently distributed normal with mean zero and variance $\mathbf{\Omega} = (\mathbf{\Gamma}^{-1})'\mathbf{\Sigma}(\mathbf{\Gamma}^{-1})$. When the primary objective of modelling is for forecasting purposes interest centers on $\mathbf{\Pi}$ and $\mathbf{\Omega}$.[46] Assuming that the reduced form parameters are estimated directly and the exogenous variables are known constants the LS estimator $\hat{\mathbf{\Pi}} = (\mathbf{X}'\mathbf{X})^{-1}\mathbf{X}'\mathbf{Y}$ is unbiased as well as $\hat{\mathbf{\Omega}}$, estimator of $\mathbf{\Omega}$, whose typical $ij$-th element is

$$\hat{\omega}_{ij} = (\hat{\mathbf{v}}_i', \hat{\mathbf{v}}_j)/(N-4) = (\hat{\mathbf{y}}_i - \mathbf{X}\hat{\boldsymbol{\pi}}_i)'(\mathbf{y}_j - \mathbf{X}\hat{\boldsymbol{\pi}}_j)/(N-4), \tag{5.6}$$

where $\hat{\mathbf{v}}_i$, $\mathbf{y}_i$ and $\hat{\boldsymbol{\pi}}_i$ denote the $i$-th column of the relative array.[47]

From the distributional assumption on the error terms follows that (Judge et al., 1988, p. 52)[48]

$$N\text{vec}(\hat{\boldsymbol{\Pi}} - \boldsymbol{\Pi})'\boldsymbol{\Theta}^{-1}\text{vec}(\hat{\boldsymbol{\Pi}} - \boldsymbol{\Pi}) \sim \chi_8^2 \qquad (5.7)$$

with $\text{vec}(\hat{\boldsymbol{\Pi}} - \boldsymbol{\Pi})$ the column vector obtained by stacking the columns of $(\hat{\boldsymbol{\Pi}} - \boldsymbol{\Pi})$ and $\boldsymbol{\Theta}$ the covariance of the reduced form parameters defined as $\boldsymbol{\Theta} = \boldsymbol{\Omega} \otimes (\mathbf{X}'\mathbf{X}/N)^{-1}$.[49] However, $\boldsymbol{\Theta}$ is usually unknown and it is replaced by a consistent estimator, for instance, $\hat{\boldsymbol{\Theta}} = \hat{\boldsymbol{\Omega}} \otimes (\mathbf{X}'\mathbf{X}/N)^{-1}$. In this case (5.7) holds asymptotically.

To obtain a finite sample result when the covariance is unknown, system (5.5) is rewritten as

$$\mathbf{Y} = \mathbf{W}\boldsymbol{\Psi} + \mathbf{V} \qquad (5.8)$$

with $\mathbf{W} = \mathbf{X}\mathbf{S}^{-1/2}$, $\boldsymbol{\Psi} = \mathbf{S}^{1/2}\boldsymbol{\Pi}$, where $\mathbf{S}^{-1/2}$ is a positive definite symmetric matrix $4 \times 4$, and $\mathbf{W}'\mathbf{W} = \mathbf{I}_4$.[50] It can be shown that (Tucci, 1995)

$$N^{1/2}(\hat{\boldsymbol{\psi}}_i - \boldsymbol{\psi}_i) \sim \mathcal{N}(0, \boldsymbol{\Omega}), \quad i = 1, 2, 3, 4, \qquad (5.9)$$

where $\boldsymbol{\psi}_i$ contains the parameters of the $i$-th row and $\hat{\boldsymbol{\psi}}_i$ their LS estimates. An exact confidence region for the transformed parameters of the $i$-th row can be derived from

$$(\hat{\boldsymbol{\psi}}_i - \boldsymbol{\psi}_i)'\hat{\boldsymbol{\Omega}}^{-1}(\hat{\boldsymbol{\psi}}_i - \boldsymbol{\psi}_i) \sim T^2 \qquad (5.10)$$

with $T^2$ the Hotelling statistic distributed as $[2(N-4)/(N-5)]F_{2,N-5}$. By exploiting the fact that these rows are independently distributed, a region simultaneously valid for all the parameters is obtainable. Four ellipses as in (5.10) are constructed and the probability that all the rows are captured by their own confidence region is $(1-\alpha)^4$, with $\alpha$ the significance level associated with each region.

If an exact multidimensional confidence region for the yet to be realized values of the jointly determined endogenous variables at some future period $N+h$ is needed, Hooper and Zellner (1961) results are available. The forecasts for (5.5) come from

$$\hat{\mathbf{y}}'_{N+h} = \mathbf{x}'_{N+h}\hat{\boldsymbol{\Pi}} \qquad (5.11)$$

with $\hat{\mathbf{y}}_{N+h}$ and $\mathbf{x}_{N+h}$ the vectors of endogenous and exogenous variables, respectively, and $\hat{\boldsymbol{\Pi}}$ containing the LS estimates of the reduced form parameters. They have shown that

$$(\hat{\mathbf{y}}_{N+h} - \mathbf{y}_{N+h})'\hat{\boldsymbol{\Omega}}_{\hat{\mathbf{y}}}^{-1}(\hat{\mathbf{y}}_{N+h} - \mathbf{y}_{N+h}) \sim T^2 \qquad (5.12)$$

with $\hat{\boldsymbol{\Omega}}_{\hat{\mathbf{y}}} = \hat{\boldsymbol{\Omega}}[1 + \mathbf{x}'_{N+h}\mathbf{X}'\mathbf{X})^{-1}\mathbf{x}_{N+h}]$ and $T^2$ distributed as before. Using this result, a joint forecast region for $\mathbf{y}_{N+h}$ can be constructed.[51]

If more efficient estimators of the reduced form parameters are desired or estimates of the structural parameters in **B**, **$\Gamma$** and **$\Sigma$** are needed and some prior information is available, more sophisticated techniques should be used.[52] Assuming that the restrictions in (5.4) hold, the vector form of (5.3) is[53]

$$\mathbf{y} = \mathbf{X}\boldsymbol{\delta} + \mathbf{e}, \tag{5.13}$$

where $\mathbf{y} = \text{vec}(\mathbf{Y})$ and $\mathbf{e} = \text{vec}(\mathbf{E})$ are $2N$-vectors, $\mathbf{Z}$ is a $2N \times 6$ matrix partitioned in four blocks with $\mathbf{Z}_i = [\mathbf{Y}_i \ \mathbf{X}_i]$, where $\mathbf{Y}_i$ contains the observations on the endogenous variables, excluded the $i$-th one, of the $i$-th equation and $\mathbf{X}_i$ on the exogenous variables, in the $i$-th position for $i = 1, 2$ and zeroes elsewhere and $\boldsymbol{\delta} = (\boldsymbol{\delta}'_1 \ \boldsymbol{\delta}'_2)'$ is the vector of unknown structural parameters with $\boldsymbol{\delta}_i = (\boldsymbol{\gamma}'_i \ \boldsymbol{\beta}'_i)'$.[54] Confidence regions for the structural parameters **B** and **$\Gamma$** are derived from (Judge et al., 1985, p. 614)

$$N(\hat{\boldsymbol{\delta}} - \boldsymbol{\delta})' \Sigma_{\hat{\boldsymbol{\delta}}}^{-1} (\hat{\boldsymbol{\delta}} - \boldsymbol{\delta}) \overset{\text{asy}}{\sim} \chi_6^2 \tag{5.14}$$

with $\hat{\boldsymbol{\delta}}$ the estimator of unknown structural parameters and $\Sigma_{\hat{\boldsymbol{\delta}}}$ the relative asymptotic matrix.[55] The latter is usually unknown and is replaced by a consistent estimator.

From $\hat{\boldsymbol{\delta}}$ the derived reduced form parameters $\hat{\boldsymbol{\Pi}}^*$ can be easily obtained. Their asymptotic variance is

$$V(\hat{\boldsymbol{\pi}}^*) = \boldsymbol{\Theta}^* = \mathbf{A}\boldsymbol{\Sigma}^*\mathbf{A}' \tag{5.15}$$

with $\hat{\boldsymbol{\pi}} = \text{vec}(\hat{\boldsymbol{\Pi}})$, $\mathbf{A} = (\boldsymbol{\Gamma}^{-1})' \otimes (\boldsymbol{\Pi}\mathbf{I}_4)$ and $\boldsymbol{\Sigma}^*$ a function of $\boldsymbol{\Sigma}_{\hat{\boldsymbol{\delta}}}$. Namely, $\boldsymbol{\Sigma}^*$ is composed of submatrices $\boldsymbol{\Sigma}^*_{ij}$ of dimension $(2+4) \times (2+4)$ containing the asymptotic variances of the structural parameters appearing in the $i$-th and $j$-th equations for $i, j = 1, 2$.[56] For system (5.3–5.4) the submatrix in the top left corner is estimated by

$$\hat{\boldsymbol{\Sigma}}^*_{11} = \begin{bmatrix} 0 & 0 & 0 & 0 & 0 & 0 \\ 0 & 0 & 0 & 0 & 0 & 0 \\ 0 & 0 & V(\hat{\beta}_{11}) & * & * & 0 \\ 0 & 0 & \text{cov}(\hat{\beta}_{11}, \hat{\beta}_{21}) & V(\hat{\beta}_{21}) & * & 0 \\ 0 & 0 & \text{cov}(\hat{\beta}_{11}, \hat{\beta}_{31}) & \text{cov}(\hat{\beta}_{21}, \hat{\beta}_{31}) & V(\hat{\beta}_{31}) & 0 \\ 0 & 0 & 0 & 0 & 0 & 0 \end{bmatrix}, \tag{5.16}$$

where the nonzero elements come from a consistent estimator of $\boldsymbol{\Sigma}_{\hat{\boldsymbol{\delta}}}$ and the star indicates that the $ij$-th element is equal to the $ji$-th element.[57]

The prediction for period $N + h$, based on the derived reduced form parameters, is obtained from (5.11) with $\boldsymbol{\Pi}$ substituted by $\hat{\boldsymbol{\Pi}}^*$.[58] Indicating the new forecast error by $\hat{\mathbf{y}}^*_{N+h} - \mathbf{y}_{N+h}$, it can be shown that

$$(\hat{\mathbf{y}}^*_{N+h} - \mathbf{y}_{N+h})' [(1/N)(\mathbf{I}_2 \otimes \mathbf{x}'_{N+h}) \boldsymbol{\Theta}^* (\mathbf{I}_2 \otimes \mathbf{x}_{N+h}) + \boldsymbol{\Omega}]^{-1}$$
$$\times (\hat{\mathbf{y}}^*_{N+h} - \mathbf{y}_{N+h}) \overset{\text{asy}}{\sim} \chi_2^2, \tag{5.17}$$

which is consistently estimated when $\Theta^*$ and $\Omega$ are substituted by their estimators $\hat{\Theta}^*$ and $\hat{\Omega}^*$, with $\hat{\Omega}^* = (\mathbf{Y} - \mathbf{X}\hat{\Pi}^*)'(\mathbf{Y} - \mathbf{X}\hat{\Pi}^*)/N$ (Judge et al., 1988, pp. 355 and 766). Then an asymptotic forecast region for the dependent variables can be constructed.[59]

Equation (5.17) is not correct when some of the predetermined variables are stochastic (Feldstein, 1971). If consistent estimates of these variables, with covariance $\mathbf{Z}$, are computed and they are independent of the estimated parameters, the term in square bracket should be replaced by $\Sigma^{**}$ with typical element (Fomby et al., 1984, p. 523)

$$\sigma^2_{\hat{y}_r \hat{y}_s} = \mathbf{x}'_{N+h}\Theta^*_{ij}\mathbf{x}_{N+h} + \boldsymbol{\pi}'_i \mathbf{Z} \boldsymbol{\pi}_j + \mathrm{tr}(\Theta^*_{ij}\mathbf{Z}) + \omega_{ij} \quad \text{for } i,j = 1,2, \quad (5.18)$$

where $\omega_{ij}$ is the $ij$-th element of $\Omega$ and $\Theta^*_{ij}$ is the asymptotic covariance between the derived reduced form estimates of the $i$-th and $j$-th equations.[60] This produces an asymptotic region larger than that described in (5.17) due to the presence of the second and third term. As usual all the unknowns are replaced by consistent estimates to have an operational formula.[61]

The prediction of predetermined variables is common in dynamic econometric models, i.e. models where some of the exogenous variables are lagged dependent variables.[62] In this case (5.18) is clearly inappropriate because the forecasts for the lagged dependent variables are not independent of the estimated parameters. When (5.3–5.4) are modified to include lagged dependent variables, regressors and coefficients are rearranged as (Judge et al., 1988, p. 665)[63]

$$\mathbf{x}'_n = (\mathbf{x}'_{1n}\ \mathbf{x}'_{2n}), \quad \Pi = \begin{bmatrix} \Pi_1 \\ \Pi_2 \end{bmatrix}, \quad (5.19)$$

with $\mathbf{x}_{1n} = [1\ K_n\ L_n\ A_n]'$ and $\mathbf{x}_{2n} \equiv \mathbf{y}_{n-1} = [Y_{n-1}\ \Delta\mathcal{E}_{n-1}]'$ the vector of truly exogenous variables and of lagged dependent variables for period $n$, respectively, $\Pi_1$ the $4 \times 2$ submatrix of reduced form parameters associated with $\mathbf{x}_{1n}$ and $\Pi_2$ the $2 \times 2$ submatrix associated with $\mathbf{y}_{n-1}$.[64] It is, furthermore, assumed that the model is stable.[65]

Denoting by $\tilde{\Pi}$ any consistent estimator of the reduced form coefficients $\Pi$, the vector of dependent variables at yet to be realized period $N+h$ can be forecasted, at time $N$, by (Fomby et al., 1984, p. 545)[66]

$$\tilde{\mathbf{y}}'_{N+h} = \sum_{j=1}^{h} \mathbf{x}'_{1,N+j}\tilde{\Pi}_1 \tilde{\Pi}_2^{h-j} + \mathbf{y}'_N \tilde{\Pi}_2^h = \mathbf{p}'_{N+h}\tilde{\mathbf{Q}}_{N+h}, \quad (5.20)$$

with $\mathbf{p}'_{N+h} = (\mathbf{x}'_{1,N+h}, \mathbf{x}'_{1,N+h-1}, \ldots, \mathbf{x}'_{1,N+1}, \mathbf{y}'_N)$ and $\tilde{\mathbf{Q}}_{N+h}$ accordingly defined. When the reduced form parameters are consistently estimated with $\tilde{\pi}$, a $2(4+2)$ vector defined as $\tilde{\pi}' = [\tilde{\pi}'_1\ \tilde{\pi}'_2]'$ with $\tilde{\pi}_i = \mathrm{vec}(\tilde{\Pi}_i - \Pi_i)$ for $i = 1, 2$, distributed as

$$N^{1/2}\tilde{\pi} \overset{\mathrm{asy}}{\sim} \mathcal{N}(\mathbf{0}, \Theta^\dagger), \quad (5.21)$$

the asymptotic variance of the forecast error is

$$T/N = (1/N) \text{plim}\, \mathbf{F}' \mathcal{M}_{N+h} \Theta^\dagger \mathcal{M}_{N+h} \mathbf{F} + \sum_{j=0}^{h-1} (\Pi_2^j)' \Omega \Pi_2^j, \quad (5.22)$$

with $\mathbf{F}' = (\mathbf{I}_2 \otimes \mathbf{p}'_{N+h})$, $\mathcal{M}_{N+h}$ partitioned in $h+1$ blocks $\mathcal{M}_{N+h}^i = [\mathbf{M}_{1i} \; \mathbf{M}_{2i}]$ where $\mathbf{M}_{10} = \mathbf{I}_8$, $\mathbf{M}_{20} = 0$, $\mathbf{M}_{1h} = 0$, $\mathbf{M}_{2h} = \sum_{j=0}^{h-j-1} (\Pi_2^{h-j-1}) \otimes \tilde{\Pi}_2^j$, $\mathbf{M}_{1i} = (\Pi_2^i)' \otimes \mathbf{I}_4$ and $\mathbf{M}_{2i} = \sum_{j=0}^{i-1} (\Pi_2^j)' \otimes \tilde{\Pi}_1 \tilde{\Pi}_2^{i-j-1}$ for $i = 1, \ldots, h-1$.[67] Therefore, an asymptotic forecast region for $\mathbf{y}$ is given by Equation (5.17) with $\hat{\mathbf{y}}^*_{N+h}$ replaced by $\tilde{\mathbf{y}}_{N+H}$ and the term in square bracket by (5.22). This is approximated by substituting all the unknowns with consistent estimates. The first term in (5.22) is sometimes ignored in the approximation because vanishes as the sample size N goes to infinity (Judge et al., 1988, pp. 766–767).[68]

When the vector of purely exogenous variables $\mathbf{x}_{N+j}$ is not known and $\tilde{\mathbf{p}}_{N+h}$, a consistent estimate of $\mathbf{p}_{N+h}$, is used (5.22) is replaced by[69]

$$T^*/N = (1/N) \text{plim}\, \mathbf{F}' \mathcal{M}_{N+h} \Theta^\dagger \mathbf{F}$$
$$+ \sum_{j=0}^{h-1} (\Pi_2^j)' \Omega \Pi_2^j + \mathbf{Q}'_{N+h} \mathbf{Z}^\dagger \mathbf{Q}_{N+h} + \mathcal{D}/N, \quad (5.23)$$

with $\mathbf{Z}^\dagger$ the asymptotic covariance of $\tilde{\mathbf{p}}_{N+h}$ and $\mathcal{D}$ a $G \times G$ matrix whose $ij$-th element is $d_{ij} = \text{tr}(\Lambda_{ij} \mathbf{Z}^\dagger)$ where $\Lambda = \mathcal{M}_{N+h} \Theta^\dagger \mathcal{M}_{N+h}$. As before an approximation is obtained by replacing the unknowns with consistent estimates and sometimes only the second and fourth terms are considered.[70]

## 6. An Example

The concepts discussed in the previous sections are now applied to an empirical example. Nordhaus (1994) considers the following "emissions-carbon cycle-climate" system

$$E_n = s_n Y_n \quad (6.1)$$

$$M_n = \beta E_n + (1 - \delta)[M_{n-1} - 590] \quad (6.2)$$

$$\mathcal{E}_n = \mathcal{E}_{n-1} + (1/R_1)(F_n - \lambda \mathcal{E}_{n-1}) \quad (6.3)$$

$$F_n = 4.1 \log(M_n/590)/\log(2). \quad (6.4)$$

The amount of GHGs emissions in $CO_2$ terms in period $n$, $E_n$, is determined by the level of output, $Y_n$, and a technological parameter representing the

GHGs-output ratio, $s_n$. Equation (6.2) relates the level of atmospheric concentration of GHGs at the end of the period, $M_n$, with the concentration level at the beginning of the period and $E_n$, via the transportation rate from the atmosphere to the deep oceans, $\delta$, and the marginal atmospheric retention rate, $\beta$, respectively. Finally, in (6.3) the equilibrium global mean surface temperature, $\mathcal{E}_n$, is a function of its past value, the thermal capacity parameter $R_1$, the feedback parameter $\lambda$ and the radiative forcing variable $F_n$ defined in (6.4) with 590 the preindustrial time level of concentration.[71]

When the parameters in (6.1), (6.3) and (6.4) are known only $\beta$ and $\delta$ need to be estimated. Adding an error term, normally distributed with mean zero and variance $\sigma_\varepsilon^2$, to Equation (6.2) and running a regression on Nordhaus (1994) data for period 1860–1989 it yields[72]

$$M_n^* - M_{n-1}^* = 0.72889 E_n - 0.01545 M_{n-1}^*, \quad \hat{\sigma}_\varepsilon = 0.1604, \quad (6.2a)$$

$$(0.0438) \qquad (0.0024)$$

where $M_n^* = M_n - 590$ and $E$ are measured in billions of metric tons of carbon, the standard errors of the parameters are in parenthesis and $\hat{\sigma}_\varepsilon$ is the estimated standard deviation of the error term.[73] It follows that with a probability of 95% the marginal retention rate in the atmosphere is between 0.8155 and 0.6423 and the turnover time in the oceans, the reciprocal of $\delta$, between 93 and 50 years, if taken separately.[74] However, the correct simultaneous confidence intervals are given by (3.3), namely

$$1481.38(0.72889 - \beta)^2 + 2(27386.82)(0.72889 - \beta)(0.01545 - \delta)$$
$$+ 510944.33(0.01545 - \delta)^2 \leq F_{2,128;0.05} 2\hat{\sigma}_\varepsilon^2. \qquad (6.5)$$

The projections of this ellipse, which looks like that sketched in Figure 3, on the $\beta$ and $\delta$ axes are 0.838–0.619 and 0.0214–0.0095, i.e. a turnover time between 47 and 107 years, respectively.

Most of the times the forecast for a certain future period is desired. In this case the confidence intervals for the parameters are used to construct intervals for the forecasted values. To analyze the difference between the two most common ways to derive these intervals, namely sensitivity analysis and the econometric approach, the level of concentration of GHGs in 1995 is forecasted first. This case is simple enough to permit hand calculations. Then the attention is turned toward more meaningful cases.

Assuming that $M_{94}^*$ and $E_{95}$ are known and equal to 170.215 and 9.262, respectively, the forecast for 1995, derived from (6.2a), is 174.336. A plausible candidate for the lower end of the sensitivity analysis interval is obtained by setting the estimated parameter $\beta$ at its individual 95% low, while keeping $\delta$ at its central value estimate, and yields $M_{95}^* = 173.534$. The corresponding upper bound, with $\beta$ at its upper end, is 175.139. Alternatively, if sensitivity analysis is performed on the turnover time, using the lower and upper bound of its 95% individual confidence interval, the extremes for $M_{95}^*$ are 173.542 and

175.130. In the econometric approach the estimates of $\beta$ and $\delta$ are considered simultaneously, i.e. (6.5) is applied, and the forecast interval for the expected value of $M_{95}^*$ is[75]

$$E(M_{95}^*) = 174.336 \pm 2.4761\sqrt{(0.0399)^2} \quad (6.6)$$

with extremes 174.238 and 174.435. If the actual value of $M_{95}^*$ is considered the appropriate interval is 174.009 and 174.664.[76]

As noticed in the previous sections sensitivity analysis intervals are not associated with a precise probability.[77] Moreover, from this example emerges that they are different from, in this case larger than, the econometric ones and that they depend upon the chosen parameter. These differences, however, are very small and may seem irrelevant to environmental economists which usually consider much longer time horizons and do not have, or may not be interested in, data with a precision of up to three decimal digits. It may be argued that as long as the two approaches give similar answers the problem is purely theoretical. To see what happens when some fairly distant future year is forecasted, the tools described in Section 5 are needed. Defining

$$x_{1,N+j} = E_{94+j}, \quad x_{2N} \equiv y_N = M_{94}^*,$$
$$\Pi_1 = \beta, \quad \Pi_2 = (1-\delta) \quad \text{and} \quad j = 1,\ldots,26 \quad (6.7)$$

the forecast for the level of GHGs concentration in year 2020, indicated by '20', is

$$M_{20}^* = \hat{\beta}\sum_{j=1}^{26} E_{94+j}(1-\hat{\delta})^{26-j} + M_{94}^*(1-\hat{\delta})^{26} = 294.78 \quad (6.8)$$

and its asymptotic variance, when future emissions are known, is estimated by

$$V(M_{20}^*) = 1.9377 + 0.4655 = 2.4032. \quad (6.9)$$

In general, future emissions are not known. When the technological parameter in (6.1) is given,[78] this reduces to predicting future output and estimating its variance.[79] This is done using the projections reported in (Nordhaus, 1994, Table 5.2) as forecasts and constructing a series of out-of-sample forecast variances.[80] The asymptotic variance is given then by (5.23) and an estimate is

$$V(M_{20}^*) = 2.4032 + 0.0498 + 0.001 = 2.4531. \quad (6.10)$$

The small difference between (6.9) and (6.10) in this example is probably due to the lack of an error term in (6.2) and to the fact that $s$ is considered known and future output is forecasted fairly precisely (Table 1).

At this point a 95% forecast interval for mass concentration, in excess of the preindustrial baseline, for year 2020 can be constructed and is equal to[81]

$$M_{20}^* = 294.79 \pm 1.9799\sqrt{2.4531}. \quad (6.11)$$

TABLE 1

Forecast variances (components).

| Forecasted year | Variance components | | | Total variance |
|---|---|---|---|---|
| | Deterministic | Quadratic term | Trace term | |
| 2020 | 2.4032 | 0.0498 | 0.0001 | 2.4531 |
| 2050 | 36.6045 | 0.4713 | 0.001 | 37.0768 |
| 2075 | 164.3898 | 3.8137 | 0.0079 | 168.2114 |

Notes: The second column contains the covariance estimated using (5.22), the third one the quadratic term in $Q$ in (5.23) and the fourth one the trace term in (5.23).

This interval is slightly larger than that based on (6.9) and greatly different from, in this case much smaller than (Table 2), that obtained from sensitivity analysis on $\beta$, or $\delta$. Furthermore, the extremes found using sensitivity analysis are not invariant to choice of the unknown parameter considered. The same situation holds when forecasts and intervals for years 2050 and 2075 are computed and the main findings of the hand calculations example are fully confirmed. If a simultaneous 95% forecast interval for the three years is desired the critical value 1.9799 should be replaced by the square root of 3(2.675).[82] These joint intervals appear in parenthesis in Table 2.

By solving (6.3) for a constant equilibrium global mean surface temperature it can be seen that the equilibrium impact of a change in radiative forcing is $\Delta \mathcal{E}/\Delta F = 1/\lambda$. Assuming that $\lambda$ is known and equal to 1.41 the change in equilibrium temperature, with respect to preindustrial baseline, is readily computed (Table 2).[83] As obvious uncertainty about the future level of $M^*$, and consequently of $M$ and $\mathcal{E}$, increases as the forecast gets farther into the future and in this example it ranges from 3.6 to 8.1% if simultaneous intervals of the three forecasts are considered, in terms of the increase of GHGs concentration with respect to 1994 level.

## 7. Conclusions

In the previous pages the probabilistic meaning of the numerical results obtained from sensitivity analysis is investigated. It is found that this procedure is equivalent to determining the upper, or lower, bound of the confidence interval for the expected value of tomorrow's dependent variable in a "one-unknown-parameter" model. In other words it is implicitly assumed that the underlying process is deterministic, rather than stochastic. If two unknown parameters appear in the same equation the situation is ambiguous. The combination of parameters used by the researcher performing sensitivity analysis

TABLE 2

"95% intervals" obtained with different methods.

|  | Central value | Interval | |
|---|---|---|---|
|  |  | GHGs Concent. | $\Delta$ in Eq. Mean Temp. |
| *Forecast for 2020* | 294.79 |  |  |
| 95% Sensitivity analysis on $\beta$ |  | 273.25–316.33 | 1.60–1.80 |
| 95% Sensitivity analysis on $(1 - \delta)$ |  | 272.65–319.24 | 1.59–1.81 |
| Dynamic Model |  | 291.69–297.89 | 1.69–1.71 |
|  |  | (290.37–299.23) | (1.68–1.72) |
| *Forecast for 2050* | 468.00 |  |  |
| 95% Sensitivity analysis on $\beta$ |  | 420.84–515.16 | 2.26–2.63 |
| 95% Sensitivity analysis on $(1 - \delta)$ |  | 415.05–531.60 | 2.23–2.69 |
| Dynamic Model |  | 455.94–480.06 | 2.40–2.50 |
|  |  | (450.75–485.25) | (2.38–2.52) |
| *Forecast for 2075* | 622.33 |  |  |
| 95% Sensitivity analysis on $\beta$ |  | 554.10–690.57 | 2.78–3.25 |
| 95% Sensitivity analysis on $(1 - \delta)$ |  | 539.91–726.74 | 2.73–3.37 |
| Dynamic Model |  | 596.65–648.01 | 2.93–3.11 |
|  |  | (585.59–659.07) | (2.89–3.15) |

Notes: Figures in the first and second column indicate the level of GHGs, measured in terms of contained carbon, above the preindustrial baseline. The "sensitivity" intervals are obtained using the extremes of the 95% individual confidence interval. In parenthesis the simultaneous confidence region for the three forecasts at 95% are indicated. The last column is expressed in degrees C and reports the change with respect to preindustrial time when $\lambda = 1.41$.

is either inside or outside the correct confidence region but is never on the frontier. Therefore, the results of a sensitivity analysis exercise cannot be associated with a known probability.

For this reason some of the standard econometric theory of simultaneous confidence intervals for systems of seemingly unrelated regressions and of simultaneous equations is briefly reviewed in Sections 4 and 5. Using these tools an empirical example based on Nordhaus's (1994) model and data is presented in Section 6. In this case the intervals for the GHGs concentration and temperature based on the econometric approach are much smaller than those obtained from sensitivity analysis. Furthermore the extremes of the latter are not invariant to the choice of the unknown parameter considered. Consequently Lau's (1984, p. 136) suggestion "first, ..., use the econometric approach" seems more valid than ever.

As theoretically expected, the numerical example shows that uncertainty about the future level of GHGs concentration and temperature increases as the predicted period gets farther into the future and the number of forecasts larger. This fact may be extremely important when dealing with several unknown parameters and very long time horizons, of 200 or 300 years, as suggested by (Cline, 1991). Empirical cases in which no sensible confidence intervals exist cannot be ruled out. This is a clear symptom that too much is being asked to the data. Reducing the number of forecasts to a few significant periods, for instance predicting at intervals of 25 or 50 years, or turning to tolerance intervals may help. Focusing on improving the precision of the estimators of the parameters is the other route. Whenever literature search is needed, instead of performing sensitivity analysis, it seems more appropriate to compute the mean and variance of the estimates relative to a certain parameter and to construct the relevant confidence regions.[84]

## Notes

1. The major GHGs are carbon dioxides, methane, nitrous oxides and chlorofluorocarbons. For an overview of the economics of global warming, see (Schelling, 1992).
2. Production and utility functions belonging to the class of flexible functional forms, as defined in (Diewert, 1971), seem the correct candidates. See also (Yue, 1991), and the references therein cited, for the most recent developments.
3. In general confidence intervals can be found through stochastic simulations or analytical solutions (Pindyck and Rubinfeld, 1981, ch. 13).
4. Lau (1984, pp. 130–131) argues that underidentification represents a more serious problem for the calibration procedure than for the econometric approach.
5. See, e.g., (Walley and Wigle, 1991).
6. For a comparison of the two approaches, see (Lau, 1984).
7. This model is similar to a stripped version of the DICE model (Nordhaus, 1994) with the economic and climate systems described by one equation and no explicit optimizing behavior.
8. Mean temperature is a useful index of climate change (Nordhaus, 1994).
9. When the GHGs generated by the economic process are offset by the assimilative capacity allowed by the biogeochemical cycles, i.e. $h(Y, A) = 0$, mean temperature follows a random walk.
10. In (Tucci, 1997) the effect of output on the environmental variable is lagged one period.
11. See Section 6 for further considerations.
12. These assumptions can be weakened when Diewert's flexible functional forms are used.
13. After all the restrictions imposed to go from (2.2a) to (2.3) are not that "stringent". As long as $h_1$ and $h_2$ are known, it is always possible to define $Y_n^* = h_1(Y_n)$ and $A_n^* = h_2(A_n)$ and express $y_n$ and $x_n$ in terms of these new variables in (2.3).
14. See (Johnston, 1972, p. 16).
15. See Section 5 for the case in which the future values of exogenous variables are not known.
16. This interval refers to the unknown value of a random variable and is similar to a beta expectation tolerance interval (Hooper and Zellner, 1961, p. 546; Judge et al., 1988, p. 252).
17. The same is true for (2.5). A nice discussion of the $z, t, F$ and $\chi^2$ distributions is contained in (Pindyck and Rubinfeld, 1981, pp. 31–36).
18. See (Pindyck and Rubinfeld, 1981, pp. 208–212) for further considerations.

19. See (Johnston, 1972, p. 41) and (Wonnacott and Wonnacott, 1981, pp. 42–44).
20. See Tucci (1997) for details.
21. This is the case when a second order Taylor series expansion is used to approximate the mean of the stochastic variable even if it is implicitly assumed that the third and fourth moment of the error term distribution are zero (Tucci, 1992).
22. See (Johnston, 1972, ch. 2).
23. See (Johnston, 1972, pp. 26–28).
24. If two 95% confidence intervals like (2.5) are constructed for $\beta_0$ and $\beta_2$ the probability of the associated rectangular region, when they have zero covariance, is 90.25% (Kennedy, 1985, pp. 51–58).
25. An "approximate rough and ready procedure" is described in (Miller, 1966, pp. 67–70) and consists of constructing individual intervals with $1 - \alpha/l$ level of confidence, where $l$ is the number of parameters under investigation. This approximation is very good in the orthonormal case (Judge et al., 1988, pp. 246–249). For a comparison of the different procedures, see (Miller, 1966, pp. 12–27).
26. If the error term variance is known the critical value $\chi^2_{N-2;\alpha}$ substitutes $F_{2,N-2;\alpha}$.
27. This interval is "wasteful in the sense that the probability is $1 - \alpha$ that all ... (linear combinations) ... will be included in their respective intervals. However, it is only a finite number of (them) that are ever examined in any application" (Miller, 1966, p. 69). Therefore, the actual probability is higher than the declared one. See (Judge et al., 1985, p. 244) for a generalization of (3.3).
28. Using $2F_{2,N-2;\alpha}$ in the place of $t_{N-2;\alpha/2}$ results in larger intervals. Wonnacott and Wonnacott (1981, p. 430) present a graphical representation of this problem. A formal proof appears, e.g., in (Bickel and Docksum, 1977, pp. 282–292 and problem 7.4.7 on p. 309). See also (Miller, 1966, p. 111).
29. To get an intuitive grasp of the relationship between confidence regions for the parameters and forecast intervals see (Wonnacott and Wonnacott, 1981, pp. 429–430).
30. See (Johnston, 1972, pp. 38–42).
31. Figure 1 remains valid in the presence of two unknown parameters.
32. This can be approximated using $t_{N-2;\alpha/2l}$ instead of $(lF_{l,N-K;\alpha})^{1/2}$ (Miller, 1966, p. 115).
33. Alternatively, the concept of tolerance intervals may be applied (Miller, 1966, p. 123). As far as the forecast variance term is concerned the only hope is to improve the precision of the estimator.
34. The rectangle generated by the "rough and ready" procedure described in a previous footnote is larger than that drawn in Figure 2, but presents the same characteristics. Namely, the portions of the rectangle near the vertices are not included in the ellipse and point a lies inside the ellipse (Miller, 1966, pp. 12–27).
35. The appropriate forecast band for an infinite number of future expected values is obtained by replacing $t_{N-2;\alpha/2}$ with $(2F_{2,N-2;\alpha})^{1/2}$ in (3.9). See (Miller, 1966, p. 69).
36. The interval corresponding to (3.8) is shorter than that in (3.9) if

$$V(\hat{\beta}_0) + x^2_{N+1}V(\hat{\beta}_2) + 2x_{N+1}\mathrm{Cov}(\hat{\beta}_0,\hat{\beta}_2) > x^2_{N+1}V(\hat{\beta}_2).$$

If the covariance is positive, or $2x_{N+1}V(\hat{\beta}_2)$ is less than one, this inequality is satisfied. Otherwise it depends upon the correlation coefficient. The smaller it is the more likely is that the inequality holds.
37. In general **R** is a known matrix of dimension $J \times K$, where $K$ is the number of exogenous variables in the system and $J$ the number of restrictions, **r** a known $J$-dimensional vector and $\beta$ the $K$-vector of estimated parameters (Judge et al., 1988, p. 457).
38. Equation (4.5) is similar to (3.3), and the parameters are estimated as in Section 2.
39. If the number of regressors is the same in all equations the estimated covariance matrix is unbiased when divided by $N - K/G$, where $G$ is the number of endogenous variables

## Stochastic Sustainability in the Presence of Unknown Parameters

in the system, rather than $N$. Unbiased estimates of the unknown elements of (4.5) are obtained as in Section 2.

40. Sometimes (4.4) is divided by $J$, in finite samples. The asymptotic distribution is then $F$ with $J$ and $GN - K$ degrees of freedom (Judge et al., 1988, p. 458).

41. This is equivalent to a Wald test $W = \mathbf{d}'[\text{Var}(\mathbf{d})]\mathbf{d}$ where $\mathbf{d} = \mathbf{R}\hat{\boldsymbol{\beta}} - \mathbf{y}_{N+1}$ is asymptotically normal with mean $E(\mathbf{d}) = 0$ and variance $V(\mathbf{d}) = \mathbf{R}V(\hat{\boldsymbol{\beta}})\mathbf{R}' + V(\mathbf{y})$ and $V(\hat{\boldsymbol{\beta}})$ and $V(\mathbf{y})$ are consistently estimated (Greene, 1990, pp. 189, 317, 389, 394; Judge et al., 1988, p. 452).

42. The conditions required for the existence of a solution to system (5.3) are implicitly satisfied (Fomby et al., 1984, pp. 444–445).

43. The distribution of $Y_n$ does not depend upon the $\beta_2$'s and the variance of $\varepsilon_n$ (Greene, 1990, pp. 321–326) and the relevant expectations exist (Judge et al., 1985, pp. 164–165; Schmidt, 1976, pp. 93–96).

44. The estimators of the parameters in (5.2) are no longer normal in finite sample, but the confidence intervals based on the $t$ and $F$ statistics remain valid unconditionally (Johnston, 1972, p. 32; Greene, 1990, p. 323).

45. For a discussion of the identifying restrictions, see (Judge et al., 1985, pp. 573–586). If $\boldsymbol{\Gamma}$ is triangular and $\boldsymbol{\Sigma}$ is not diagonal the procedure described in (Greene, 1990, p. 618) can be used. It is easily verified that the model (5.3–5.4) is identified. Both equations are overidentified. When $\gamma_{21}$ is unconstrained, but the other restrictions in (5.4) hold, Equation (5.1) is exactly identified and (5.2) is overidentified.

46. See (Liu, 1960).

47. When some regressors are stochastic and/or the error terms are not normally distributed, $\hat{\boldsymbol{\Pi}}$ and $\hat{\boldsymbol{\Omega}}$ are consistent (Johnston, 1972, p. 377; Judge et al., 1988, pp. 451–452 and 613).

48. If the error terms are not normally distributed and/or the $\mathbf{X}$ contains stochastic variables such as lagged dependent variables equations, (5.7) holds asymptotically (Fomby et al., 1984, pp. 446–447).

49. In general, $\boldsymbol{\Theta} = \boldsymbol{\Omega} \text{plim}(\mathbf{X}'\mathbf{X}/N)^{-1}$ and the degrees of freedom of the $\chi^2$ distribution in (5.7) are $KG$. When a set of $J$ restrictions on the parameters $\mathbf{R}\boldsymbol{\Pi} = \mathbf{R}^*$ is considered the appropriate confidence regions are derived, asymptotically when the covariance is unknown, from

$$N(\hat{\boldsymbol{\Pi}} - \boldsymbol{\Pi})'\mathbf{R}'[\mathbf{R}\boldsymbol{\Theta}\mathbf{R}']^{-1}\mathbf{R}(\hat{\boldsymbol{\Pi}} - \boldsymbol{\Pi}) \sim \chi_J^2.$$

50. This is a canonical reduction and $\mathbf{S}^{-1/2} = \mathbf{C}'\mathbf{L}^{1/2}\mathbf{C}$ with $\mathbf{C}$ an orthogonal matrix of order $4 \times 4$, in general $K \times K$, and $\mathbf{L}$ the diagonal matrix with the characteristic roots of $\mathbf{X}'\mathbf{X}$ (Judge et al., 1985, p. 24).

51. See (Hooper and Zellner, 1961, p. 550). Equation (5.12) cannot be used when some of the exogenous variables are stochastic even if $\boldsymbol{\Pi}$ is directly estimated and disturbances are normal (Feldstein, 1971).

52. The most common of them are two-stage LS (2SLS), three-stage LS (3SLS), limited information ML (LIML) and full information ML (FIML), see, e.g., (Judge et al., 1985, ch. 15; Fomby et al., 1984, ch. 21 and 22). If the model is exactly identified, estimating the reduced form parameters by LS equation by equation remains the correct procedure.

53. This procedure is valid for any set of identifying restrictions but the dimension and composition of the arrays are exclusive to this example.

54. In general, the dimension of $\mathbf{Z}$ and $\boldsymbol{\delta}$ is $GN \times \sum_{i=1}^{G}(g_i - 1 + k_i)$ and $\sum_{i=1}^{G}(g_i - 1 + k_i)$, respectively, with $g_i$ and $k_i$ the number of endogenous and exogenous variables in the $i$-th equation (Judge et al., 1985, p. 594).

55. If $\boldsymbol{\delta}$ is estimated by 2SLS, $\hat{\boldsymbol{\delta}} = [(\mathbf{Z}_i'\mathbf{X})(\mathbf{X}'\mathbf{X})^{-1}(\mathbf{X}'\mathbf{Z}_i)](\mathbf{Z}_i'\mathbf{X})(\mathbf{X}'\mathbf{X})^{-1}\mathbf{X}'\mathbf{y}_i$ and $\boldsymbol{\Sigma}_{\hat{\boldsymbol{\delta}}}$ is replaced by $\hat{\boldsymbol{\Sigma}}_{\hat{\boldsymbol{\delta}}} = \{\hat{\sigma}_{ii}(\mathbf{Z}_i'\mathbf{X})(\mathbf{X}'\mathbf{X})^{-1}(\mathbf{X}, \mathbf{Z}_i)\}^{-1}$ with $\hat{\sigma}_{ij} = (\mathbf{y}_i - \mathbf{z}_i\hat{\boldsymbol{\delta}})'(\mathbf{y}_j - \mathbf{z}_j\hat{\boldsymbol{\delta}}_j)/N$, on the other hand when 3SLS are applied $\hat{\boldsymbol{\delta}} = \{\mathbf{Z}'[\hat{\boldsymbol{\Sigma}}^1 \otimes \mathbf{X}(\mathbf{X}'\mathbf{X})^{-1}\mathbf{X}']\mathbf{Z}\}^{-1}\mathbf{Z}'[\hat{\boldsymbol{\Sigma}}^{-1} \otimes$

$\mathbf{X}(\mathbf{X}'\mathbf{X})^{-1}\mathbf{X}']\mathbf{y}$ where the elements of $\hat{\boldsymbol{\Sigma}}^{-1}$ are $\hat{\sigma}_{ij}$ and $\boldsymbol{\Sigma}_{\hat{\boldsymbol{\delta}}}$ is estimated by $\hat{\boldsymbol{\Sigma}}_{\hat{\boldsymbol{\delta}}} = \{\mathbf{Z}'(\hat{\boldsymbol{\Sigma}}^{-1} \otimes \mathbf{X}(\mathbf{X}'\mathbf{X})^{-1}\mathbf{X}']\mathbf{Z}\}^{-1}$ (Judge et al., 1985, pp. 596 and 600–601).

56. In general, $\boldsymbol{\Sigma}^*$ and $\boldsymbol{\Sigma}^*_{ij}$ are $G(G+K) \times G(G+K)$ and $(G+K) \times (G+K)$ matrices and $i, j = 1, \ldots, G$.
57. The zero elements in (5.16) are associated with the restricted structural parameters.
58. See, e.g., (Fomby et al., 1984, p. 518; Schmidt, 1976, p. 244).
59. Equation (5.17) holds under more general conditions than (5.12) but is not valid in finite samples.
60. If the reduced form parameters are estimated directly $\boldsymbol{\Theta}$ replaces $\boldsymbol{\Theta}^*_{ij}$.
61. Given the lack of finite sample results in this case, Feldstein (1971) proposes the use of a multidimensional Chebyshev inequality which provides outer bounds for the forecast region of the dependent variables regardless of the distribution of the error terms.
62. See (Judge et al., 1985, p. 660) for an interpretation of this kind of models as part of vector autoregressive moving average processes.
63. As noted previously the restrictions in (5.4) are not necessary to make system (5.3) identified.
64. Even this version of system (5.3–5.4) is identified as can be shown checking the rank and order condition (Judge et al., 1988, p. 622). In general, the dimensions are $K$, $G$, $K \times G$ and $G \times G$, respectively.
65. The system is stable if and only if $\lim_{s \to \infty} \boldsymbol{\Pi}_{s+1} = 0$. It is assumed that the probability that an otherwise stable system would be unstable because of random disturbances is zero (Fomby et al., 1984, pp. 534–536).
66. Both the estimator $\hat{\boldsymbol{\Pi}}$ and $\hat{\boldsymbol{\Pi}}^*$ discussed above are consistent.
67. Arrays $\mathcal{M}_{N+h}$, $\mathbf{M}_{1i}$, $\mathbf{M}_{2i}$, $\tilde{\mathbf{Q}}_{N+h}$ and $\mathbf{p}'_{N+h}$ correspond to $\mathbf{R}_h \mathbf{Q}_h$, $\mathbf{D}_n$, $\mathbf{A}_n$, $\tilde{\mathbf{A}}_n$, and $\mathbf{w}'_h$, respectively, in (Fomby et al., 1984, pp. 540–546). In general $\mathbf{F}' = (\mathbf{I}_G \otimes \mathbf{p}'_{N+h})$, $\mathbf{M} = \mathbf{I}_{GK}$ and $\mathbf{M}_{1i} = (\boldsymbol{\Pi}^i_2)' \otimes \mathbf{I}_K$.
68. This is equivalent to (5.18) without the terms vanishing as $N \to \infty$ (Schmidt, 1978, p. 1229).
69. It is assumed that $\mathbf{p}_{N+h}$ is determined independently of $\boldsymbol{\Pi}_1$ or $\boldsymbol{\Pi}_2$ (Fomby et al., 1984, p. 547).
70. See (Fomby et al., 1984, pp. 524–526 and 576–590) for systems with an autocorrelated error structure.
71. Combining (6.1), (6.2) and (6.4) it yields

    $$1/R_1(F_n - \lambda \mathcal{E}_{n-1}) = h(Y_n, M_{n-1}, \mathcal{E}_{n-1})$$

    and the temperature equation becomes

    $$\mathcal{E}_n = \mathcal{E}_{n-1} + h(Y_n, M_{n-1}, \mathcal{E}_{n-1}) = \mathcal{E}_{n-1} + h_n(Y_n, \mathcal{E}_{n-1})$$

    which is the same as (2.2), except for the time subscript of $h$, with $A_n$ set identical to $\mathcal{E}_{n-1}$. A clear discussion of (6.3) is contained in (Nordhaus, 1994, pp. 30–47).
72. The values for 1860, 1880, 1900, 1920, 1940 and 1965 are read from Figure 3.1 and those for 1965, 1975 and 1985 from Table 5.4 in (Nordhaus, 1994). Given that the latter are higher than the former by 5%, for the overlapping period, these are increased accordingly. The intermediate years are obtained by interpolation.
73. The same procedure is used in (Nordhaus, 1994, p. 27).
74. This is within the range 50–200 indicated by IPCC (1990). The critical value used is 1.9799 which corresponds to t. For parameters five-decimal accuracy and for variances and critical points four-decimal accuracy is maintained for comparative purposes. It is not implied that this degree of accuracy is required nor necessarily desirable in general.
75. If only some of the estimated parameters are considered critical, the subvector of regressors associated with these parameters and the relevant submatrix of the full covariance matrix are used in the construction of the confidence regions (Greene, 1990, p. 191).

76. These extremes are derived from (6.6) with 1.9799 and 0.1653 in the place of 2.4761 and 0.0399. The interval (6.6) corresponds to the light band in (Wonnacott and Wonnacott, 1981, p. 47).
77. See Section 3 for details.
78. This parameter reflects the trend in $CO_2$-equivalent emissions per unit of gross output. For the future it is assumed to decline at 1.25 percent annually, as in (Nordhaus, 1994). The values used here are derived dividing the projections of uncontrolled emissions by those of world output, Tables 5.4 and 5.2 in (Nordhaus, 1994) respectively.
79. This is only a "partial" estimation of emissions. Whenever possible the technological parameter should be treated as unknown and the correlation between $s$ and $Y$ considered.
80. To take into account the fact that forecast variance increases over time, an index of out-of-sample variance is constructed. Assuming that the growth rate is 9.75%, as in (Nordhaus, 1994) from 1975 to 1985, forecast errors are first calculated and then divided by "1985 error". This index is then multiplied by the in-sample variance, estimated from 1965, 1975 and 1985, to obtain the forecast variances used in this example. It is also assumed that $M_{94}$ is estimated and its variance is given by (5.18), with $\mathbf{\Pi}' = [\beta\,(1-\delta)]$, $V(\mathbf{\Pi}) = \mathbf{\Theta}^{\dagger}$, $\mathbf{x} = [E_{95}\ M_{94}]$ and $\mathbf{Z}$ with $V(E_{95})$ in the top left corner and 0 elsewhere.
81. This approximation is based on the $t$-distribution (Judge et al., 1988, pp. 268–270).
82. Number 2.675 is the $F_{3,128;0.05}$ critical value. See Section 3 for details.
83. This is the value used by Nordhaus (1994, p. 47) in his base case. Cline (1991) proposes a value of 1.75 for $\lambda$.
84. Assuming that each "literature estimate" $\beta_i$ for $i=1,\ldots,s$ is identically and independently distributed, i.e. iid, $\mathcal{N}(\beta, \sigma_\beta^2)$ it is immediate to show that $\bar{\beta} = (1/s)\sum_{i=1}^{s}\beta_i$ is distributed $\mathcal{N}(\beta, \sigma_\beta^2/s)$ and an unbiased estimator of $\sigma_\beta^2$ is $\hat{\sigma}_\beta^2 = (1/s-1)\sum_{i=1}^{s}(\beta_i - \bar{\beta})^2$. In general, if $s$ "literature estimates" of a $K$-vector $\boldsymbol{\beta}$ are available and $\boldsymbol{\beta}_i \stackrel{\text{iid}}{\sim} \mathcal{N}(\boldsymbol{\beta}, \boldsymbol{\Sigma})$ for $i=1,\ldots,s$, the elements of $\boldsymbol{\Sigma}$ are estimated by $\hat{\sigma}^2_{\beta_k \beta_j} = (1/s-K)\sum_{i=1}^{s}(\beta_{ki} - \bar{\beta}_k)(\beta_{ji} - \bar{\beta}_j)$ for $k,j=1,\ldots,K$. When the $\beta_i$'s, or $\boldsymbol{\beta}_i$'s, are not normally distributed but still iid these results are valid asymptotically (Bickel and Docksum, 1977, p. 464).

## References

1. Bickel, P. J. and K. A. Docksum (1977). *Mathematical Statistics: Basic Ideas and Selected Topics*, San Francisco, CA, Holden Day.
2. Cline, W. R. (1991). "Scientific Basis for the Greenhouse Effect", *The Economic Journal* 101, 904–919.
3. Diewert, W. E. (1971). "An Application of the Shephard Duality Theorem: A Generalized Leontief Production Function", *Journal of Political Economy* 79, 481–507.
4. Feldstein, M. S. (1971). "The Error Forecast in Econometric Models when the Forecast-Period Exogenous Variables Are Stochastic", *Econometrica* 39(1), 55–60.
5. Fomby, B. T., R. C. Hill and S. R. Johnson (1984). *Advanced Econometric Methods*, Berlin, Springer-Verlag.
6. Greene, W. H. (1990). *Econometric Analysis*, New York, MacMillan.
7. Hooper, J. and A. Zellner (1961). "The Error of Forecast for Multivariate Regression Models", *Econometrica* 29(4), 544–555.
8. IPCC, Intergovernmental Panel on Climate Change (1990). *Climate Change: The IPCC Scientific Assessment*, Cambridge, U.K., Cambridge University Press.
9. Johnston, J. (1972). *Econometric Methods*, 2nd ed., New York, McGraw Hill.
10. Jorgenson, D. W. and P. J. Wilcoxen (1992). "Reducing U.S. Carbon Dioxide Emissions: The Cost of Different Goals", in *Energy, Growth and the Environment: Advances in the*

*Economics of Energy and Resources*, Vol. VII, J. R. Moroney (ed.), Greenwich, CT, JAI Press, pp. 125-158,
11. Judge, G. G., W. E. Griffiths, R. C. Hill, H. Lutkepohl and T. C. Lee (1985). *The Theory and Practice of Econometrics*, 2nd ed., New York, Wiley.
12. Judge, G. G., R. C. Hill, W. E. Griffiths, H. Lutkepohl and T. C. Lee (1988). *Introduction to the Theory and Practice of Econometrics*, 2nd ed., New York, Wiley.
13. Kennedy, P. (1985). *A Guide to Econometrics*, 2nd ed., Cambridge, MA, The MIT Press.
14. Lau, L. J. (1984). "Comments", in *Applied General Equilibrium Analysis*, H. Scarf and J. Shoven (eds.), Cambridge, MA, Cambridge University Press, pp. 127-137.
15. Liu, T. (1960). "Underidentification, Structural Estimation and Forecasting", *Econometrica* 28, 855-865.
16. Mansur, A. and J. Whalley (1984). "Numerical Specification of Applied General Equilibrium Models: Estimation, Calibration and Data", in *Applied General Equilibrium Analysis*, H. Scarf and J. Shoven (eds.) Cambridge, MA, Cambridge University Press, pp. 69-126.
17. Miller, R. G. (1966). *Simultaneous Statistical Inference*, New York, McGraw Hill.
18. Mood, A. M., F. A. Graybill and D. C. Boes (1974). *Introduction to the Theory of Statistics*, 3rd ed., New York, McGraw Hill.
19. Nordhaus, W. (1991). "Economic Approaches to Greenhouse Warming", in *Global Warming: Economic Policy Responses*, R. Dornbusch and J. Poterba (eds.), Cambridge, MA, The MIT Press, pp. 33-66.
20. Nordhaus, W. D. (1994). *Managing the Global Commons: The Economics of the Greenhouse Effect*, Cambridge, MA, The MIT Press.
21. Pindyck, R. and D. Rubinfeld (1981). *Econometric Models and Economic Forecasts*, 2nd ed., New York, McGraw Hill.
22. Schelling, T. C. (1992). "Some Economics of Global Warming", *The American Economic Review* 82(1), 3-14.
23. Schmidt, P. (1976). *Econometrics*, New York, Marcel Dekker.
24. Schmidt, P. (1978). "A Note on Dynamic Simulation Forecasts and Stochastic Forecast-Period Exogenous Variables", *Econometrica* 46, 1227-1230.
25. Tucci, M. P. (1992). "Sustainable Growth: A Stochastic Approach", Nota di Lavoro 10.92, Fondazione Eni Enrico Mattei, Via S. Sofia 27, 20122 Milano, Italy.
26. Tucci, M. P. (1995). "An Exact Test for the Reduced Form Parameters of a System of Simultaneous Equations", Facoltà di Giurisprudenza, Università di Siena, Piazza S. Francesco 7, 53100 Siena, Italy, mimeo.
27. Tucci, M. P. (1997). "Stochastic Sustainability", in this volume.
28. Whalley, J. and R. Wigle (1991). "The International Incidence of Carbon Taxes", in *Global Warming: Economic Policy Responses*, R. Dornbusch and J. Poterba (eds.), Cambridge, MA, The MIT Press, pp. 233-262.
29. Wonnacott, T. H. and R. J. Wonnacott (1981). *Regression: A Second Course in Statistics*, New York, Wiley.
30. Yue, P. (1991). "A Microeconometric Approach to Estimating Money Demand: The Asymptotically Ideal Model", *Review of The Federal Reserve Bank of St. Louis* 73(6), 36-51.
31. Zellner, A. (1962). "An Efficient Method of Estimating Seemingly Unrelated Regressions and Tests of Aggregation Bias", *Journal of American Statistical Association* 57, 348-368.

ANDREA BELTRATTI*

## 3.7. Climate Change and Emission Permits

### 1. Introduction

Climate change is slowly entering the policy and research agenda. As the prospect of a human-induced increase in the temperature becomes more realistic, scientists and policy-makers are called upon to tackle problems of enormous complexity. A structural change in the climatic conditions is likely to have a very large impact on the structure of many areas of the world economy.

Unfortunately, the phenomenon is not well understood from either a physical or an economic point of view. Scarcity of scientific certainties magnify different attitudes of various countries about the costs and benefits of immediate restrictions of greenhouse gases; such attitudes are largely determined by the level of economic development and by the expected effects of the new climate on welfare and economic activity. Countries which might benefit from an average increase in the temperature are obviously against decreasing emissions, while countries which are expanding rapidly are not willing to give up the possibility of future increases in income per capita by slowing down the use of materials connected to emissions of dangerous gases.

Heterogeneity of attitudes, while an interesting topic per se, is not the main concern here, where it is assumed that a consensus has been reached on the need to decrease emissions. If the possibility of reaching a world agreement mandating signatories to curb emissions is regarded unrealistic, perhaps one may think of the case of an economy which has unilaterally decided to reduce emissions of dangerous gases.

In this case one interesting economic question is how to effectively implement policy measures inducing decentralized decision-makers to change production processes, decreasing certain types of production, and the measures

---
* I thank William Baumol and Geoffrey Heal for comments on a previous version of this paper. All errors remain my own.

which allow to reach the goal. Clearly, this issue is part of a more general comparison among alternative environmental policy instruments.

As pointed out by Cropper and Oates [9], authorities in the US, if not in Europe, have emphasized the role of marketable permits, as opposed to effluent fees, in the regulation of the environmental effects of economic activity. Marketable permits may be preferred to fees on the basis of various considerations also discussed in Cropper and Oates [9], for example, revenue-raising arguments, efficiency considerations, asymmetric information, market imperfections. Even more to the point of this paper, there have been recent proposals, see [23], for the use of permits as an efficient instrument for managing emissions of $CO_2$, in the context of the climate change issue.

Most of the studies about the properties that the prices of such permits are likely to have push to the extreme the equivalence between permits and taxes due to their considering static frameworks of analysis. It is contended here that a richer framework, based on a dynamic model, can highlight potential differences between the two systems, which may become relevant to policy-makers.

Emission permits define, like stocks and bonds and other financial assets, property rights. A stock, for example, can be bought and then resold on organized markets, and the resulting capital gain is the essential element in the evaluation of the current market price. Depending on the specific characteristics of the pollutant under consideration and of the contractual agreements, emission permits may be considered in a similar way. To the extent that they attach to the owner the possibility to emit for a certain time period a given amount of polluting substances, they incorporate characteristics which are similar to those offered by financial assets.

Such considerations point out that theoretical analyses of emission permits may be fruitfully based on an explicitly dynamic framework giving rise to equilibrium pricing considerations similar to those prevailing for asset prices. Surprisingly, even though emission permits are financial instruments, there is a general lack of formal analysis of their market price in the context of dynamic models. The traditional concern of the literature has been to show the equivalence between permits and taxes as instruments in the reduction of polluting emissions under conditions of perfect information, and the superiority of permits in a context where the planner lacks the information about heterogeneous costs of abatement on the part of the various polluters. Such static analyses are useful to compare alternative policy instruments, and can explain the market price of permits as a function of demand and supply, but cannot by definition incorporate future elements.

Financial assets are traded on organized markets at prices depending on the perceptions of traders about a few fundamental variables. In the case of bonds, fundamentals are represented by future short term interest rates; in the case of stocks, interest rates plus dividends are important. In the case of permits one would expect by analogy that the price should be some present discounted value of similar variables, even though such a conjecture cannot be made more precise without an analytical scheme.

This paper presents a dynamic analysis of emission permits, within the context of an overlapping generations model, which seems suited to consider elements related to asset pricing, externalities and contrasts of interests between generations. The basic questions considered by this paper are the following: is there a useful way to model emission permits in a dynamic context? Does such an analysis provide a perspective to understanding permits that is different from that coming from static models? Does environmental policy have more or less impact on the market price of permits in a dynamic context?

The result that market prices at a point in time do not only reflect conditions for the same time period, but also involve expectations about the future, is likely to have important implications for environmental policy, and for the comparisons among different instruments. To the extent that prices are set in liquid financial markets populated by speculators, one may expect a large volatility in price, due to changing expectations or internal dynamics of speculation, which is going to affect firms buying permits as inputs into production processes. This increases the links between financial markets and the real economy, but may induce the environmental agency to revise the results of the comparison between permits and taxes.

The plan of the paper is as follows: Section 2 presents a brief discussion of climate change and of some elements which are of interest in a discussion of emission permits in a stochastic model. Section 3 describes emission permits and their equivalence to financial assets, while Section 4 uses an overlapping generations model developed in [3] to formally analyze permits in a dynamic context. Section 5 uses the model to discuss the implications for the price of permits, while Section 6 concludes emphasizing policy considerations.

## 2. Climate Change

According to the greenhouse effect, accumulation of carbon dioxide ($CO_2$) and other greenhouse gases (GHGs) permit the sun's radiation to penetrate to the earth surface but trap a portion of the earth's outbound radiation. This linkage between gases and temperature is not bad for life as we know it today: without the greenhouse effect the earth's average surface temperature would be $-18°C$ rather than $+15°C$. What may potentially be dangerous for life as we know it today is that the further increase in the concentration of gases that is expected to take place in the near future, largely as a consequence of the activities performed to create consumption and investment goods and services, might produce an increase in the average temperature over the earth and other significant climatic changes that are likely to negatively affect humanity. This suggests that a model to study the climate change issue should include two interacting dynamic systems, representing economic and climatic considerations. These characteristics are in fact part of the overlapping generations model described in this paper.

It has been proposed that $CO_2$ permits are used to control total emissions [23]. Before starting with the analysis, it is necessary to say that the introduction of emission permits for the global warming problem depends on the existence of some coalition of countries that is willing to overcome the free rider problem and take positive actions in restricting emissions. Lacking any coalition, countries will never agree to observe the requirements imposed by permits in the first place, and a market would never arise. However, these coalitions may not be easy to form, and may depend on the existence of increasing returns to scale [13], or on the possibility of tying the environmental problem to other bargaining problems, as pointed out by Carraro and Siniscalco [5]. This paper will not consider this problem, and will just assume that the world economy has reached an agreement that is sufficient to operate a system of emission control based on taxes or permits. As observed by Sandor [18], this is likely to be the crucial step in organizing a market for permits.

Which sources of uncertainty could one consider with respect to the climate change problem? Recent research has shown the existence of many dimensions of uncertainties that surround the links from economic activity to the environment and viceversa. As to the first link, there is uncertainty over some parameters, especially over the feedback multiplier [8]. The various feedbacks are in general complex, and their interactions are even more complex. Two examples are the following: (a) an increase in temperature decreases the amount of ice and snow, and this in turn decreases the reflectivity of the planet to the sun, therefore, more radiations are absorbed (positive feedback loop), (b) an increase in the temperature of the earth leads to increased evaporation that increases the clouds and decreases the temperature (negative feedback loop). Difficulties in measuring these interactions have led the Intergovernmental Panel on Climate Change [14] to assign a minimum value of 1.1 and a maximum of 3.4 to the feedback multiplier. Moreover, the empirical evidence is on the other hand even more controversial, and induces some to deny the very existence of the problem. As a result nobody can predict with great safety the rise in temperature associated with the level of economic activity and gases that are likely to be produced in the future.

The second link between the economic and climatic system goes from global warming to economic activity and more in general to welfare. Nordhaus [16] has produced some estimates for the US economic system, suggesting that the damage is likely to be relatively minor. The effects on the industrial sector are small since productivity of factors of production by and large does not seem to depend on the temperature, while the effects on agriculture may certainly be large, but are not uniformly negative. As long as the losses of some areas can be compensated with the gains from other areas there may well be an overall balance. These estimates are certainly very interesting, but should be taken with caution; in fact others are more pessimistic [8, 14]. The IPCC study points out the large ignorance about the precise effects of the temperature on agriculture, and to the extreme heterogeneity that a given mean increase in the temperature might have on different areas (higher warming in the high altitudes, poleward advance of monsoon rainfall, etc.). Moreover, there are various other impacts that seem no less important than the ones on agriculture, that is on natural terrestrial ecosystems, hydrology and water resources, human settlements, that are both poorly understood and difficult to measure, especially in terms of damages to future generations. Relatively more is known about the costs of cutting down emissions [15, 17].

## 3. Emission Permits

### 3.1. *Types of Instruments*

Baumol and Oates [2] and Cropper and Oates [9] compare permits to other forms of regulation aimed at reducing the level of pollution, especially command-and-control and emission fees. Roughly, one can say that the advantage of both emission permits and emission fees over measures of command-and-control lies in their greater efficiency.

Indeed, one way to go about reducing pollution towards socially optimal levels is to proceed in a "bottom-up" fashion, by first obtaining information on the productive processes of the different plants or units involved in pollution, and then fixing targets for all of them in such a way to reach an overall level that is compatible with the target. In this command-and-control approach the central regulator has, therefore, to distribute control responsibilities among different points of discharge, and this requires an incredible amount of information in order to implement the system in an efficient way.

Such information may be impossible to obtain because of incentive problems; as Tietenberg [21] puts it "The fundamental problem with the command-and-control approach is a mismatch between capabilities and responsibilities. Those with the incentive to allocate the control responsibility cost effectively, the control authorities, have too little information available to them to accomplish this objective. Those with the best information on the cost-effective choices, the plant managers, have no incentive either to voluntarily accept their cost-effective responsibility or to transmit unbiased cost information to the control authority so it can make a cost-effective assignment".

The other possibility is to give a price to emissions, and ask that each polluter pays such a price for each unit of emission. This tax obtains equivalent results to command-and control in terms of physical reduction of emissions, even though each polluter responding optimally to market prices will spontaneously set emissions at the desired level. When plants have different costs of reducing emissions, those plants which can reduce emissions at a lower cost will find it profitable to do so by a large amount and at the same time sell part of the permits to those plants which abate less due to larger costs. This ensures that the total cost of achieving a certain reduction in pollution will be lower with a tax than with a command-and-control strategy.

Emission permits can in general be thought of as a tax, even though they seem to have some advantages: (a) permits may reduce the uncertainty and adjustment costs involved in reaching a certain level of pollution, (b) permits decrease the financial burden put over firms, especially if some form of grandfathering in their initial distribution is adopted, and (c) they can solve the problem of spatial heterogeneity of pollution sources. The disadvantage connected with (b), from the point of view of public budget, is lack of tax revenue raising.

## 3.2. Types of Permits

The distinction between uniformly mixed assimilative pollutants and uniformly mixed accumulative pollutants is important for proper modelling. In the former case the absorption capacity of the environment is so large with respect to the flow of emissions over one unit of time, that pollutants do not accumulate over time; the cost-effective emission reduction credit design is defined in terms of an allowable emission rate. This means that one does not need, for the specific purpose of modelling emission permits, to consider explicitly a dynamic description of environmental assets, as the spontaneous regeneration is much larger than the use connected with economic activity. In this case a model which is only concerned with flows is appropriate. In the case of accumulative pollutants the distinction between stocks and flows is instead important, as the rate of emission in general exceeds the absorption capacity. In the extreme case in which the capacity to absorb is zero, the stock of pollutant at time t is the sum of all past flows of emissions.

The assumptions made about environmental dynamics become of fundamental importance to the way permits are issued. For accumulative pollutants, emission permits of a completely exhaustible type, like those described by Tietenberg [20], should be issued: holders do not have any constraint about using the permits, but the permits die down after the corresponding emission of pollutant. One unit of permit would give the owner the right to emit a certain amount of substance, e.g. one ton, with no time limitation. This implicitly assumes that it is necessary to come to a complete phase-out of the pollutant in question, since it is not possible to produce or consume forever if the pollutant is essential. Exhaustible permits are therefore uncommon, as in most cases, at least at a general level, the main effort lies in designing instruments useful for the coexistence of pollution and economic activity.

In the case of assimilative pollutants one can instead imagine a situation where a flow of new permits is issued every time period. Here one could assume that, even though the reproduction capacity of the environment is so large, it is necessary to control emissions because of direct effects on human health. One unit of emission permit in this case gives the owner the right to emit a certain amount of substance within a given time period, e.g. one ton within the year 2001. Again, one might conceive of a system where permits are valid only until the owner actually emits the amount corresponding to them; firms would have to buy, before emissions, enough units of permits, which under this system would again be exhaustible.

## 3.3. Emission Permits as Financial Assets

Can emission permits be considered as financial assets? As pointed out in the introduction, the essential characteristic of the latter is their representing tradable property rights, assigning certain well-specified privileges to their owners. Usually, the flow of payments associated with a financial asset is the reason why the latter is traded in an organized secondary market; the purchase of the asset on the market gives the holder the right to receive future cash flows and/or the possibility to resell it to others in the future.

Such characteristics are also present in the types of exhaustible emission permits which were described in the previous subsection. This is especially true in the case of accumulative pollutants, where the owner of one permit may be interested in exploiting the existence of a secondary market and selling the permit to other producers in case that there is no more need to emit the pollutant to carry out production. It is easy to imagine many situations where this can happen, the most common being the case of a technological innovation which allows production with no use of the pollutant.

Clearly, the existence of a secondary market may facilitate the efficient use of emission permits. Indeed, this is one fundamental reason why permits may be more desirable than other instruments. The possibility of reselling permits on a secondary market may also increase initial demand. If there were no possibility of selling the permits, firms would have to solve a complicated intertemporal problem, in order to understand what is the convenience to buy the permits at a given price, and calculating therefore the costs of the inputs, the probability of technical changes which affect future demand, and so on. Such calculations are enormously simplified with a secondary market, since the buyer knows that there is always the possibility of a future sale. The problem is still difficult to solve, but increased flexibility is certainly positively related to demand.

The existence of a secondary market may, moreover, bring into the picture agents who are not directly concerned with the purchase of emission permits for their direct use in production processes, but rather for the opportunity to buy the permits given expectations of a large rate of return from a future sale to other agents, be their producers or speculators. These agents would certainly increase the liquidity of the market, and might be beneficial even to producers, even though the welfare of the latter might also decrease due to the volatility of prices caused by a class of speculators.

In the case of assimilative pollutants such considerations are not so appropriate, because the secondary market would be limited to permits valid for emissions before the end of the time period, e.g. one year. The dimension of the market would not necessarily be smaller than the one for accumulative pollutants, depending on the supply of permits, in turn a function of the importance of the pollutant under consideration in production processes. However one would certainly observe a progressive decline of trading as time goes by and there are fewer and fewer permits which allow for emission during the specific time period. The problem could be eliminated by trading simultaneously permits for different time periods, e.g. for emissions in the year 2000 and in the year 2001, and by issuing permits for the future time periods as soon as one type of permit disappears.

Even though there seem to be many similarities between emission permits and financial instruments, most of the literature has been set in the context of models which are not only static, but also of a partial equilibrium nature. Chichilnisky et al. [7], building on Chichilnisky and Heal [6], instead adopt a general equilibrium framework, and study the role of emission permits as instruments traded in financial markets to help facing the global warming problem in a decentralized system. One of the important results achieved in these papers is to relate the burden of reduction of costs to welfare; for example, when there are many polluters, the optimal solution consists of equalizing the product of marginal costs of abatement times the marginal utility of consumption, not simply the former. This has important consequences about who should abate in order to reduce the total stock of pollutant.

Extending analytical models to an intertemporal framework seems to be important, as the demand functions of polluters in the presence of intertemporal considerations are likely to be very different from those emerging from a static model. Indeed, in an intertemporal framework producers may well demand permits not simply for their possible future use, but also for the rate of return which may be expected from the operation of immediate purchase and future sale. Moreover, this introduces into the picture considerations related to the comparison of expected rates of return from different assets, e.g. permits and bonds. Finally, equations connecting rates of return for different assets may give rise to present discounted value formulas, explaining the price level in terms of fundamentals. Most of these considerations will be formalized in the model to be presented in what follows, who extends a general equilibrium framework to an intertemporal context.

## 4. A Dynamic Model of Emission Permits

In the model considered by Beltratti [3], the economy is inhabited by agents who live for two periods and maximize:

$$u(c_t^0, T_t) + \delta u(c_{t+1}^1, T_{t+1}), \tag{1}$$

where $u$ is a utility function that respects all the standard regularities conditions, $c_t^0$ is consumption when young, $c_{t+1}^1$ is consumption when old, $T_t$ is the level of temperature at time $t$, $\delta$ is the discount factor due to the existence of time preference. Utility is, therefore, derived from consumption of both a private and a public good, so that $u_1(.,.) > 0$, $u_2(.,.) < 0$, where $u_i(.,.)$ represents marginal utility with respect to the i-th argument of the utility function.

The history of the economy starts at time 0 and goes on forever, $t = 0, 1, 2, \ldots$ At time 0 there is a first generation (generation 0) which is born old and lives only for one period, and another generation which is born young and goes through the standard two-period life-cycle which is followed by all subsequent generations (for a discussion of such a structure, see [1]).

Each agent is also a producer, by means of a domestic technology using physical capital and emissions to produce goods, $y_t = f(k_t, e_t)$, where $f(0, e_t) = f(k_t, 0) = 0$, $f_i(.,.) > 0$ $i = 1, 2$, $f_{ii}(.,.) < 0$. The production function is of the Brock [4] type, where emissions $e$ enter the production function because producing with no worries about pollution makes other factors available for operations of direct production rather than for cleaning purposes.[1] Such a production function is useful to model a permanent trade-off between production of goods and use of environmental resources, since, as pointed out below, emissions increase the stock of a pollutant.

It is assumed that there is an institution which can enforce the rule of having to buy emission permits before polluting. Permits can be bought on a secondary market. Given the assumptions made about the structure of population, the result of such assumptions is that young agents buy from the old agents the number of emission permits which is suggested by the utility maximization problem. It follows that, since savings earn a gross rate of interest equal to $(1 + r_t)$, the budget constraint is:

$$c_t^0 = f(k_t, e_t) - p_t e_t - s_t - (1 + r_t)k_t, \tag{2}$$

$$c_{t+1}^1 = s_t(1 + r_{t+1}) + p_{t+1} e_t, \tag{3}$$

where $s_t$ is savings at time $t$, $e_t$ is both emissions and the number of permits bought when young and then resold to the next young generation at price $p_{t+1}$. According to (2) young agents produce by means of a production function using capital and emissions as inputs. Emissions can be used only if an equal amount of permits is available, which has to be bought by the old generation at price $p_t$. Capital is obtained from the savings of the past young generation, at a cost equal to $(1+r_t)k_t$. Of course, $k_t = s_{t-1}$, as in equilibrium savings of one generation become capital for the next generation.

According to (3) consumption when old depends on savings when young and on sale of permits to the next generation of producers. The model therefore assumes that agents have to emit when young in order to have resources for consumption in both periods. From now on, and without loss of generality, the number of total consumers will be normalized to 1.

The institutional arrangement prevailing in this economy, therefore, requires that in order to emit one unit of pollutant it is necessary to buy from the old generation one unit of permit at price $p_t$; the holder of one permit is entitled to emit one unit per period of time for the indefinite future. Of course, in the model agents live for two periods and produce for one only, so that each agent will buy the permit when young in order to produce, and then will sell it when old to the next young producer. From the point of view of the single agent, therefore, the right to emit one unit for each period for the indefinite future is not directly relevant for production purposes, but becomes essential when it comes to selling the permits to a future generation.

Such a modelling framework is connected with that used by Chichilnisky et al. [7] and Tietenberg [20]. The relation between the model of this paper and the one of Tietenberg can be explained by assuming that the problem (1) subject to the constraints (2) and (3) has a bliss point at $e_t = B(k_t)$, which, therefore, would be the optimal choice of emissions in an unregulated system. The equations could be reformulated in order to assume that the public authority wants to establish a price for emission reductions. Net emissions would, therefore, be equal to bliss emissions minus reductions $R_t$, so that the constraints of the problem would become:

$$c_t^0 = f(k_t, B(k_t) - R_t) - p_t(B(k_t) - R_t) - s_t,$$
$$c_{t+1}^1 = s_t(1 + r_{t+1}) + p_{t+1}(B(k_t) - R_t).$$

This problem is equivalent to the one that was just presented when one sets $e_t = B(k_t) - R_t$. Tietenberg also assumes that the permits are distributed across polluters, and asks questions about equity of the initial distributions and about effects of alternative distribution schemes on the efficiency of abatement. In the model of this paper the only heterogeneity is between agents living in different generations, and the permits are then sold from one generation to the other, so that the only relevant problems about distributional equity lies in the discrimination which is performed in favor of the old generation to which permits are assigned for the first time in history. It would be easy however to complicate the model by allowing for horizontal heterogeneity at each point in time, see, for example, the comprehensive treatment by Azariadis [1].

Finally, it is assumed that the level of the public good for period $t$, $T_t$, is connected with a stock of pollution, such that:

$$T_t = \gamma P_t, \tag{4}$$

where the stock of emissions $P$ affects the temperature and evolves dynamically according to:
$$P_t = e_t + (1-h)P_{t-1}.$$
It follows that the current stock is a weighted sum of past emissions:
$$P_t = e_t + (1-h)e_{t-1} + (1-h)^2 e_{t-2}$$
$$+ (1-h)^3 e_{t-3} + \cdots = \sum_{j=0}^{\infty}(1-h)^j e_{t-j}.$$

By assuming that $h = 1$, one obtains a flow formulation $T_t = \gamma e_t$, where the flow of emissions determines the temperature. Such formulation may describe situations where the assimilative rate of a natural resource is large, so that in each time period it is only the net flow which may be harmful, corresponding to assimilative pollutants. The stock formulation may describe an accumulative pollutant, for example the global warming scenario, where emissions exceed the assimilative rate, and it is the stock of $CO_2$ which is responsible for the level of the temperature.

## 5. Equilibrium and Prices in the Permits Markets

After describing preferences and technologies, it is possible to derive demand functions. As to capital, one has the standard equality between the interest rate and the marginal productivity:
$$(1 + r_t) = f_1(.,.).$$
Optimal savings decisions is derived from the budget constraint and the usual necessary condition ($T_t$ and $T_{t+1}$ are taken as exogenous by the single agent):
$$\frac{\partial u}{\partial c_t^0} = \delta(1 + r_{t+1})\frac{\partial u}{\partial c_{t+1}^1}. \tag{5}$$

According to (5), marginal utilities have to be equal across periods of time, after considering the interest rate and time preference. Demand for emission permits instead derives from:
$$\frac{\partial u}{\partial c_t^0}\left[\frac{\partial f}{\partial e_t} - p_t\right] + \delta\frac{\partial u}{\partial c_{t+1}^1}p_{t+1} = 0, \tag{6}$$
according to which the marginal cost in terms of consumption must be equal to the sum of the current and future marginal benefits: buying one permit costs $p_t(\partial u/\partial c_t^0)$ in terms of utility, and yields $(\partial u/\partial c_t^0)(\partial f/\partial e_t)$ immediately in terms of emissions and $\delta(\partial u/\partial c_{t+1}^1)p_{t+1}$ in the next period when the permits will be sold on the market.

The equilibrium of the economy is represented by prices and rates of return such that the demand for capital at time $t$ is equal to the supply of savings decided at time $t-1$, and the demand for emission permits is equal to supply. Here it is assumed that the supply of permits is fixed over time, and was given as a gift to generation 0.

From the equilibrium conditions it is possible to derive an asset pricing formula considering the price as a present value of future fundamentals, and can be obtained by solving forward the first order condition (6):

$$p_t = \sum_{j=0}^{\infty} \delta^j \Pi_{i=0}^{j}(1+r_t)^{-i} \frac{\partial f}{\partial e_{t+j}}. \tag{7}$$

According to the present value equation (7), the equilibrium market price at time $t$ depends on future fundamentals, given by the discounted values of the marginal productivity of permits. In particular, the price is not simply equal to the current marginal productivity of permits, as the static model predicts, but the whole equilibrium path is relevant. The equation closely resembles that for stocks, when future dividends are discounted at the interest rate.

Note that participants in the market need to have a large degree of foresight in order to compute this price, that depends on both the marginal productivity of capital and the future environmental policy. This is also true of other pricing formulas, for stocks and bonds. The latter equations have not performed well empirically, being subject to many findings of excess volatility [19]. It should not be forgotten that such equations are difficult to test, and that many auxiliary hypotheses need to be made in order to have an empirical counterpart to the equation. It follows that the model for permits should be thought of as providing a general equilibrium structure giving some precise meaning to the price of permits in an intertemporal framework.

One important implication of the equation is the precise meaning which is assigned to the difference between temporary and permanent environmental policies. Being a present value of future elements, it illustrates clearly that current environmental policy is only one factor in the determination of prices in the market for permits, as future policy conditions are also relevant. For example, a temporary reduction in the supply of permits will not have a large impact on the price if the policy is known to be reverted shortly. Conversely, markets are going to react immediately to any credibly announced modification of future environmental policy.

## 6. Climate Change and Emission Permits

As was mentioned in the second section, in reality there are many elements of uncertainty in the climate change problem. The various elements compound in a situation in which the supply of permits is likely to be a stochastic process rather than a constant. Behind this is the hypothesis of a complicated learning process which is not specified explicitly.

All these elements of uncertainty have of course an impact over the market price and consumption, which become random variables. The first order condition becomes:

$$\frac{\partial u}{\partial c_t^0}\left[\frac{\partial f}{\partial e_t} - p_t\right] + \delta E_t \frac{\partial u}{\partial c_{t+1}^1} p_{t+1} = 0$$

and the price becomes the expectation of future fundamentals:

$$p_t = E_t \sum_{j=0}^{\infty} \delta^j \Pi_{i=0}^{j}(1+r_t)^{-i}\frac{\partial f}{\partial e_{t+j}}.$$

The equation suggests the factors that may be important for determining the volatility of prices in the permits market, that is changes in present and future consumption, to be interpreted as recessions and expansions, or changes in future standards, which modify the quantity of permits and therefore their future marginal productivity, or changes in technological relations. For example an innovation that increases the productivity of permits by lowering the permits-production ratio, would increase the market price.

In particular, elements like scientific discoveries about the physical model of the climate change problem should have a large impact on market prices, and the same should happen of any new estimate of the damage produced by the climate change on the economic system and welfare. Such new elements should modify the optimal supply of permits, and be incorporated in market prices even before the changes take place, as soon as the expectation materializes.

Also, the equation points out that climate change may have immediate effects on the price of permits, as well as of other assets, particularly in the case that it affects the marginal productivity of capital and therefore the interest rate. In this case in fact both the numerator and the denominator of the equation would be affected. However, climate change is not likely to have a large impact on prices if the damages it produces are mainly on utility and welfare, e.g. an increase in the mean temperature makes everybody worse off but does not significantly affect the amount of output produced by the economy. This, for example, is the scenario implicit in the estimates of Nordhaus [16].

Different effects of climate change on productivities and utilities are important not only for volatility of asset and permits prices per se, but mainly in connection with the hedging opportunities that private agents may hope to derive by using financial instruments. Considering two extreme cases is a good way to make this point. First, take the case where climate change has no effect whatsoever on the amount of production. Then, lacking other changes in the structure of the economy, and assuming that asset valuation depends only on expectations of future production, there would be no movements in asset prices following the change in the climate. As a consequence, there would be no possibility for private investors to use such markets in a counter-cyclical way, i.e. the representative investor of country $i$ which is negatively affected in utility terms by the change in the climate could not increase his wealth by holding assets representative of the production opportunity set of country $j$.

On the other hand, imagine that climate change has heterogeneous effects on productivities of factors in various countries, with consequent heterogeneous effects on expected returns and correlations of returns of the financial assets. For example climate change increases the productivity of factors in country $i$ and decreases it in country $j$. In this case the cross-sectional variability in the effects of climate change on various economies produces different reactions of national asset markets. This provides greater hedging opportunities: a portfolio composed of representative stock indices of many countries is more stable (across states of nature) than a portfolio concentrated in assets of only one country. The representative agent of countries $i$ and $j$ can stabilize their wealth across states of nature by holding shares of companies present in both country $i$ and country $j$.

## 7. Conclusions

This paper starts from the observation that emission permits are financial assets, in the sense of representing property rights on the use of a common good that can be exercised at some time in the future. The possibility of using them for valuable production processes is what gives them a price on the secondary market. Contrary to this intuition, the economics literature has usually considered permits within the context of static partial equilibrium models, apart from recent attempts discussed in the introduction to treat them within the context of static general equilibrium models.

The model proposed here considers emission permits within an intertemporal general equilibrium framework. Such a shift of focus allows the derivation of a present value equation connecting market prices to current and future market fundamentals, like rates of marginal substitution, marginal productivities of emissions and the rate of return on capital. The market price is not simply a function of current demand and supply, as in static models, but may depend on the expectations of future variables. The use of an overlapping generations model is not a limitation to the analysis. Similar valuation formula may be derived for representative agent economies, and there are previous examples of the use of the OLG structure for the analysis of market prices.

These features seem to be relevant in discussing the current proposals for the organization of spot and futures markets, and to point out the role that expectations about future prices have on the current price. In turn, this brings to attention the role of future policy decisions about the level of emissions;

in a dynamic market that prices assets with an eye to present discounted valuation all the current and expected future conditions are relevant to current prices. It follows that the market price of emission permits will incorporate all the expectations and risks of many factors related to environmental policy and to the formation of coalitions of countries that agree on controlling global emissions [5, 12].

Also, there seem to be interesting possibilities of using the model to study the possible use of financial markets as an instrument for hedging against risks, see the discussion of the preceding section and the ideas advanced by Chichilnisky and Heal [6].

## Note

1. By considering an exogenous rate of technical change it would be possible to model a situation where the emission-production ratio goes down over time, but this would not add to the main points made in the paper. For certain problems, for example the global warming, the possibility of finding back-stop technologies could be modelled by assuming that at some future time the emission-output ratio drops to zero.

## References

1. Azariadis, C. *Intertemporal Macroeconomics*, Oxford, U.K., Blackwell, 1993.
2. Baumol, W. J. and W. E. Oates. *The Theory of Environmental Policy*, Second Edition, Cambridge, U.K., Cambridge University Press, 1988.
3. Beltratti, A. "Emission Permits in a Dynamic Model with Overlapping Generations", mimeo, University of Turin, 1995.
4. Brock, W. A. "A Polluted Golden Age", in *Economics of Natural and Environmental Resources*, V. L. Smith (ed.), New York, Gordon and Breach, 1973, pp. 441–461.
5. Carraro, C. and D. Siniscalco. "Strategies for the International Protection of the Environment", *Journal of Public Economics* 52, 1993, 309–328.
6. Chichilnisky, G. and G. Heal. "Global Environmental Risks", *Journal of Economic Perspectives* 7, 1993, 65–86.
7. Chichilnisky, G., G. Heal and D. Starrett. "International Emission Permits: Equity and Efficiency", mimeo, Stanford University, CA, 1993.
8. Cline, W. R. *The Economics of Global Warming*, Washington DC, Institute for International Economics, 1992.
9. Cropper, M. L. and W. E. Oates. "Environmental Economics: A Survey", *Journal of Economic Literature* 30, 1992, 657–740.
10. Diamond, P. A. "National Debt in a Neoclassical Growth Model", *American Economic Review* 5, part 1, 1965, 1126–1143.
11. Heal, G. "Interactions between Economy and Climate: A Framework for Policy Design under Uncertainty", in *Advances in Applied Microeconomics*, Vol. 3, V. K. Smith and A. D. White (eds.), London, JAI Press, 1984, pp. 151–168.
12. Heal, G. "The Optimal Use of Exhaustible Resources", in *Handbook of Natural Resources and Energy Economics*, A. V. Kneese and J. L. Sweeney (eds.), Amsterdam, North-Holland, 1993.
13. Heal, G. "The Formation of Environmental Coalitions", in *Trade, Innovation, Environment*, C. Carraro (ed.), Dordrecht, Kluwer Academic Publisher, 1994.

14. Intergovernmental Panel on Climatic Change (IPCC). *Policy Makers Summary of the Scientific Assessment of Climate Change*, New York, WMO and UNEP, 1990.
15. Manne, A. S. and R. G. Richels. "Global $CO_2$ Emission Reductions – The Impacts of Rising Energy Costs", *The Energy Journal* 12, 1991, 87–107.
16. Nordhaus, W. "Economic Approaches to Greenhouse Warming", in *Economic Policy Responses to Global Warming*, R. Dornbusch and J. Poterba (eds.), Cambridge, MA, MIT Press, 1991, pp. 33–66.
17. Nordhaus, W. "The Costs of Slowing Climate Change: A Survey", *The Energy Journal* 12, 1991, 37–65.
18. Sandor, R. "Implementation Issues: Market Architecture and the Tradeable Instrument", in *United Nations Conference on Trade and Development, 1992, Combating Global Warming*, New York, United Nations, 1992, Chapter 10.
19. Shiller, R. J. *Market Volatility*, Cambridge, MA, MIT Press, 1991.
20. Tietenberg, T. "Emission Trading: An Exercise in Reforming Pollution Policy", Washington DC, Resources for the Future, 1985.
21. Tietenberg T. "Implementation Issues: A General Survey", in *United Nations Conference on Trade and Development, 1992, Combating Global Warming*, New York, United Nations, 1992, Chapter 8.
22. Tirole, J. "Asset Bubbles and Overlapping Generations", *Econometrica* 53, 1985, 1071–1100.
23. United Nations Conference on Trade and Development, Combating Global Warming, New York, United Nations, 1992.

FONDAZIONE ENI ENRICO MATTEI (FEEM) SERIES ON ECONOMICS, ENERGY AND ENVIRONMENT

This series serves as an outlet for the main results of FEEM's research programmes in the areas of economics, energy and environment.

1. C. Carraro and D. Siniscalco (eds.), *The European Carbon Tax: An Economic Assessment*. 1993 ISBN 0-7923-2520-6
2. C. Carraro (ed.), *Trade, Innovation, Environment*. 1994 ISBN 0-7923-3033-1
3. C. Dosi and T. Tomasi (eds.), *Nonpoint Source Pollution Regulation: Issues and Analysis*. 1994 ISBN 0-7923-3121-4
4. C. Carraro, Y. Katsoulacos and A. Xepapadeas (eds.), *Environmental Policy and Market Structure*. 1996 ISBN 0-7923-3656-9
5. C. Carraro and A. Haurie (eds.), *Operations Research and Environmental Management*. 1996 ISBN 0-7923-3767-7
6. I. Musu and D. Siniscalco (eds.), *National Accounts and the Environment*. 1996 ISBN 0-7923-3741-7
7. C. Carraro and D. Siniscalco (eds.), *Environmental Fiscal Reform and Unemployment*. 1996 ISBN 0-7923-3750-6
8. A. Beltratti: *Models of Economic Growth with Environmental Assets*. 1996 ISBN 0-7923-4032-9
9. G. Chichilnisky, G. Heal and A. Vercelli (eds.), *Sustainability: Dynamics and Uncertainty*. 1998 ISBN 0-7923-4698-X
10. R. Roson and K.A. Small (eds.), *Environment and Transport in Economic Modelling*. 1998 ISBN 0-7923-4913-X

KLUWER ACADEMIC PUBLISHERS – DORDRECHT / BOSTON / LONDON